ROLF GIESEN

Golem, Caligari, Nosferatu

A CHRONICLE OF
GERMAN FILM FANTASY

BEAR MANOR
MEDIA

Golem, Caligari, Nosferatu:
A Chronicle of German Film Fantasy

© 2021 by Rolf Giesen

All rights reserved.

No portion of this publication may be reproduced, stored, and/or copied electronically (except for academic use as a source), nor transmitted in any form or by any means without the prior written permission of the publisher and/or author.

Published in the United States of America by:
BearManor Media

BearManor Media
1317 Edgewater Dr #110
Orlando FL 32804

bearmanormedia.com

Cover design and typesetting by Brian Phillips Design

Cover photo: Nosferatu replica created by Peter Day.
Courtesy of the Artist.

ISBN—XXX-X-XXXXX-XXX-X

Printed in the United States.

CONTENTS

Introduction v

Acknowledgments vii

Peculiar Problems of Producing Fantasy and Horror Films in Germany
A Brief Experience Report by Robert Sigl ix

Chronicle: 1808—2021 1

The Orwellian Age of Phantomology 443

Bibliography 453

Index 473

INTRODUCTION

There seemed to have been, in the realm of Gothic fiction, an interesting Anglo-German interaction. The groundbreaking novels came from British (and Irish) writers: John Polidori, Mary Shelley, Robert Louis Stevenson, Joseph Sheridan Le Fanu, Bram Stoker, H. G. Wells. But the early films were, due to the bad shape of the British film industry in those days, German. Right before WWI members of the Imperial Family, including one son of the Kaiser, attended a screening of a German *Hound of the Baskervilles*. F. W. Murnau adapted (unauthorized) *Dr. Jekyll and Mr. Hyde* (retitled *The Head of Janus*) and *Dracula* (retitled *Nosferatu*) for the silent screen. Ten years before Hollywood made *Island of Lost Souls* from H.G. Wells' 1896 novel *The Island of Dr. Moreau* there was (unauthorized as well) a German *Island of the Lost*. Even Edward Bulwer-Lytton's *Zanoni* was on the agenda—but alas, due to the bankruptcy of the production company, not filmed. Some of the German films left an impact on American films: The influence of *The Golem* and *The Cabinet of Dr. Caligari* is clearly felt when viewing James Whale's *Frankenstein* or Robert Florey's *Murders in the Rue Morgue*. And German filmmakers contributed directly to American mystery, fantasy and horror flicks: Paul Leni, Curt Siodmak, John Brahm, in recent years Roland Emmerich. Reason enough to focus on the schizophrenic world of German gore and fantasy: Nightmares and children's stories, fairies, witches and warlocks, giants, dragons and talking animals, vampires, golems, living statues, doppelgänger, vanishing shadows and the incarnation of the Devil, robots, alchemists and mad scientists, occultism and stories of the supernatural, miracle weapons, rockets and spaceships, aliens, zombies and post-apocalyptic fiction.

Following therefore is the first attempt to chronicle German film fantasy, year by year: birthdays, dying days, special events and film premieres of fairy tales, animation, science fiction, and horror, beginning with the great writers of the 19th century whose work influenced domestic cinema, the early fairy tale films, Germany's first robot movie made at a time when the term robot wasn't even coined, the silent period that includes *Dr. Mabuse*, *Faust* and the dystopian *Metropolis*, National Socialist trickfilms with *Munchausen* (Hans Albers) riding on a cannonball (in front of a process screen, all in Agfacolor) and a Snow Man melting in summer at a time when German war atrocities became rather authentic, leading to post-war films in West (the Edgar Wallace series, *Space Patrol*) and East Germany (*First Spaceship on Venus* inspired by Stanisław Lem, a Jew who survived the Nazi occupation of Poland), the New German Cinema of Alexander Kluge's *The Big Mess*, Rainer Werner Fassbinder's TV adaptation of Daniel Francis Galouye's *Simulacron-3: World on a Wire* and his failed attempt to base a movie on George Orwell's groundbreaking *1984* right before his untimely death, Werner Herzog's *Nosferatu* homage (read why it is not to be called a remake of F. W. Murnau's silent) starring the erratic Klaus Kinski, Wolfgang Petersen's *Neverending Story, Independence Day* (a rather Teutonic military fantasy produced in America) up to the ill-fated *Cloud Atlas*: an astounding compendium of hundreds, sometimes virtually unknown films (particularly with the era of cheap video and digital production) and projects that didn't survive preproduction.

Alas, the baker's dozen or so of so-called classics quoted in every standard work of film history is outnumbered by those countless mediocre films of low quality, average product at best that you won't find in film literature. With the advent of digital media, all that amateurish product (made for € 2000, 10,000 or 20,000) came through the back door and was not released theatrically or seen on TV. Since then, it's almost impossible to draw a line between professional, semi-professional and nonprofessional work. A lot of these titles are mentioned in this book, but as they are only an edge phenomenon, product of a new media era that is no more cinematic, we can easily do without them.

ACKNOWLEDGMENTS

Forrest J Ackerman, Henri Alékan, Hans Joachim Alpers, Karlheinz Böhm, Artur Brauner, Ferdinand Diehl, Hanns Eckelkamp, Bernd Eichinger, Michael Ende, Gerhard Fieber, Elfriede Fischinger, Peter A. Hagemann, Ray and Diana Harryhausen, Werner Hierl, Alfred Hirschmeier, Antonín Horák, Gerhard Huttula, Jürgen Klauss, Manfred Korytowski, Christopher Lee, Stanisław Lem, Curt Linda, Kurt Marks, Fritz Maurischat, Ferdy Mayne, Dr. William Moritz, Theo Nischwitz, Thilo Rothkirch, Karl Ludwig Ruppel, Ulrich Schamoni, Niklaus Schilling, Herbert K. Schulz, H. O. Schulze, Curt and Henrietta Siodmak, Albert Uderzo, Wolfgang Urchs, Albert Whitlock, Jürgen Wohlrabe who have passed away since and Frank Arnold, Stefan Birckmann, John Boorman, Dr. Ralf Bülow, Michael Coldewey, Martin Compart, Jim Danforth, Holger Delfs, Roland Emmerich, Volker Engel, Marc Fehse, Dr. Michael Flintrop, Dieter Geissler, Terry Gilliam, Nina Goslar, F.-B. Habel, Ronald M. Hahn, Caroline Hagen Hall, Andreas Hartung, Michael "Bully" Herbig, Josef Hilger, Wolfgang Jacobsen, Udo Kier, Volker Kronz, Volker Lange, Holger Mandel, Theo Mezger, Thomas Mulack, Dr. Gerd Naumann, Gerd J. Pohl, Dr. Volker Petzold, Hans Helmut Prinzler, Bernd Reichert, Hanns-Georg Rodek, Horst Schäfer, Friedhelm Schatz, Ivo Scheloske, Cornelius Schick, Mario Schühly, Thomas Schühly, Uwe Sommerlad, Olaf R. Spittel, Michael Skowronski, Angela & Karlheinz Steinmüller, Christel Strobel, Tom Tykwer, Rolf Zehetbauer and to the staff of Deutsche Kinemathek Berlin, Filmmuseum Dusseldorf and Schongerfilm (Franziska Schonger and Michael Seidel), once Germany's leading producers of fairy-tale films.

Grateful thanks are due to Robert Sigl, one of Germany's most talented directors of the fantastic, for the foreword, to my wife, Anna Khan, for helping me with the images, to Stone Wallace (who checked the manuscript) and to Peter Day for the cover. Peter is no professional but sure did professional work.

PECULIAR PROBLEMS OF PRODUCING FANTASY AND HORROR FILMS IN GERMANY

A BRIEF EXPERIENCE REPORT BY ROBERT SIGL

Legend has it that it was none other than David Cronenberg who once famously said: "Censors tend to do what only psychotics do: they confuse reality with illusion."

Actually, the film industry in Germany has been breeding a lot of such psychotics.

Many Germans, and particularly those responsible for distributing the money for film productions, have a load of taboos and these taboos extend from daily life into the arts resulting in a devastating effect on cinema—such as:

Horror. Horror Films. Homosexuality. Holocaust. Death. Corpses. Concentration Camps. Black humor. The occult. The supernatural. Incest. Suicide. Female antagonists. Realistic violence not played for amusement. Children's sexuality and/or the sexual awakening in pre-teens…

And so on.

The occult and the supernatural are only accepted in Kids Programs and in dulled-down, *über*-harmless fairy tale films. In fact, they have been dulled down to an extent that even the smallest children start to yawn.

Thus, the reactions to my work and unrealized screenplays from most producers, Film Boards and TV editors—the so-called *Redakteure*—have been quite psychotic, in the way that Mr. Cronenberg described above. Back in 1989 when watching my movie ***Laurin*** the owner of the respectable Munich Cinema "Kino am Sendlinger Tor" turned away in disgust: Ein blutrünstiges Machwerk für ein Nischenpublikum. *A blood-thirsty piece for a very restricted audience.*

The political influence on the media, on films with State subsidies and on the non-private TV stations ARD and ZDF always has been enormous and much more so than for instance in the often-maligned United States—a fact that most Germans would dispute and deny maniacally if confronted with it. Yet their artistic output bears witness to their asexual and unsensual tendencies while their "humor" and their "comedies" are adolescent, quite primitive and vulgar—and homophobic.

Self-censorship also helps the puppeteers enormously in avoiding uncomfortable material and subject matters from the get-go.

Those puppeteers have also successfully made the filmmakers to avoid deep (or depth) psychology—"Tiefenpsychologie"—and the artists themselves seem to have lost any intimate and profound access to the human soul. As particularly horror films need to touch and open the locked gates to the soul and excavate concealed human fears, they consequently are a red rag for the majority of Germans, men and women alike. You just have to picture it: you have more than a dozen women and men sitting around a table, each of them a member from another guild or institution such as the Church, having brought their personal problems, sensitivities (and deficits for that matter) with them. In an atmosphere like this it is hardly possible to get projects with scary, daring, challenging, controversial, provocative and offensive content funded, let alone horror films. Similar to the times of the Third Reich, it is still the censors watching their gates like 'Cerberuses' and denying any courageous filmmakers to slip through the entrance of their Fort Knox of film subsidies and get access to funds.

NATIVE filmmakers, that is.

Whenever directors and producers of fame from abroad such as Lars von Trier or Hollywood with a horror film like Gore Verbinski's *A Cure for Wellness* come knocking at our Fort Knox the gates open wide for them. Forgotten are the problems with the despised genre and the depiction of violence (e.g., the mutilations of sex organs in *Antichrist*) when those guardians of moral can decorate themselves with famous names and stars.

All my projects following my debut picture *Laurin* have been turned down by the Film Boards and refused any production funds—even those that previously had been granted a screenplay fund: an adaptation of Dan Simmons' vampire bestseller *Children of the Night* was among them. *Medusa* (which had a similar plot to *A Cure for Wellness* and had been submitted years before the aforementioned Hollywood picture) was refused funds, too, with one of the board members of the Bavarian Film Board telling my producer that in the future no more projects expecting a *FSK 16* [1] and upwards would receive any more state money. Most of us know: Lars von Trier's *Antichrist* got an *18* then—and a lot of German subsidy money.

To explain *FSK 16*: in Germany we have a rating system that refuses patrons under 16 entrance to the movies that had received a FSK 16 and patrons under 18 entrance to a film with a *FSK 18*.

This rating system applies to television as well, meaning that films with a *FSK 16* and upwards may not be aired on prime time and before 10 pm. As it is impossible to get any funds from Film Boards for a movie without any co-financing from a German TV station this has been another nail in the coffin for genre films.

Now in the wake of ever-growing political *über*-correctness (over-correctness)

---

1   FSK Freiwillige Selbstkontrolle der Filmwirtschaft: a German self-regulatory Body for the legally regulated protection of youth and minors.

and with all its accompanying enforced regulations the genre faces yet the biggest nail in its coffin—and not only in Germany but world-wide.

Just don't expect another 13-year-old girl brandishing a crucifix, then jabbing it into her vagina yelling: "Let Jesus Christ fuck you, let Jesus Christ fuck you."

CHRONICLE: 1808–2021

1808

Johann Wolfgang von Goethe's tragic play *Faust* in print.

1812

DECEMBER 20

The first copies of the *Children's and Household Tales (Kinder- und Hausmärchen)* collected by Jacob and Wilhelm Grimm, two philologists doing cultural research. Fairy tales are, in essence, tales about loss: the loss of childhood and innocence. They are telling us, however, that at the same time every loss is a gain making the protagonist a prince or a princess after having sex with a frog.

1813

SUMMER

Adelbert von Chamisso writes a fantastic tale about a man who sells his shadow: *Peter Schlemihls wundersame Geschichte (Peter Schlemihl's Strange and Wonderful History*, published in 1814).

1815

Die Elixiere des Teufels (The Devil's Elixirs) by **E. T. A. Hoffmann**, a psychedelic novel about a Capuchin monk who finds a mystical bottle and drinks from it: *As if on the transprarent medium of phantasmagorie, one bright and smiling image chased another before the mind's eye—before that mind, which now, for the first time, seemed to be awoke from deep sleep...*

1822

JUNE 25

E. T. A. Hoffmann died in Berlin. Hoffmann, born on January 24, 1776 in Königsberg, East Prussia, was a Prussian judge, much celebrated during his lifetime, both as writer of dark romances, and a composer of music.

1829

JANUARY 19

Premiere of Goethe's *Faust, Part One* on stage in Braunschweig.

1832

MARCH 22

Johann Wolfgang von Goethe died in Weimar.

1848

APRIL 20

Kurd Lasswitz, gymnasium teacher and founder of German Utopian literature, born in Breslau (today Wrocław).

1859

DECEMBER 16

Wilhelm Carl **Grimm** died in Berlin.

1863

JANUARY 8

Paul Carl Wilhelm **Scheerbart**, a pioneer of fantastic literature, born in Danzig.

SEPTEMBER 20

Jacob Ludwig Karl **Grimm** died in Berlin.

1866

NOVEMBER 22

Film pioneer **Oskar** Eduard **Messter** born in Berlin.

1867

JANUARY 17

Karl Lämmle (Carl Laemmle), founder of Universal City Studios, born in Laupheim, Swabia.

MARCH 30

Paul Davidson, founder of PAGU Projektions-AG "Union", born in Lötzen, East Prussia.

1868

JANUARY 19

Gustav Meyrink, occultist and author of *The Golem*, born in Vienna as Gustav Meyer, the illegitimate son of Baron Karl von Varnbüler von und zu Hemmingen, Württembergian minister of state, and Maria Meyer, a Bavarian-Jewish court actress.

1869

APRIL 30

Architect **Hans Poelzig** born in Berlin.

OCTOBER 3

Robert Kraft, a German Jules Verne, born in Leipzig.

OCTOBER 22

Director **Otto Rippert** born in Offenbach.

1871

NOVEMBER 3

Novelist **Hanns Heinz Ewers** born in Dusseldorf.

1872

NOVEMBER 15

Hans Joachim **Dominik,** science fiction author, science journalist and engineer, born as son of a veterinarian in Zwickau. While attending the gymnasium one of his teachers was **Kurd Lasswitz** who inspired him deeply.

1873

APRIL 27

Director **Robert Wiene** born as son of actor Karl Wiene and Pauline Loevy in Breslau (Wrocław).

SEPTEMBER 9

Famed stage director and producer **Max Reinhardt** born as Maximilian Goldmann, son of Jewish merchant Wilhelm Goldmann and his wife Rachel Lea Rosi "Rosa" née Wengraf, in the spa town of Baden near Vienna.

1874

DECEMBER 11

Actor and film pioneer **Paul Wegener** born as son of a cloth manufacturer in Arnoldsdorf, West Prussia.

1877

MARCH 12

Actor **Alfred Abel** born in Leipzig.

1879

MARCH 4

Author **Bernhard Kellermann** born in Fürth.

JUNE 22

Cameraman Friedrich Konrad **Guido Seeber** born in Chemnitz. Seeber's father Clemens owned a photographer's studio.

SEPTEMBER 6

Max (Friedrich Gustav Maximilian) **Schreck,** Count Orlok in *Nosferatu*, born as son of an accountant in Berlin Friedenau.

Max (*Nosferatu*) Schreck | Art by Albin Grau, Courtesy of Gerd J. Pohl

1880

JULY 4

Director **Stellan Rye** born in Randers, Denmark.

NOVEMBER 5

Director **Richard Oswald** born as Richard W. Ornstein in Vienna.

NOVEMBER 7

Julius Otto Mandl, the future director **Joe May**, born in Vienna.

1881

JANUARY 7

Actor and writer-director **Henrik Galeen** born as Heinrich Wiesenberg in Stry, Galicia, Austria-Hungary.

Autograph by Henrik Galeen (addressed to Joe May) | Author's collection.

JANUARY 15

Actor **John Gottowt**, Galeen's future brother-in-law, born as Isidor Gesang in Lemberg (Lwiw).

John Gottowt (r.) with Paul Wegener in Der Student von Prag | Author's collection.

1882

OCTOBER 20

Actor **Béla Lugosi** born as Béla Ferenc Dezső Blasko in Lugos, then Austria-Hungary, today part of Romania.

SEPTEMBER 28

Actor-director-producer **Rudolf Meinert** born as Rudolf Bürstein in Vienna.

NOVEMBER 7

Nosferatu composer **Hans Erdmann** born in Breslau (today Wrocław) as Hans Erdmann Timotheos Guckel.

1884

JANUARY 2

Fairy tale producer Aloys **Alfons (Alf) Zengerling** born in Heyerode, Thuringia.

JUNE 2

Actress **Mia May** born as Hermine Pfleger in Vienna.

Mia May | Author's colletion

JUNE 5

Actor **Bernhard Goetzke** born in Danzig.

JUNE 23

Actor **Werner** Johannes **Krauss**, *Dr. Caligari* himself, born in Gestungshausen near Coburg.

JULY 23

Actor **Emil Jannings** born in Rorschach.

OCTOBER 21

Director **Max Mack** born as Moritz Myrthenzweig in Halberstadt.

DECEMBER 5

Cameraman **Fritz Arno Wagner** born in Schmiedefeld am Rennsteig in Thuringia.

DECEMBER 22

Albin Grau, artist, occultist, and art director, born in Schönefeld near Leipzig.

1885

JULY 8

Designer and director **Paul Leni** born as Paul Josef Levi to a Jewish family in Stuttgart.

NOVEMBER 24

Actor Friedrich **Rudolf Klein-Rogge** (*Dr. Mabuse*) born in Cologne as son of a court judge.

1887

MARCH 11

Composer **Gottfried Huppertz** born in Cologne.

SEPTEMBER 30

Actress **Lil Dagover** born as Martha Seubert in Madiun, Java.

DECEMBER 28

Experimental filmmaker **Walter Ruttmann** born in Frankfurt.

1888

JUNE 25

Director **Artur** (Arthur) **Robison** as son of a German American born in Chicago, Illinois.

NOVEMBER 7

Actor-director **Reinhold Schünzel** born in Hamburg.

DECEMBER 27

Author and screenwriter **Thea** Gabriele **von Harbou**, a Prussian officer's daughter, born in Tauperlitz (today Döhlau).

DECEMBER 28

Friedrich Wilhelm Plumpe (a.k.a. **Friedrich Wilhelm Murnau**) born as son of cloth manufacturer Heinrich Plumpe and his wife Ottilie, a teacher appreciative of art, in Bielefeld.

1889

FEBRUARY 8

Siegfried Kracauer, sociologist and film theorist, born in Frankfurt/Main.

MAY 5

Art Director **Hermann** Georg **Warm (*Caligari*)** born in Berlin.

JULY 20

Producer **Erich Pommer** born in Hildesheim as son of a Jewish laundry dealer, Gustav Pommer, and his wife Anna née Jacobson.

1890

JANUARY 16

Karl Freund, future cinematographer, born in Königinhof (Dvůr Králové), Bohemia, as son of a glasser.

APRIL 18

Actor **Alexander Granach** born as Jessaja Gronach in Werbowitz, Eastern Galicia.

Alexander Granach as Knock in *Nosferatu* | Art by Albin Grau | Courtesy of Gerd J. Pohl

DECEMBER 2

Caligari's co-writer **Hans Janowitz** born in Podiebrad, Austria-Hungary.

DECEMBER 5

Friedrich Christian Anton **(Fritz) Lang** born in Vienna, the second son of Anton Lang, architect and municipal construction company manager, and his wife Pauline "Paula" née Schlesinger.

1891

JANUARY 6

Rochus Gliese, production and costume designer and director, born in Berlin.

MAY 13

Actor **Fritz** Heinrich **Rasp** born in Bayreuth.

SEPTEMBER 7

Margarete (Greta) Schröder, in 1921 to star in *Nosferatu*, born in Dusseldorf.

1892

JANUARY 6

Director **Ludwig Berger**, son of banker Franz Bamberger, born in Mainz.

JANUARY 29

Ernst Lubitsch born as son of a prosperous ladies' tailor in Berlin.

JULY 12

Stunt actor and director **Harry (Heinrich) Piel** born in Benrath, a suburb of Dusseldorf, as son of a landlord and a farmer's daughter

1893

JANUARY 22

Actor Hans Walter **Conrad Veidt** born in Berlin.

JULY 21

Artist, cameraman and inventor **Eugen Schüfftan** born in Breslau (Wrocław).

NOVEMBER 1

Art director **Erich Kettelhut** born in Berlin.

Harry Piel in later years starring in a science fiction movie | Author's collection

Conrad Veidt as Devil in a fantasy movie produced by Richard Oswald: *Kurfürstendamm* | Author's collection

1894

NOVEMBER 20

Carl Mayer, the second *Caligari* writer, born in Graz, Austria, the son of a stock speculator who committed suicide.

1895

NOVEMBER 1

Max Skladanowsky screened his Bioscop images, such as a *Boxing Kangaroo*, at the Berlin Wintergarten music hall.

1896

MARCH 5

Lotte Henrietta Regina **Eisner**, future film critic and chronicler of the German silent screen, born as daughter of a Jewish merchant in Berlin.

1897

OCTOBER 19

Film and fairy tale producer **Hubert Schonger** born in Bachhagel, Dillingen.

Hubert Schonger | Courtesy of Schongerfilm

Most likely the first German fantasy films were short adaptations of Grimm's *Hänsel und Gretel (Hansel and Gretel)* and *Rapunzel* produced by movie pioneer **Oskar Messter.**

NOVEMBER 13

Heinrich Otto Karl Eduard **Dieckmann,** the future manager of Prana Film that produced *Nosferatu*, born in Berlin.

1899

JUNE 2

Silhouette film artist **Charlotte (Lotte) Reiniger** born in Berlin Charlottenburg.

Lotte Reiniger working on a silhouette movie | Courtesy of Caroline Hagen Hall and Christel Strobel

JUNE 10

Anita Berber born in Leipzig as daughter of a violin virtuoso and a chanson singer.

1900

OCTOBER 31

Projection GmbH established in Berlin by **Oskar Messter**.

JUNE 22

Animator **Oskar Fischinger** born in Gelnhausen.

1901

At age 17 **Albin Grau** entered the Dresden Academy of Fine Arts as working student with Eugen Bracht (1842-1921).

MAY 20

Stop-motion filmmaker **Ferdinand Diehl** born in Unterwössen, Bavaria.

Ferdinand Diehl | Author's collection

1902

MAY 29

Producer and talent agent **Paul Kohner** born in Teplitz-Schönau, Austria-Hungary (now Teplice, Czech Republic).

AUGUST 10

Writer **Kurt (Curt) Siodmak**, the younger brother of director **Robert Siodmak**, born in Dresden.

Curt Siodmak | Author's collection

1904

JUNE 26

Actor **Peter Lorre** born as László Loewenstein in Rosenberg, Austria-Hungary.

1905

MAY 15

Actor and fairy-tale producer **Fritz Genschow** born in Berlin as son of a baker.

Fritz Genschow (standing, with hat, checking sky) while Gerhard Huttula prepares camera
Author's collection

1906

Henrik Galeen and **Paul Wegener** joined **Max Reinhardt** in Berlin.

Frau Holle (Mother Holly), a short fairy tale picture.

1907

MARCH

Pathé Frères released the highly successful (tinted) *Passionsspiele (Passion Plays)* to the German market.

A sound-on-disc picture based on Engelbert Humperdinck's fairy-tale opera *Hänsel und Gretel (Hansel and Gretel)* produced by Internationale Kinematograph- und Lichtbild-Gesellschaft.

The Heinrich Ernemann Aktiengesellschaft für Camerafabrikation Dresden released a series of fairy-tale shorts: *Frau Holle (Mother Holly)*, *Rapunzel*, *Schneewittchen (Snow White)* and once again *Hänsel und Gretel*.

1908

Heinz Widtmann's German translation of Bram Stoker's *Dracula* offered by Max Altmann, an occult Leipzig publisher.

MARCH 17

Brigitte Helm (Schittenhelm) born in Berlin.

JULY 9

Director **Harald Reinl** born in Bad Ischl, Austria.

1909

DECEMBER 31

Two trickfilm shorts by **Guido Seeber** who was promoted chief cameraman of Deutsche Bioscop company: *Prosit Neujahr! (Happy New Year)* and *Geheimnisvolle Streichholzdose (A Match Box Mystery)*: A legless seller of matches falls asleep and dreams of (stop-frame animated) matches performing tricks. Seeber was an admirer of Georges Méliès.

Trick Shot: Six times Guido Seeber | Author's collection

1910

OCTOBER 17

Kurd Lasswitz died in Gotha.

Sergei Pankejeff, widely known in the history of psychoanalysis as *Wolf Man*, became one of **Sigmund Freud's** most famous patients in Vienna:

I dreamt that it was night and that I was lying in bed. (My bed stood with its foot towards the window; in front of the window there was a row of old walnut trees. I know it was winter when I had the dream, and night-time.)

Suddenly the window opened of its own accord, and I was terrified to see that some white wolves were sitting on the big walnut tree in front of the window. There were six or seven of them. The wolves were quite white, and looked more like foxes or sheepdogs, for they had big tails like foxes and they had their ears pricked like dogs when they pay attention to something.

In great terror, evidently of being eaten up by the wolves, I screamed and woke up. My nurse hurried to my bed, to see what had happened to me.

It took quite a long while before I was convinced that it had only been a dream; I had such a clear and life-like picture of the window opening and the wolves sitting on the tree. At last, I grew quieter, felt as though I had escaped from some danger, and went to sleep again.

The dream intrigued Freud who soon discovered that it marked a turning point in Pankejeff's childhood, the result of Pankejeff having witnessed his parents having sex.

Dornröschen (Sleeping Beauty) released by Heinrich Ernemann AG, Dresden.

In a sound-on-disc picture produced by DMB Deutsche Mutoskop- und Bioscop G.m.b.H. Berlin one could hear the flute of the Pied Piper of Hamelin: *Der Rattenfänger von Hameln*.

1911

MARCH

Max Reinhardt discovered **Friedrich Wilhelm Plumpe** in Heidelberg. Plumpe followed Reinhardt to Berlin and became a member of Reinhardt's acting classes.

JULY 15

Karl August Geyer established the first big film laboratory in Berlin: Kino-Kopier-Gesellschaft, later known as Geyer Werke.

Henrik Galeen left Reinhardt to become a director at Berlin Volksbühne and met **Hanns Heinz Ewers**.

The publishing house of Georg Müller Munich and Leipzig published **Hanns Heinz Ewers'** novel *Alraune. Die Geschichte eines lebenden Wesens.*

Alraune, a novel by Hanns Heinz Ewers | Author's collection

1912

FEBRUARY 12

In a newly erected glass stage in Neubabelsberg near Berlin Bioscop started production on the first movie. *Totentanz (Dance of Death)* starred Danish actress Asta Nielsen. Director: Urban Gad. Cinematographer: Guido Seeber.

MARCH 23

Wernher Magnus Maximilian Freiherr **von Braun** born in the small town of Wirsitz, Posen Province. His father was the East Prussian landowner and future Minister of Agriculture Magnus Freiherr von Braun.

JUNE 8

Actor **Henry Brandon** born as Heinrich von Kleinbach in Berlin.

SEPTEMBER

For the first time **Friedrich Wilhelm Plumpe** appeared as actor under the name **F. W. Murnau** (named after Murnau, a market town in Bavaria) in a play directed by Max Reinhardt in Vienna.

DECEMBER 7

Der Schatten des Meeres (Specter of the Sea): The tragic love story of Evelyne, a painter (Henny Porten), and Sven Nansen, a fisherman (played by director Curt A. Stark), ends with the fisherman's suicide. The dead fisherman reappears as ghost and takes Evelyne with him. Cinematographer: Carl Froelich. A two-reeler based on an East-Friesian ballad (*Der Gonger*) and produced by **Messter's** Projection GmbH (in its studios at Blücherstrasse in Berlin) and on location on the Swedish island Kullen.

Max Altmann Leipzig published Heinz Widtmann's translation **Frankenstein oder Der moderne Prometheus**.

1913

FEBRUARY 15

Premiere at Mozartsaal cinema in Berlin: In *Der Andere (The Other)* directed by **Max Mack** end of 1912 **Albert Bassermann** played a split personality. Dr. Hallers, a Berlin lawyer, refers the existence of split personality, a neurosis in which the personality becomes dissociated, to the realm of fantasy—until he transforms into a criminal after a riding accident and joins a burglar (Léon Resemann) in robbing his own home. Based on 1893 play by dramatist Paul Lindau (1839-1919) that seemed to have been inspired by Robert Louis Stevenson. Produced by Jules Greenbaum's Vitascope company.

MAY

First screen version of Johann Nestroy's magic play about an evil ghost: *Lump-aci Vagabundus*.

APRIL

S. Fischer published **Bernhard Kellermann's** novel *Der Tunnel (The Tunnel)* in which the ambitious project of a Transatlantic Tunnel is finished, in spite of all accidents.

Spring: **Conrad Veidt** joined **Max Reinhardt** and the group around **F. W. Murnau**. Alexander Granach, Lothar Müthel, Ernst Hofmann and perhaps Ernst Lubitsch are part of that circle.

AUGUST 22

Premiere of *Der Student von Prag (The Student of Prague)* at the Mozartsaal cinema in Berlin. The doppelganger story was concocted by **Hanns Heinz Ewers** from elements of *Faust* and Adelbert von Chamisso's *Peter Schlemihl* with shades of **E. T. A. Hoffmann** and Edgar Allan Poe (*William Wilson*):

Balduin (played by **Paul Wegener**), a poor student of 19th Century Prague, the best fencer in town, sells his mirror image (and with it his soul) for the price of 100,000 guilders to an uncanny shylock named Scapinelli (**John Gottowt**), hoping for social advancement and prestige. Yet the mirror image hunts him like an evil demon. In a duel, the doppelganger kills Count Waldis, a rival for the hand of beautiful Countess Margit (Grete Berger, a personal friend of Ewers). To get rid of the mirror image Balduin shoots it but only kills himself.

Thanks to Guido Seeber's skilled cinematography, the *doppelganger* scenes turned out well enough to convince the audience. Seeber, Bioscop's chief cameraman, had to photograph Wegener twice on the same film strip for his dual role by putting a matte in front of the camera lens, then rewinding the film and using a counter-matte to create the effect: "For the first time I executed the Split Screen in the production of *doppelganger* shots well and truly, and as the technique proved flawless the impact of the film was incredible."

Stellan Rye directed on location in Prague and at Deutsche Bioscop's studio in Neubabelsberg.

Paul Wegener (left) and Hanns Heinz Ewers on location in Prague
Der Student von Prag (The Student of Prague) | Author's collection

Max Reinhardt signed **Werner Krauss** for Deutsches Theater.

OCTOBER 3

Greta Schröder and Ernst Mátray who was going to marry her were seen in a screen comedy directed by **Max Reinhardt**: *The Island of Bliss—Die Insel der Seligen*—turns out to be the home of Greek gods who chase away mortal intruders. Paul Davidson produced the film for his Projektions-AG Union.

OCTOBER 23

Ein Sommernachtstraum in unserer Zeit (A Midsummer Night's Dream in Our Time) passed the Board of Censors. **Hanns Heinz Ewers** brought Shakespeare's play up to date.

OCTOBER 31

Amerika—Europa im Luftschiff. Ein Zukunftsbild aus dem Jahre 2000 (America—Europe in an Airship: A Vision of the Future in Year 2000).

NOVEMBER 3

Die Eisbraut (The Ice Bride) written by **Hanns Heinz Ewers** (based on his novel *John Llewellyn Hamiltons Ende* published in 1905) and directed by **Stellan Rye** right after *Student von Prag*: An artist falls in love with a museum exhibit, the frozen body of a woman who died 20,000 years ago (found somewhere in Siberia and now on display in the British Museum in London).

NOVEMBER

An 8-year-old girl, Gertrud Siefert, was murdered at Holstenwall in Hamburg. **Hans Janowitz** was going to use the crime as premise for the *Caligari* story.

DECEMBER

Der Herr der Welt (Master of the World): sci-fi drama about the ancient alchemist dream of creating gold. Produced in Karl Werner's film studio located at Grosse Frankfurter Str. 105 in Berlin.

1914

JANUARY 9

Premiere *Die Augen des Ole Brandis (The Eyes of Ole Brandis)* directed by **Stellan Rye**:

Trieste-born **Alexander Moissi** (1879-1935), one of Germany's most prominent stage actors, played the title character, a painter who, thanks to some mysterious gift of a crippled Jewish antiques dealer (Lothar Körner), got the ability to recognize man's true nature. **Hanns Heinz Ewers,** who wrote the story, was not pleased with Moissi's play: *Moissi set his mind on doing pantomime; all my begging and pleading was useless—he was downright goofy.*²

JANUARY 23

A French release: *Die Mumie (The Mummy)* produced by Gaumont, announced as vaudeville in 2 acts.

Actor postcard: Ernst Reicher | Author's Collection

MARCH 13

Premiere of *Die geheimnisvolle Villa (The Mysterious Villa)* with Ernst Reicher, half-brother of Frank Reicher (Captain Englehorn in *King Kong*) as Sherlock Holmes-like sleuth Stuart Webbs: A woman is kidnapped by *The Black Triangle*, a secret society. Directed by **Joe May.**

---

2   Hanns Heinz Ewers, *Anfänge des Films*. Typescript.

APRIL 3

Der andere Student von Prag (The Other Student of Prague), Deutsche Bioscop's parody of their own movie, starring Hugo Fink and Emil Albes.

APRIL

Das Geheimnis der M-Strahlen Drama in 3 Akten (The Mystery of the M Rays)

Dr. Buchmann's special research topic is the secret of the *M rays* which have an enormous healing power, but after a while the effect is deadly. Bella Mira, a tightrope artist he has fallen in love with, sacrifices herself in a self-experiment, a martyr of love and science. The shocked scientist commits suicide too.

Viggo Larsen, the director and star, was born in Copenhagen. Together with Wanda Treumann who played Bella Mira and her husband Karl Treumann he formed a ménage à trois: the Treumann-Larsen-Film-Vertriebs Company. Wanda Treumann withdrew from the movies in 1922.

JUNE 12

Premiere of the 1st part of *Der Hund von Baskerville (The Hound of the Baskervilles)* starring Alwin Neuss as Sherlock Holmes. Produced by Vitascope from a script by **Richard Oswald**, directed by **Rudolf Meinert** and photograped by **Karl Freund**.

JULY 28

Begin of **World War I**.

Der Spuk im Hause des Professors (Spook in the House of the Professor), another part of the Stuart Webbs series with Ernst Reicher. In the United States released as *Trapped by the Camera*.

OCTOBER

F. W. Murnau was drafted.

NOVEMBER 14

Danish film director **Stellan Rye** (*Der Student von Prag*) died in French war imprisonment.

DECEMBER 6

Premiere *Ein seltsamer Fall (A Strange Case)* directed by **Max Mack** (*Der Andere*) which was based on **Richard Oswald's** stage adaptation *The Strange Case of Dr. Jekyll and Mr. Hyde*. Mack and Oswald call Jekyll Siles (played by Alwin Neuss). Siles is suffering from depression and transforms (not by an in-camera effect but by a simple cut) into an apeman. The whole story turns out to be a nightmare.

DECEMBER

Conrad Veidt got drafted.

1915

JANUARY 14

Premiere at U.T. Lichtspiele Kurfürstendamm in Berlin: **Paul Wegener** as *Der Golem (The Golem)* pursues the daughter of a a Jewish Prague antiques dealer who has revived him. The frightened girl tries to escape the uncanny wooer and flees to her aristocratic lover who at that time is holding a reception. The rejection brings the colossus-turned-into-a-monster to the verge of sexual rage. The 'Stalker' creates havoc and causes panic among the summer guests invited by the Count to a masquerade ball. The nobleman and the girl flee the stairways up the tower of the castle:

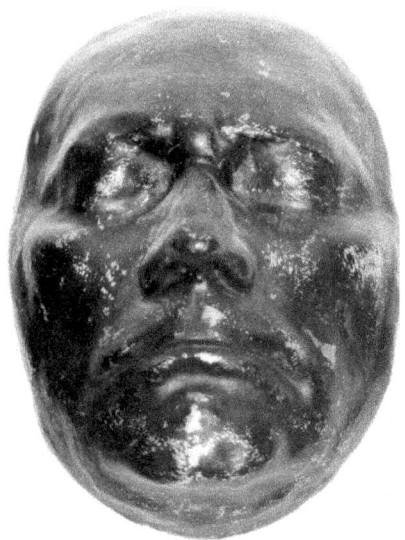

Life mask of Paul Wegener
Photograph by Anna Khan | Author's collection

A small round tower, ivy-covered. Count and daughter arrive. He opens the door with a key he had in the pocket. Slams the door behind him. Golem appears, approaches the door. Platform of the tower. View to the treetops. Sideways ahead a circular opening of the spiral staircase. Count and daughter appear, sink down exhausted on the cornice of the battlements. She lays her head onto his heart, he embraces and consoles her. Suddenly their faces distort fearfully, they hear the splintering of the door and the heavy step of the Golem. They rush to the rearmost battlement, pressed to each other.

Expecting the horrible.

Golem's head appears from the deep, he looks around searching, sees the group. Slowly he ascends and strides with a childlike smile towards the scared couple. Count plants himself protectively in front of the girl. Golem makes a step. The girl signals that she wants to talk to the Golem. She passes the Count and with a smile approaches the Golem. Hand and eye aim at the Schenn [sic! Shem]. *Golem spreads his arms as if to lift her. Wants to embrace her. Count misconceives the gesture, sees his beloved in danger, leaps at Golem. Golem's smiling good-naturedness distorts into anger. He grabs the Count and lifts him up, strides with him towards the edge of the tower, desperate wrestling. Highest danger. Desperate resistance. Change of position. In the last moment the girl is able to rip the Schenn out of the Golem's breast. For a moment Golem stays with closed eyes at the rim of the tower, then he stumbles and falls into the deep. In this moment the head of the old Jew appears at the platform. He sees the couple, runs towards his daughter, daughter knees in front of him, pointing downwards.*

At the bottom of the tower lies the figure of the Golem: smashed.

Platform of the tower. The silhouettes of those who bow over the rim. They look up shocked. The girl sinks into the arms of the Count, the Count extends his hand towards the Jew. The Jew takes it after some hesitation and blesses the couple.[3]

The Golem's iconic face was created by sculptor Rudolf Belling.

Emil Jannings signed with Reinhardt and Deutsches Theater.

Gustav Meyrink's *Golem* novel published as book illustrated by **Hugo Steiner-Prag** after its serialization as early as December 1913 in the Leipzig periodical *Weisse Blätter*.

FEBRUARY 16

Erich Pommer and Fritz Holz established Deutsche Eclair Film und Kinematographen GmbH "Decla" as independent company that no longer is linked to French Éclair.

AUGUST

Das Geheimnis von D.14 (The Mystery of D.14) written and directed by **Harry Piel**.

---

3   *Der Golem. Phantastisches Filmspiel in vier Akten* by Paul Wegener and Henrik Galeen. The title page is labeled Lyda Salmonova—Praha—Berlin and was given to Wegener's biographer Kai Möller by Mrs. Salmonova-Wegener in December 1949.

SEPTEMBER

First movie version based on **Bernhard Kellermann's** novel *Der Tunnel*. Written and directed by William Wauer. Produced by **Paul Davidson**. Photographed by Axel Graatkjær. Art Director: **Hermann Warm**. Starring Friedrich Kayssler, Hermann Vallentin and Fritzi Massary.

OCTOBER

Premiere *Die Toten erwachen (The Dead Awake)* at Marmorhaus in Berlin, another entry in the Stuart Webbs series with Ernst Reicher.

OCTOBER 15

Author **Paul Scheerbart** died in Berlin.

NOVEMBER

Der Vampyr des Schlosses (The Vampire of the Castle) produced by DMB Deutsche Mutoskop- und Biograph G.m.b.H., Berlin.

Der Kraftmeyer (The Bruiser): **Ernst Lubitsch** as wimpy homebody who thanks to a tonic develops superpowers.

NOVEMBER 19

*Premiere **Und wandern sollst du ruhelos... (You Will Be a Restless Wanderer...)** at Admiralstheater in Berlin.* The appearance of a female ghost, wife of a medieval knight, is part of a curse. Based on sources by **E. T. A. Hoffmann** and Edgar Allan Poe. Directed by **Richard Oswald**.

DECEMBER

Board of Censors *Die große Wette (The Big Bet)*

Austria: Der Elektromensch (The Electro-Man)

Ein phantastisches Erlebnis aus dem Jahre 2000

Maybe the first robot movie of film history. The plot is set in the year 2000 in America and concerns two male rivals for the hand of Lee Kennedy (Mizzi Wirth), a beautiful, rich widow. One, an engineer named Ardan, strikes a bet with Fogg, the film's hero, that he will not be able to cope three days living with a person that the engineer will send to his home at midnight. The guest turns out to be an electro-man whose actions are monitored by Ardan but finally an explosion destroys the inventor's laboratory and Fogg wins the widow's hand. The movie is lost and it is not known if **Harry Piel**, the film's director, played the part of the robot. Fogg (the name comes from Jules Verne) is played by Ludwig Trautmann, his rival Ardan by Victor Janson.

Die grosse Wette (The Big Bet) | Courtesy of Dr. Ralf Bülow

Another **Piel** movie released this year was *Der Bär von Baskerville (The Bear of the Baskervilles)* that has a bear instead of Conan Doyle's Hound.

Aschenbrödel (Cinderella), fairy tale produced by Jules Greenbaum and directed by Dr. Hans Oberländer.

1916

JANUARY 6

William Voss. Der Millionendieb (William Voss, the Million Thief) written, produced and directed by **Rudolf Meinert**. A count who has passed way is substituted by a mechanical puppet. The culprit is Count Chamberley's valet William Voss. A detective named Holmes (!) solves the case.

FEBRUARY 25

Premiere at Marmorhaus Berlin: *Hoffmanns Erzählungen (The Tales of Hoffmann)* directed by **Richard Oswald**.

Episodes from the life of Ernst Theodor Wilhelm (later changed to Amadeus in honor of Mozart) Hoffmann: **E. T. A. Hoffmann**, a true representative of *Dark Romanticism*, was Germany's premier creator of spooky Gothic, supernatural and fantastical stories that gave him the nickname *Ghosts-Hoffmann* and inspired Jacques Offenbach's operetta.

MARCH

Board of Censors *Das Phantom der Oper:* The first film version of *The Phantom of the Opera* was written by actress **Greta Schröder**. The phantom was portrayed by a Swedish actor, Nils Chrisander (1884-1947).

Und das Wissen ist der Tod (The Knowledge of Death) produced by Deutsche Bioscop in Neubabelsberg and approved by the Board of Censors: Dr. Alfred Bergmann (played by Arthur Bergen) inherits Ahasver's ability to foresee death.

Richard Oswald established Richard Oswald Film GmbH in Berlin.

MARCH 11

Ferdy Mayne (*Dance of the Vampires*) born as Ferdinand Philip Mayer-Horckel in Mainz.

APRIL 24

In the auditorium of Berlin Singakademie **Paul Wegener** talked about *Neue Kinoziele (New cinematic frontiers)*:

You have all seen films in which suddenly a line appears, curves and changes its form. Out of it grows faces and the line disappears. To me the impression seems highly remarkable. But such things are always shown as an intermezzo and nobody has ever thought of the colossal possibilities of this technique. I think the film as art should be based—as in the case of music—on tones, on rhythm. In these changeable planes, events unreel which are partly identified with natural pattern, yet partly beyond real lines and forms. Imagine one of [Arnold] Böcklin's sea paintings with all the fabulous tritons and nereids. And imagine an artist duplicating this work in hundreds of copies but with each copy having small displacements so that all copies revealed in succession would result in continuous movement. Suddenly we would see before our very eyes a world of pure fantasy come to life. Such effects can also be achieved with specially constructed little models animated like marionettes… We are entering a new pictorial fantasy world as we would enter a magic forest. We are setting foot in the field of pure kinetics—or optical lyric as I call it. This field will perhaps be of major importance and will open new, beautiful sights. This eventually is the final objective of each art, and so cinema would gain an autonomous aesthetic domain for itself. A movie could be created which would become an experience of art—an optical vision, a great symphonic fantasy! That it will happen one day, I am sure—and beyond that, I am certain, later generations will look upon our early efforts as upon childish stuttering.

MAY 10

Author **Robert Kraft** died in Haffkrug near the Baltic Sea.

JUNE 10

Premiere *Die Wunderlampe des Hradschin (The Magic Lamp of the Prague Castle)* at the Tauentzien Palace in Berlin.

The plot combined the Arabian Nights fable of Aladdin's Magic Lamp with the Jewish mysticism of Old Prague.

JUNE 19

Ernst Lubitsch starred as *Dr. Satansohn*, the Devil himself, who operates (of all things!) a beauty parlor. (At the end everything turns out a bad dream.) Premiere at Filmhaus Polo in Vienna.

JULY

Board of Censors approved *Das lebende Rätsel (The Living Enigma)* written and directed by **Harry Piel**. The premise was inspired by H. G. Wells. In his novel *When the Sleeper Wakes* (first published in 1899) the protagonist sleeps for two hundred and three years. Piel contented himself with one hundred years. Professor Mikett (Hermann Vallentin) is going to revive Olaf Peer (Ludwig Trautmann), a millionaire, after hundred years of deep sleep. Peer is not only staggered by the progress but also falls in love with Mikett's daughter Melya (Leontine Kühnberg). Marston (Victor Janson), Mikett's assistant, gets jealous and kills Peer with deadly *Mars Rays* developed by the Professor.

JULY 16

Titanenkampf (Titan Struggle): Erich Kaiser-Titz in a dual role as two antagonist brothers. One of them has developed a pill that is going to solve the feeding problems and win the fight against hunger in the world.

AUGUST 18

Premiere of a six-part Bioscop serial *Homunculus* at Marmorhaus in Berlin. Danish actor Olaf Fønss (who collected the highest money ever paid for a film actor in Germany up to that time) as Richard Ortmann, a Homunculus, an artificial human being created by Professor Ortmann (Ernst Ludwig) and his assistant Dr. Hansen (Albert Paul). The unhappy creature is going to take revenge on mankind. Elements of Mary W. Shelley's *Frankenstein* story appear in modern day setting. **Otto Rippert** directed from a script by Robert Reinert. The climax confronts Homunculus in a showdown with a second Übermensch (superhuman).

The episodes *Homunculus; Das geheimnisvolle Buch (The Mysterious Book); Die Liebeskomödie des Homunculus (The Love Tragedy of Homunculus); Die Rache des Homunculus (The Revenge of Homunuculus); Die Vernichtung der Menschheit (The Extermination of Mankind); Das Ende des Homunculus (The End of Homunculus)* were screened between August 1916 and January 1917.

Homunculus | Author's collection

SEPTEMBER 1

Premiere of the **Messter** production *Das wandernde Licht (The Wandering Light)* at Mozartsaal Nollendorfplatz in Berlin. Anna (Henny Porten), the bride of Count von Fahrenwald (Bruno Decarli), is warned that the bridegroom is mentally disordered. Actually, not the Count is mad but his valet (Theodor Becker). The film was an adaptation of a novel by Ernst von Wildenbruch. **Robert Wiene** directed with **Karl Freund** behind the camera.

A short French documentary film about cross spiders became the springboard for a movie about a vampire: *Nosferatu*. A scene from it and some microscopic shots from other movies were later used in this cinematic adaptation of Bram Stoker's *Dracula*. Another documentary used in *Nosferatu* was titled *In der Welt des Unsichtbaren*.

Nosferatu
Bitten by mosquitoes?
Courtesy of Christian Dörge (Apex Verlag)

SEPTEMBER

Premiere of **Richard Oswald's** *Das unheimliche Haus (The Scary House)* with **Werner Krauss** at Skalatheater in Cologne. An unemployed young man is hired to work as secretary in a house which turns out to be haunted. Out of a mirror a woman appears and asks him for help. A detective is consulted and solves the case. More parts of Oswald's *Haunted House* detective series to follow.

Der Yoghi (The Yoghi) approved by the Board of Censors. **Paul Wegener** in a dual role: as Rasmus, a natural scientist, and a Yoghi, who lives remotely in a village where he hides Myra (Lyda Salmonova), a beauty from India. The Yoghi is able to render himself invisible. Doors open and close automatically, ghostly footsteps appear in the sand and, at the end, drops of blood spill from the mortally wounded invisible man. Co-directed by Wegener and his friend **Rochus Gliese**. Wegener had left Deutsche Bioscop and worked now for **Paul Davidson's PAGU**.

OCTOBER

Rübezahls Hochzeit (Rübezahl's Wedding) approved by the Board of Censors, however with a ban on young people (because of some amorous scenes). *As early as 1662 a mountain ghost, Rübezahl, has found his way out of the secret mutterings of spinning rooms and long winter nights into printed literature—to which he was introduced by Johannes Praetorius under the Latin title "Daemonologia Ruebenzalia Silesii" solemnly as well as awkwardly—living his double existence in the mind of our people:*

To big and small children, he is known as well as to those who did not get tired of doing research about his nature and his origin. The cornerstone to this work was laid in 1782 by a former Pagenhof master and later professor at Weimar gymnasium, Karl August Musaeus.[4]

Paul Wegener's film is the first to bring the character, modeled after Wotan a.k.a. Odin, on the screen showing the towering ghost that has fallen in love with a fairy played by Lyda Salmonova. At that time, Wegener was really in love with his fellow performer and would marry her soon.

---

4   Frank Maraun, *Der Deutsche Film.* Special Issue 1940/41.

WINTER

Albin Grau, serving as anesthesist in war hospitals, then as artist drawing maps. Later he talked about having met that winter a Serbian peasant who claimed that his father was a vampire.

Hanns Heinz Ewers was interned in the United States where he met Aleister Crowley and Hitler's later chohort Ernst "Putzi" Hanfstaengl.

NOVEMBER 3

Premiere *Homunkulieschen Parodistischer Scherz in 2 Akten* at the Tauentzien Palace in Berlin. Homunkulieschen (Lo Vallis) is no real Homunculus but an interchanged twin who plays the artificially inseminated girl just for the sake of science. Sequel: *Homunkulieschen wird Filmdiva (Homunkulieschen Becomes a Screen Goddess.* 1916).

Hanns Heinz Ewers | Author's collection

NOVEMBER 10

Richard Oswald's detective story *Freitag, der 13: Das unheimliche Haus, 2. Teil (Friday the 13th/Back Friday: The Scary House, 2nd Part)* with **Reinhold Schünzel** as Engelbert Fox, Max Gülstorff as Fix, and **Werner Krauss** as Professor Cardallhan was said to be based (somehow) on Edgar Allan Poe: Superstition has it that the heads of the Eulenstein family will die on Friday the 13th. Detective Fox and his friend Fix are chosen to protect the new lord of the manor.

DECEMBER 1

Premiere of a modern version of *Aschenbrödel (Cinderella)* starring Danish actress Asta Nielsen.

1917

JANUARY

Due to bad health **Conrad Veidt** was officially dismissed from the battlefields and had already returned to Berlin and **Max Reinhardt**.

JANUARY 13

Oberste Heeresleitung, the German High Command, established a Bild- und Filmamt (Bufa) to produce and distribute propaganda films.

FEBRUARY 7 OR 9

Premiere *Nächte des Entsetzens (Nights of Terror)* written and directed by **Arthur Robison**: Werner Krauss as artist who disguised as ape (in appropriate costume) and murdered everybody who came near to his wife. **Lu Synd** a.k.a. Pauline Müller, the female star, was also the film's producer. **Emil Jannings** was cast as a banker.

The Golem and the Dancer | Paul Wegener on the right | Author's collection

FEBRUARY

The Board of Censors approved *Die Entdeckung Deutschlands (The Discovery of Germany)*.

German wartime propaganda intended for release in neutral countries like Switzerland, the Netherlands and Scandinavia: Martians travel to Earth in a flying ball and land in Germany. After having seen everything they declare the country fit for winning the war.

APRIL

The Board of Censors approves *Der Golem und die Tänzerin (The Golem and the Dancer)*: **Paul Wegener** falls in love with a young dancer, who has seen him as the Golem on screen. But Jela Olshevska (Lyda Salmonova) is not interested in the actor, only in the clay figure which she wants to purchase. But instead of the figure Wegener has himself delivered in full Golem outfit.

JUNE

Premiere *Das Bildnis des Dorian Gray (The Picture of Dorian Gray)* in Berlin. **Richard Oswald** directed Bernd Aldor in the fourth screen adaptation of Oscar Wilde's novel. A dozen will follow.

AUGUST 31

Hilde Warren und der Tod (Hilde Warren and Death), directed by **Joe May** from a script by **Fritz Lang**, doesn't belong in this book—if there would not be a brief scene at the end: Mia May who played Hilde yearns for death and finally meets him, in the person of versatile actor Georg John who perished in November 1941 in the Ghetto Litzmannstadt (Łódź).

SEPTEMBER 21

Furcht (Fear) premiered at Mozartsaal in Berlin: Count Greven (Bruno Decarli) who took a Buddha figure from India feels haunted by an Indian Priest (**Conrad Veidt**) and fears for his life.

Premiere of the first part of *Ahasver*

Second part: *Die Tragödie der Eifersucht (The Tragedy of Jealousy)*, third part: *Das Gespenst der Vergangenheit (The Spook of the Past)*:

Again the "Eternal Jew", Ahasver, was made the central character of a film project that tells three love stories each ending in tragedy.

OCTOBER

Board of Censors approved *Hans Trutz im Schlaraffenland*: **Paul Wegener** as Hans Trutz, a poor peasant, who encounters **Ernst Lubitsch** as Satan. Satan Lubitsch offers him a living on the fat of the land of the Schlauraffen, the Land of Milk and Honey, in exchange for his soul. The film was made during the Turnip Winter, a period of profound civilian hardship in Germany due to World War I. **Fritz Rasp** was cast in a supporting role.

EARLY DECEMBER

F. W. Murnau who had landed on a plane in Basel was interned in Switzerland.

DECEMBER 18

Formation of Ufa Universum Film AG with a share capital of 25 Mio. Goldmark by a consortium led by Deutsche Bank and with secret participation of the German Reich. Ufa was established by absorbing Nordisk Film, **Messter** and **Paul Davidson's** PAGU. Chairman of the Board: Emil Georg von Stauss (Deutsche Bank).

DECEMBER 20

Premiere *Dornröschen (Sleeping Beauty)* directed by **Paul Leni** in Berlin.

1918

Cinemas: 2299
Number of feature films produced: 340

JANUARY

A deadly influenza pandemic began to rage: the so-called Spanish Flu. In Germany both, the lost war and the flu, served as springboard to all kind of fantasy and horror films, notably *Nosferatu* that was going to tell what happened during the Great Death in Wisborg. Maybe Stephen King was probably right when he once defined horror fiction as a rehearsal for death: *It's a way to get ready.*

FEBRUARY

F. W. Murnau began to direct stage plays in Luzern. He hoped to find a permanent job as director in Switzerland.

AUGUST 1

Producer **Artur** (Abraham) **Brauner** born as son of Jewish timber merchant Moshe Brauner and his wife Brana in Łódź, Poland.

AUGUST

Der fliegende Holländer (The Flying Dutchman) approved by the Board of Censors. The legend of Captain Jan van der Straaten (played by Guido Schützendorf), whose ghost ship can never make port and is doomed to sail the oceans for all time until he finds a woman who will break the curse. Young Senta Daland (Olga Desmond) is the one who redeems him by her death. Directed by Hans Neumann and photographed by **Guido Seeber** and Edgar S. Ziesemer on location at Stettin Lagoon, Baltic Sea.

Henrik Galeen back to Berlin. He had stayed with his wife in Sweden.

AUGUST 18

Der Weltspiegel (The World Mirror) by Lupu Pick with Bernd Aldor who has invented a device which enbables one to see *everything*.

OCTOBER 3

Premiere of *Die Augen der Mumie Ma (The Eyes of the Mummy)* at U.T. Kurfürstendamm in Berlin. Pola Negri as a kidnapped Oriental dancer held captive in an Egyptian temple. She is freed but her guardian (**Emil Jannings**) pursues her to England: *All the charm and mystery of the East caught into a passion-swept romance of irresistible appeal.* **Ernst Lubitsch** directed from a screenplay by Hans Kräly and Emil Rameau.

NOVEMBER 11

Armistice of Compiègne.

NOVEMBER 12

Elimination of Censorship in Germany.

Hans Janowitz who had served as an officer returned from war as pacifist. At Residenz Theater in Berlin he met dramaturge **Carl Mayer**. Both decided to try and write a film script for actress Gilda Langer who longed to be a movie star.

DECEMBER 19

Premiere *Der Rattenfänger (The Pied Piper)* at U.T. Nollendorfplatz in Berlin: Grimm Brothers' fairy tale of a rat-catching pied piper (**Paul Wegener**) who was called in by the councilmen to get rid of the rats that plagued the town of Hamelin. Some wooden rats were animated by **Lotte Reiniger**.

1919

Cinemas: 2836
Number of feature films produced: 470

German film industry experienced an illusory boom. Soldiers of fortune and gamblers hoped to get rich quick by investing in movies. Some producers dreamt of establishing film trusts and hurried to issue stock. Because the import of foreign films was restricted German films had no competitors on the domestic market. But the appearances were deceptive.

JANUARY 17

Premiere *Die Dame, der Teufel und die Probiermamsell (The Lady, the Waitress, and the Devil)* written by **Robert Wiene** at Mozartsaal Nollendorfplatz in Berlin. Henny Porten, in the role of a food taster, is that fascinated by an ermine coat she has seen in a shopwindow that the customer, a baron, who bought the item appears in her dream. He looks like the Devil, takes her to hell and offers her the coat provided she would accept his conditions. Baron and Devil are played by **Alfred Abel**.

FEBRUARY 28

Premiere *Alraune, die Henkerstochter, genannt die rote Henne* at Asta Nielsen Theater in Dusseldorf. A childless Duchess has recourse to the magic of a mandrake root, with fatal results for the whole family. Hungarian-born Eugen Illés photographed and directed.

MARCH 20

Premiere at Marmorhaus in Berlin: *Die Reise um die Erde in 80 Tagen (Around the World in 80 Days)*, a modest Jules Verne screen adaptation by **Richard Oswald** with **Conrad Veidt** (as Phileas Fogg), **Reinhold Schünzel**, **Anita Berber** and Max Gülstorff as Detective Fix, filmed in and around Berlin.

JUNE

Producer Peter Ostermayr purchased real estate in Geiselgasteig near Munich and established the nucleus of the future Bavaria studio complex.

SEPTEMBER

The Book of *Hiob* as popular cinematic tale produced by Ideal-Film and premiered at Kantlichtspiele in Berlin. Eduard von Winterstein as Hiob, Sibyl Smolowa as Esther, and Hans Adalbert Schlettow as Satan.

SEPTEMBER 11

The first issue of *Illustrierter Film-Kurier*.

SEPTEMBER 16

First part of *Die Arche (The Ark)* at director **Richard Oswald's** cinema in Berlin. While diving in a submarine the devastating effects of a comet wiped out mankind. Based on a novel by Werner Scheff published by Ullstein in 1917, with Georg Heinrich Schnell as submarine commander Klaus Donken. Second part: *Die letzten Menschen (The Last Men)*.

SEPTEMBER 18

Ufa's flagship cinema opened in Berlin Charlottenburg: Ufa Palast am Zoo (Ufa Zoo Palace).

OCTOBER 3

Premiere of the first part of *Die Spinnen (The Spiders): Der goldene See (The Golden Lake)* by **Fritz Lang**. The hero, Carl de Vogt as Kay Hoog, fights a criminal secret society named *The Spiders*. Hoog is clearly an ancestor of James Bond.

OCTOBER 15

Premiere of *Wahnsinn (Madness)* produced and directed by **Conradt Veidt** who also starred as Friedrich Lorenzen, a jealous banker who is convinced that his girlfriend Marion (Gussy Holl, then married to Veidt) cheats with his procurist. A gypsy fortune teller (Grit Hegesa) gives him the key to a lost trunk and tells him that the trunk's contents will lead him either to happiness or death. Both prophecies come true: Lorenzen finds the trunk and hides inside. He learns that the procurist (**Reinhold Schünzel**) has forced desperate Marion into prostitution and that Marion isn't cheating, but when the procurist locks the trunk Lorenzen is suffocating to death.

OCTOBER 23

Die Pest in Florenz (Plague in Florence) at Marmorhaus in Berlin. A production intended by Decla for international release, proudly labeled *Decla World-Class:* The story takes place in Florence in 1348 just before the first outbreaks of the Black Death in Italy, which rapidly spread across Europe. Thanks to the activities of an evil courtesan named Julia (Marga Kierska), Florence transforms into a cesspool of iniquity and is punished by the plague (similar to the Spanish Flu the world was confronted with after the war). Fritz Lang, the author of the screenplay, seems to have used motives from Poe's *The Masque of the Red Death*. **Otto Rippert** directed.

Die Pest in Florenz (Plague in Florence)

Author's collection

OCTOBER 29

Decla-Film-Gesellschaft-Holz & Co. became a joint-stock company, Decla-Film KG.

Seed capital: 15 Million Mark. Funding came from Nationalbank Bremen and the banking houses Schröder, Heye & Weyhausen and Friedmann & Co.

OCTOBER 30

Prinz Keo. Der Raub der Mumie (Prince Keo: The Rape of the Mummy) approved by the Board of Censors: Albert Steinrück as Professor Skrupello, a depauperate excavator, is asked to steal a mummy, but he refuses as the mummy has appeared in his dreams and he fears the curse.

NOVEMBER 6

Richard Oswald-Film AG released the episodic *Unheimliche Geschichten (Eerie Tales/Tales of Horror)*, an anthology of stories by Edgar Allan Poe (*The Black Cat*), Robert Louis Stevenson (*The Suicide Club*), Anselma Heine (*Die Erscheinung*), Robert Liebmann (*Die Hand*) and an original story by Oswald himself (*Der Spuk*). The Trio infernal of actors was represented by **Conrad Veidt** as Devil, **Reinhold Schünzel** as Death and **Anita Berber** as Prostitute.

DECEMBER

A professor discovers a bacillus that could wipe out all humanity: *Der Würger der Welt (The Strangler of the World)*, a detective thriller directed by Ewald André Dupont.

DECEMBER 19

Paul Wegener recommended his protégé **Lotte Reiniger** to Dr. Hans Cürlis, head of the recently established Institut für Kulturforschung e.V. in Berlin. Cürlis produced Reiniger's first silhouette short *Das Ornament des verliebten Herzens (The Ornament of the Lovestruck Heart)*.

Alraune und der Golem (Alraune and the Golem): Although **Paul Wegener** was no longer with Deutsche Bioscop, the company still tried to capitalize on his Golem teaming him with the equally successful female magic of Alraune. Nils Chrisander directed from a tale by Achim von Arnim (1781-1831): *Isabella von Ägypten, Kaiser Karl des Fünften erste Jugendliebe.*

1920

Cinemas: 3422
510 feature films produced

JANUARY 9

Premiere of *Nachtgestalten (Night Creatures)* at director **Richard Oswald's** cinema in Berlin: **Paul Wegener** as Thomas Bezug, a screwy billionaire, who is the richest man in the world and father of a son one would call an apelike freak (played by Erik Charell). He surrounds himself with musclemen and dwarfs and has set his mind on buying all countries in the world together with other moguls. Cast included **Reinhold Schünzel, Conrad Veidt** and **Anita Berber.**

Gustav Meyrink, Hanns Heinz Ewers and Austrian-born Karl Hans Strobl (1877-1946), the author of the literary source this picture was based on (titled *Eleagabal Kuperus* and published in 1910), were the Great Three of German Speculative Fiction after 1900. 1919-1921 Strobl edited, in collaboration with Alfons von Czibulka, a magazine for speculative fiction and erotic literature called *Der Orchideengarten*, most likely the oldest fantasy magazine in the world. During Austrofascism (since 1933) he campaigned for Hitler and the NSDAP. After the annexation of Austria, he became NS country director of *Reichsschrifttumskammer* in Vienna. In 1945 he was temporarily arrested by the Red Army and died penniless in an old folk home after a series of strokes.

JANUARY 10

The Treaty of Versailles was signed.

JANUARY 30

Satanas (played by **Conrad Veidt**) works his way through episodes of world history, from Ancient Egypt (Fritz Kortner as Pharaoh Amenhotep) to Renaissance and present age, in an episodic picture supervised by **Dr. Robert Wiene** and directed by **F. W. Murnau**. The movie seemed to have been inspired by Marie Corelli's novel *Satans sorger (The Sorrows of Satan)* and the start of Carl Theodor Dreyer's production *Blade af Satans bog* that was filmed at the same time but released later.

FEBRUARY 5

Premiere of the 2nd part of Fritz Lang's *Die Spinnen (The Spiders): Das Brillantenschiff (The Brillant Ship)*. Two more parts *Das Geheimnis der Sphinx (The Secret of the Sphinx)* and *Um Asiens Kaiserkrone (For Asia's Imperial Crown)* were not made.

FEBRUARY 26

Dr. Robert Wiene's *Das Cabinet des Dr. Caligari (The Cabinet of Dr. Caligari)* premiered at Marmorhaus Cinema in Berlin: The director of an asylum (**Werner Krauss**), modeled after a military doctor who examined co-author **Carl Mayer** during an army physical, slips into the role of Dr. Caligari and abuses one of his patients, somnambulist Cesare (**Conrad Veidt**), to kill people who attend a fair in Holstenwall.

Reportedly **Hans Janowitz**, who wrote the script together with **Mayer**, had suggested the Austrian graphic artist Alfred Kubin as set designer but naturally the regular film architect of Decla's Lixie Studios, a small glass stage outside Berlin in Weissensee, was commissioned. Thus, **Hermann Warm** became the supervising art director. Under the headline *Gegen die Caligari-Legende* [*Against the Caligari Legend*] [5] he wrote:

The screenplay conceived and written by Carl Mayer and Hans Janowitz was given

---

[5] In: *Caligari und Caligarismus*. Deutsche Kinemathek. Berlin 1970. pp. 11-16.

Holstenwall: *Caligari* drawing by art director Hermann Warm

Photograph by Anna Khan | Author's collection

Caligari caricature found in the estate of Joe and Mia May | Author's collection

to me by [Decla production manager] **Rudolf Meinert** *in the presence of director* **Dr. [Robert] Wiene** *whom I got to know at that occasion.*

A brief conversation without any particular clue what the screenplay was about, only an appointment for the next day when I should make my suggestions considering design and sets, At the afternoon, after repeated lecture, making excerpts and working through this screenplay which was so completely different with a nod to the settings I was fascinated more and more by the bizarre atmosphere. I recognized that one had to deviate in styling and design from the regular naturalist kind.

The movie images, turned away from the real, must receive a fantastic graphic styling. The images must be visionary, nightmarish. No real construction elements should be recognized. Instead a kind of bizarre painting that would serve the topic should dominate the screen.

If the film shouldn't be built with real or naturalist elements then painters should have the word, that is, hold the brush…

I informed my two painter friends Walter Reimann and Walter Röhrig who already had painted for various films backgrounds, images, and tapestries for me. The time period was one year after World War I—no profitable time for freelance artists. Until night the three of us painters read and discussed the screenplay, talked about my opinion concerning the style which I have described, and which should form the basis for the sets.

Reimann who used in his art the technique of aggressive painting cut through with his opinion that this topic must have an expressionist style for sets, costumes, actors, and direction.

The same night we did some sketches.

The next morning, I outlined to Rudolf Meinert and Dr. Wiene the result of the previous night. Based on the first art sketches, I explained briefly that only a consequent execution all around, in short: expressionist design would lend this film its absolute and strong effect.

Dr. Wiene recognized immediately the possibilities and agreed to adopt this style.

Production manager Meinert, thoughtfully contemplating, promised to let us know his decision the next day. It was positive and he explained it as follows:

He wanted to call the style and its execution mad, but one has to stick with it, everything as mad as possible. Then the film would become a sensational success, no matter if the press would publish positive or negative reviews, if the reviews are damning or acknowledging the artistic approach—in both cases the experiment would be worth.

Thanks to this decision it happened that the **Caligari** *film was made in the form that we had conceived, at least in the design that prevails in film. [...]*

In one-and-a-half to two weeks we did all preproduction, designed sets and costumes, made lists of props, and planned the construction work, selected from production designs, many of which existed in several versions.

There was a lot of work, layout planning and the classification for the studio plan, blueprints for the manufacture of individual components, furniture, props etc.

Walter Reimann did additional sketches for costumes and make-up of the actors who had been hired in the meantime.

Director's meetings and presentation of the designs only in the presence of Dr. Wiene and Rudolf Meinert and cameraman [Willy] Hameister. [...]

With furor we went to work; even the stagehands enjoyed it. Us three painters worked always till night, as if in a frenzy. This was the new wave that washed around all participants and carried them away.[6]

---

6   Collection of Deutsche Kinemathek Berlin.

Das Cabinet des Dr. Caligari (The Cabinet of Dr. Caligari) | Author's collection

All enthusiasm for Hermann Warm's formula aside, that the moving image must become graphic art, one shouldn't overlook that most likely this demand was caused by different, more materialistic circumstances outside the realm of art. German émigré author **Curt Siodmak**, who later penned *The Wolf Man* for Universal, knew **Erich Pommer**, one of the heads of Decla-Bioscop. He claimed—and even this might be only half of the truth that *during production a fire destroyed the sets. The producer of the film, Erich Pommer, didn't have enough money to rebuild the expensive sets. His inventive architects, Hermann Warm, Walter Reimann and Walter Röhrig, saved the movie by painting the backgrounds in the Expressionist style of those days on packing paper. A legend was born.* [7]

Siodmak added another legend to a legend. The fire is no more than a figment of the imagination. Contemporaries cannot recall such an event. Nevertheless, the expressionist style helped to save electricity, which was rationed in postwar

---

7   Curt Siodmak quoted from Rolf Giesen, *Lexikon des phantastischen Films. Horror—Science Fiction—Fantasy.* Volume 1. Berlin; Vienna; Frankfurt/M.: Ullstein, 1984, p. 8. [Reprint Munich: Apex Verlag, 2018]

Berlin, while lighting the sets. Light and shadow were simply painted, and everything was erected in a hurry: a compromise that made film history.

According to Hans Feld, a film critic who worked for *Film-Kurier*, Robert Wiene himself said *distinctly that the expressionist style of* **Caligari** *could be simply explained with one reason: lack of money. Film funding was difficult to find and Wiene was assigned the project because they knew that he was an all-rounder. An art connoisseur and collector—he was the first to track down the expressive Benin sculptures, pride of his home, that are sought after today—he combined the know-how with a solid knowledge about the commercial substructure.*

The sets of the previous Decla production *Die Pest von Florenz (The Plague of Florence)* were so costly and took so much time to build that they jeopardized the productions scheduled to follow. This—and mainly this—was the reason for all experimenting. Expressionist sets were simply built, didn't cost much money and were easy to light.

Erich Pommer: *The German film industry made 'stylized films' to make money. Let me explain. At the end of World War, I the Hollywood industry moved toward world supremacy. The Danes had a film industry. The French had a very active film industry, which suffered an eclipse at the end of the war. Germany was defeated; how could she make films that would compete with the others? It would have been impossible to try and imitate Hollywood or the French. So we tried something new: the expressionist or stylized films. This was possible because Germany had an overflow of good artists and writers, a strong literary tradition, and a great tradition of theater. This provided a basis of good, trained actors. World War I finished the French industry; the problem for Germany was to try to compete with Hollywood.* [8]

Germany tried hard over the next decades, but when they left the path of finding a new expression in art and just imitated the money was spent on failures like *Metropolis* or *Cloud Atlas*.

---

8   George A. Huaco, *The Sociology of Film Art*. New York City and London: Basic Books, 1965, pp. 35-36.

Werner Krauss and Conrad Veidt in *Das Cabinet des Dr. Caligari (The Cabinet of Dr. Caligari)*
Author's collection

APRIL 6

Decla-Film KG merged with Deutsche Bioscop AG and became Decla-Bioscop AG. **Erich Pommer** was promoted head of foreign sales department while **Rudolf Meinert** remained in charge of production.

MAY

A former aircraft factory in Berlin Johannisthal (Albatros) was transformed into a movie studio (Johannisthaler Film-Anstalten "Jofa").

MAY 12

Censorship was reintroduced in Germany by issuing a new *Reichslichtspielgesetz* (Reich Moving Images Law).

JULY 8

Premiere at Marmorhaus Berlin: **Friedrich Wilhelm Murnau's** *Der Bucklige und die Tänzerin (The Hunchback and the Dancer)* from an original script by *Caligari* co-author **Carl Mayer** (titled *Der grüne Kuss/The Green Kiss*), produced by Erwin Rosner's Helios production and distributed by Unitas Film. **John Gottowt** as James Wilton, a weatlthy hunchback, kills all men who dare to kiss Gina, a beautiful dancer, by using a mysterious elixir, first her fiancé, then her lover.

JULY 12

The Board of Censors approved *Kurfürstendamm Ein Höllenspuk in 6 Akten*: Out of boredom the Devil (**Conrad Veidt**) takes a trip to Berlin, but the Kurfürstendamm, the famous avenue, is even too much for him. **Richard Oswald** produced and directed. Asta Nielsen and Erna Morena were seen in the female leads.

JULY 28

Die Maske des Todes (The Mask of Death) produced by and starring Hans Mierendorff.

AUGUST 27

Die Luftpiraten (The Air Pirates) by **Harry Piel** who also starred. Most likely inspired by a pulp series called *Der Luftpirat und sein lenkbares Luftschiff*, also known as *Captain Mors the Air Pirate* (modeled after Jules Verne's Robur and Captain Nemo). Piel, by the way, had his own pulp series written by Karl Lütge (1895-1965) and published by Speka Verlag Leipzig.

EARLY AUGUST

After six years in American "exile" **Hanns Heinz Ewers** returned to Berlin. The same year he published his novel *Vampir*, the third part of his Frank Braun trilogy. Braun is the writer's alter ego, a cultured German stranded in America at the beginning of WWI. But he takes the advantage to mobilize the German masses living in the United States with his speeches and writing. During this time, he encounters a woman named Lotte Levi. She is a German Jewish bohemian and believes in occult powers as well as in a bond between Jews and Germans. After a while, Braun thinks he may have contracted some rare kind of disease.

AUGUST 26

The same year Paramount presented John Barrymore in *Dr. Jekyll and Mr. Hyde*, Decla released **F. W. Murnau**'s *Der Januskopf (The Head of Janus)*, freely adapted from Robert Louis Stevenson's novel by *Caligari* co-writer **Hans Janowitz** and starring **Conrad Veidt** of *Caligari* fame in one of the most famous dual roles as Dr. Warren (Dr. Jekyll) and Mr. O'Connor (Mr. Hyde): *One has hailed him [Conrad Veidt] justifiably as the film artist of expressionism. His intensity is burning, incinerating. If we study his suggestive-drawing movements and gestures, we discover that the acting lines that occasionally prortrude into the grotesque and draft awesome outlines also are unleashed by Jugendstil [art nouveau] that never really was removed by expressionism.*[9] Hungarian actor **Béla Lugosi** was seen as Warren's butler.

SEPTEMBER 2

Genuine with American-born actress Fern Andra (Fern Edna Andrews) was Decla's scecond try with expressionist movies, again directed by **Robert Wiene** and produced by **Rudolf Meinert** who ignored all warnings of his partner **Erich Pommer** that the chance of a second *Caligari* was zero: A hairdressing

---

9 Walter Kaul, *Pikant pointiert*. In: Film International. Unabhängige Zeitung zu den 25. Internationalen Filmfestspielen Berlin. July 7, 1975, p. 8. Walter Kaul had seen the lost film at the time of its Berlin release.

apprentice (Hans Heinrich von Twardowski) falls in love with a slave girl who thirsts for male blood. *Genuine is an expressionist film because expressionism was a success. But rather than a method of composition, it became the content of the film, so to speak. With this paradoxical discrepancy, the expressionist film faded. Genuine was the official proof that these films do not constitute a business. The "boom" was over.*[10] Interesting is one of the actors', Ernst Gronau's Lord Melo mask that seemed to have inspired **Albin Grau** in creating the iconic *Nosferatu* face. In fact, **F. W. Murnau** was going to cast Gronau—no, not as Count Orlok but as Professor Bulwer. The sets were designed by César Klein who was assisted by his brother Bernhard.

SEPTEMBER 3

Premiere at U.T. Kurfürstendamm in Berlin: *Algol eine Tragödie der Macht (Algol: Tragedy of Power)*. An evil alien (**John Gottowt**) from Planet Algol (a star called Demon, Arabian *al-gul*, according to astrology an unlucky star), 93 light years from earth, gives an ordinary miner who works in a coal mine but is dissatisfied with his life (**Emil Jannings** played him) a gift of mysterious power that transforms the Algol waves in energy. The Algol machine makes Robert Herne, the former miner, rich but its radiation destroys his family. The late Paul Scheerbart isn't mentioned in the credits, but certain futuristic design ideas in this film seem to refer to his work. *Algol* was directed by Hans Werckmeister.

SEPTEMBER 10

Das fliegende Auto (The Flying Car), another production directed by and starring **Harry Piel**, was screened in two parts in the Schauburg cinema in Berlin: Part 1. *Das Blumenmädchen von der Rialto Brücke (The Flower Girl from the Rialto Bridge)*, Part 2. *Der Klub der Teufelsbrüder (The Club of the Devil Brothers)*. A criminal named Gusson steals construction plans and prototype of a flying car.

---

10 Rudolf Kurtz, *Expressionism and Film*. New Barnet, Herts: John Libbey Publishing Ltd., 2016, p. 75.

SEPTEMBER 17

Die Tarantel (The Tarantula): An American-style crime story producd by **Messter** Film that deals with a world-shaking invention, a radium motor. Georg Heinrich Schnell played Frank Davis, a detective of the millionaires.

OCTOBER 8

Premiere at the Tauentzien Palace in Berlin *Die Legende von der heiligen Simplicia (The Legend of Saint Simplicia)*, a melodrama directed by **Joe May** from a script by **Thea von Harbou**. Rochus, a knight, tries to seduce a young nun. Under his spell Simplicia commits mortal sins, but the deeds always turn to good account. Finally, Simplicia daggers herself. The knight regrets what he has done. At the end both are united in death. Simplicia was played by Eva May, the erratic daughter of Joe and Mia May. After an unfortunate love affair Eva committed suicide in real life too (and her mother quit acting).

OCTOBER 29

Premiere *Der Golem, wie er in die Welt kam (The Golem: How He Came into the World)* at the Ufa Zoo Palace in Berlin. In 16th-century Prague, Rabbi Loew (Albert Steinrück) brings to life a man of clay (**Paul Wegener**) to protect his people from persecution, but the titan runs amok.

TITAN OF THE SCREEN

A Paramount Super Special that
STRIDES AMONG ORDINARY FILM DRAMAS
LIKE A GIANT AMONG PYGMIES!
THE GOLEM

Now terrible as all the passions of earth let loose. Now tender as a child's caress. Sweeping into its mighty scenes, whole multitudes of living men and women. The most compelling figure in screen history. Not merely a photoplay; an EVENT in the life of the city. A strange, inspiring, beautiful thing! Resembling n o t h i n g you've ever seen before. See it! [11]

The Golem city, full of nocks and crannies, was erected by architect Hans Poelzig on the backlot of the Ufa (former PAGU) Studios in Berlin Tempelhof. Edgar Ulmer who had met Poelzig (but didn't work on this picture as he had sometimes claimed) used Poelzig's name for Boris Karloff's villain in *The Black Cat* (1934) and even Universal's *Frankenstein* productions referred to Paul Wegener's film.

Paul Wegener in *Der Golem, wie er in die Welt kam (The Golem: How He Came into the World)*
Author's collection

DECEMBER 3

Harry Piel's ***Das Gefängnis auf dem Meeresgrunde (The Prison on the Ocean Floor)*** at the Schauburg in Berlin.

---

11   Film advertisement of the American distributor.

1921

Cinemas: 3851
370 feature films produced

JANUARY 28

Premiere at Richard Oswald Cinema: *Das Haus zum Mond (The House to the Moon)*:

An astronomer owns an old house, called the Moon. Strange figures lurk throughout the house's floors, from the scholar with his observatory on the roof, to an old actor and a waxworks maker à la E. T. A. Hoffmann, on down to the coal cellar and the bordello. The waxwork maker shapes a figure that resembles the astronomer's wife, which he embraces. This arouses the suspicion of unfaithfulness in the husband, who perceives only vague outlines at a window. The wife bears a daughter, Luna, who has a mysterious relationship to the moon, and sleepwalks. Conflict unfolds around her, causing the old man's ruin, death, insanity, and the destruction of the house. And above it all, the moon shines softly, mysteriously, as though it channeled destiny; its beams have infused the blood of all the inhabitants of the house with otherworldliness. [12]

Fritz Kortner played Jan van Haag, the waxwork maker, Erich Pabst Nathanel, the astronomer, and Leontine Kühnberg was seen as Luna his daughter (as well as his wife Bettina). Also in the cast: Gustav von Wangenheim as son of a coal dealer. The film directed by stage director Karlheinz Martin wasn't well received.

JANUARY 31

Heinrich Dieckmann joined artist Albin Grau in founding Prana Film GmbH. Dieckmann claimed to be able to line up a whole series of occult horror films, particularly *Nosferatu* (loosely based on Bram Stoker's

---

12 Rudolf Kurtz, *Expressionism and Film*. New Barnet, Herts: John Libbey Publishing Ltd., 2016, p. 76.

Dracula novel) and *Non Mortuus*, an adaptation of Edward Bulwer-Lytton's 1842 Rosicrucian novel *Zanoni* whose title character knows the secret of eternal life.

Book cover: Zanoni by Edward Bulwer-Lytton | Author's collection

FEBRUARY 10

Premiere of *Der Graf von Cagliostro (The Count of Cagliostro)* at Marmorhaus Berlin: **Reinhold Schünzel** who directed himself was seen as alchemist and con man Joseph Balsamo. His film partners were Anita Berber and Conrad Veidt. Produced jointly by Lichtbild-Fabrikation Schünzel-Film Berlin and Micco-Film Victor Micheluzzi Vienna.

FEBRUARY

Drakula halála, an Austrian-Hungarian horror film from a screenplay by Mihaly Kertesz (in Hollywood soon to become Michael Curtiz) directed by Károly Lajthay. Paul Askonas played Dracula, inspired by but to be confused with Bram Stoker's character.

FEBRUARY 3

Premiere at U.T. Berlin Kurfürstendamm: *Der verlorene Schatten (The Lost Shadow)* that **Rochus Gliese** and his friend **Paul Wegener** based on the novel *Peter Schlemihls wundersame Geschichte* (1813) by Adelbert von Chamisso. Wegener played a musician who falls in love with a young woman (Lyda Salmonova) but is too shy to confess his love. Then, all of a sudden, a shadow player (Hans Sturm) presents him with a magic violin in exhange for his shadow. Art titles designed by **Lotte Reiniger**.

Paul Wegener in *Der verlorene Schatten (The Lost Shadow)* | Author's collection

FEBRUARY 4

A fairy tale with Arabian background written by Wilhelm Hauff: *Der kleine Muck (Little Muck)* was directed by Wilhelm Prager and produced by Ufa Kulturfilm.

MARCH 3

Perhaps for the first time a merchandise-conscious toy factory produced a fairy tale film: once again, *Hänsel und Gretel*. The Bing Company was founded in 1866 by the Bing Brothers Adolf and Ignaz.

APRIL 27

Walter Ruttmann's abstract animation *Lichtspiel Opus 1* consisted of 10,000 frames and was shown in Berlin at the Marmorhaus cinema.

MAY 11

The Board of Censors approved *Der Vampyr (The Vampyre)* produced and directed by Fred Stranz who had cast **Max Schreck** in his previous movie, *Der unheimliche Chinese (The Uncanny Chinese)*. This film written by Franz Seitz, Sr. and photographed by August Arnold (later to become co-inventor of the Arriflex camera) seemed to have been one of the first German films dealing with the subject of vampirism (set in circus milieu). World Sales: Filmhaus Bavaria, Munich.

Nosferatu's shadow over Gustav von Wangenheim
Courtesy of Christian Dörge (Apex Verlag)

22ND CALENDAR WEEK:

The recently founded Prana Film (**Grau** and **Dieckmann**) announced for the first time their "Grossfilm" (A picture) *Nosferatu*.

Nosferatu | Courtesy of Christian Dörge (Apex Verlag)

JUNE 21

Die Teufelskirche (The Devil's Church) by Hans Mierendorff and Friedrich Degener: The Devil (played by Paul Rehkopf) builds his own church to destroy the local priest. Produced by Mierendorff's Lucifer (!) Film Company and released after a temporary ban for reasons of blasphemy.

JULY 4

Board of Censors approved *Der Unsichtbare (The Invisible Man)* produced by Martin Kopp (Kopp-Filmwerke Munich).

AUGUST 8

Die schwarze Spinne (The Black Spider): Film adaptation of a novel with supernatural background written by Jeremias Gotthelf in 1842.

AUGUST 15

Von morgens bis mitternachts (From Morn to Midnight) by Karlheinz Martin approved by the Board of Censors. Japan was the only country where they seemed to understand and appreciate this largely experimental drama: Ernst Deutsch as the cashier of a bank, who has embezzled a large sum of money, goes to the graveyard to discuss the case with a skeleton and shoots himself when the police is arriving to arrest him.

AUGUST 19

In an article *Streit um Nosferatu* published in *Film-Kurier*, No. 193 we read of another screenplay titled *Nosferatu*. The screenwriter blamed Prana Company of plagiarism but in turned out that both projects were different from each other. The case was settled out of court.

Murnau, Grau and their crew shot scenes for *Nosferatu* in and around Oravský hrad (Orava Castle) situated on a high rock above Orava river near the village of Oravský Podzámok, Slovakia. Around the same time Franz Kafka was not far away in a lung sanatorium and might have used Orava Castle as model for his posthumously published fragment *The Castle*.

MID-SEPTEMBER

The *Nosferatu* team back to Berlin ready to start shooting interiors at Jofa Studios.

SEPTEMBER 14

Lotte Reiniger's silhouette short *Der fliegende Koffer. In beweglichen Schattenbildern erzählt (The Flying Trunk)* adapted from a story by Hans Christian Andersen was shown at the Terra Theater Motivhaus in Berlin.

Nosferatu on board the sailing ship

Courtesy of Christian Dörge (Apex Verlag)

Max Schreck and Max Nemetz aboard the sailing ship "Jürgen" at the Old Harbor of Wismar *Nosferatu*

Author's collection

SEPTEMBER 23

Die Abenteuer des Dr. Kircheisen (The Adventures of Dr. Kircheisen) at U.T. on Kurfürstendamm in Berlin:

Hermann Thimig as Dr. Theopil Kircheisen, a chemist, who has invented a serum and proves its strange effects on the human body right before death.

39TH CALENDAR WEEK:

Der Film, No. 39 reported **Nosferatu** *ready for release end of October.*

Enrico Dieckmann, **Albin Grau** and their creative team that consisted of actor Ernst Reschke and composer Dr. Hans Erdmann Guckel announced an ambitious future production schedule for Prana Film: *Niccolò Paganini*; *Saptaparna*; *Gold*, a four-part serial *Höllenträume (Hell Dreams)*; *Non Mortuus*.

OCTOBER 6

Der müde Tod Ein deutsches Volkslied in sechs Versen (The Weary Death/Behind the Wall/US: Destiny) by **Fritz Lang** and **Thea von Harbou** at U.T. Berlin Kurfürstendamm and Mozartsaal on Nollendorfplatz. A young, grief-stricken woman's desperate attempt to bring her dead lover back to life is contrasted with episodes of tragic love that happened in the Caliph's city, during Carnival in Venice and in the Middle Kingdom of China. **Lil Dagover** played the woman, **Bernhard Goetzke** was Death. For Fritz Lang the production marked a personal loss too: His mother died while he prepared the movie.

OCTOBER 11

Jumbo merger of Decla-Bioscop AG and Ufa. Ufa took over Decla's studios in Neubabelsberg. Decla's debt relief caused some financial trouble.

OCTOBER

At Jofa Studios, the former aircraft factory in Berlin-Johannisthal, *Nosferatu* wrapped shooting. The Silesian funding had fallen through that month and new investors had to be found who were lured with the prospect of making a fortune in media business. Prana arranged a press shooting with director **F. W. Murnau** and actors **Max Schreck** and Wolfgang Heinz in the belly of the ship. The reporters also noted some rats that didn't act as directed.

OCTOBER 22

At Ufa's Zoo Palace, **Joe May's** two-part *Das indische Grabmal (The Indian Tomb)* was premiered. A story of Indian love and obsession: Ayan (**Conrad Veidt**), the Maharajah of Bengal, awakens Yogi Ramigani (**Bernhard Goetzke**) from his holy sleep. The Yogi has the power to transcend space and time, read people's minds and readily grant their wishes. Asked by the Maharajah to fetch a renowned English architect (Olaf Fønss), he rematerializes in Herbert Rowland's living room in England and asks him to build the most lavish and most beautiful tomb in the world for the Maharajah's wife. But Princess Savitri (Erna Morena), the Maharajah's wife, isn't dead. She is still alive and has no intention to die for the sake of a building devoted to her death.

From a series of lovely drawings illustrating work on Joe May's *Das indische Grabmal (The Indian Tomb)* by Ludwig von Wohl (a.k.a. Louis de Wohl, 1903-1961) | Author's collection

NOVEMBER 18

Die goldene Pest (The Golden Plague) by **Richard Oswald** has Paul Bildt play a student of chemistry who has found the philosopher's stone, making gold from natrium, but an anarchist is going to use the invention to flood the world with gold and drown society. The inventor goes insane and blows up his factory that is situated on an island.

NOVEMBER 21

Die Insel der Verschollenen (The Island of the Lost) premiered at Terra Theater in Berlin was an unauthorized film adaptation of H. G. Wells' 1896 novel *The Island of Dr. Moreau* directed by Urban Gad: On an island in the South Seas Professor McClelland experiments with humans. He creates monsters but his goal is the perfect man, the artificial man.

DECEMBER 9

A fairy tale produced by Ufa: *Tischlein deck dich, Eselein streck dich, Knüppel aus dem Sack (The Wishing-Table, the Gold-Ass, & the Cudgel in the Sack)*.

DECEMBER 15

Peggy Longard (Peggy Löwenthal) in *Die Tochter Ahasvers: Das flackernde Licht (Ahasver's Daughter)*.

DECEMBER 16

The German Board of Censors approved *Nosferatu*.

DECEMBER 19

Die Tochter Ahasvers: Höllenreigen (Ahasver's Daughter 2nd part) with Peggy Longard.

DECEMBER 21

Der Stern von Bethlehem (The Star of Bethlehem), a silhouette short (one reel) by **Lotte Reiniger**.

Nosferatu's downfall
Courtesy of Christian Dörge (Apex Verlag)

DECEMBER 24

Enrico Dieckmann offered F. W. Murnau a 2% interest in *Nosferatu* and a new picture. According to Murnau's tax records, he received Reichsmark 25,000 for directing *Nosferatu* from July to October. Furthermore, Dieckmann mentioned that *Nosferatu* was pre-sold to Scandinavia, Benelux, Austria-Hungary (Apollo Film Aktiengesellschaft Vienna) and Czechoslovakia (Primax).

Rejected *Nosferatu* artwork by Jürgen Maassen for 2022 marionette play

Courtesy of Gerd J. Pohl

1922

Cinemas: 3647

240 feature films produced

JANUARY 1

Film-Kurier ran an advertisement by Prana: ***Immortuus*** (originally: ***Non Mortuus***). The project was to be based on an 1842 published novel by Edward

Bulwer-Lytton: *Zanoni,* a Rosicrucian story of love and occult aspiration. Scheduled director was Ernst Reschke with Dr. Hans Erdmann Guckel composing the musical score at the same time the screenplay was prepared, ahead of shooting, a practice unheard of at that time.

FEBRUARY 17

Nosferatu screened in The Hague (Flora and Olympia).

MARCH 4

Because Prana Film, fallen into disrepute because of obscure company policy and unsteady funding, was unable to book a cinema, the Berlin premiere of *Nosferatu—Eine Symphonie des Grauens (Nosferatu: A Symphony of Horror)* took place enshrined by a great festive evening (announced as *Feast of Nosferatu*) in the Marble Hall of Zoologischer Garten. Among the many guests were **Ernst Lubitsch** and **Richard Oswald** who left after the screening and didn't participate in the party. **Murnau** smuggled one of the actresses, Ruth Landshoff who wasn't full-aged, into a loge. There was a supporting program: *After the screening of the film Elisabeth Grube and Ines Mesina of the State Opera danced with the ballet the pantomime* **The Serenade** *by Hans Erdmann who has composed the score for* **Nosferatu** *played by the ball orchestra O[tto] Kermbach. But the whole feast begins with an odd item on the programme: Kurt Alexander has written exclusively for this occasion a prelude and an interlude that refers to the introduction of Goethe's* **Faust**. *The persons: the theater director, the singer, the actor. Max Schreck as actor of modern days is selected to explain to an impresario of the past* [13] *what the art of film means. At the prelude 'Herr Schreck claimed that he can do everything', notes the Film-Echo of* Berlin Lokal-Anzeiger. *Maybe Max Schreck even appeared as a kind of master of ceremonies who gave the signal to start the film. An interlude and a brief postlude followed in which the theater director bows appreciatively to the new art the actor has demonstrated to him. [...]* [14]

---

13   Played by Leopold von Ledebur.
14   Stefan Eickhoff, *Max Schreck. Gespenstertheater.* Munich 2009. pp. 138/140.

One assures that some ladies who on Saturday had attended the **Nosferatu** *premiere had a bad night. And that doesn't seem unlikely. To pour such horror into the form art has been achieved in this perfection until now only by Hoffmann, Poe and Ewers in the field of literature. And the man who in Grimm's fairy tale went forth to learn what fear was would have got his money's worth watching this film. The* **Nosferatu** *film is a—sensation; for he leaves radically the well-trodden tracks of the hundredfold only slightly refurbished love stories and the mechanistic adventure. It scoops from presuppositionless speculative fiction whose source is the horrifying superstition of the vanpire who drinks human blood. The story of the spectral vampire Nosferatu who spreads death, plague and terror is shaped into a moving picture with spellbinding intensity. Mood-creating elements were used wherever the camera lens found them. Gloomy high mountain cliffs, roaring sea, storm-beaten clouds, creepy ruins. A perfect example of how the film can make use of the atmosphere of landscape to its advantage.* [15]

Alexander Granach as Knock in *Nosferatu* | Author's collection

---

15 H.W. [=Hans Wollenberg] in: Licht-Bild-Bühne No. 11, March 11, 1922, p. 49.

Contrary to Bram Stoker's *Dracula* novel the film was loosely based on it's a woman (**Greta Schröder**) who sacrifices herself to stop the plague that was brought from the East by Transylvanian vampire Count Orlok (**Max Schreck**), his army of rats, messengers of the Black Plague, and his accomplice in conspiracy, Knock (**Alexander Granach**), a Jewish realtor who acts as the vampire's fifth column in the Biedermeier town of Wisborg (in the script the English Whitby, same as in Stoker's novel). There are anti-Semitic overtones in *Nosferatu* as well as in Stoker's novel (which named Dracula's accomplice Immanuel Hildesheim).

MARCH 15

Finally, a Berlin cinema was willing to show *Nosferatu*, the recently opened Primus Palace located at Potsdamer Str. 19/corner Margarethenstraße 9 in the Tiergarten district of the German capital. The cinema was operated by Hulke & Isenheim (and destroyed in 1938).

Max Schreck's makeup was almost iconic:

Max Schreck, who played Dracula, underwent subtle changes of makeup throughout the film so that, while one wasn't aware of it, his looks got progressively more repellent; one never took him for granted as a standard bogeyman. He was totally without the redeeming social graces of Bela Lugosi, in the later Hollywood version, and literally looked like a sallow, living corpse. In many scenes of attack and depradation, his grotesque, elongated shadow preceded him like an evil omen, and he was constantly surrounded by indirect as well as immediate victims, the trappings of death—funerals, disease, pestilence, rats—following in his wake. The imagery is both terrifying and richly romantic by turn, and the film—a remarkable achievement, especially given the prevailing standards in Germany at that time—is still one of the very best vampire essays... [16]

---

16 William K. Everson, *Classics of the Horror Film: From the Days of the Silent Film to The Exorcist.* Secaucus, NJ: Citadel Press, 1974, p. 192.

Greta Schröder played Ellen, Nosferatu's voluntary victim
Courtesy of Christian Dörge (Apex Verlag)

Cameraman **Fritz Arno Wagner** remembered *Nosferatu* as a rather short film.

The same day producer **Horst Wendlandt** was born as Horst Otto Grigori Gubanov in Criewen near Schwedt as son of a German mother and a Russian peasant.

APRIL 10

Fundraising matinee at Staatsoper Unter den Linden Berlin: *Hanneles Himmelfahrt (The Assumption of Hannele)*, the first film adaptation of an 1893 play by Gerhart Hauptmann directed by Urban Gad: A mistreated orphan child has, right before dying, a vision of heavenly peace and afterlife. Hannele was played by Margarete Schlegel, her tormentor Mattern, a bricklayer, by Hermann Vallentin and the Angel of Death by Walter Rilla. Professor Max von Schillings conducted the orchestra.

APRIL 22

Florence Stoker, Bram Stoker's widow, authorized Berlin lawyers Dr. Wronker-Flatow and Dr. Schneider to represent her against Prana Film and *Nosferatu* for plagiarism.

Nosferatu a.k.a. *Dracula* | Author's collection

APRIL 25

Premiere of the first part of **Fritz Lang's** *Dr. Mabuse, der Spieler: Der große Spieler—Ein Bild der Zeit (Dr. Mabuse the Gambler: The Great Gambler. An Image of the Time)* at Berlin's Ufa Zoo Palace based on a character invented by Luxembourgist novelist Norbert Jacques in 1921 (serialized in the *Berliner Illustrierte*): Dr. Mabuse (played by **Rudolf Klein-Rogge,** former husband of screenwriter **Thea von Harbou**) is a master criminal, a clever hypnotist with many faces and disguises, just like his French counterpart *Fantomas*.

...Lang's film was originally received as a realistic portrayal of the situation in a corrupt, inflation-ridden Germany. The Spartakist rising in 1919 had been defeated with the brutal murders of Rosa Luxemburg and Karl Liebknecht, and political as well as entrepreneurial gangsterism ruled virtually unchallenged. According to Lang, the film was first shown with a prologue: a dynamic montage of scenes of the socialist rising and the murderous right-wing backlash, organized under state control, which eventually triumphed. [17]

Rudolf Klein-Rogge as *Dr. Mabuse the Gambler*
Author's collection

In those days Lang sympathized more with bourgeois nationalism. The supporting cast of **Mabuse** consisted of **Alfred Abel, Bernhard Goetzke**, Aud Egede-Nissen, Paul Richter, Hans Adalbert Schlettow and **Anita Berber** as herself, a scandal-ridden dancer.

---

17 Phil Hardy, *The Overlook Film Encyclopedia Science Fiction*. New York City: The Overlook Press, 1995.

APRIL 27

Florence Stoker applied for membership in British Incorporated Society of Authors with the objective to get support in her legal actions against Prana Film and *Nosferatu*.

Premiere of the second part of *Dr. Mabuse, der Spieler: Inferno, ein Spiel von Menschen unserer Zeit (Dr. Mabuse the Gambler: Inferno. A Game of People of Our Time)*:

Lang himself claimed that his major interest in making **Dr. Mabuse** *was that it enabled him at the same time to attack the shocking conditions of crime and perversion that were rampant in postwar Germany. It is true that none of Mabuse's victims are very sympathetic. Most of them are society parasites, living empty, useless lives. Mabuse feeds on them like a wolf on a dying carcass, not from necessity, but because playing with human destinies is the only exciting game left in a jaded and decadent world. For the most part, the socialites look and behave like debauched sleepwalkers...* [18]

MAY 18

Adrian Hoven born as Wilhelm Arpad Peter Hofkirchner in Wöllersdorf, Tyrol.

JUNE 9

Short film episode of the *Nobody* detective series starring Bohemian-born artist, magician and juggler Georg Sylvester Schäffer. Schäffer later refused to entertain Hitler in a private show and to separate from his Jewish agent. He died in Hollywood exile in 1949. In the 25th entry of the *Nobody* series G. H. Schnell, the shipowner in *Nosferatu*, co-starred as a criminal who called himself (according to the film title) *Lucifer*.

---

18   William K. Everson, *Classics of the Horror Film: From the Days of the Silent Film to The Exorcist*. Secaucus, NJ: Citadel Press, 1974, p. 30.

JULY 10

The business manager of British Incorporated Society of Authors informed **Florence Stoker** that Prana Film went into receivership but that it might be possible to lay hands on its production *Nosferatu*.

JULY 31

Der falsche Prinz (The False Prince) was the third fairy tale directed by Wilhelm Prager.

Der unsichtbare Mensch (The Invisible Man) and *Im Express-Zuge zum Mars (Express Train to Mars)*, animated one-reelers produced by Plastrick-Film AG Berlin.

SEPTEMBER 12

Johann Nestroy's play *Der böse Geist Lumpaci Vagabundus (The Evil Ghost Lumpazivagabundus/Lumpaci the Vagabond)* filmed with Hans Albers in the title role.

NOVEMBER 13

Phantom adapted from a Gerhart Hauptmann novel by **Thea von Harbou** and directed by **F. W. Murnau** has a clerk in a minor government office who longs to be a poet become obsessed with the vision of a mysterious lady in a carriage. Lorenz Lubota played by **Alfred Abel** ends in jail where he swears off all phantasm and delusion. Murnau's film was premiered in Breslau (today Wrocław) celebrating Gerhart Hauptmann's 60th birthday.

DECEMBER 14

Director **Gottfried Kolditz** born in Altenbach, Saxonia.

DECEMBER 23

Lotte Reiniger's silhouette short *Dornröschen (Sleeping Beauty)*.

1923

Cinemas: ca. 2700
253 feature films produced

JANUARY 23

Premiere at U.T. Berlin Kurfürstendamm: *Der steinerne Reiter (The Stone Rider)*, a ballad written by **Thea von Harbou** with **Rudolf Klein-Rogge** as sinister Master of the Mountain who is struck by lightning and petrified at the end of the picture.

JANUARY 25

Director **Francesco Stefani** born in Offenburg.

FEBRUARY 22

Enrico Dieckmann, joined by Willy Seibold and Guillarmo Lorey, incorporated a new film company: Pan Film GmbH was supposed to continue where Prana ended. **Albin Grau** was in charge of designing new projects.

MARCH 6

A one-reel silhouette *Aschenputtel (Cinderella)* by **Lotte Reiniger** who was assisted by Toni Raboldt and Alexander Kardan.

APRIL 10

Kalif Storch (Caliph Stork), a two-reel silhouette adaptation of Wilhelm

Hauff's fairy tale animated by Ernst Mathias Schumacher and produced by Colonna-Film GmbH, Hanns Walter Kornblum Berlin.

JULY

A former Zeppelin hangar in Berlin Staaken was transformed into a film studio (Filmwerke Staaken).

JULY 13

In *Der Film*, Nr. 34 Willy Seibold published the new distribution program of Pan films to be released by DAFU Deutsch-Amerikanische Film-Union: After *Schatten (Warning Shadows)* adapted and designed by Albin Grau a *Blaubart* picture was in preparation and a reissue of *Nosferatu*. The medieval *Bluebeard* fantasy film was not made although some costume designs by Grau survive.

JULY 14

32-minute *Die Mysterien eines Frisiersalons (The Mysteries of a Barbershop/ The Mysteries of a Hairdresser's Shop)* passed the Board of Censors. A surreal, whimsical slapstick comedy by Erich Engel and Bert Brecht with the comedy team Karl Valentin as hairdresser and Liesl Karlstadt. **Max Schreck** has a supporting role as bearded customer.

JULY 27

Censorship approval of *Der Geisterseher. The Ghost Seer* based on a fragment by Friedrich von Schiller that included spiritism and the conspiracy of a Jesuit secret society was adapted by **Hanns Heinz Ewers** in a 1922 story. Heinrich Brandt directed. Georg Heinrich Schnell was in the cast.

Hyperinflation at its peak.

OCTOBER 16

Premiere *Schatten Eine nächtliche Halluzination (Warning Shadows)* in Berlin at U. T. Nollendorfplatz. **Albin Grau**'s story, originally titled *Schatten der Nacht (Shadows of the Night)*, was based on the novel *Das unbewohnte Haus (The Uninhabited House)* by A. M. Frey. A shadowplayer (**Alexander Granach**) shows a wealthy but sadistically jealous husband (Fritz Kortner) what might happen if his guests, all bachelors, date the lusty lady of the house (Ruth Weyher). The shadows reveal the consequences of the characters' desires and hatreds. The original version coped without intertitles which was considered by professional circles (including Alfred Hitchcock and Ivor Montagu) a sensation.

NOVEMBER

Der Puppenmacher von Kiang-Ning (The Puppet Maker of Kiang Ning) produced and directed by **Robert Wiene** from a script by **Carl Mayer** wasn't received favorably: The story of a mad Chinese puppet maker (**Werner Krauss**) who is going to kidnap a woman because she is more beautiful than the best of his works. He can be stopped at the last moment. The woman (played by Lia Eibenschütz) is rescued, but the puppet maker falls to death.

NOVEMBER 16

Currency reform.

DECEMBER 5

Der verlorene Schuh (The Lost Shoe), Ludwig Berger's charming interpretation of *Cinderella*, opened at the Ufa Zoo Palace.

DECEMBER 19

Das kalte Herz (The Cold Heart) based on a fairy tale by Wilhelm Hauff: A Black Forest charburner sells his heart to an evil ghost who spooks around the woods and in return receives a heart of stone that kills any empathy.

DECEMBER 25

Premiere at Mozartsaal in Berlin: *I.N.R.I.* The story of Jesus Christ based on a 1905 novel by Peter Rosegger. **Robert Wiene** directed. Hans Neumann produced in the former Zeppelin hangar of Berlin Staaken. Judas Iscariot is portrayed by **Alexander Granach** as a social revolutionary, who wants Jesus (Ukrainian-born Grigori Chmara) to lead an uprising against the Roman occupation forces. The all-star cast included Henny Porten (Mary), Asta Nielsen (Mary Magdalene), **Werner Krauss** (Pontius Pilatus) and Erik Ode (Young Jesus). The lavish sets were designed by Ernö Metzner.

1924

Cinemas: 3669
220 feature films produced

JANUARY 15

First episode of a two-part *Helena (Helen of Troy)* written by Hans Kyser and directed in Munich by Manfred Noa approved by the Board of Censors.

FEBRUARY 1

The second part of *Helena* approved.

FEBRUARY 14

At Berlin's Ufa Zoo Palace, the first part of **Fritz Lang's** *Nibelungen* epic adapted by **Thea von Harbou** was premiered, the *Game of Thrones* of those days: *Siegfried* starring Paul Richter as Teutonic hero who slew Fafnir, a dragon, and courted Kriemhild (Margarete Schön), the sister of King Gunther of Burgundy (Theodor Loos), but was killed by a traitor, Hagen von Tronje (Hans Adalbert Schlettow), from the ambush. **Bernhard Goetzke** played minstrel Volker von Alzey.

Die Nibelungen: Siegfried vs. Fafnir | Author's collection

For the central Fafnir sequence Lang vetoed the use of a living lizard in a miniature set plus a large replica of the lizard's head steering upon the hero. Instead, he ordered the construction of a full-sized mechanical dragon designed by Otto Hunte and **Erich Kettelhut** and built by Karl Vollbrecht and his team. The dragon's long serpent neck was assembled with gradually enlarging iron rings, as was the tail. The neck's curve was created using stabilizing beechwood frames which were fastened vertically into the ring forms. Wire tackles made it maneuverable. In all, the beast measured approximately fifty feet from head to tail and was mounted on wheels. Inside its hollow body, a man was positioned to manipulate the eyes and the mouth. Other technicians, hidden beneath the dragon's body in a trench, provided motivation for the legs. In the monster's giant head was a petrol can with a hose leading to a pair of bellows concealed within the torso. On the other side of the can was a hole, and in front of that a little basin filled with lycopodium and the acetylene flame was lit. The bellows set the flammable lycopodium powder in motion over the flame, which in turn produced a fiery burst twenty to thirty feet long.

In his memoirs Kettelhut described the shooting of the dragon sequence in detail:

The dragon's first duty was to stand at the edge of a pond and sip some water. After this shot had gone well, Siegfried—played by Paul Richter—had to ride his splendid white horse through the giant trees of the dim forest until he spotted the dragon. Pushed uphill to the highest point of the canyon, the monster came down scouting left and right. Its eyes followed the movements of the approaching enemy and the mouth opened a little bit. Then it marched on until reaching the edge of the pond. This procedure was repeated several times. After each take about twenty grips had to shove the monster uphill to its starting point. Naturally, that took a while. Lang used the time to photograph the approaching Siegfried from different angles in order to get enough footage for editing. Finally, Siegfried attacked the fire-breathing beast with his sword. Karl Vollbrecht and his men inside the dragon had their hands full executing the commands Lang was shouting by megaphone.

For a few hours I experienced this myself when I had to replace Karl, who was needed elsewhere, inside the dragon. Though all I had to work was the movement of the beast, including the mouth and eyes, I felt the muscular exertion from it for days. Paul Richter's task wasn't enviable either. The head and the neck of the dragon were as hard as iron and moved around hastily and incalculably. An unfortunate stroke of this heavy mass could have broken a man's bones. First Siegfried had to get in under the monster's fiery breath and dig out one of its eyes. The dragon then craned its neck and stopped as did the camera. At that point, Karl was able to replace the dragon's painted eye with a prepared pig's bladder. When the cameramen cranked again, a milky, glutinous mass flowed out. With the dragon now half-blinded and unable to fully defend itself, Siegfried drove his sword into the beast's left breast and then jumped out of the frame. The cameramen stopped again cranking while Vollbrecht provided a large rubber bag and disappeared with it inside the dragon's body. There he fixed it firmly at the reverse side of the point Siegfried had hit. Meanwhile, I stood outside with a pocketknife. As the cameramen started cranking, I cut the bag and disappeared quickly out of the frame. Meanwhile, Vollbrecht rhythmically pressed the bag from inside, causing the amber-colored blood of the mortally wounded monster to flow out into the pond. After some convulsive movements, it died.

At the end, Paul Richter refused to bath in the dragon's blood. **Rudolf Klein-Rogge** volunteered and stepped in as his double.

Karl Vollbrecht's *Nibelungen* dragon reconstructed en miniature

Courtesy of Filmpark Babelsberg

The contemporary reviews were as pathetic as the movie itself:

Like Volker von Alzey the bard once played his fiddle to spread the epic of the Nibelungs all over the world, Fritz Lang today grabs the silent chords of the film to present to the demanding eye what rested in the dark womb of an ominous past. He resurrects the Germanic heroic song and confesses himself to a deed whose audacity most Germans will not grasp. A defeated people: poetizing its belligerent heroes in an epic of pictures like the world has never seen before—this is a powerful achievement! Fritz Lang accomplished it and a whole people remains steadfastly at his side. A whole people because he grabs its innermost heart. [19]

Emile Vuillermoz, a French critic, called Lang's monumental film the first heavy-calibered projectile fired at the superstudios of Los Angeles by European

---

19 Die Filmwoche No. 7, 1924, Special issue *Die Nibelungen*.

batteries destined to confront the American film with a genuinely European production. [20] It remained a pious hope.

Paul Richter as Siegfried in *Die Nibelungen* | Author's collection

Margarete Schön as Kriemhild in *Die Nibelungen*

Author's collection

---

20 Emile Vuillermoz, *Ein europäischer Film*. In: Temps, April 29, 1925, quoted from Der Bildwart, Blätter für Volksbildung, Berlin, issue 1, January 1, 1926.

MAY 10

Premiere of the *Nibelungen* 2nd part: *Kriemhilds Rache (Kriemhild's Revenge)* with **Rudolf Klein-Rogge** as Etzel (Attila), King of the Huns, who serves as Kriemhild's instrument of vengeance.

Siegfried's death: *Die Nibelungen*
Author's collection

JULY

Florence Stoker asked for 5,000 Pound sterling from the new distributors of *Nosferatu*, DAFU Deutsch-Amerikanische Film-Union.

AUGUST

DAFU was not willing to pay the sum to Stoker's widow and appealed a judgement.

OCTOBER

Greta Schröder married **Paul Wegener**.

FALL

Occultist Heinrich Tränker learned that Aleister Crowley, a Master of Black Magic (and self-promoter), was in Paris and invited him telegraphically to be a guest of the Berlin lodge.

OCTOBER 6

Vienna premiere of **Paul Leni**'s *Das Wachsfigurenkabinett (Waxworks)*, an episode film written by **Henrik Galeen** (who had to sue the producers for money) starring **Emil Jannings** as Harun al-Rashid, **Conrad Veidt** as Ivan the Terrible and **Werner Krauss** as Jack the Ripper.

OCTOBER 20-22

Harry Hill im Banne der Todesstrahlen (*Harry Hill Under the Spell of Death Rays*), a crime film directed by and starring Valy Arnheim, banned by the Board of Censors.

OCTOBER/NOVEMBER

Director **Fritz Lang** and producer **Erich Pommer** visited New York and Hollywood. In Burbank they witnessed the shooting of *The Lost World*.

NOVEMBER 5

A 7-minute animated experimental short film *Symphonie Diagonale (Diagonal-Symphonie)* by Swedish-born Dadaist Viking Eggeling was seen in a private screening at Berlin's Gloria Palace.

NOVEMBER 13

German premiere of *Waxworks* at U.T. Berlin Kurfürstendamm.

DECEMBER 16

The Pansophic Lodge Berlin was founded by Heinrich Tränker (Mstr. Recnartus) with **Albin Grau** serving as chairman.

1925

Cinemas: 3878
212 feature films produced

JANUARY 29

Erich Pommer's production *Der Turm des Schweigens (The Tower of Silence)*, a mystic melodrama directed by Johannes Guter (born Jānis Guters), premiered at the Tauentzien Palace in Berlin: Eva (Xenia Desni) is kept in the decayed ruin of a high tower by her grieving widow father. The situation changes when not a prince (as in fairy tales) but an attractive explorer (Nigel Barrie) appears on the scene. Loosley based on William Shakespeare's *Tempest*. Sets designed by Rudi Feld.

Der Turm des Schweigens (The Tower of Silence) | Author's collection

JANUARY 30

German premiere of *Orlacs Hände (The Hands of Orlac)* by **Robert Wiene** at U.T. Nollendorfplatz Berlin. Based on 1920 novel *Les Mains d'Orlac* by French author Maurice Renard. **Conrad Veidt** played famous pianist Paul Orlac who in a terrible train crash lost both hands and begins a steady descent into madness when he learns that a surgeon replaced his hands with the hands of an executed murderer.

MARCH 10

Hans Neumann's film version of Shakespeare's: *Ein Sommernachtstraum (A Midsummer Night's Dream/Wood Love)* starring Charlotte Ander as Hermia, Hans Albers as Demetrius, **Werner Krauss** as Zettel (Nick Bottom), Valeska Gert as Puck, Wilhelm Bendow as Flaut (Francis Flute), **Fritz Rasp** as Schnauz (Tom Snout) and **Alexander Granach** as wood gnome. Photography by Reimar Kuntze and **Guido Seeber**. Art Director: Ernö Metzner.

MAY

London trade show of an Anglo-German co-production based on H. Rider Haggard's *She*: *Mirakel der Liebe* written by Walter Summers and directed by Leander De Cordova, with Betty Blythe as Ayesha and Heinrich George as Horace Holly. Producers were G. B. Samuelson (Reciprocity Films London) and left-wing entrepreneur Willi Münzenberg (Prometheus Film-Verleih, the German distributor of Eisenstein's *Battleship Potemkin*).

MAY 3

A unique matinee of *Der absolute Film (Absolute Film)* organized by the artists' association November Group with the culture film division of Ufa at U.T. Berlin Kurfürstendamm. Screened were films by Fernand Léger, Viking Eggeling and **Walter Ruttmann** (*Opus 3* and *Opus 4*).

MAY 10

In a rerun of *Der Absolute Film* a short by Hans Richter *Rhythmus 21* was included.

MAY 12

Premiere *Lebende Buddhas (Living Buddhas)* at Theater on Nollendorfplatz in Berlin.

In 1923 **Paul Wegener** was persuaded to establish his own production company. Being a partisan of Buddhism, Wegener decided the first production of his own to be *Living Buddhas,* and asked his friend architect Hans Poelzig, who had transformed Circus Schumann into Reinhardt's *Grosses Schauspielhaus*, to build some lavish Tibetan sets in the dirigible hangar in Berlin Staaken. The story written by Wegener and Hans Sturm, a fellow actor who passed away in 1933, featured two British explorers who rescue a beautiful Tibetan girl (Danish actress Asta Nielsen) about to be sacrificed to a hideous goddess. Their attempt to escape to London, however, is thwarted by a Buddha-like Lama priest—played by Wegener, who also directed. He commands the girl's return through his magical powers. In his 1927 book *Der Trickfilm in seinen grundsätzlichen Möglichkeiten (The Fundamental Principles of Trickfilm)*, cinematographer **Guido Seeber** explained the technique employed to produce the movie's most impressive effects shot in which Wegener's Buddha head rises gigantically on the horizon and guides an ocean liner with the sheer power of his eyes:

For the execution of this problem a method was used which was already described in French literature as early as 1912. A person garbed in dark clothes is filmed against an entirely white background. From this shot a positive is printed which shows a dark person in front of an entirely transparent background. If this master positive is placed directly in front of a dupe negative—emulsion to emulsion with both strips running in bipack fashion through the camera—in addition to the objects of the now-filmed scene, the scene of the positive is also copied onto the dupe negative. In our case, the ship was filmed as it crossed against a cloudless sky. From this shot, as clear and as transparent as possible a negative was printed, Buddha's head was supposed to rise at the horizon line. To accomplish this, there was a white background which consisted of two parts. One was only as high as the horizon line of the previously shot sea picture, which was useful for hiding the body of the actor rising in the rear. About two-and-a-half feet behind was the second white background which—as seen from the front—formed with the other part one big equally white plain. This white background was illuminated considerably from the front to achieve, by reflection of strong light, the printing of the bipack-run master positive. When the liner appeared in the positive, behind the lower white wall, the actor's head arose looking upon the crossing ship.

For a scene in which the Lama priest walked above the water a travelling matte was employed.

Despite its fantastic effect shots and sets, *Living Buddhas* was way too bizarre to become a success. It was rarely screened and turned out a costly failure.

Danish actress Asta Nielsen was the female star of Paul Wegener's *Living Buddhas*

Author's collection

MAY 19

Artist-Animator **Viking Eggeling** died in Berlin.

MAY 22

Fritz Lang started shooting *Metropolis* from a script by his wife **Thea von Harbou**.

JUNE 1

One the occasion of Deutsche Verkehrsausstellung in Munich a short film *Zwischen Mars und Erde (Between Mars and Earth)* was screened that was produced by Friedrich Karl Möhl, Eku (Emelka-Kulturfilm GmbH). Camera: Gustav Weiss. Animation: Rudolf Pfenninger. The exhibition lasted until October 12.

JUNE 22

Aleister Crowley, deported from France and Belgium, sought asylum in Germany and accepted fellow occultist Heinrich Tränker's hospitality. In Crowley's honor a conference of occultists was announced at Tränker's country seat in Thuringia.

JULY 20

Florence Stoker might have been given the right to destroy negatives as well as positives of *Nosferatu*, but in the end, it was no more than a storm in a teacup. Like any Undead, *Nosferatu* survived.

AUGUST

Weida Conference in Hohenleuben, Tränker's country seat in Thuringia: Aleister Crowley proclaimed himself world savior which led to a schism of German occultists into three groups: Tränker's O.T.O. Pansophy, the Thelema Verlag of publishers Martha Küntzel and Karl Germer and a new development of the

Pansophical Working Group in Berlin, the Fraternitas Saturni. **Albin Grau** was present and was said to have shot film footage of Crowley.

SEPTEMBER 14

At Kammerlichtspiele located at Potsdamer Platz in Berlin a semi documentary was shown: *Wunder der Schöpfung (Miracle of Creation/In the World of the Stars)* was co-produced by Colonna Film GmbH, Hanns Walter Kornblum and Ufa Kulturfilm division and showed contemporary German special effects technique at its peak. It's an extraordinary feature-length educational about the history of astronomy which describes a fictitious space trip to the Moon and Beyond (at a time when Pluto wasn't yet even known). At the end, there is some thrilling speculation about Earth and Mankind being destroyed by asteroids.

15 special effects experts and 9 cameramen were involved in the production of this film which combines documentary scenes, historical documents, fiction elements, animation scenes and educational impact. It is beautifully colored, using tinting and toning in a very elaborated way. Some visual ideas in the sequences with a space shuttle visiting different planets in the universe seem to have to be the inspiration for Stanley Kubrick's **2001: A Space Odyssey.** [21]

In the context of Germany's Kulturfilm phenomenon, **Wunder der Schöpfung** *was among the greatest achievements of the 1920s. The production was constructed, rehearsed, and shot over a period of two and a half years, under the supervision of Hanns Walter Kornblum. The idea to describe the universe and man's place in it well suited UFA's Grossfilm mentality, one year before the* **Metropolis** *catastrophe. Hundreds of skilled craftsmen participated in the project, building props and constructing scale models drawn by 15 special effects draughtsmen, while 9 cameramen in separate units worked on the historical, documentary, fiction, animation, and science-fiction sequences.* [...]

The film's symbol to progress and the new scientific era is a spacecraft, travelling through the Milky Way, making all the planets and their inspiring worlds familiar

---

21 Film Museum Munich.

to us, with the extravaganza of their distinctive features. The film's educational intentions, however, become steadily more obscure, humorous, or even campy as this popularization project proceeds. With the excuse of presenting the end of the world a not-so-new concept as a new, undeniably scientific truth, the film veers happily along a new path, displaying detailed apocalyptic scenes of the end of mankind. [22]

Margarete Schön and Theodor Loos of *Nibelungen* fame were among the actors.

There are some fantasy scenes on a Lilliputian planet à la Jonathan Swift, one of the favorite projects of inventor-cameraman **Eugen Schüfftan**. Parts of *Wunder der Schöpfung* were re-used in an American documentary *Our Heavenly Bodies*.

OCTOBER

The recently founded Film Society in London (Ivor Montagu, Sidney Bernstein, Adrian Brunel, Iris Barry, Hugh Miller, Walter C. Mycroft, Frank Dobson who helped to liberalise the London film scene by importing avant-garde films from across the world) screened *Nosferatu*. **Florence Stoker** asked them where they got the print.

DECEMBER 19

Debt-ridden Ufa signed a distribution deal with Paramount and Metro-Goldwyn that opened Ufa theaters to even more American films. Its distribution organization was accordingly named Parufamet.

DECEMBER 20

Das Mädchen mit den Schwefelhölzern (The Girl with the Matchsticks/The Little Match Girl), a short film based on the fairy tale by Hans Christian Andersen that used the new Tri-Ergon Sound System (optical sound). The sound didn't

---

22 Juha Kindberg, Helsinki 2002.

convince the viewers. The system was later bought by Fox and turned into a worldwide success.

1926

Cinemas: 4293
Attendance figure: 332 million
185 feature films produced

JANUARY 22

Criticized for the cost explosion of *Metropolis* producer **Erich Pommer** left Ufa and tried his luck in America.

JANUARY 28

In Schneekönigs Reich (In the Kingdom of the Snow King), a silhouette short produced by Ernst Mathias Schumacher for Deulig Film AG.

MARCH 24

Premiere at the Gloria Palace in Berlin: *Geheimnisse einer Seele (Secrets of a Soul)* by Georg Wilhelm Pabst: **Werner Krauss** is tormented by an irrational fear of knives tied with the compulsion to murder his wife. Film includes a Freudian fantasy dream sequence full of tricks and visual effects conceived by cinematographer **Guido Seeber**.

APRIL

Disappointed with the use of his mirror process that in Germany was mainly used to combine full-sized sets with miniatures by selectively scraping away the silvering from a mirror that was positioned in front of the camera lens at a 45-degree angle, inventor **Eugen Schüfftan** went to America to prepare a favorite project of his: *Gulliver's Travels*.

The Los Angeles Times published an article about this project:

In a projection room at Universal the other day I saw two reels of what is probably the queerest film ever made. They were comprised of a collection of random "shots" taken by the Schuefftan method.

Certain views of the film version of **Gulliver's Travels,** *which Universal plans to produce soon, will perhaps best illustrate the inner works of this clever Teutonic device.*

In one scene Gulliver is shown peering over a high wall into a courtyard. A Lilliputian regards him with awe from the court, while another appears in the second-story window of the building which serves as a background.

Although he appears to be gazing at him on the screen, Gulliver didn't see the dwarfs when the scene was made. He was standing behind a wall that came up to his shoulders. The tiny man in the courtyard was situated on a vacant lot and his little friend in the window was off somewhere else in front of a black curtain. The building itself was merely a photograph several feet square which was placed in front of one of the mirrors.

Here are four separate scenes scattered around without apparent regard for the location of the camera.

Looking through the finder, all four scenes magically converge. The wall over which Gulliver leans fits perfectly into and becomes part of the building. The ground on which the dwarf is standing appears to be the site on which both building and wall rest.

On the screen it was impossible to detect where the matching had taken place. [...]

The all-important thing, of course, is the adjustment of the mirrors. This is accomplished by means of intricate gears, which permit adjustments to the thousandth part of an inch.

Lenses which magnify or reduce are used to balance the perspective. Lighting of the "various" sets is a phase that demands careful attention, particularly as regards matching. Through the use of curved mirrors distorted images are focused on the lens—a feat with great comedy possibilities as witness the giving of the cinematic Andy Gump a chin in one of his recent films. [23]

It is not clear if the *Gulliver* scenes were tests made in Germany and brought by Schüfftan to the United States or actually made at Universal City Studios. Alas, the project proved too costly for Universal. Schüfftan returned to Germany after having participated in some effect shots of Old Vienna in Ewald André Dupont's *Love Me and the World is Mine*.

MAY 2

At a Volksbühne matinee in Berlin **Lotte Reiniger's** feature-length silhouette picture *Die Abenteuer des Prinzen Achmed (The Adventures of Prince Achmed)* was screened. During Germany's financial crisis, Louis Hagen, a banker, had invested in a large quantity of raw film stock as a shelter from inflation, but the gamble hadn't paid off—and so Lotte Reiniger was allowed to use it to make her animated *Adventures of Prince Achmed*, a *Thousand and One Night Fantasy*, in the magnificent tradition of the Shadow Theatre.

Describing the process of *Achmed's* animation over a period of three years Lotte Reiniger explained that before any acting there is a lot of technique involved to move the flat silhouette puppets around:

When you are going to play with your figure seriously, make sure that you are seated comfortably. The shooting will take up a long time and you will have to keep yourself as alert as possible. Don't wear any bulgy sleeves; they might touch your figure unexpectedly and disturb its position. If possible, arrange to place an iron or wooden bar 5 in. above the set along your field of action and let your arms rest on it, so that you touch your figure only with the finger-tips, or with your scissors. […]

---

23   Moulton, Herbert, *Magical Effects Brought to Screen by Unique Process. Virtually No End of Startlingly Clever Things Can Be Done by Schuefftan Method.* In: Los Angeles Times. April 18, 1926.

The most cautiously executed movements must be the slow ones, where you have to alter the position only the fraction of an inch. A steady, slow walk is one of the most tricky movements to execute. Here the most frequent mistake at the beginning is to let the body lag behind the legs, so that they seem be running away from under the body. If you touch the centre of the body first and move it forward, holding the legs in the initial position, you will notice that they fall into the next position almost by themselves.

Tall, lean figures are more prone to these errors than round, short ones, which roll along easily, whilst the balance of the long ones is more difficult to establish. [...]

If a figure is to turn round it had best to do so in a quick motion. If you want the movement slower, you might partly hide it in a convenient piece of the setting. [24]

Lotte Reiniger's animated silhouettes: *Die Abenteuer des Prinzen Achmed (The Adventures of Prince Ahmed)*
Courtesy of Caroline Hagen Hall and Christel Strobel

---

24   Lotte Reiniger, *Shadow Theatres and Shadow Films*. London and New York: B. T. Batsford Ltd. and Watson-Guptill, 1970, pp. 105-108

MAY 3

At Capitol Cinema in Dresden *Die Biene Maja und ihre Abenteuer (The Adventures of Maya the Bee)*: Waldemar Bonsels's 1915 book about the adventures of a honey bee fighting the evil hornets was all portrayed by real bees and insects with the action awkwardly described in intertitles. Wolfram Junghans started shooting in 1924. **Albin Grau** was hired to design the hornet castle.

SEPTEMBER 3

Ufa released *Abenteuer des Prinzen Achmed* to Gloria Palace in Berlin.

Die Abenteuer des Prinzen Achmed (The Adventures of Prince Achmed)
Courtesy of Caroline Hagen Hall and Christel Strobel

SEPTEMBER 25

F. W. Murnau was signed by William Fox.

OCTOBER 14

F. W. Murnau's last German film *Faust* was premiered at Ufa Zoo Palace. Faust the alchemist makes a pact with the devil in exchange for his soul. **Emil**

Jannings dominated the picture as Mephistopheles (a part originally intended for **Conrad Veidt**) while Swedish actor Gösta Ekman as Faust remained weak. For director Murnau it was no more than commissioned work. It was Jannings who asked Ufa to seek Murnau's services. Among the premiere guests were Reich Chancellor Wilhelm Marx, foreign minister Gustav Stresemann, Reich bank president Hjalmar Schacht and **Max Reinhardt**.

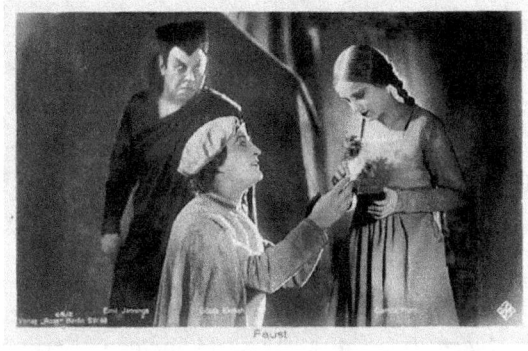

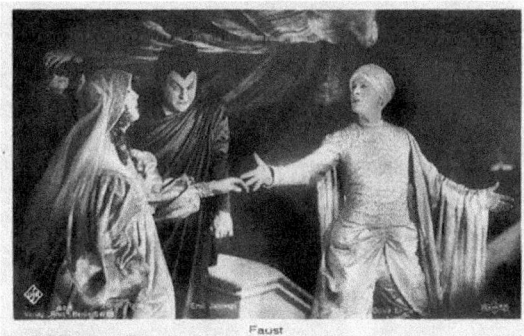

F. W. Murnau's version of *Faust* | Author's collection

OCTOBER 18

Klaus Kinski born as Klaus Günter Karl Nakszynski, son of a pharmacist and a nurse, in Zoppot, Danzig.

OCTOBER 24

Metro-Goldwyn released *The Magician (*German release title: *Der Dämon/ The Demon)* made in Rex Ingram's studios in Nice (French Riviera) to American cinemas. **Paul Wegener** played Oliver Haddo, a character that the author of the original novel, W. Somerset Maugham, had modeled after Aleister Crowley. After the *Living Buddhas* debacle Wegener was happy that he was in demand again.

OCTOBER 25

Premiere of *Der Student von Prag* at Capitol Cinema in Berlin. In the remake of **Paul Wegener's** *The Student of Prague* (this time directed by **Henrik Galeen**) **Conrad Veidt** played the student and **Werner Krauss** the evil Jew Scapinelli who buys his mirror image. Only from a photo we know that Horst Wessel, later to become a martyr of the Nazi movement, was among the corps student extras.

1927

Cinemas: 4462
Attendance figure: 337 million
242 feature films produced

JANUARY 10

Premiere of **Fritz Lang's** *Metropolis* at Berlin's Ufa Zoo Palace: In *Metropolis* Lang's writer wife Thea von Harbou combined ideas from Jules Verne (the little-known novel *The Black Indies,* also called *The Child of the Cavern* or *The*

Underground City) and H. G. Wells (the underground morlocks fom *The Time Machine*) and linked them with **E. T. A. Hoffmann's** idea of a female automaton, Olimpia. The term robot had been coined by Czech writer Karel Čapek in the play *R.U.R.* that dealt with a rebellion of machine people, which Lang must have known or even seen during its Berlin run.

The film's highlight was the duplication of the human, divine Mary/Maria (**Brigitte Helm**) into an evil automaton witch who leads the workers to a revolution that was instigated by mad Jewish inventor C. A. Rotwang who is going to overthrow the regime of the Master of Metropolis (played by **Alfred Abel**).

Rudolf Klein-Rogge as mad scientist and Brigitte Helm in *Metropolis* | Author's collection

The transformation scene was quite challenging for trick cinematographer Günther Rittau. When virgin Maria's flesh is transferred onto the metallic body of sculptor Walter Schulze-Mittendorf's "Machine Woman" as constructed per script by Rotwang, the mad alchemist played by **Rudolf Klein-Rogge**, the automaton is encircled by glittering light rings, halos, and electric flashes. Lap-dissolves made it possible to change the robot's face into Maria's right there on the set (although a little incorrect even if you don't watch closely). The rings and flashes, however, were more complicated and needed to be done in postproduction in a blackened barrack on Ufa's backlot in Neubabelsberg. Two Mitchell cameras were imported from the States for the production of *Metropolis*, one for **Karl Freund**, 1st cinematographer, one for Rittau. H[ugo] O[tto] Schulze, Rittau's assistant, handled the tedious work but never saw Fritz Lang coming to the barrack where this work was done.

In front of Rittau and Schulze's rigidly mounted Mitchell camera, a plywood silhouette of the previously filmed Machine Maria—garbed in black velvet for matte purposes—was carefully positioned. Just over the silhouette, a simple lift was erected to maneuver two parallel rings attached to three fine wires. The rings themselves were made of a special grease-proof paper that dispersed light. To further diffuse the imagery, Rittau placed a sheet of glass smeared with thin layers of grease in front of the camera lens. After running some test footage, each ring was double-exposed six times onto the original negative, resulting in twelve glittering rings encircling the automaton. Electric flashes were superimposed to complete the effect.

The traffic of the futurist city of light, the *Metropolis* itself, was enlivened by stop-frame animation. **Erich Kettelhut:**

From our tests we knew that the aeroplanes had to be animated .6 inch after a single frame of film was exposed, the high-speed rail cars .4 inch, the automobiles about .3 inch and the pedestrians just minimally to get fluid movements in a believable tempo. An animation team was assembled by Edmund Ziehfuss, the chief modelmaker. Each man was assigned to a specific job. A blue light signaled the move. Cars, trains and pedestrians had to be animated conscientiously and for exactly the required distance. The aeroplanes were animated with the aid of wires. The work had to be done sometimes in uncomfortable positions since frontages and railway bridges and lamp sockets hindered our efforts enormously. When everybody had done his requested animation, the gaffer switched on full shooting light and another frame of film was exposed.

Released by Parufamet.

APRIL 17

The New York Times published a damning review of *Metropolis* by one of the founding fathers of modern science fiction, H. G. Wells:

Then comes the crowning absurdity of the film, the conversion of the Robot into the likeness of Mary. Rotwang, you must understand, occupies a small old house, embedded in the modern city, richly adorned with pentagrams and other reminders of the antiquated German romances out of which its owner has been taken. A quaint smell of Mephistopheles is perceptible for a time. So even at Ufa, Germany can still be dear old magic-loving Germany. Perhaps Germans will never get right away from the Brocken. Walpurgis Night is the name-day of the German poetic imagination, and the national fantasy capers insecurely for ever with a broomstick between its legs. By some no doubt abominable means Rotwang has squeezed a vast and well-equipped modern laboratory into this little house. It is ever so much bigger than the house, but no doubt he has fallen back on Einstein and other modern bedevilments. Mary has to be trapped, put into a machine like a translucent cocktail shaker, and undergo all sorts of pyrotechnic treatment in order that her likeness may be transferred to the Robot. The possibility of Rotwang just simply making a Robot like her, evidently never entered the gifted producer's head. The Robot is enveloped in wavering haloes, the premises seem to be struck by lightning repeatedly, the contents of a number of flasks and carboys are violently agitated, there are minor explosions and discharges. Rotwang conducts the operations with a manifest luck of assurance, and finally, to his evident relief, the likeness is taken, and things calm down. The false Mary then winks darkly at the audience and sails off to raise the workers. And so forth and so on. There is some rather good swishing about in water, after the best film traditions, some violent and unconvincing machine-breaking and rioting and wreckage, and then, rather confusedly, one gathers that Masterman has learnt a lesson, and that workers and employees are now to be reconciled by 'Love'.

Never for a moment does one believe any of this foolish story; for a moment is there anything amusing or convincing in its dreary series of strained events. It is immensely and strangely dull. It is not even to be laughed at. There is not one good-looking nor sympathetic nor funny personality in the cast; there is, indeed, no scope at all for looking well or acting like a rational creature amid these mindless, imitative absurdities. The film's air of having something grave and wonderful to say is transparent pretence. [...]

The theatre when I visited it was crowded. All but the highest-priced seats were full, and the gaps in these filled up reluctantly but completely before the great film began. I suppose everyone had come to see what the city of a hundred years hence will be like. It was, I thought, an unresponsive audience, and I heard no comments. I could not tell from their bearing whether they believed that **Metropolis** *was really a possible forecast or no. I do not know whether they thought that the film was hopelessly silly or the future of mankind hopelessly silly. But it must have been one thing or the other.*

In the United States *Metropolis* was distributed by Paramount Pictures in a version "butchered" by Channing Pollock, an American playwright.

JULY 18

Producer **Paul Davidson,** founder of the Union theater chain and PAGU, unhappy with his Ufa deals, died by suicide.

SEPTEMBER 7

Premiere at Beba Palace Atrium in Berlin: *Svengali*: **Paul Wegener** in the title role as a hypnotist and music lover who dragoons innocent singer Trilby (Anita Dorris) into becoming a diva. When George Du Maurier's novel was published in 1894 the portrayal of Svengali was highly criticized for anti-Semitism. One of the supporting actors was **Alexander Granach** as Gecko, a violonist.

SEPTEMBER 9

In the United States the success of Universal's *The Cat and the Canary* (German release title: *Spuk im Schloss*) directed by German **Paul Leni,** who was hired by **Carl Laemmle,** led to a wave of mystery films.

SEPTEMBER 19

Am Rande der Welt (At the Edge of the World), a parable directed by Karl Grune in Neubabelsberg about a mill that is situated between two unnamed countries that become engaged in a war. With Albert Steinrück as miller, **Brigitte Helm** as his daughter Magda, Wilhelm Dieterle as his son Hans and **Max Schreck** as a spy of the enemy who is disguised as a peddler.

OCTOBER 21

The German branch of First National Pictures released *Ramper, der Tiermensch*, in the United States known as *The Strange Case of Captain Ramper:* During a pioneering flight across the Arctic Ramper, an aviator played by **Paul Wegener**, crashes and, when found many years later, has mutated into a beastlike creature. In a supporting role: **Max Schreck** (*Nosferatu*). The movie still exists as fragment.

Paul Wegener as *Captain Ramper*
Author's collection

1928

Cinemas: 5267
Attendance figure: 353 million
24 feature films produced

JANUARY 25

In Berlin's Capitol Cinema *Alraune* directed by **Henrik Galeen** (originally announced as director: Mario Bonnard) from the novel by **Hanns Heinz Ewers** was premiered: the decadent and blackly humorous tale of an artificially birthed *femme fatale*. Ewers' friend **Paul Wegener** in the role of Professor ten Brinken, a veritable alchemist, who had impregnated a prostitute with the semen of a hanged murderer to create the girl Alraune played by **Brigitte Helm** of *Metropolis* fame. Production manager Helmut Schreiber, later involved with the Nazis, was in charge. Schreiber was also known as a professional magician who appeared on stage under a name borrowed from Rudyard Kipling's *Jungle Book*: *Kalanag*.

MARCH 21

Der geheimnisvolle Spiegel (The Mysterious Mirror), the first directorial effort of cinematographer Carl Hoffmann: At full moon a magic mirror found in a castle foretells the future. The new lord of the castle (**Fritz Rasp**) is a brute. When he looks into the mirror, he sees how he is being murdered.

There are new plans for a reissue of *Nosferatu Eine Symphonie des Grauens*. Of course, all references to Bram Stoker's novel would have to be eliminated and some sequences of the original changed or rearranged. We assume that a different film title would have been used.

SEPTEMBER 24

Rotkäppchen (Little Red Riding Hood), a two-reel fairy tale produced by Fama Film.

NOVEMBER 4

Paul Leni's greatest triumph as director for Universal Pictures was *The Man Who Laughs* based on a novel by Victor Hugo with **Conrad Veidt** as Gwynplaine.

NOVEMBER 10

Drug-addicted dancer and actress **Anita Berber** died in Berlin.

DECEMBER 5

Schneewittchen (Snow White) by **Alf Zengerling**.

DECEMBER 15

Lotte Reiniger's silhouette version of *Doktor Dolittle und seine Tiere (Dr. Dolittle and his Animals)*.

DECEMBER 16

Nosferatu screened under the title *Dracula* at New Gallery Kinema in London in the 27th Program of the Film Society. **Florence Stoker** asked her lawyer to intervene. In the meantime, she corresponded with Universal concerning the film rights to her late husband's vampire novel.

DECEMBER 20

Frau Holle (Mother Holly) produced by Colonna Film GmbH, Hanns Walter Kornblum.

In addition:

Vormittags-Spuk (Ghosts Before Breakfast), a 6-minute experimental film by Dadaist Hans Richter who shows a rebellion of objects: clocks, coffee cups, bow ties, hoses, ladders, pistols and bowler hats.

1929

Cinemas: 5078
Attendance figure: 328 million
183 feature films produced

FEBRUARY 7

Florence Stoker asked Ivor Montagu to hand out the print of *Nosferatu*. At first, Montagu refused to have the print destroyed which he considered a piece of art.

FEBRUARY 27

The first German sound cartoon, *Die chinesische Nachtigall (The Chinese Nightingale)* produced by Julius Pinschewer's advertising film company, with silhouette animation by Rudi Klemm.

END OF MARCH

Film Society handed *Nosferatu* to Mrs. Stoker.

CA. APRIL 1

Finally, **Florence** Stoker had one single print of *Nosferatu* destroyed.

MAY 18

Nosferatu the Vampire was shown in New York, later in Detroit: *inspired by motives from 'Dracula'…a symphony in gray…moods macabre and mordant…a powerful psychopathic study of blood-lust…* **F. W. Murnau's** name wasn't mentioned. Screenings organized by International Film Arts Guild (Symon Gould).

Nosferatu | Author's Collection

AUGUST 27

Der Würger (The Wrecker), an Anglo-German co-production from a mystery novel by Edgar Wallace adapted by Angus MacPhail (and directed by Géza von Bolváry) with poor sound (optical sound and needle sound).

AUGUST 28

Richard Oswald's remake of *Der Hund von Baskerville (The Hound of the Baskervilles)* with Carlyle Blackwell Sr. as Sherlock Holmes and Livio C. Pavanelli as Sir Henry Baskerville.

AUGUST 30

Geheimnisse des Orients (Secrets of the Orient), a French-German co-production by Russian expatriates (director: Alexander Wolkoff), with impressive hanging miniatures, premiered in France: Ali (Nikolaj Kolin), a cobbler out of the Arabian Nights, gets hold of a magic pipe.

SEPTEMBER 2

Paul Leni died in Hollywood, unable to realize *Dracula* with **Conrad Veidt**.

SEPTEMBER 24

On the Neubabelsberg lot Ufa erected four sound film stages arranged in a cross pattern.

OCTOBER 15

Premiere of **Fritz Lang's** *Frau im Mond* at Ufa's Zoo Palace, one of the last big silent films. The first rocket to the moon: a triangular love story and a conspiracy thriller all in one. **Fritz Rasp** plays a ruthless American conman. He and his backers are after the gold that Professor Manfeldt believes is to be found on the moon. Fritz Lang's newest love affair, Gerda Maurus, was cast in the female lead as *Woman in the Moon*.

Special photography by **Oskar Fischinger**.

Among Lang's consultants was Hermann Oberth, one of the founding fathers of German rocketry and mentor of **Wernher von Braun**. Oberth was supposed to launch a modest rocket at the time of the premiere but failed to do so.

In America Ufa arranged a limited release of the picture under the title *By Rocket to the Moon*.

NOVEMBER 6

Sterntaler (Star Money), a fairy tale by **Alf Zengerling** following the financial crash.

NOVEMBER 12

Author **Michael** Andreas Helmuth **Ende** born in Garmisch as son of surrealist artist Edgar Ende and his wife Luise Bartholomä.

NOVEMBER 23

Erich Pommer returned to Ufa as head of his own production unit.

DECEMBER 11

Brüderchen und Schwesterchen (Brother and Sister), a Grimm story filmed by Alf Zengerling.

DECEMBER 14

Das Ungeheuer von Kamimura (The Monster of Kanimura), an animation short by Paul Nikolaus Peroff.

DECEMBER 16

The International Film Arts Guild offered again *Nosferatu the Vampire*, this time with better conceived intertitles by Benjamin de Casseres.

1930

Cinemas: 5059
Attendance figure: 290 million
146 feature films produced

JANUARY

An agent, on behalf of Universal, indicated interest in purchasing the *Nosferatu* print of International Film Arts Guild. Gould was asked about a negative.

JANUARY 17

The first *Mickey Mouse* sound cartoon to pass the Board of Censors was *The Barn Dance*. *The Barn Dance* was screened as supplement to Ufa feature film *Wenn Du einmal Dein Herz verschenkst* at the Universum Cinema in Berlin.

Distributor Südfilm's *Mickey* campaign was designed by Karl Ritter, a follower of the Nazi movement and later one of the regime's faithful film directors and producers:

Mickey is born in the country of Black Bottom, Slow Fox, Nigger Songs, in the country of jazz, in a word: the U.S.A. Mickey is the sound film mouse. Father: Walt Disney, an American artist and cartoonist. A marvelous, ingenious, extremely witty, splendid guy! A whiz par excellence, a virtuoso of humor up to date, a universal genius in all things technical, obsessed by the sense of motion and rhythm as only few of his contemporaries are. […]

Mickey's language is international: Old and young, Chinese or Eskimo and Nigger [sic!], *white or red, everybody understands him: a new Esperanto […] the divine language of the laughing human heart!* [25]

FEBRUARY 15

The first Disney-Iwerks *Silly Symphony: Skeleton Dance*, in Germany released as *Die Geisterstunde (The Witching Hour)*:

Another hit from the **Mickey Silly Production**. *An owl dialogues with its sitting tree, a ghost dog and two ghost cats intervene as the clock strikes 12, and a skeleton rise from its grave. Before you know it, it quadruplicates and a danse macabre of horrifying comedy begins, culminating—a splendid idea—in a xylophone solo which one of the skeletons plays on skull, vertrebrae and ribs of one of its companions. Then the rooster crows, and the haunting is over; two forgotten feet remain lonely outside till a bone hand grabs out of the grave and collects the desperate parts to join it with the others—The End.* [26]

---

25   Filmwoche No. 12, 1930.
26   Ton und Bild No. 37, 1930.

FEBRUARY 17

Südfilm invited all Berlin cinema owners to a trade show with *Mickey Mouse* and *Silly Symphonies* that took place at Marmorhaus Theater. Südfilm screened *Ein Schiff streicht durch die Wellen (Steamboat Willie), Das Dampfross steigt, Jedermann seine eigene Jazzband, Im Tiervarieté (The Opry House)*, the Sillys *Die Geisterstunde (The Skeleton Dance)* and *Im wunderschönen Monat Mai (Springtime)*.

FEBRUARY 27

Das Waldhaus (The Hut in the Forest), one of the lesser known fairy tales of the Grimm Brothers, and *Die Wichtelmänner (Heinzelmännchen/Brownies)* by Alf Zengerling.

MAY 16

Waldemar Roger followed the example of *Schatten* that was rereleased in 1929 under the title *Die Nacht der Erkenntnis* with sound-on-disc (and a commentary by Dr. Kurt Thomalla). Roger's newly edited Organon needle sound version of *Nosferatu* released under the title *Die zwölfte Stunde (The Twelfth Hour)* opened in Vienna (to negative reviews). The role names were changed and, except for Orlok who became Wolkoff, germanized: Knock was renamed Karsten, Hutter Kundberg, Ellen Margitta, Harding Hartung. Some sound scenes and landscape views were added, and in the end, when the vampire is dead, we hear the choral *Grosser Gott, wir loben dich (Holy God, we praise thy name)*.

Nosferatu marionette
Courtesy of Gerd J. Pohl

MAY 27

The Comenius feature film *Die Jagd nach dem Glück (The Pursuit of Happiness)* by **Rochus Gliese** had some shadow play and silhouette animation by **Lotte Reiniger** and Berthold Bartosch.

JULY

Symon Gould offered Universal his *Nosferatu* print for $1000.

AUGUST 12

Premiere of the sound film remake of *Der Andere (The Other)* at Capitol in Berlin. **Robert Wiene** directed. Fritz Kortner played the split personality of attorney Hallers.

AUGUST 13

Finally, Universal paid $400 for Symon Gould's print of *Nosferatu*.

OCTOBER 30

Producer **Erwin C. Dietrich** born in Glarus, Switzerland.

NOVEMBER 14

Waldemar Roger's *Die zwölfte Stunde (The Twelfth Hour)* approved by the German Board of Censors.

Nosferatu marionette
Courtesy of Gerd J. Pohl

DECEMBER 2

Premiere of **Richard Oswald's** sound film remake of *Alraune* at Gloria Palace in Berlin. **Brigitte Helm** repeated her part from the silent while **Paul Wegener** as Professor ten Brinken was substituted by Albert Bassermann. Thanks to screenwriter Charlie Roellinghoff (who also did some work for George Pal's comic strips published by Scherl), parts of the script were slightly comedy.

Major Hans Ewald's company that specialized in industrial films released a short film with animated plasticine dinosaurs inspired by Willis O'Brien's stop-motion animation for *The Lost World*: *Aus der Urzeit der Erde (From Primordial Times)*.

1931

Cinemas: 5066
Attendance figure: 273 million
144 feature films produced

JANUARY 17

Ferdinand Diehl, who had served as trickfilm cameraman at the now defunct Emelka in Munich, finished a 20-minute silhouette short in the tradition of **Lotte Reiniger**: *Kalif Storch (Caliph Stork)* from the fairy tale by Wilhelm Hauff.

MARCH 11

Friedrich Wilhelm Murnau died in a hospital in Santa Barbara from injuries he had sustained in a car accident.

MARCH 17

Posthumously *Die zwölfte Stunde (The Twelfth Hour)* and **Murnau's** original *Nosferatu* were shown at the Kamera Arthouse Cinema in Berlin.

MARCH 18

Director **Rolf Losansky** born in Frankfurt/Oder.

APRIL 11

F. W. Murnau entombed in Southwest Cemetery in Stahnsdorf outside of Berlin. Among the mourners were **Emil Jannings, Erich Pommer**, Georg Wilhelm Pabst, and Robert Flaherty. Eulogy held by **Fritz Lang**.

MAY 11

Premiere of **Fritz Lang's** *M* at Ufa Zoo Palace. The child murderer Hans Beckert was played by **Peter Lorre**, a Jew, a fact often overlooked but obviously highly important for Germany's right-wing scene. Berlin's NS Gauleiter Goebbels rejoiced in his diary: *Finally, a film voting for death penalty.*

OCTOBER 15

Joined by Paul Wittke Jr., a Berlin businessman, George Pal who had left Ufa recently founded Trickfilm-Studio G.m.b.H. Pal, besides preparing a 2D series from his *Hababuk* comic strips, turned to dimensional animation which became the basic principle of his later *Puppetoons* replacement series. *Metropolis* alumnus H. O. Schulze who was Pal's cinematographer recalled: *"I became acquainted with George Pal at Ufa Werbefilm where I was responsible for model animation photography and for the photographic quality of the cartoons. In 1932, when he decided to leave Ufa and establish his own company, Pal asked if I was interested in joining him. He told me that he had in mind something really unusual and that he wanted to equip his new studio in a very up-to-date manner. Always interested in experiments, I accepted. Our first commission was an advertising film for Oberst Cigarettes. Pal didn't want to have it drawn frame by frame in the common cartoon fashion, but to do it instead with dimensional animation. A blade of tobacco would fold up by itself, glide into a paper husk, stand up, get legs, and a head and so on. Then the twenty cigarettes from one package would form a squadron, with an oberst (colonel) commanding in front, and would march through a futuristic setting which consisted of cigarette packages. The main street of our set was about thirty feet long and ran the whole length of the studio. The cigarettes for each animation step were mounted on boards. All in all, we had approximately sixteen or eighteen boards with squadrons of cigarettes in various walking positions to complete one single walking step which, repeatedly used, resulted in a walking cycle."*

A cigarette tobacco leaf standing on two legs, complete with Plasticine mouth movements, is going to introduce the process of cigarette production that is shown in live-action scenes.

The humanized lead tells the audience that the tobacco leaves keep moist, not by drinking (from a small milk bottle), but that they generate moisture from the air to keep themselves smooth.

We see female workers sort out leaves.

From the process of shredding, the leaf returns, from the netherworld so to speak, in ghostly 2D animation, to continue its narration. Then it is rolled into the paper.

Finally, we have a humanoid cigarette, with wire legs and wire arms and clods for feet and hands.

This stop motion cigarette takes over as Colonel Oberst with paper mouth movements and a small paper hat as a helmet. He then proceeds to command a small army:

Stand at attention!
Eyes front!
Count off!

Gold filter soldiers count off and form a marching column: six cigarettes in front, six in the middle, two behind, with the colonel marching ahead to Prussian and Bavarian march music.

NOVEMBER 4

Aschenbrödel (Cinderella) by **Alf Zengerling**.

DECEMBER 1

With the short *Zwischpaduri, der Strolch (Zwischpaduri the Rascal)* animator **Ferdinand Diehl** switched from silhouette to puppet animation.

1932

Cinemas: 5059
Attendance figure: 238 million
132 feature films produced

FEBRUARY 18

Der Geheimagent. Ein Mann fällt vom Himmel (Secret Agent) at Mozartsaal on Nollendorfplatz, Berlin: **Harry Piel** as secret agent Harry Parker who represents a society that fights chemical warfare and mustard gas is sent to a country where Professor Managan (Eduard von Winterstein) has developed a dangerous lethal gas. His adversary is Soviet intelligence officer Salit (Leonard Steckel).

MARCH 24

Das blaue Licht. Eine Berglegende aus den Dolomiten (The Blue Light: A Mountain Legend from the Dolomites), Leni Riefenstahl's debut as film director (at least she claimed that credit while actually Béla Balázs directed): a mystic yarn of a village girl named Junta who lives in an isolated village in the Dolomites. She is ostracized by the superstitious villagers who consider he a witch. They believe that numerous young men, lured by Junta's beauty, have followed her towards a mysterious blue light located in a crystal grotto on Monte Cristallo and fallen to their deaths. Vigo (Mathias Wieman), an artist, wins her affection and reveals the secret which leads to Junta's fatal death. The result of Riefenstahl's work looked rather amateurish.

MAY 6

Berlin premiere of Carl Theodor Dreyer's Franco-German co-production *Vampyr—Der Traum des Allan Gray,* loosely based on Joseph Sheridan Le Fanu's novel *Carmilla: The young, ethereal Carmilla is very unlike the aged, solid Marguerite Chopin (Henriette Gérard), though the two successive girl victims in the Le Fanu [story] might have transformed into the sisters Léone (Sybille Schmitz) and Gisèle (Rena Mandel).* **Vampyr** *seems more like a screen original that tries to feel like an oft-told tale, with silent-movie-style prose captions between scenes and characters who drift through the plot as if trapped in a recurring nightmare. Still, the evocation of Le Fanu's female vampire is significant—just as* "**Carmilla**" *established a countertradition of the seductive female vampire.* **Vampyr** *is the first film to make much of such a figure, as incarnated by the dour crone Marguerite and the semitransformed Léone.* [...]

The character of Marguerite Chopin remains unusual, if not unique, in vampire literature and film. Vampires may be centuries old, but they tend not to look as ancient as Gérard's white-haired "woman from the graveyard", unless the light of day or a stake through the heart transforms them into a crone [...] *Though Gérard's Marguerite is not as extravagantly repulsive as Max Schreck's Dracula stand-in Graf von Orlok in* **Nosferatu** *or Chaney's bogus vampire [in the lost* **London After Midnight***], Dreyer makes her frightening simply by dwelling on her careworn face and blank eyes, which the audience invests with malevolence...* [27]

Photographed by Rudolph Maté. **Hermann Warm** of *Caligari* fame was the art director.

---

27   Kim Newman, *Vampyr* and the Vampire. https://www.criterion.com/current/.../560-vampyr-and-the-vampi...

Vampyr by Carl Theodor Dreyer | Author's collection

MAY 18

Frankenstein released to Germany by Universal's Berlin branch office.

JULY 22

Der Hexer (The Witcher) based on a novel (*The Ringer*) by Edgar Wallace (that was repeatedly filmed in Germany) with Paul Richter and **Fritz Rasp**.

Cotta in Stuttgart published Hanns Heinz Ewers' Fascist *Horst Wessel* novel.

AUGUST 25

Wupp lernt Gruseln (Wupp Learns What Fear Is), a stop-motion puppet film short by Ferdinand and Hermann **Diehl**.

SEPTEMBER 6

German premiere of the Franco-German co-production *Die Herrin von Atlantis (L'Atlantide)* based on a novel by Pierre Benoit which was turned into a movie already in 1921 by Jacques Feyder. The sound version was directed by Georg Wilhelm Pabst. **Brigitte Helm** played Antinea, the ruler of lost Atlantis sunk (for a change) not in the ocean but in desert sand.

SEPTEMBER 7

Richard Oswald's talkie remake of his own *Unheimliche Geschichten (Tales of Horror)* at Ufa Theater Kurfürstendamm in Berlin. Instead of five this time there are only three stories anthologized cinematically: Robert Louis Stevenson's *Suicide Club*, *The Black Cat* by Edgar Allan Poe and, for the first time, *The System of Dr. Tarr and Professor Fether* by Poe as well. **Paul Wegener** starred. Future futurologist Robert Jungk assisted Oswald. **John Gottowt** was seen for the last time on a German screen in a small supporting role.

DECEMBER 1

A 10-minute Universal short with the title *Boo* with excerpts from *The Cat Creeps* (1930) and *Frankenstein* (1931) and—lo and behold!—not their own Lugosi *Dracula* but *Nosferatu*.

The Lugosi *Dracula* was released to Germany the same year in a dubbed version.

DECEMBER 4

Gustav Meyrink died in Starnberg.

DECEMBER 13

Geheimnis des blauen Zimmers (The Secret of the Blue Room) produced and directed by Erich Engels from a screenplay by Arnold Lippschitz: Three friends (Hans Adalbert Schlettow, Wolfgang Staudte and Peter Wolff) who visit a girl named Irene (Else Elster) who lives in a castle with her father (Theodor Loos) go for a test of courage and decide to explore the mystery of a blue room that has been locked for 20 years.

DECEMBER 22

F.P. 1 antwortet nicht (F.P. 1 Doesn't Answer) premiered at Ufa Zoo Palace. **Kurt Siodmak's** novel about a huge floating platform in the Atlantic that makes long-distance flights viable was filmed in three sound versions (German with Hans Albers as heroic flier Ellissen and **Peter Lorre** as sidekick, French with Charles Boyer, English with **Conrad Veidt** released in the United States by Fox). Critic Willy Haas called the movie *a symphony of machines, a song of a mechanized world.* [28]

For a brief time, a sound film remake of *Metropolis* with **Conrad Veidt** and **Peter Lorre** was considered.

1933

Cinemas: 5071
Attendance figure: 245 million
114 feature films produced

JANUARY 30

Adolf Hitler was sworn in by Reich President Paul von Hindenburg as Chancellor of Germany.

A planned sound film version of *The Golem* by **Henrik Galeen**, *Das steinerne Phantom (The Phantom of Stone)*, fell through. Galeen was going to leave the country.

---

28 Film-Kurier, Nr. 302, 23. December 1932.

The same year a German pulp series was created by Paul Alfred Müller, a fan of the Hollow Earth theory (that was popular with some Nazis too) using the nom de plume Lok Myler: *Sun Koh—Der Erbe von Atlantis*. *Sun Koh: The Heir of Atlantis* is sort of an "Aryan" prince from the past sent to the present to escape the sinking of his island. The series was published by Bergmann Verlag Leipzig.

MARCH 13

Dr. Joseph Goebbels was appointed Reich Minister of Public Enlightenment and Propaganda.

MARCH 29

Germany's new Minister of Enlightenment and Propaganda banned **Fritz Lang's** second talkie *Das Testament des Dr. Mabuse (The Testament of Dr. Mabuse)* to be released by the German branch office of Universal (**Paul Kohner**). A premiere at the Ufa Zoo Palace in Berlin was canceled. Instead, a heroic documentary was shown: *Blutendes Deutschland (Bleeding Germany)*. In interviews after the war Lang claimed to have consciously critized the Nazi movement with this picture although, at that time, he sympathized with Germany's nationalist "elatedness". His former writer wife **Thea von Harbou** was already a member of NSDAP and the Nazis allegedly courted Lang because they liked *Nibelungen* and *Metropolis*. Nevertheless, Goebbels had problems with the portrayal of a criminal organization masterminded by the spirit of Dr. Mabuse (**Rudolf Klein-Rogge**) who succeeds in brainwashing Prof. Dr. Baum's (Oscar Beregi, Sr.) mind and bends the head of an insane asylum to his will.

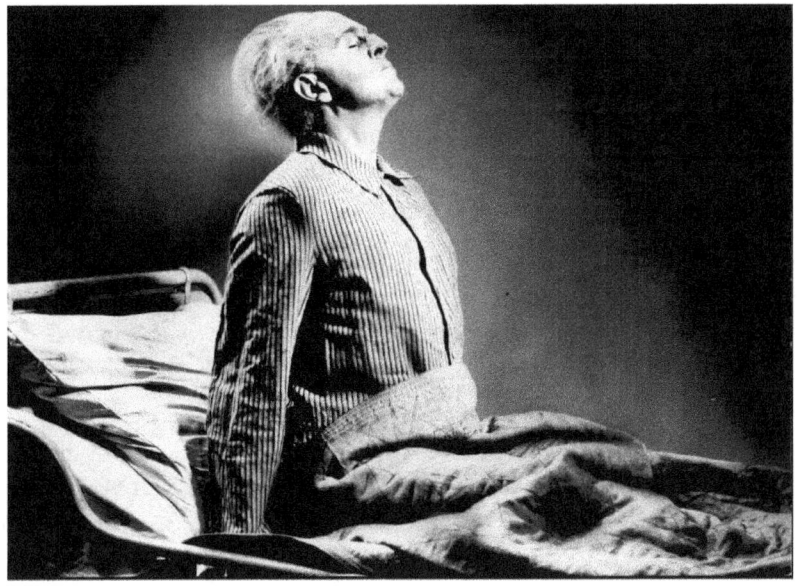

Rudolf Klein-Rogge in *Das Testament des Dr. Mabuse*
Author's collection

APRIL 12

Frank Wysbar's film ***Anna und Elisabeth***, a strange salvation story, was shown at the Capitol Cinema in Berlin. In a village in the Canton of Grisons one who was already declared dead recovers thanks to the prayers of Anna (Hertha Thiele), a young peasant girl. Soon after, Elisabeth (Dorothea Wieck), a middle-aged aristocratic woman who is paralyzed, can walk again—and Anna finds herself in the role of a faith healer. When Anna fails to heal a city-dweller named Mathias Testa (played by Mathias Wieman) the slightly lesbian relationship between Anna and Elisabeth breaks up: Elisabeth commits suicide.

AUGUST 26

Director **Rainer Erler** born in Munich.

SEPTEMBER 29

When Universal announced its production of James Whale's *The Invisible Man* that turned out to be quite faithful to H. G. Wells' novel **Harry Piel** hurried and jumped on the bandwagon with *Ein Unsichtbarer geht durch die Stadt (An Invisible Man Walks the City)* to beat Claude Rains to the screens by two months:

Piel plays Harry, a Berlin taxi driver. In a suitcase that was lost in his cab he finds some bizarre gadgetry that renders the carrier invisible, like Siegfried's camouflage cap of the *Nibelungs*, a cloak of concealment. As invisible man Harry fixes a horse race and wins 96,000 Marks. With a fortune at his hand, he indulges himself in a lazy lifestyle but Lotte, his girlfriend, doesn't want to join in. She realizes that something is wrong with Harry: that the man she loves is changing. Instead Lissy, an actress, steps in and gets kept by him. But then Fritz (played by Fritz Odemar), Harry's new valet, runs away with the "magic box". Hot on the invisible man's track, Harry prevents a bank robbery. He pursues Fritz in a car, riding a motorbike and up into the air aboard a zeppelin. Fighting Fritz, he wakes up and realizes that all was a nightmare. The gadgetry found in his taxi was just a pilot's helmet with blind flight transmitter. The finder's reward pays for Lotte's back rent and for the engagement of the couple.

Written by Hans Rameau. Premiered at U.T. Kurfürstendamm in Berlin.

OCTOBER 19

Premiere of the short films *Das Wunder des gezeichneten Tones, Pitsch und Patsch* and *Kleine Rebellion* in Munich, a day later at Marmorhaus in Berlin. The films were based on Rudolf Pfenninger's experiments with *Tönende Handschrift*, graphical sound that was drawn on the film strip.

OCTOBER 27

Der Tunnel (The Tunnel), the second screen adaptation of **Bernhard Kellermann's** utopist novel with Paul Hartmann as Mac Allan, engineer, and Gustaf

Gründgens as Woolf, a dubious Wall Street financier who tries to sabotage Mac Allan's achievements in building a Transatlantic Tunnel. **Max Schreck** was seen in a pipe-smoking bit part for less than a minute. Directed by Kurt Bernhardt who left Germany after this work was finished and became a Hollywood director (Curtis Bernhardt) filming with Bette Davis, Ronald Reagan, Humphrey Bogart, Charles Laughton, Joan Crawford and Peter Ustinov.

DECEMBER 1

After some problems with censorship a cut version of *King Kong* became a huge success in Germany too, released by Europa Filmverleih as *Die Fabel von King Kong: Ein amerikanischer Trick- und Sensationsfilm (The Fable of King Kong: An American Trick and Sensation Film)*. Hitler was said to have seen it at least 18 times and often talked about it.

1934

Cinemas: 4889
Attendance figure: 259 million
129 feature films produced

MARCH 9

Premiere of **Harry Piel's** *Die Welt ohne Maske: Ein Film vom Fernsehen (The World Without a Mask: A Film about Televison)* at Capitol Cinema in Berlin: Two tinkerers, Dr. Tobias Bern (Kurt Vespermann) and his neighbor Harry Palmer (Piel) accidentally invent fully fledged television: "We not only teleview, we see all through!" The invention enables the two to see right through walls. A South American radio industrialist (Hubert von Meyerinck) sics his gangsters (**Rudolf Klein-Rogge** and others) on them to bring the device under his control. To accomplish televised pictures on screen Piel and his cameraman Ewald Daub used a special A.E.G. rear projector developed by Emil Mechau (1882-1945).

MARCH 29

Following *F.P. 1* Ufa and director Karl Hartl launched a second science fiction talkie starring Hans Albers as modern-day alchelmist at Ufa's Zoo Palace in Berlin: *Gold*. Albers is seen as engineer Werner Holk who tries to restore the good name of his mentor Professor Achenbach (Friedrich Kayssler) who was killed in an explosion that destroyed his idea to win gold through atomic fragmentation. His adversary is a Scottish speculator, John Wills (Michael Bohnen) who has copied Achenbach's device. **Brigitte Helm** plays Wills' daughter. Parts of the film were reused in 1953 by producer Ivan Tors and **Curt Siodmak** for *The Magnetic Monster*. A French version *L'or* that was filmed simultaneously starred Pierre Blanchar and Brigitte Helm.

APRIL

Backed by Zeiss Ikon A.-G. in Dresden, Richard Groschopp, who began as a film amateur before he entered professional ranks, presented a puppet film in 9.5mm format, *Die wundersamen Abenteuer des kleinen Mutz (The Miraculous Adventures of Little Mutz)*: A boy's rocket flight to Planet X won the silver medal of the 1935 International Amateur Film Festival in London. The same year Groschopp animated another short using chess figures titled *Eine kleine Königstragödie (A Little King's Tragedy)* that was so impressive that Dresden producer Fritz Boehner (Boehner Film) asked him to re-do it in 35mm.

APRIL 13

Hanneles Himmelfahrt (Hannele's Assumption), a sound film remake of Gerhart Hauptmann's play about an abused orphan girl (Inge Landgut, one of **Peter Lorre's** victims in *M*) who has heavenly dreams while dying. The Angel of Death is played by Lothar Warsitz, Hannele's brutal stepfather by **Rudolf Klein-Rogge**. **Thea von Harbou** wrote and directed this entry for Jewish producer Gabriel Levy (Aafa Film A.G.) who left Germany the same year.

AUGUST 11

Premiere at Ufa Zoo Palace in Berlin: *Der Herr der Welt (Master of the World)*,

Harry Piel's second robot film: While idealistic factory owner Dr. Heller (Walter Janssen) only wants to create working robots his colleague, Professor Wolf (Walter Franck), is going to create a gigantic fighting machine as means to put down strikes and rebellions and secure world domination. *Such robots are beneficial—this demonstrates* **The Master of the World**—*basically for entrepreneurs who are enabled to throw their workers on the dole. Only when an engineer who falls in love at the right time with the right woman, the widow of the robot manufacturer, takes a stand for his workmates they are regarded: With a share of the profits made from the leasing of the robots they are settled as farmers. While in this half of the story the blessing of technology reaches everybody, the fear of technology prevails in the other half, the horror plot of super robots, a fear that is fed from an experience made in the production process—the experience of the subject being at the mercy of a mechanical object world. As the film allows this everyday horror only in the image of the super robot, it can ban it with the self-destruction of the moloch. Albeit how much this horror resonates in the image of the working robot too, one feels realizing the seriousness of other scenes that are supposed to prove the harmlessness of the sheet metal monsters, for instance when [actor] Otto Wernicke repairs one and talks to it like to a buddy.* [29]

The writer, Georg Mühlen-Schulte, belonged to a group of authors who had signed an oath of allegiance vowing for Adolf Hitler. The group included Gottfried Benn, Max Halbe, Hanns Johst, Walter von Molo and Will Vesper.

OCTOBER

Ufa commissioned cartoonist Otto Waffenschmied [a.k.a. Otto Wawrzyckek] to develop a new animated cartoon character. After some research Waffenschmied came up with an old German fairy-tale silvan elf, *Tilo Voss*, whom he thought would fit the purpose. Screen and color tests were made but a year later the project was finally disbanded.

---

29 Kraft Wetzel, *Liebe, Tod und Technik. Utopie und NS-Ideologie im Phantastischen Kino des Dritten Reiches*. In: *Liebe, Tod und Technik. Kino des Phantastischen 1933-1945*. Berlin: Stiftung Deutsche Kinemathek, 1977, pp. 27-28.

Tilo Voss was abandoned by Ufa | Courtesy of J. P. Storm

NOVEMBER 20

Lotte Reiniger's 12-minute silhouette short *Das gestohlene Herz (The Stolen Heart)* based on a fable by Ernst Keienburg screened at Marmorhaus in Berlin celebrating the Day of German Folk Music.

DECEMBER 2

Trickfilm expert **Helmut Herbst** born in Escherhof.

DECEMBER 9

Bayerische Film GmbH compiled a Walt Disney short film program: *Die lustige Palette—Im Reiche der Micky Maus (The Funny Palette: In the Reich of Mickey Mouse)*. It consisted of four Technicolor *Silly Symphonies* and two black-and-white *Mickey Mouse* cartoons: *Der Rattenfänger von Hameln (The Pied Piper)*, *Die Nacht vor dem Weihnachtsabend (The Night Before Christmas)*, *Die mechanische Micky Maus (Mickey's Mechanical Man)*, *Die drei kleinen Schweinchen (Three Little Pigs)*, *Micky im Lande der Riesen (Giantland)*, *Die Arche Noah (Father Noah's Ark)*. Premiere at Marmorhaus in Berlin.

DECEMBER 19

Premiere of *Liebe, Tod und Teufel (Love, Death and Devil)* at Gloria Palace in Berlin, an Ufa adaptation of Robert Louis Stevenson's *The Bottle Imp* by directors Reinhart Steinbicker and Heinz Hilpert. The working title was *Der gläserne Fluch (The Glass Curse)*. A French language version was titled *Le Diable en bouteille*.

1935

Cinemas: 4782
Attendance figure: 303 million
92 feature films produced

SPRING

Hitler and his entourage visited the shooting of *Amphitryon* at Ufa Studios Neubabelsberg.

MAY 3

Premiere of **Oskar Fischinger's** experimental Gasparcolor short *Komposition in Blau (Lichtkonzert Nr. 1/Composition in Blue: Light Concert No. 1)* at a special screening. Official release date June 5 at Capitol in Berlin.

JUNE 12

Stop-motion animator **Ferdinand Diehl** applied for a patent "*Puppe mit lösbaren auswechselbaren Teilen zur Herstellung von Filmen nach dem Einbildaufnahmeverfahren*" [Puppet with soluble, exchangeable parts for film production in stop-frame process, patent no. 404937, Reichspatentamt Berlin].

A Diehl film that used this patent was the 33 minute *Von einem, der auszog, das Gruseln zu lernen (The Story of the Youth Who Went Forth to Learn What Fear Was)*.

JULY 18

Premiere *Amphitryon. Aus den Wolken kommt das Glück (Amphitryon: Happiness from the Clouds)* at Gloria Palace in Berlin. **Reinhold Schünzel's** amorous comedy about Jupiter's escapades was based on Maccius Plautus, Molière and Heinrich von Kleist. Willy Fritsch as Jupiter and Paul Kemp as Mercur switched parts with mortals Amphitryon and Sosias thanks to background transparency process. Director of Photography: **Fritz Arno Wagner** who had photographed *Nosferatu*. Adele Sandrock as Jupiter's wife Juno. French language version was titled *Les Dieux s'amusent*.

AUGUST 11

Papageno, a silhouette short by **Lotte Reiniger**, screened at Kamera Unter den Linden in Berlin.

OCTOBER 12

Der gestiefelte Kater (Puss in Boots) by **Alf Zengerling**. Exteriors were shot in Dresden. Paul Walker in cat costume.

OCTOBER 20

Director **Arthur Robison** died in Berlin.

OCTOBER 30

U.S. Premiere of émigré **Max Reinhardt's** *A Midsummer Night's Dream* (co-directed with Wilhelm Dieterle) released by Warner Bros.

DECEMBER 7

Galathea, another short film, was shown right after its creator, **Lotte Reiniger**, had left Germany to live and work for some time in London.

DECEMBER 10

Soundfilm remake of *Der Student von Prag (The Student of Prague)* directed by **Arthur Robison** (posthumously released): Austrian actor Adolf Wohlbrück (in British emigration he changed his name to Anton Walbrook to avoid sharing his first name with Hitler) as Balduin who sells his mirror image to the uncanny Dr. Carpis (Theodor Loos) to win the hand of singer Julia Stella (Dorothea Wieck) who is engaged to Baron Waldis (Erich Fiedler). **Hanns Heinz Ewers,** the author of the original, is briefly glimpsed on screen.

Adolf Wohlbrück (a.k.a. Anton Walbrook) as *Der Student von Prag* with Theodor Loos (r.) as Dr. Carpis
Author's collection

Neues Deutsches Lichtspiel-Syndikat, a Berlin-based company, was reportedly interested in financing a stop-motion project by Władysław Starewicz: *Die Reise nach dem Mond (The Journey to the Moon)*, but the final movie didn't materialize.

1936

Cinemas: 5259
Attendance figure: 362 million
112 feature films produced

JANUARY 7

Fährmann Maria (Ferryman Maria) premiered at Bernward Cinema in Hildesheim. Sybille Schmitz as the title character struggling with Death for the life of her lover.

Goebbels disliked the picture. In his diary we find a note: *Tonight films:* **Fährmann Maria**, *an experiment but not a good one. Wilfully! Literature!*

Director Frank Wysbar left Germany in 1938 as his wife Eva was considered non-Aryan under Nazi law.

JANUARY 18

Graf Habenichts, an animated short by Kurt Stordel based on *Puss in Boots*, passed the Board of Censors. It was the first entry in a series *Deutscher Märchenkranz*.

FEBRUARY 20

Nosferatu actor **Max Schreck** suffered a heart attack and died in Munich.

MAY 1

George Moorse born in New York City. Moorse was going to direct films in Germany.

Max Schreck at the time of his death | Author's collection

JUNE 14

Architect **Hans Poelzig** who had done film work for **Paul Wegener** died in Berlin.

JULY 27

Ufa 12-minute short with parts animated Curt Schumann and Hans Neuberger: *Unendlicher Weltenraum (Infinite Outer Space)* by Dr. Martin Rikli.

NOVEMBER 10

Alf Zengerling's *Dornröschen (Sleeping Beauty)* with Ilse Petri.

NOVEMBER 13

Another *Dornröschen (Sleeping Beauty)*, this one in an animated short film by Kurt Stordel.

DECEMBER 31

According to Goebbels' diary, Adolf Hitler suggested a *Nibelungen* sound film remake: *"entirely monumental. Syllabus for the schools. A standard reference. Probably already in color."* [30]

1937

Cinemas: 5302
Attendance figure: 396 million
94 feature films produced

FEBRUARY 7

Composer **Gottfried Huppertz** (*Die Nibelungen, Metropolis*) died in Berlin.

MARCH 19

The German Reich (via Cautio Treuhand) purchased 72.6 percent of Ufa shares. The Nazis nationalized German film industry: Terra, Tobis and fledgling Bavaria.

MAY 27

Florence Stoker died in London.

OCTOBER 3

Premiere of a sound version of Władysław Starewicz' *Reineke Fuchs (Le Roman de Renard)* funded by Ufa (production unit: Erich Neusser) in Berlin. The original silent was produced between 1929 and 1931 in France. The commentary of the German version was written by Wilhelm Krug and narrated by Leo Peukert with a score composed by Dr. Julius Kopsch. Starewicz came

---

30 Goebbels diary entry, December 31, 1936.

to Berlin hoping that the Germans would finance more of his projects, but this didn't happen.

DECEMBER 2

The first feature-length stop-motion film of the **Diehl Brothers** (Ferdinand, Hermann, and writer Paul) was premiered at Primus Palace in Berlin with an audience of 500 orphans: *Die sieben Raben (The Seven Ravens)* adapted from a tale by the Grimm Brothers about seven brothers who are cursed to become ravens. The project developed into a box-office failure.

DECEMBER 4

Rotkäppchen und der Wolf (Little Red Riding Hood and the Wolf) at Ufa Pavillon Nollendorfplatz in Berlin, the first fairy tale directed by **Fritz Genschow** with a framework plot (Mother tells the story to her daughter) in black-and-white and the main story filmed in a bi-pack color process.

Bavaria Filmkunst prepared the production of an ambitious 24-minute science fiction film written and directed by Anton Kutter: *Weltraumschiff I startet (Spaceship I Starts)* with the spaceship (under the command of actor Carl Wery) surrounding the Moon and returning to Earth. Willi Horn, for some time associated with Schüfftan's unit, designed the project.

DECEMBER 12

Alfred Abel, known for his part as Fredersen in *Metropolis*, died in Berlin.

1938

Cinemas: 5446
Attendance figure: 100 million
100 feature films produced

SPRING TO AUTUMN

Two leading German distribution companies in competition for the release rights of Walt Disney's *Snow White and the Seven Dwarfs*: Bavaria and Ufa.

JUNE

Disney commissioned a German dubbing of *Snow White* in Amsterdam. Dubbing director: Kurt Gerron (in 1944 murdered in Auschwitz as were Dora Gerson, the first [Jewish] wife of Veit Harlan, and Otto Wallburg who were in the dubbing cast).

The **Diehl Brothers Ferdinand and Hermann** made a 14-minute short *Der Wettlauf zwischen dem Hasen und dem Igel (The Race between the Hare and the Hedgehog)* that introduced a stop-frame animated hedgehog character that after the war became known as *Mecki*.

JULY 17

Director **Dr. Robert Wiene** died in Paris exile.

OCTOBER 1

Tischlein deck dich, Esel streck dich, Knüppel aus dem Sack! (The Wishing-Table, the Gold Ass, and the Cudgel in the Sack) produced by **Hubert Schonger** and starring Paul Henckels as master tailor Zwirn (yarn).

OCTOBER 10

Sonne, Erde und Mond (Sun, Earth, and Moon), a 16-minute Ufa documentary by Dr. Martin Rikli, premiered at Gloria Palace in Berlin.

OCTOBER 22

Hubert Schonger's second fairy tale *Schneeweisschen und Rosenrot (Snow White and Rose Red)* at the Planetarium in Dusseldorf. The evil dwarf who transforms the prince into a bear was played by Wilhelm Blase, the "smallest lilliputian of the Berlin Scala vaudeville".

NOVEMBER 22

Georg Woelz and Gerhard Krüger created the cartoon short *Hansemanns Traumfahrt (Hansemann's Dream Journey)* by employing the Agfa-Bipack color process.

DECEMBER 7

Ein Märchen (Purzel, Brumm und Quack)—A Fairy Tale: Purzel, Brumm, and Quack, a ten-minute cartoon by Kurt Stordel released by Terra Filmkunst. The National Socialist *Völkischer Beobachter* hailed *Purzel, Brumm und Quack* as a first-rate German cartoon: *Nobody should ask which fairy tale shall be filmed. There is no answer to this question. Nothing will be turned into a film what German people possess in treasures of fairy tales. Stordel loaned his creatures from cartoonists, draughtsmen and painters and one should let them go as they were conceived by their creators. If we wouldn't be able to newly invent nice and funny plots things would be looking bad for us. The trickfilm is an absolutely modern invention and so the contents which he deals with have to be new and topical.* [31]

One should be anxious to see if Stordel will succeed in breaking Walt Disney's present autocracy over the 'German fairy tale forest'. In fact, in the interest of German filmmaking it should be wished that this gap in the field of short films will be filled if one considers the many excellent attempts for instance in the advertising films. [32] In another interview Kurt Stordel stressed that he didn't want to become a Walt Disney. [33]

---

31 Völkischer Beobachter April 30, 1939.
32 *Konkurrenz für Micky Maus? Gespräch mit Kurt Stordel*. In: 12 Uhr Blatt, December 22, 1938.
33 *20 000 Zeichnungen—ein Film. Interessante Versuche mit bunten Märchentrickfilmen*. In: Hamburger Fremdenblatt December 24, 1938.

Purzel der Zwerg (Purzel the Dwarf) | Courtesy of J. P. Storm

Filmwelt let Purzel introduce himself:

I take off my pointed cap and make a low bow. I am allowed to introduce myself to the readers of "Filmwelt": My name is Purzel the Dwarf, and I am a film actor. Do not compare the size of my body impression to my abilities as an actor. What I am able to do and mean you will see yourself in the film theatre where my first picture will be premiered around Christmas. Without any doubt I am a talent for I have formed myself quietly. Nobody foresaw my coming. I appeared extremely sudden. All famous movie people are being interviewed now, but I, as a creature of fable, cannot communicate with humans. I must take the miracle of Christmas for help. My father lived for a long time in Hamburg, studied at the Academy in Berlin, read years ago a newspaper advertisement that they were looking for artists to make an advertising film, bought himself a camera, opened a studio in the kitchen of his home and thus entered animated films and finally got the idea to film me. At Ufa he trained himself in trickfilm technique, for Tobis he made a film **Der gestiefelte Kater** *and now for Terra has drawn and painted the first color fairy tale featuring myself. As you all know I have predecessors. In America, besides the Mickey Mouse, many colorful characters have been brought to life on screen. I myself do not want to be confused or identified with them. It's very important to me to stress that I am German. My father in his pictures consciously strives for mood and not only mere grotesque. Contradictory to the Americans he prefers not the contour drawing but water colors. He designed me as well as my partners, Quack the Frog and Brumm the Fly, with whom I have in the picture "A fairy tale by Kurt Stordel" immense* *adventures with the deadly enemy spider and in a strange kingdom. I save my life and that of my comrades and provide the King with a beautiful wife.* [34]

1939

Cinemas: 6923
Attendance figure: 624 million
111 feature films produced

JANUARY

The Nazis decided in favor of Ufa to bid for *Snow White and the Seven Dwarfs*. Bavaria was out.

FEBRUARY 26

Tanz der Farben (Dance of the Colors) in Gasparcolor by Hans Fischinger, Oskar's brother, shown at the Waterloo Theater in Hamburg.

JULY 7

Robert und Bertram, Gustav Raeder's 1856 farce about two vagabonds, Robert (played by Rudi Godden) and Bertram (Kurt Seifert), is turned into an anti-Semitic musical comedy with the protagonists cheating a "parasitic" Jewish money lender named Nathan Ipelmeyer (*Ipel*, by the way, is a South German variation of *übel*, translating evil) during a rather grotesque fancy-dress ball. Finally, the two escape in a balloon up into the sky where they are welcomed by angels and rewarded by the heavenly hosts. Produced by Helmut Schreiber a.k.a. Kalanag.

---

34   *Filmwelt. Das Film- und Foto-Magazin*. No. 52, 1938.

SUMMER

Leni Riefenstahl planned to star in her own studio (funded by Hitler and the Party), as *Penthesilea*, Queen of the Amazons. Riefenstahl talked at length about this pet project of hers to Herman Weigel, later to write the screenplays for *Christiane F.* and Wolfgang Petersen's *The NeverEnding Story*:

Penthesilea *was one of my favorite topics.* Originally, *Penthesilea* was a play written by Heinrich von Kleist in 1808. But Riefenstahl thought that this rarely staged play about the Queen of the Amazons, telling about a clash of genders, didn't fit the theatrical stage very well: *Either it would be a wonderful radio play or, if you do it right, a great movie.* So she wrote a screenplay and hired Jürgen Fehling as co-director.

…the reliefs of antique art that depict the Amazons for us are that impressive that I saw a visual direction of the Penthesilea drama stylistically in form of reliefs. And as the speech of Kleist is irreplaceable in its beauty, I just wanted to shorten here and there. Story and mise-en-scène I envisioned in a way that the movements of the actors, including the mass scenes, would be stylized. I wanted to shoot in color, but the color would have been very thrifty, graphical, like stone.

And then I wouldn't have shot with clouds in the background but also nature would have been stylized, the sun ten times as big, a tree, much, much bigger and exceptional in its shape. As the words were excessive, so should have been the real elements and the movements and gestures of the actors. I didn't imagine those as for instance in **Hamlet**, *where they act just normally but so as if these characters from antique days, as the heads in the prologue of* **Olympia**, *which you have seen, would move and speak that way. And when somebody talks, it should get darker and you only hear the sound because it is essential. And then light comes back on heads and figures.* […]

The screenplay, Riefenstahl said, is lost: *I had withdrawn to Kampen to write the screenplay. And I had to train myself. As Amazon I had to ride splendidly, without saddle and backwards sitting on the horse. After that was done, we got to location scouting. Parts would have been shot in Kampen, others, the big battle scenes, in*

Libya. Roughly hundred girls were being trained. No girls but real females you would believe to fight a war.

The battle scenes Riefenstahl wouldn't have been done in a way that they looked realistic: *If a warrior grabs a girl and she falls from the horse, she has to fall really. But photography and lighting are handled in a way that it looks like a relief. Nevertheless, these are people of flesh and blood. But not as stylized that they would appear like puppets. It is perfectly realistic and sanguine and on the other hand not realistic in light and imagery.*[35]

But while she prepared all this, war intervened. Riefenstahl's dream to produce *Penthesilea* in her own studio and achieve stardom failed.

AUGUST 21

Kurt Stordel's second color animation short for Terra: *Purzel, der Zwerg und der Riese vom Berg (Purzel and the Giant from the Mountains).*

SEPTEMBER 1

Hitler's troops invaded Poland. Begin of WWII.

SEPTEMBER 24

Carl Laemmle died in Beverly Hills.

OCTOBER 6

Premiere of Heinz Hilpert's Tobis production *Die unheimlichen Wünsche (The Sinister Wish)* in Karlsruhe. The movie was based on a novel by French playwright Honoré de Balzac: *La Peau de chagrin* (1831). An elderly shopkeeper sells a mysterious piece of shagreen that is inscribed with "Oriental" writing. It is said to fulfill wishes but at the end it destroys the respective owners.

---

35 Herman Weigel, *Interview mit Leni Riefenstahl*. In: Filmkritik No. 188, August 1972.

OCTOBER 7

Premiere at Ufa Pavillon Nollendorfplatz in Berlin: When Ufa stopped to bid for Disney's *Snow White*, Naturfilm producer **Hubert Schonger** and Willy Wohlrabe, Jugendfilm distributor, provided as substitute a black-and-white live-action version *Schneewittchen und die sieben Zwerge* with Marianne Simson (a declared Nazi sympathizer) as Snow White, Elisabeth Wendt as evil queen and, as dwarfs, "real midgets" from Berlin Scala Vaudeville. Score composed by Norbert Schultze who also wrote Lilli Marleen.

Marianne Simson as *Snow White* | Courtesy of Schongerfilm

OCTOBER 17

The Phenomenology and Psychology of Cartoon Films: Analytical investigations (analysis) of the phenomenological, psychological and artistic structures of the animation group, a doctoral thesis by Reinhold Johann Holtz at Hansische Universität in Hamburg.

OCTOBER 28

Die verzauberte Prinzessin (The Enchanted Princess), an oriental fairy tale by **Alf Zengerling** based on a story (1837) and play (1849) by Friedrich Hebbel, at Ufa Pavillon Nollendorfplatz in Berlin. The Bagdad scenes were filmed in

Sarajevo. The German trade press reported that Jews agitated against the film team and that there was a scuffle during shooting.[36]

NOVEMBER 11

A 48-minute fairy tale *Die Heinzelmännchen (The Brownies)* directed by **Hubert Schonger** at Ufa Pavillon Nollendorfplatz in Berlin.

Harry Piel prepared a second *Invisible Man* for Tobis Filmkunst, but the project remained unrealized.[37]

Bavaria in Munich announced *Zwischenfall im Weltenall (Incident in Outer Space)* to be directed by Robert Adolf Stemmle: *The eternal wishful dream of mankind culminates in the daring idea to reach the Moon with the support of technically advanced means in order to explore the strangest of all planets* [sic!]. *Not only shall the steel sheeting of the space rocket include delegates of ultramodern sciences, the celebrities of the international press and a choice of the most progressive technology but also bring, in its lightning "fall upwards", to the infinite space between the stars the most important item Earth has to offer: love.*[38] *The movie most likely was to use some special effects footage from* **Weltraumschiff I startet**.

Ufa was going to produce an even bigger space *Weltraumschiff 18 (Spaceship 18)* budgeted a 1.8 million Reichsmark and based on a 1934 book by **Hans Dominik:** *Ein Stern fällt vom Himmel (A Star Falls from the Sky). Ufa films that depicted the audacious presentation of technical, future-oriented problems were always the highlights of the annual program, startling, spectacular events that guaranteed success—one should remember* **F.P. 1 antwortet nicht** *and* **Gold**. *With* **Weltraumschiff 18** *Ufa continues this tradition by producing a movie that will not only be a worthy sequel of the previous features but even surpass these in the dynamic order of events, in its adventurousness and the feasibility of the resolving of technical problems, in the modern selection of its location and in the emphasis of*

---

36 Zengerlings *Märchenfilm die verzauberte prinzessin. Bei den Außenaufnahmen in Sarajewo hetzten Juden.* In: Film-Kurier, August 16, 1939.
37 Filmwelt, No. 44, November 3, 1939.
38 Ibid.

human relations.—The most sensational plot requires the existence of large airplanes fast beyond belief—so-called "spaceships" that can perform polar flights in only a few hours and can be stationed for research goals in the Antarctic. During such a flight, they observe the downfall of a giant, earthshaking meteor. As they examine the aerolith, they discover new, unknown elements which spark enormous energies. A fight of science and a battle of nations ensue for these elements, for mysterious powers that could set the world on fire. … Subject, direction and cast point to a film that is great in every respect! The cast was to include Willy Birgel, René Deltgen and Brigitte Horney. Directed by Eduard von Borsody. Produced by Hans Tost. [39]

Due to the outbreak of war neither movie was made.

NOVEMBER 30

Max Skladanowsky, German pioneer of moving images, died in Berlin.

Ferdinand Diehl finished the puppet film *Der Wolf und die 7 Geisslein (The Wolf and the Seven Little Goats)* for Reichsstelle für den Unterrichtsfilm, the educational film department.

1940

JANUARY 12

The Invisible Man Returns with Vincent Price and Cedric Hardwicke was conceived and written by two German émigrés, **Joe May** and **Curt Siodmak**. May, once one of Germany's most prominent directors, was soon forgotten while Siodmak's star rose at Universal City Studios.

JANUARY 15

Silent film director **Otto Rippert** (*Homunculus*) passed away in Berlin.

---

39   Ufa Jahresprogramm 1939-40.

FEBRUARY

Henrik Galeen left Denmark and settled in the United States.

JULY 2

Guido Seeber, veteran cinematographer, died in Berlin.

SEPTEMBER 12

Hubert Schonger's *Hänsel und Gretel* at Ufa Pavillon Nollendorfplatz in Berlin: Gunnar Möller as Hansel, Gisela Bussmann as Gretel, and Elsa Wagner as the witch. In the days of Auschwitz, the "traditional" European burning of witches had a fatal subtext.

Hänsel und Gretel | Courtesy of Schongerfilm

SEPTEMBER 20

In a matinee at Ufa Pavillon Nollendorfplatz in Berlin **Hubert Schonger's** *Der süsse Brei (Sweet Porridge)* from a Grimm tale that has the countryside flooded by millet porridge. Directed by Dr. Erich Daudert.

OCTOBER 2

The Board of Censors approved **Alf Zengerling's** *Der Froschkönig (The Frog Prince)* with Paul Walker.

OCTOBER 3

Zengerling's *Rumpelstilzchen (Rumpelstiltskin)* with Paul Walker approved.

OCTOBER 11

Matinee at Ufa Pavillon Nollendorfplatz in Berlin: **Hubert Schonger's** production of *Der kleine Häwelmann (The Little Haverman)* from an 1849 children's story by Theodor Storm about a boy whose bed begins to roll towards the Moon.

OCTOBER 14

Alexander Korda's Technicolor production *The Thief of Bagdad* was partly directed by a German, **Dr. Ludwig Berger**, and had a German villain as well: **Conrad Veidt** as Jaffar the Grand Vizier.

Die Sterntaler (The Star Money/The Star Talers) produced by **Hubert Schonger** and starring Heidelore Rutkowski as poor orphan girl who is presented by the nightly sky with stars that turn out hard smooth pieces of money.

NOVEMBER 4

Der Störenfried (The Intruder), a Bavaria Agfacolor cartoon by Hans Held. All the animals in the forest unite against the red (!) intruder, a fox, who troubles the peaceful Teutonic environment: hedgehogs wearing *Wehrmacht* helmets as well as wasps forming sounding *Stuka* squadrons vividly attack the enemy.

Der Störenfried (The Intruder), animation by Hans Held | Courtesy of J. P. Storm

NOVEMBER 7

Anton Kutter's *Weltraumschiff I startet* shown at Kulturfilmwoche in Munich and at the Capitol Cinema in Berlin.

NOVEMBER 28

Premiere of the anti-Semitic propaganda film *Der ewige Jude (The Eternal Jew)* at Ufa Zoo Palace.

In one exposing sequence the "director", SS Hauptsturmführer Fritz Hippler, interjected images of rats:

In the Polish and Russian sections of Eastern Europe, the nineteenth century, with its muddled ideas about human quality and freedom, gave the Jews a great lift.

From Eastern Europe they spread across the entire continent during the nineteenth and twentieth centuries, and then across the world. Parallel to these Jewish wanderings throughout the world, is the migration of a similarly restless animal [sic!], *the rat. Rats have been parasites on mankind from the very beginning. Their home is Asia, from where they migrated in gigantic hordes over Russia and the Balkans into Europe. By the middle of the eighteenth century, with the growing shipping traffic, they took possession of America as well, and eventually Africa and the Far East. Wherever rats turn up, they carry destruction to the land, by destroying mankind's goods and nourishment and spreading diseases and plagues such as cholera, dysentery, leprosy, and typhoid fever. They are cunning, cowardly and cruel, and usually appear in massive hordes. They represent the elements of sneakiness and subterranean destruction among animals. Just as the Jews do among mankind.*

A 9-minute color cartoon *Vom Bäumlein, das andere Blätter hat gewollt (The Little Tree That Longed for Other Leaves)* animated by Heinz Tischmeyer for Naturfilm **Hubert Schonger** presented an anti-Semitic, *Stürmer*-like caricature of a bearded Jew who is after the golden leafs of an innocent little tree, freely based on a poem by Friedrich Rückert (1813): *...ging der Jude durch den Wald mit grossem Sack und grossem Bart/Der sieht die goldnen Blätter bald;/Er steckt sie ein, geht eilends fort/und lässt das leere Bäumlein dort.* The Jew came through the woods with a big bag and a big beard/Soon he sees the golden leafs/He pockets them and goes away/and leaves the little tree empty.

1941

Cinemas: 7043
Attendance figure: 892 million
67 feature films produced

MARCH 3

Die Wiesenzwerge (The Meadow Dwarves), a 16-minute Gasparcolor cartoon by Gerhard Krüger based on a picture book by Ernst Kreidolf, premiered with other short films at Capitol Cinema in Cologne.

Die Wiesenzwerge (The Meadow Dwarves) | Courtesy of J. P. Storm

MARCH 14

Wolfgang Petersen born in Emden, Eastern Frisia.

MAY 30

Under the headline *The Color Puppet Trickfilm: What it is—what it could be—what it will cost?* Herbert Pohris and Jürgen Clausen of Gasparcolor Werbefilm GmbH/Gasparcolor Naturwahre Farbenfilm GmbH provided a memorandum for Tobis Filmkunst to promote a stop-motion film manufacture:

We have to proceed from Pal technique!

Georg Pal is a Hungarian with a specific Balkan joy for the color and love for good-natured grotesque. He comes from hand-drawn animation but has produced color dimensional trickfilms for many years. Almost exclusively commercials for Philips, Holland. Although he lost much of his original instinct—in the service of advertisement he has become a little bit Americanized—even his most abstract ideas reflect a little bit the childlike narrator. Therefore, too, his films are so sympathetic to us in spite of their American outfit.

What appeals most to us Germans is the special wooden puppet style of Pal's films and the precision of his stop-frame technique. Behind the moving grotesque there is an, albeit originally more technical than artistic, seriousness and diligence. If one observes a Pal animator at the making of technical blueprints, one could think that it would be about the construction of valuable machines.

Color Dimensional Trickfilm will enlighten the whole process of filmmaking—especially color feature films

Pal's films today represent not only an outstanding achievement in the field of color dimensional trickfilm but—and this is essential—in this technique rest possibilities of expression resp. shaping of incredible simplicity and depth. The solution of these tasks will raise the puppet animation film finally into the ranks of artistic high-grade dimensional trick creation, and so will demonstrate what essentially a Film-Spiel [Picture Play] is. ("Film-Spiel" should be written as motto above the whole process of filmmaking!)

If one reminds that not only an according score (in German tradition) will be added but also the color of these simple wooden forms (one should think only about Cézanne's space principle of painted space, of "cone, ball and cylinder") will achieve the most glorious, striking performance so that finally, what hasn't been tried before, one can go to a kind of synchronized element of color and its dramatic assessment—not only aesthetical—(which color film development needs so badly) … if one considers all of this than one will understand why we should proceed from Pal's technique and should acknowledge it as a textbook example sine qua non by those offices responsible for German culture.

Who will win—has to dare!

We Germans have to make up a lot in the field of trickfilm: today and particularly after this war which burdens us a pleasant as well as heavy responsibility for all of Europe.—We have the power and the artistic impulse to create exemplary things: open the road—as generous as possible!—An operation like this should not be introduced with calculations of profitability: otherwise, it will never make a profit. –

Planning in advance

Although one has to make estimates of cost and find out about all financial possibilities—it should be done due to the dimensions of such a project. In this regard we should learn from the American who is not glued on the maxim that time is money but modifies it occasionally:

A big business—much time, much money!

For sceptics, finally this suggestion: run Pal's films in a cinema... when one realizes the excitement of the audience and the box-office receipts, each objection would vanish and would be replaced by insight and understanding:

Color dimensional trickfilm as feature-length film play will have a bright future.

Concerning style

which people who are tied in tradition—contrary to people who are conscious and aware of tradition—might consider at first a little abstract, we have to conclude that the times of Baroque and Biedermeier are finally over. One should remember the way fashion has become in the past thirty years, architecture, machine building, yes—how could it be else—our style of living and, especially, the form of state: more and more our whole life tends to simplicity, the outspoken, the clear and plain.

"Deutsch sein heisst klar sein," the Führer once said: "To be a German means to be clear in mind."

Pal's technique proceeds from such clarity, onto purity of style—in its field of cinematic dream world.

A Postscript:

Puppet trickfilm and German toy industry.

With regard to American animation film, a unique insemination of the toy has occurred, which results for instance in the fact that after release of the Mickey Mouse or Pig films and later after **Snow White** *and* **Pinocchio** *not only children's books were published in millions of copies based on the artwork and characters of the Disney production, but also toys, puppets and records invaded European countries (bijouterie: necklaces, buttons, stickers etc.). In Paris, for instance, many shop windows were decorated with characters of the* Snow White *picture. The same is true for the Georg Pal production in Holland. Here too the most prominent characters from various Pal films were absorbed by the toy industry and were exploited.*

The German toy industry up until now was leading the whole world, especially the German children's puppet industry. We are absolutely sure that out of German puppet film production an equally extensive as well as necessary insemination of German toy industry will result, so that later an interaction will occur: puppet trickfilm will support toy industry and vice versa. Add to it that Pal's technique (use of simple work forms like cone, ball, cylinder etc.) is well suited for mass production. This is the technically best prerequisite for animated film featuring plastic color bodies and on the other hand simplifies the transfer into efficient production methods of the toy industry.

The toy industry will have to learn from color spatial trickfilm if it wants to play the role again, particularly as an export industry, in the wide world as it has done before.—

The memo was ignored as the Nazis were longing for drawn animation Disney-style, not puppets.

JUNE 8

A note in Goebbels' diary re: a feature-length animated film produced by Cracow-born Max Fleischer for Paramount release: Color trickfilm *Gulliver. An American production. Very good, very witty, very skillfull. I must succeed with that here too and will care for that issue in spite of the war. We have the people who are able to achieve this. One only has to find them.* [40]

---

40 Die Tagebücher von Joseph Goebbels. Volume 4: January 1, 1940-July 8, 1941. Munich 1987.

JUNE 22

Hitler launched *Operation Barbarossa*, the attack on the Soviet Union.

JULY

Two cartoon film productions were abruptly stopped, *Quick macht Hochzeit (Quick Marries)* at Ufa and *Rübezahl* at Tobis, to transfer the units to a new state-controlled cartoon factory.

Rübezahl, an abandoned Tobis animation project | Courtesy of J. P. Storm

JULY 15

Experimental filmmaker **Walter Ruttmann** died in Berlin.

AUGUST 7

Deutsche Zeichenfilm Gesellschaft mit beschränkter Haftung, the German Animation Film Company, was founded by Universum-Film A.G. (Ufa) and

Cautio Treuhand, backed by Goebbels' ministry with the clear intention to compete with Disney. Managing director was to be Karl Neumann who had worked as proxy in a sausage factory before he joined the Ministry of Enlightenment and Propaganda. According to his ambitious plans the Zeichenfilm Company was destined to train artists to start short films and then finish feature-length German cartoons in Disney style until 1950.

OCTOBER 24

Das tapfere Schneiderlein (The Brave Little Tailor), Hubert Schonger's screen version of the Grimm fairy tale with Hans Hessling and as giants Wolfgang Ritter von Schwind, an opera singer, and Kurt Zehe, Germany's tallest wrestler (height: 7'18").

Das tapfere Schneiderlein (The Brave Little Tailor) | Courtesy of Schongerfilm

DECEMBER 12

The Wolf Man, a Universal production by George Waggner, written by **Curt Siodmak**.

1942

Cinemas: 7042
Attendance figure: 1,062 billion (including occupied countries)
57 feature films produced

AUGUST 29

John Gottowt, who had played Scapinelli in the original *Student of Prague* and Professor Bulwer in *Nosferatu*, murdered by the SS in Wieliczka, Poland, during the deportation of Jews.

SEPTEMBER 5

Werner Herzog Stipetić born in Munich.

NOVEMBER 21

Dr. Hans Erdmann Guckel, the composer of *Nosferatu*, died in Berlin at age 60.

1943

Cinemas: 6561
Attendance figure: 1,116 billion
78 feature films produced

JANUARY 12

Hanns Heinz Ewers died in Berlin.

FEBRUARY 2

The Battle of Stalingrad ended with the surrender of Hitler's 6th Army.

MARCH 5

Premiere of the Agfacolor extravaganza *Münchhausen (The Adventures of Baron Munchausen)* in celebration of the 25th jubilee of Ufa at the company's Zoo Palace.

So lively a descendant of the famous Baron Münchhausen narrates the fantastic adventures of his famous ancestor: riding on a cannonball (thanks to Gerhard Huttula's rear projection) and traveling by montgolfier to the Moon as if he had been present himself—and indeed he had been. The gift of immortality was bestowed to him by Cagliostro—until, weary of a long life, he returns this present of magic and immediately grows old.

Author Erich Kästner, banned in the Third Reich, was granted a special permission to write the screenplay anonymously that was destined to rival Alexander Korda's *Thief of Bagdad*. Hans Albers as tale-spinning Münchhausen led an all-star-cast that included Brigitte Horney as Czarina Catherine the Great, Leo Slezak as Sultan Abdul-Hamid, Ilse Werner as Italian Princess Isabella d'Este, Hermann Speelmans as Münchhausen's faithful servant Christian Kuchenreutter, Wilhelm Bendow and Marianne Simson as Moon People and Veit Harlan's *Jud Süss* Ferdinand Marian as Count Cagliostro. A legion of actors was added to the cast: Käthe Haack, Michael Bohnen, Hans Brausewetter, Andrews Engelmann, Eduard von Winterstein, **Bernhard Goetzke**, Victor Janson, and Gustav Waldau as Casanova.

Berlin.—In a festive company plea held by Ufa on the occasion of its 25th anniversary at Ufa Palace at Zoo and in parallel events in other big Ufa theaters, Reich Minister Dr. Goebbels explained the German film as spiritual power and talked about its organization. Besides the Ufa fellowship and numerous filmmakers, among those who appeared to the ceremony were Reich Minister [Walter] Funk, Reich Organization Leader Dr. [Robert] Ley, state secretary [Leopold] Gutterer, Private Counsillor Dr. [Alfred] Hugenberg and Reich film intendant Dr. Fritz Hippler.

After the Leonore Overture No 3 by Beethoven and a tribute to fallen comrades, the first speaker was general manager Ludwig Klitzsch who talked about the history of

French poster: Hans Albers as *Münchhausen* | Author's collection

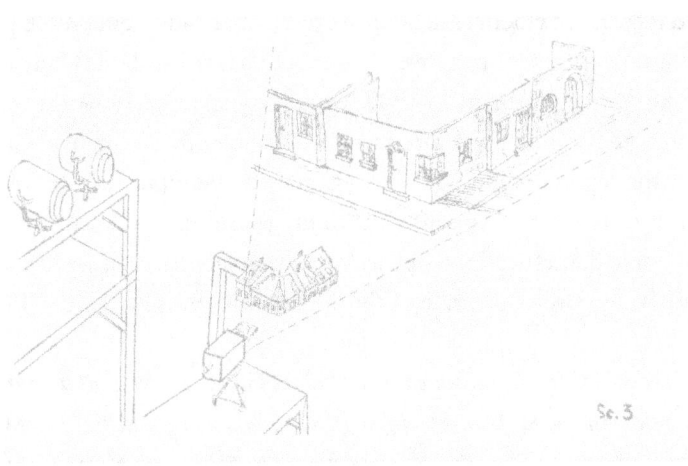

Original design for hanging miniature, *Münchhausen*
by Gerhard Huttula, head of Ufa Process Department Babelsberg | Author's collection

Ufa. He said i.a., "When the National Socialist state one year ago put German film under a central leadership it named this leading organ 'Ufa'. This honor satisfies us deeply. Ufa is a foundation of the world war. It was initiated by Generalquartiermeister [chief of the general staff] Ludendorff on behalf of Oberste Heeresleitung [top army command]. We had to abide very painful experiences re: enemy propaganda by photographs and film until it was decided to get down to action. Ludendorff put an end to this dishonorable state with the postulate of combining the economical, artistic, and technical facilities to an influential company under state control. This task was consigned to the former head of the Deutsche Bank, Emil Georg von Stauss [who had died in December 1942]. *On December 18, 1917, it was solved. The Universum Film Aktiengesellschaft was founded. End of February 1918 the company was registered. The following years were under the burden of political and economical instability. They were shaped by the Versailles Treaty. During inflation it was defenselessly exposed to Jewish and economically irresponsible forces. The State withdrew its interests in year 1921 under the influence of leftist circles.*

Then, in 1933, it came to that fertile wedlock between time and film. National Socialists' struggle for the soul of the German people took this unspent, so highly effective weapon. Reich Minister Dr. Goebbels became the patron of the German film. He taught us to lead the film in a new way. The never expected increase of cinema attendance exceeded already a billion the previous year but is only an exterior expression for today's intrinsic bonds between film and people. When Germany in 1939 was forced again into a world war, there was a completely different picture than 1914. In weekly 32 languages and over 30 prints the reports of our PK [Propaganda company] men who fight heroically in front line are woven into a thrilling sound film work. More than 50 million people domestically as well as internationally see each week a thrilling image about the fateful struggle of the German people.

Right in the middle of the increased service of all forces, the art of film approaches a new era in its history. It's a convincing signal of the unbroken initiative of German filmmaking that in this time after ten years of laboratory experiments of Ufa and Agfa German color film based on the Agfacolor process was developed. [41]

---

41   *Im alten Geist zu neuen Zielen.* In: Der Film, March 6, 1943.

The same day as Goebbels spoke at the *Münchhausen* premiere Universal released in the United States *Frankenstein Meets the Wolf Man* written by **Curt Siodmak**: Originally Lon Chaney, Jr. was supposed to play both parts, Frankenstein's Creature, and the Wolf Man via split screen, but then it was decided to cast **Béla Lugosi** as the Monster, with disastrous results for the actor.

APRIL 3

Conrad Veidt died in Hollywood.

JULY 1

One of the most innovative authors of German silent films, *Caligari* co-author **Carl Mayer**, F.W. Murnau's favorite writer, died of cancer in London exile, maltreated, poor and almost forgotten. Buried at Highgate Cemetery.

OCTOBER 1

Because Deutsche Zeichenfilm Company couldn't supply cinemas with a reasonable number of cartoons, Dr. Heinrich Roellenbleg, in charge of German newsreels, commissioned cartoon film producer Hans Fischerkoesen (i.e., Hans Fischer born in Koesen) to produce a short film *Verwitterte Melodie (Weather-Beaten Melody)* from an idea conceived by Horst von Möllendorff to be premiered at Intercine Newsreel Cinema in Brussels.

On a sunny summer day, a wasp, reminding distantly Waldemar Bonsels' *Maya the Bee* (a favorite but unrealized project of Deutsche Zeichenfilm GmbH), discovers an abandoned phonograph box in a meadow. There is a technically rather complicated shot of the wasp flying down from the sky and entering the picture through 12 multiplane layers of grass and flowers and circling around the three-dimensional phonograph box. Accidentally, she touches the record with her sting and is surprised to hear some chords. Astonished she checks her sting. Then she runs along the record and produces more sound while she manages to use her sting as stylus to play the record. The weather-beaten phonograph starts to produce some jazz and swing (!) music which attracts more insects. But dust makes the wasp come to a standstill, the music sounds distorted. A stately caterpillar, which has watched curiously, volunteers. He comes to the rescue and cleans the record. On the now mirror-like surface the wasp, however, starts to slip and skid. Only with the support of two helpful beetles she gets onto her legs again. Pairs of beetles dancing and swaying to the music in the branches. Even the hedgehog, the snail and the frogs are in the best mood.

After a while, from intense recording, the wasp's sting starts to glow. Beetles refresh with dewdrops from the cup of a bellflower. A stag beetle whirls the wasp around until the wasp is thrown out with a broken sting. The sting has to be sharpened and the show goes on.

Original artwork from *Verwitterte Melodie (Weather-Beaten Melody)* that survived the war in the collection of J.P. Storm

The late animation historian and Fischinger biographer Dr. William Moritz proved a good observer and even discovered some subtle "bit of forbidden information" in Fischerkoesen's little cartoon:

...the discovery of an abandoned phonograph takes on a new meaning, especially when the record on the turntable is a swing number with lyrics that say, "The week wouldn't be worthwhile without a weekend when we can get away to enjoy nature." Near the phonograph lies an "abandoned" clasp from a woman's garter belt (with a lucky four-leafed clover growing out of it!), which suggests that the interrupted picnic that left behind the musical instrument had also involved erotic play—something also strictly forbidden by the puritanical Nazi codes. So from beneath the charming surface of this cartoon emerges a subversive message: women, far from the unnatural Nazi-designated stereotype of "children, church and kitchen," can escape into Nature to be self-reliant and adventurous, erotic and free—they can discover or revitalize a suppressed world of forbidden joy in music and friendship between diverse creatures who may be brown or white, frog or caterpillar—or even a pair of ladybug beetles who may be a same-sex couple. [42]

According to Moritz, **Verwitterte Melodie** is *quite the opposite of the Nazi requirements for a dedicated Aryan citizen.* One should remember, however, that later in the war the image of women had changed, as females were "invited" to work in the armament factories and take on the jobs of males who were dying at the front.

Fischerkoesen transformed the idea with the support of 14 employees in his Potsdam studio. Colorization was outsourced to a studio in The Hague where another 17 employees were kept busy.

Möllendorff (interviewed by J. P. Storm in the late 1980s): *Fischerkoesen and his studio worked effectively and very fast on the cartoon. He was in straight competition with Reich-owned Deutsche Zeichenfilm G.m.b.H. which for some time worked on* Hansi. *Based on his long-year experience with advertising films and commercials Fischerkoesen had developed his own style and as I was not experienced in manufacturing cartoons, I only submitted the idea for him.*

---

42 William Moritz, *Resistance and Subversion in Animated Films of The Nazi Era: the Case of Hans Fischerkoesen*. In: Animation Journal, Fall 1992.

More artwork from *Verwitterte Melodie (Weather-Beaten Melody)* | Courtesy of J. P. Storm

OCTOBER 4

A few days later, Karl Neumann and the state-controlled and funded Deutsche Zeichenfilm Company presented their first (and only) finished cartoon *Armer Hansi (Poor Hansi)* which was less effective than Fischerkoesen's work. In his cage Hansi, a canary, listens to the voices of freedom, love, and adventure. Hansi hears the song of a chickadee and carelessly leaves his prison birdcage. However, Hansi's wings grow weak too early. The tender wooing is rejected rude sparrows. Hunger, thirst, rain and finally a cat drive Hansi back to the safety of prison. In the end it is only a dream.

Having read the basic idea Horst von Möllendorff, who acted as one of the company's many advisers before he left and joined German Newsreel, suggested changes:

I want to comment on two important issues:

1. *The canary who only dreams about the flight into freedom leaves an unsatisfied desire.*

2. *The ending leaves an unfree feeling, the cage becomes a prison as the canary returns because he is unable to live in freedom.*

But to a National Socialist mind the aspect of freedom was not plausible. On the contrary, this story appealed to the National Socialist way of thinking. A canary that escapes from prison, gets sick of freedom and returns into his cage where he is safe.

The staging of some scenes was rotoscoped from a print of Disney's *Snow White* by the way.

Original artwork *Armer Hansi (Poor Hansi)* | Courtesy of J. P. Storm

Following the Ufa release of *Münchhausen*, Bavaria Filmkunst presented an animated cartoon by Hans Held: *Die Abenteuer des Freiherrn von Münchhausen—Eine Winterreise (The Adventures of Baron Münchhausen: A Winter Journey)*.

Germans Richard Dillenz and Josef Pfister finished a pretty realistic but lame animated version of Johann Wolfgang von Goethe's *Der Zauberlehrling (The Sorcerer's Apprentice)*.

*Die Abenteuer des Freiherrn von Münchhausen—Eine Winterreise
(The Adventures of Baron Münchhausen: A Winter Journey)* | Courtesy J. P. Storm

OCTOBER 31

Max Reinhardt died in New York.

DECEMBER

Two German émigrés, **Henrik Galeen** and Paul Falkenberg, suggested a film manuscript to director **Fritz Lang** that revived the *Golem* legend in Nazi-occupied Prague:

Did Hitler know what he was doing when he deported a helpless crowd of Jews, of all walks of life, from all European nations to Chelm in the district of Lublin?

Did he know that at this very spot 350 years ago the holy Rabbi Baal Shem had brought to life an image of clay, called the **Golem,** *in order to save his people from ruthless persecution?*

Did Hitler know that the now lifeless clay figure of this Golem was underneath the narrow streets where modern Jews were thronging this new Ghetto?

The Synagogue is half in ruins, but it keeps the mystery:

Neither walls nor moats could keep off this superhuman monster. Bullets could not hurt it. Swords were powerless against Baal Shem's magic... The enemies were smitten by the sign of God and the community was saved... Baal Shem took the Shem from the Golem and buried the lifeless figure of clay... here...

Rabbi Jonah taps the floor with his cane. The crowd demands that he should bring the Golem to life again to save their community. The Rabbi raises his hand and tells them that the time has not come yet.

In the meantime, more and more Jews are deported to the already overcrowded Ghetto near Chelm. Among them a young woman from Norway, Elna, who catches the eye of Steinhardt, the German district governor. To him, Elna looks pretty Aryan. He invites her into his car. In a narrow street a bomb hits the automobile. The driver is killed, Steinhardt (unlike his role model Reinhard Heydrich) remains uninjured. Elna escapes and is saved by Sholem, a young member of the underground.

Sholem goes to see the Rabbi. There he learns that the Governor has given an ultimatum that if Elna, kidnapped by the Jews, is not brought to him within 24 hours the Ghetto will become another Lidice. Elna is devastated: "Hundreds of human lives against one ... can there be any choice?"

German guns are pointing towards the Ghetto.

Elna returns to Steinhardt. But Steinhardt's days are numbered.

In the midst of a feast a service telegram is handed to the Governor: "Immediate retreat... after destruction of all commodities that might be of value to the enemy."

Before Steinhardt's orders can be carried out a gigantic shadow appears on the wall of Steinhardt's castle, illuminated by the moonlight.

In the distance they hear shots. Soviet troops? Steinhardt follows Elna to the window: "Not yet… Those are German guns! Their target… the Ghetto! But before I leave here, you will be mine…"

As Elna rushes towards the door, Steinhardt bars the way.

The girl tears herself away—flees into a corner…

He laughs… She cannot escape…

Triumphantly he walks towards her… The girl stares at him wide eyed, silent… no tears left… A gust of wind rushes into the room… the door has opened… Steinhardt turns around… In the door stands the Golem… Steinhardt draws his revolver… shoots. But the Golem walks into the room… Steinhardt draws back to the wall… speechless. The Golem, relentless hunter, stalks his quarry… but as he walks on, he leaves a trail of blood…

Elna covers her face in her hands… a body thuds to the floor… Elna looks up… the Golem turns…

The Germans are in full retreat. The Ghetto has fought off the attack. The guerillas have led the thrust, now they follow the fleeing Nazis.

Elna bends over Sholem whose head rests on her lap. She dresses his wounded arm… On the floor lies a mask… slanted eyes over mongolic cheekbones, lips frozen in a grin…

The drone of many planes is heard in a distance…

Elna smiles…

"The Russians!" Sholem says.

Sholem—he was chosen to substitute for the Golem.

Alas, Fritz Lang was not able to find producers backing the project and do this anti-Fascist down-to-earth version of the *Golem*.

DECEMBER 7

Oskar Messter died in his home at Tegernsee in Bavaria.

1944

Cinemas: 6484
Attendance figure: 1,101 billion
64 feature films produced

SEPTEMBER

Margrith Helena Karbe and Horst von Möllendorff proposed a cartoon series with four well-known fairy-tale characters:

Their lasting success in cartoons Americans have reached by creating series. Mickey Mouse, Donald Duck, Silly Symphonies etc. are examples of how popular singular cartoon characters resp. groups of characters might become. Only after Mickey Mouse had become a household name the audience longed all the more for mire humorist films with this main character.

Until now Germany hasn't found a topic which would suit very well for the production of cartoon series. The following proposal for the first German cartoon series to my estimate brings all prerequisites which are necessary for a series.

The series bears a title which is well known from the German treasure trove of fairy tales among our people and abroad.

Die Bremer Stadtmusikanten
[The Town Musicians of Bremen].

The characters (appearing separately, by two, three or four) are sympathetic in nature and well to animate: a dog, a cat, a donkey, and a rooster.

The first film of the series **Bremen Town Musicians** *will feature the original fairy tale, i. e. the four musicians meeting on the country road and forming a quartet. On their trip the four prankster musicians have 4 to 5 funny adventures, the last being the famous expulsion of the robbers from the lonely forest hut.*

Of course, the four Town Musicians of Bremen are equipped with all possible and impossible instruments, from tuba, piccolo, and violin to mere imaginary instruments with novel clang colors. Each of the animals will command all instruments and all gags will be musically conceived.

The second film, under the headline Bremen Town Musicians, would show the adventures of the funny quartet, for instance **Im Strandbad [On the Beach]**. *All different animals basking in the sun. It is hot, the mood is tired. The four funny musicians arrive and turn the whole beach upside down. Out of a scene on the water slide a crazy splashing develops which mounts into the blown fountains of elephant and walrus. Later the four guys ride on the back of the walrus through the water; and when it dives all is continued under water, with the music of the four now gurgling and producing water bubble effects. The fantasy under water world will play a lively part and so on and so on. [...]*

Topics of that kind for the four funny animals of the Bremen Town Musicians are countless in number. One could show the **Bremen Town Musicians on a Trip to the Stratosphere, On a Persian Market, With the Devil in Hell, At a Soccer Game, On a Bicycling Tour, Among Polar Bears, Among Zulu Twerps, At Billards, At the Races, In a Movie Studio** *and on and on. Such a series starring these well-known, sympathetic, and easily to draw characters from German fairy tale treasure trove should be quite useful for a German animation film production.*

The series was not made.

OCTOBER 14

Udo Kier born as Udo Kierspe in Cologne.

NOVEMBER

Horst von Möllendorff was asked to check animation production in occupied Prague. Result was an Agfacolor short *Hochzeit im Korallenmeer (Wedding in the Coral Sea):*

"My activities in Prague were a totally new task for me. Now I was creative director of more than one-hundred artists. They worked, contrary to German animation, on a high, professional level. I always thought that there were some artists with Disney experience involved. To create the optical illusion of underwater life they clamped two panes of glass on top of each other under the camera lens. Between the panes of glass some drops of oil dissolved and, due to the heat and fast photography, left the impression of life in the sea. They have built even some kind of multiplane camera. On the floor there were 10 mtr. (30 feet) tracks and a camera moved towards the different layers to produce depth of focus." Möllendorff worked with the nucleus and cream of the future Czech animation industry: Jiří Brdečka, Eduard Hofman, Stanislav Latal, Josef Kandel and Jilis Kalaš.

The story left enough room for action and imagination: A pirate polyp kidnaps a fish bride and hides in the wreck of a sunken ship. To please her and win her over he performs wild Cherkessian dances (that reveal him as aggressive Russian type) but this frightens the fish girl who starts to cry. In the meantime, the bridegroom isn't idle. He assembles auxiliaries and frees his beloved with the assistance of other fish, mostly sword and saw fish. Ufa purchased the release rights for RM 337,134.28 as a supplementary short for Martin Fric's *Dir zuliebe*. They ordered 158 prints for a total cost of RM 61,569.68.

DECEMBER 19

The 13-minute Agfacolor cartoon *Der Schneemann (The Snowman)* was shown as supplement feature to Heinz Rühmann's *Der Engel mit dem Saitenspiel* at

Marmorhaus, U.T. and Sternlichtspiele in Berlin. One evening caricaturist and writer Horst von Möllendorff who had already written *Weather-Beaten Melody* and "supervised" Prague animation sat in a Berlin beer garden to find a suitable topic for another cartoon, and eventually came up with the story of a snowman who has a warm spot in his heart. He wakes up in a full moon night on a quiet market place. After some adventures he creeps into a house to rest on a sofa. There he discovers a calendar. The calendar page for January shows a snowman like himself, in a winter landscape. He browses through February, March and stops in July. For the first time he learns about that loveliest of seasons: summer. Under all circumstances he longs for that experience. He gets himself frozen in the refrigerator and leaves it with the advent of summer. Everything looks exactly like the promising picture in the calendar. The snowman grins from ear to ear and is all smiles when he leaves the house. He enjoys the sun tremendously and welcomes "the summer of his lifetime" singing:

This is the summer of my life,
How beautiful in your dress of flowers.
Who ever saw you did not live in vein,
My Heart melts in sheer bliss!

The snowman picks flowers and spreads them around. He sticks a red rose into his cold breast. An excited hen he surprises with an egg made of ice and snow. The warm July sun begins to burn. Slowly the snowman starts to melt leaving only a top hat and his carrot nose which is picked up and eaten by a little rabbit.

...the snowman, an average person with some good and bad qualities, is trapped in a given environment, Winterland. Although it is functional, it is cold and, in some ways, inhospitable. He reads that there is another place, sunny and free, and arranges to escape there for some thrilling moments of warmth and freedom, even at the cost of his life, as we hear him gurgle in the death throes of song, twisting and melting in the hot sun. The snowman's tragicomic death in some odd way also reflects the millionfold death that had become a firm part of German society in those years. A number of German leaders seemed to belong to a suicide club themselves and, when the war was lost, committed suicide: Joseph

Goebbels (he and his wife took their children who had so much enjoyed the *Snowman* into death), Heinrich Himmler, Hermann Göring, Robert Ley and Adolf Hitler (with his recently married wife) himself.

Original artwork from *Der Schneemann (The Snowman)* | Courtesy of J. P. Storm

Möllendorff had smeared the story onto A 5 pages which he pinned, then posted to Deutsche Wochenschau not forgetting to ask for a sizable fee. Newsreel, in turn, asked for a typewritten manuscript which he immediately reforwarded to get his money.

From Newsreel the manuscript went to Fischerkoesen who was still busy finishing *Weather-Beaten Melody* for a budget of RM 148,650.-. In the beginning scenes, the master animator and his inventive cameraman Kurt Schleicher again used his Fleischer-type revolving miniature set left over from an earlier advertising film depicting a 2D snowman as he approached the nightly house during a frozen winter night.

Protocol of a Radio Broadcast:

Started with the title melody from *Der Schneemann* (composed by Rudolf Perak).

Then Dr. Jürgen Petersen was going to interview the writer, Horst von Möllendorff.

JP Dear Listeners! The melody that you just heard has a special meaning: for to its rhythm there doesn't move a man but—a drawing. For the first time new animated cartoons have been closely linked with music and fine arts.

To this melody a snowman is dancing in a new cartoon that you will know very soon. With his first move he seems to look familiar; with almost affecting happiness he smiles all over his face and this is no miracle. The father of the little smiling character that you all will know from the newspapers is nobody else than the artist Horst von Möllendorff who has contributed the idea for this film which was produced in the animaton studios of Fischerkoesen. We have asked Horst von Möllendorff to join us to tell us a little bit. Many of you will like to hear him once; the snowman's sister in spirit many of you will already know. This is the wasp, the star of the animated cartoon *Weather-Beaten Melody*, which accidentally draws some sound out of an old phonograph record according to an idea by the same Horst von Möllendorff.

Melody from *Verwitterte Melodie* (by Lothar Brühne).

Herr von Möllendorff, we know that the artist's idea is a big secret but as you will know us laymen are always eager to learn more about. Please would you kindly tell how you came across the idea for the *Snowman* film?

vM To conceive an idea you need two things: open eyes to walk around the world and the imagination. With my very eyes I once have seen a snow man which was surrounded by snowdrops which meddlesomely were watching out of the snow. And in my creative mind this image became an idea. In my mind I have transferred a snow man who never has seen the splendor blossoming in summer to summertime. In the cartoon the snowman really experiences the summer.

JP How long did it take to transform the lovely idea into a cartoon?

vM The animated cartoon *The Snowman* was produced in 5 month's work in the animation studio of Fischerkoesen Film Production. That is an extremely brief working period if one considers that each frame of the whole film strip has to be drawn separately. Before it will be drawn each frame has to be sketched. Besides that, in one frame often appear several characters so that again for each character an individual animation drawing is necessary. In this brief period in the studio of Fischerkoesen, for a single film that runs for approximately 15 minutes, 52,000 individual drawings were produced.

JP One barely can grasp this surprisingly great and versatile work if one sees the color screen adventure of the snowman.

vM That is a good proof for our work.

JP We only can agree; for the strongest impact of the film was the great serenity which affects all of us, shining and liberating with every laugh that has been born of true humour.

JP How does it come, Herr von Möllendorff, that this cheerfulness is so outrageously affecting?

vM Well, Herr Doktor Petersen, that is almost more difficult to explain than to do but I will try. As much as beauty must be painted into a painting if it should reflect true beauty delight has to be drawn into a drawing if it should have a delightful effect. And I do my work with great joy and hope that our cartoon film will come off the screen radiant with joy onto you.

JP Herr von Möllendorff, in the name of all listeners I assume I can assure that we will accept the cartoon with similar joy.

In a letter addressed to Cautio Treuhand the Propaganda Ministry informed Max Winkler that the minister had viewed *The Snowman* on November 20: "He liked the picture very much."

Commendation signed by Dr. Joseph Goebbels for Horst von Möllendorff and *Weather-Beaten Melody*

Courtesy of J. P. Storm

DECEMBER

Der kleine Muck (Little Muck), a German fairy tale based on a play by Friedrich Forster (=Waldfried Burggraf) who wrote a National Socialist propaganda play in 1933: *Alle gegen einen Einer für alle*. Muck (Willi Puhlmann who died in a plane crash in 1996) is a brave boy who fights a witch (Elise Aulinger) and her giant brother Bumbo (Viktor Gehring) to win the hand of Princess Mareille (Christa Berndl). Filmed in Munich.

DECEMBER 21

Ulrich Manfred **"Ulli" Lommel** born as son of actor-entertainer Ludwig

Manfred Lommel and actress Karla von Cleef in Zielenzig, today Suleçin, Poland.

Naturfilm **Hubert Schonger** finished a puppet short: *Der kleine Däumling (Tom Thumb)*.

1945

MAY 8

War ended in Germany.

MAY 31

Rainer Werner Fassbinder born in Bad Wörishofen, Bavaria.

AUGUST 14

Wim Wenders born in Düsseldorf.

DECEMBER 9

Hans Dominik died in Berlin.

1946

Cinemas Western zones: 2125
Attedance figure: 300 million (estimated)
Only 1 feature film produced

Cinemas Eastern Soviet zone: unknown
Attendance figure: unknown
3 feature films produced

MAY 17

DEFA Deutsche Film AG was established in the Soviet Zone.

JULY 11

Eric (Erich) Pommer returned as American chief film officer, with assimilated rank as Colonel, to Germany.

1947

West Zones
Cinemas: 2500 (estimated)
Attendance figure: 460 million (estimated)
9 feature films produced

Soviet Zone:
Cinemas: unknown
Attendance figure: 180 million (estimated)
4 feature Films produced

FEBRUARY 20

Finished in Nazi Germany (November 1943-March 1944), the mystery *Spuk im Schloss (Ghost in the Castle)* was finally released after the war.

JUNE 13

Helmut Käutner's *In jenen Tagen (In Those Days/Seven Journeys)* has a car tell the story of its seven owners in Nazi Germany. Film was premiered in Hamburg.

NOVEMBER 30

Ernst Lubitsch died of a heart attack in Beverly Hills.

Princeton University Press published *From Caligari to Hitler* by **Siegfried Kracauer**.

1948

West Zones
Cinemas: 2975
Attendance figure: 443 million
23 feature films produced

Soviet Zone
Cinemas: unknown
Attendance figure: unknown
7 feature films produced

FEBRUARY 28

Actor-director Walter Oehmichen opened his marionette theater Augsburger Puppenkiste (puppet box or puppet chest) with *Der gestiefelte Kater (Puss in Boots)*.

JUNE 1

Chemie und Liebe (Chemistry and Love): DEFA Comedy set in "Kapitalia", a fictitious country: Hans Nielsen as Dr. Alland who has invented a way to turn grass into butter without the intervening cow is courted by all sort of profiteers. Based on a rough draft by Béla Balázs that was transformed into a screenplay by Marion Keller and Frank Clifford, i.e., Hans Heinrich Tillgner, a Tobis sound film pioneer. In the early 1930s Tillgner was sent to Paris to produce films, including René Clair's 1931 *À Nous la Liberté* and *Le Million*. *Chemistry and Love* was directed by Arthur Maria Rabenalt.

JULY 30

Heinz Rühmann as extraterrestrial who has the skill to travel the universe simply by concentration encounters some negative issues about mankind: *Der Herr vom anderen Stern (The Man from Another Star)* directed by Heinz Hilpert and produced by Rühmann in Munich proved a box-office bomb. The job bringing Rühmann to Earth in a brief sequence was handled by animator Heinz Tischmeyer.

SEPTEMBER 13

Paul Wegener died in Berlin.

NOVEMBER 16

Hubert Schonger had left Berlin and settled in Inning/Ammersee near Munich where he continued his production of fairy tales for Jugenfilm release: *Frau Holle (Mother Holly)*.

Frau Holle (Mother Holly) | Courtesy of Schongerfilm

NOVEMBER 23

Der Apfel ist ab (The Apple Fell/U.S.: The Original Sin): Bavaria-produced satire with fantasy touch and many optical effects shots, directed by Helmut Käutner. Bobby Todd as Adam, Bettina Moissi as Eva, Arno Assmann as Lucifer and Käutner himself as Petrus.

DECEMBER 21

Rotkäppchen (Little Red Riding Hood), an 18-minute short film animated by Kurt Stordel for Schongerfilm.

1949

Federal Republic of Germany (West Zones):
Cinemas: 3360
Attendance figure: 467 million
62 feature films produced

German Democratic Republic GDR (Soviet Zone)
Cinemas: unknown
Attendance figure: 184 million
14 feature films produced

JANUARY 1

Animator Hans Held tried to launch a feature-length *Kalif Storch (Caliph Stork)* in his studio in Hamburg. The project wasn't made.

FEBRUARY 4

Jenny Jugo has some fantastic daydreams in *Träum' nicht, Annette (Don't Dream, Annette)!*, a DEFA production originally finished by Terra under the title *Sag' endlich ja!* in December 1944. Annette Müller, a French teacher by profession, has two ardent admirers, both of whom would like to marry her. But she cannot decide who is the right one: the diplomat or the architect. There was only one reason for DEFA to rework the old picture: A highly remunerated contract with Jenny Jugo was at stake. Visual effect scenes created by Ernst Kunstmann and Heinrich Weidemann.

APRIL 11

Producer **Bernd Eichinger** born in Neuburg/Danube.

MAY 23

In the western zones the Federal Republic of Germany was formed.

JULY 30

Henrik Galeen suffering from cancer passed away in American exile in Vermont.

AUGUST 16

Ilse Kubaschewski's Gloria Film Distribution Company in Munich was initially based on releasing old Republic serials in recut form.

SEPTEMBER 5

Kasper reist ins Märchenland/Kaspers Reise ins Märchenland (Kasper's Trip to Fairy Tale Land): a hand-puppet film with Hohenstein Kasper directd by Curt A. Engel who bascially did documentaries and produced by F.F.E. Dautert (Hamburg).

OCTOBER 7

In the Soviet Zone German Democratic Republic GDR was established.

Poster *Kaspers Reise ins Märchenland (Kasper's Trip to Fairy Tale Land)* | Author's collection

DECEMBER 18

Hans im Glück (Hans in Luck): Schongerfilm production with Gunnar Möller and Erich Ponto.

DECEMBER 21

Die seltsame Geschichte des Brandner Kaspar (The Strange Story of Brandner Kaspar) directed by *Münchhausen's* Josef von Baky at Bavaria Studios Munich from a play by Joseph Maria Lutz: A peasant, Kaspar Brandner (Carl Wery) who doesn't want to die, outwits Death (Paul Hörbiger, son of Austrian engineer Hanns Hörbiger who concocted the pseudoscientific World Ice Doctrine).

Hans im Glück (Hans in Luck) | Courtesy of Schongerfilm

1950

Federal Republic of Germany
Cinemas: 3962
Attendance figure: 487 million
Feature films produced: 80

German Democratic Republic
Cinemas: unknown
Attendance figure: unknown
Feature films produced: 10

JANUARY 2

Emil Jannings passed away in Strobl, Austria.

JANUARY

Das Blümlein Wunderhold (Little Flower Wunderhold), a 22-minute hand-puppet film from **Schonger**.

FEBRUARY 24

Immer wieder Glück (Always Lucky), the second attempt of the **Diehl Brothers** releasing a feature-length stop-motion puppet film, this time starring their character Kasper Larifari, based on an 1858 puppet character originally created by Munich puppeteer Count Pocci.

APRIL 1

Constantin Film, soon to become Germany's leading distribution company, was co-founded by Danish entrepreneur Constantin Preben Philipsen and Waldfried Barthel, his German partner. Constantin was going to release the Edgar Wallace series and some of Toho's Japanese Kaiju films.

MAY

Georg Wilhelm Pabst was scheduled to direct a color production based on Homer's *Ulysses* for Milan-based ICET production company. The movie was postponed and eventually made in 1954 with American star Kirk Douglas, Silvana Mangano, Anthony Quinn, and wrestler Umberto Silvestri as Polyphem. But Pabst was no more involved. Instead, Mario Camerini directed.

SEPTEMBER 30

Kaspers Reise um die Welt (Kasper's Trip Round the World), a hand-puppet film featuring the Hohenstein Kasper, directed by Curt A. Engel and jointly produced by Boehner Film and Förster Film for Jugendfilm release, premiered at Mercedes Palace in Berlin Neukölln.

DECEMBER 8

Das kalte Herz (Heart of Stone), first (and best) of a series of color fairy tales (this one written by Wilhelm Hauff) produced by East-German DEFA that now occupied the former Ufa Studios lot in Babelsberg. To fulfill an older contract (and because the originally scheduled director Erich Engel left DEFA) Paul Verhoeven was trusted with directorial chores: Lutz Moik as Peter Munk, a poor Black Forest charcoal burner, meets two spirits who fight for his soul: Little Glassman (played by Paul Bildt) and Dutch Michael (Erwin Geschonneck, a member of the Communist Party since 1919 and prisoner in several Nazi concentration camps who survived the RAF sinking of the Cap Acona). He decides to go with evil Dutch Michael who promises Peter all the riches on earth if he is willing to exchange his heart for a cold stone. In a bit part for a fraction of a second **Bernhard Goetzke** is glimpsed in his last film part as poor peasant. Agfacolor photography by Bruno Mondi who had worked with Veit Harlan on *Jud Süss, Der grosse König* and *Kolberg*. Trick shots by Ernst Kunstmann who made the Glass Man small and Dutch Michael a giant by using mirror technique.

Director Verhoeven, by the way, died on stage of Munich Kammerspiele (March 22, 1975) during a tribute for the late actress Therese Giehse. When he began his obituary, he suddenly keeled over dead.

1951

Federal Republic of Germany
Cinemas: 4547
Attendance figure: 555 million
76 feature films produced

German Democratic Republic
Cinemas: 1494
Attendance figure: 188 million
8 feature films produced

JUNE 6

The first edition of Berlin International Film Festival opened at Titania Palace in West Berlin. The festival was founded by Dr. Alfred Bauer who was involved with the Nazi Ufa. Walt Disney's *Cinderella* won the *Golden Bear*.

SEPTEMBER 21

Spuk mit Max und Moritz: **Diehl** puppets acting out Wilhelm Busch's story of *Two Bad Boys in Seven Tricks*. First published in Munich in 1865, the book could rightly be called a precursor of modern comic strips including the *Katzenjammer Kids*.

OCTOBER 17

Author **Bernhard Kellermann** died in Klein Glienicke near Potsdam.

1952

Federal Republic of Germany
Cinemas: 4853
Attendance figure: 615 million
75 feature films produce

German Democratic Republic
Cinemas: 1414
Attendance figure: 197 million
6 feature films produced

MARCH 18

King Kong rerelease opened in Düsseldorf under the German title *King Kong und die weisse Frau (King Kong and the White Woman)*. Fay Wray was dubbed by Veit Harlan's daughter Maria Körber.

King Kong und die weisse Frau, German rerelease poster | Author's collection

OCTOBER 23

Alraune, the second remake of **Hanns Heinz Ewers'** novel, this time in color and with Erich von Stroheim playing Jacob ten Brinken who creates artificial Alraune played by Hildegard Knef (during her brief Hollywood stint renamed Hildegarde Neff). According to director Arthur Maria Rabenalt, Stroheim feared the actress and seemed to be quite nervous about her. Günther Stapenhorst, producer of *Amphitryon* (before he ran into trouble with the Nazis and worked for some time in London), supervised the project filmed in color by Friedl Behn-Grund. In the United States released by DCA Distributors Corporation of America in February 1957 under the title *Unnatural…The Fruit of Evil.*

…Alraune and Ten Brinken share a most perverse father-daughter relationship, which sizzles with barely repressed sexual tension and seems always ready to devolve into incest. Although she performs many malicious acts, some bordering on outright murder, in essence Alraune in **Unnatural** *is little more than an amoral "brat" of industrial society, born of permissive, ethically complicit parents and unleashed on a world which*

has no concept of how to contain her. Ten Brinken has even attempted to make Alraune "go straight" by sending her to a nunnery, but the slippery lass escapes the convent after being imprisoned for possessing "obscene literature" (which, according to Ten Brinken, was his own copy of the 1911 novel **Alraune** *by Hanns Heinz Ewers!).* [43]

NOVEMBER 14

Robert Louis Stevenson's *Der Flaschenteufel (The Bottle Imp)* produced by the **Diehl Brothers** but this time not using the time-consuming stop-motion process but rod puppets of Kasper Larifari and other characters.

NOVEMBER 19

Austrian premiere of *1. April 2000* a social utopist propaganda film about a World Global Union that is going to intervene when Austria's newly elected president (Josef Meinrad) declares the independence of the country. Finally, the Global Union President, a female (Hilde Krahl) who arrives in Vienna by Flying Saucer is convinced the Austria not only gave the world operetta (*Die Fledermaus* by Johann Strauss) and waltz but also is completely peace-loving. That Hitler was Austrian is not mentioned. Directed by Goebbels' favorite filmmaker Wolfgang Liebeneiner with a cast that included every big name available at that time: Waltraud Haas, Curd Jürgens, Hans Holt, Judith Holzmeister, Paul Hörbiger, Hans Moser, the Spanish Riding School and the Vienna Boys' Choir. Wien Film produced this atrocity on commission by the Austrian Government.

DECEMBER 25

West German television broadcast started with Nordwestdeutscher Rundfunk in Hamburg.

Lotte H. Eisner's book *L'Ecran Démoniaque* published in Paris by André Bonne.

---

43   Rob Craig, *It Came from 1957: A Critical Guide to the Year's Science Fiction, Fantasy and Horror Films.* Jefferson, North Carolina, and London 2013: McFarland & Company, Inc., Publishers, p. 52.

Cover of the German edition of Lotte H. Eisner's *Dämonische Leinwand* (The Haunted Screen)
Photograph by Anna Khan | Author's Collection

1953

Federal Republic of Germany
Cinemas: 5117
Attendance figure: 680 million
96 feature films produced

German Democratic Republic
Cinemas: 1486
Attendance figure: 211 million
7 feature films produced

JANUARY 25

Hubert Schonger's production of long-nosed *Zwerg Nase (Nose, the Dwarf/ Dwarf Nose)*, a fairy-tale by Wilhelm Hauff starring Hans Clarin in the title role (and Richard Krüger, a real dwarf, as Clarin's double in long shots). Directed by **Francesco Stefani**.

SEPTEMBER 20

Fritz Genschow continued his fairy tale production after the war with Hans Christian Andersen's *Das Mädchen mit den Schwefelhölzern (The Little Match Girl)*.

OCTOBER 9

Hans Christian Andersen's *Die Prinzessin auf der Erbse (The Princess and the Pea)* filmed by **Alf Zengerling** was approved by the censors and ready for release by Willy Karp (Düsseldorf) and Diehl-Film (Munich).

OCTOBER 15

Der Wolf und die sieben Geisslein (The Wolf and the Seven Little Goats), a silhouette film by Bruno J. Böttge, produced by DEFA in Babelsberg.

The first stop-motion puppet film of East German DEFA was created by Johannes Hempel: *Frau Holle (Mother Holly)*.

OCTOBER 25

Genschow continued his series of cinematic fairy tales with *Rotkäppchen (Little Red Riding Hood)*. Gerhard Huttula, the former head of Ufa's special effects and process department, became his regular cameraman. Huttula called it the happiest time of his life.

DECEMBER 23

Wilhelm Hauff's 1826 fairy tale *Die Geschichte vom kleinen Muck (The Story of Little Muck)* directed in color by Wolfgang Staudte for East German DEFA: A hunchback living in a small Oriental town tells kids who like to chase and tease him the story of his life. As a boy, who lost his father and was banished from home by his evil relatives, he stole a pair of magic slippers from a wicked woman and became the fastest runner in the country but was plagued by intrigues of the Sultan's courtiers and expelled from the palace. With a little more magic, however, he has the courtiers' heads fitted with donkey ears. According to Staudte, one of the favorite films of Ho Chi Minh. Planned as an interim project while Staudte was waiting for an ill-fated film adaptation of Bert Brecht's play *Mother Courage*.

DECEMBER 25

Die goldene Gans (The Golden Goose): Grimm's fairy tale adapted and produced by **Hubert Schonger** and co-directed with Walter Oehmichen.

Die goldene Gans (The Golden Goose) | Courtesy of Schongerfilm

1954

Federal Republic of Germany
Cinemas: 5640
Attendance figure: 736 million
109 feature films produced

German Democratic Republic
Cinemas: 1447
Attendance figure: 272 million
11 feature films produced

APRIL 29

Joe May died in Hollywood.

MAY 25

Caligari co-author **Hans Janowitz** passed away in New York City.

JULY 1

Thea von Harbou, who was discovered for the movies (and for **Fritz Lang,** her ex-husband) by **Joe May,** died after a tragic fall in West Berlin's Delphi Cinema connected to a reissue of her film *Der müde Tod* that she was asked to introduce. During the Third Reich she had become a member of the Nazi party. Von Harbou died in poverty as did Joe May.

AUGUST 22

Premiered at the Capitol Cinema in Berlin: *Hänsel und Gretel (Hansel and Gretel)* by **Fritz Genschow** who was going to compete with versions of the same fairy tales produced by Schongerfilm. Uwe Witt as Hansel, Heidi Ewert as Gretel, Elisabeth Ilna as the witch.

AUGUST 23

Zehn kleine Negerlein (Ten Little Nigger Boys—sic!) versus Rom-Rom-Rom the Magician. Children's film (based on the song *Ten Little Injuns*) directed by Rolf von Sydow.

SEPTEMBER 3

Superstition in a village in Thuringia: *Hexen (Witches)*, a DEFA production written by Kurt Walter Barthel and directed by Helmut Spiess, premiered at Babylon Cinema in Berlin (East).

SEPTEMBER 4

Kasper's Abenteuer in der Türkei (Kasper's Adventures in Turkey): Hand puppets directed by Hella Mora for Domo Film KG Munich.

SEPTEMBER 11

Reinhold Schünzel died in Munich.

SEPTEMBER 12

The **Schongerfilm** version of *Hänsel und Gretel (Hansel and Gretel)* at the Alhambra in Dusseldorf.

OCTOBER 10

Hubert Schonger's new version of *Rotkäppchen (Little Red Riding Hood)*.

DECEMBER 25

Kasper's Reise zu den Zwergen (Kasper's Journey to the Dwarfs): Hella Mora's second feature length hand puppet film for the Domo Film Company in Munich.

Der Froschkönig (The Frog Prince) directed by Otto Meyer on location at Charlottenburg Castle in Berlin.

1955

Federal Republic of Germany
Cinemas: 6239
Attendance figure: 766 million
Feature films produced: 122

German Democratic Republic
Cinemas: 1423
Attendance figure: 266 million
Feature films produced: 14

JANUARY 23

Struwwelpeter by **Fritz Genschow**.

MARCH 9

Walt Disney joined **Wernher von Braun** for TV's *Man in Space*.

APRIL 1

East-German DEFA established its own Studio for Animation in Dresden: DEFA Studio für Trickfilme, not exclusively but mainly a short film manufacture.

APRIL 7

DEFA Studios' fairy tale *Der Teufel vom Mühlenberg (The Devil from Mill Mountain)*, legend from the Harz Mountains: Once upon a time, during the Middle Ages, the brutal, greedy owner of a windmill farm (Willy A. Kleinau) and his comrades set a rival forest mill on fire, disguised as devils. But the evil miller is punished by three good charcoal burners, the spirits of the forest, and transformed into a stone statue.

The transformation was executed by DEFA's chief trick photographer Ernst Kunstmann who had pioneered mirror shots with his mentor **Eugen Schüfftan**:

For this scene we had to build two identical landscape sets in the studio. Each rock, and also the outlines of the mountains, had to be absolutely alike in both sets. In the set to the camera's left, the boulder in the shape of the miller-turned-to-stone was built. In front of the camera, we had the actor on the other set. Also, in front of the camera we had a large 45-degree mirror. The silvering was partially scraped away so that it reflected only the boulder and a few millimeters of the left set. In the camera's eyepiece, I could see the set in front but not the actor who was masked by the boulder's reflection. The mirror with the contours was then pulled down until I could see the actor. At first, I filmed the set with the real miller. Then my assistant slowly drew up the mirror with the contours of the miller turned to stone. The moment the silvering reached the actor's feet it began to reflect the boulder on the left set until the actor had totally turned into stone.

MAY 29

Rudolf Klein-Rogge died in Wetzelsdorf near Jagerberg, Austria.

JUNE 16

Graham Greene's *Die kleine Lok (The Little Fire Engine)*: mix of model and 2D animation photographed in color by Gerhard Huttula and produced by Gerhard Fieber (EOS Film Göttingen), an advertising film on behalf of Deutsche Bundesbahn (German Federal Railway).

JULY 29

Das Fräulein von Scuderi (The Young Woman of Scuderi) based on a novel by **E. T. A. Hoffmann** with Henny Porten and Willy A. Kleinau premiered at

Babylon Cinema in Berlin East. A GDR-Swedish co-production directed by Eugen York.

AUGUST 4

In Frankfurt/Main Science Fiction Club Deutschland was founded by writer Walter Ernsting (who had spent years in Soviet war imprisonment) and editor Walter Spiegl with some protection aid by **Brigitte Helm**, British fan Julian Parr and Americans Raymond Z. Gallun and Forrest J Ackerman.

SEPTEMBER 4

Rumpelstilzchen (Rumpelstiltskin) with Werner Krüger, produced by Alfred Förster for Jugendfilm release.

SEPTEMBER 9

Fritz Genschow's *Aschenputtel (Cinderella)* starring his wife Rita-Maria Nowottnick-Genschow [a.k.a. Rita-Maria Nowotny].

OCTOBER 30

Walter Bluhm, the German voice of Stan Laurel (even better than the original), as *Sandmännchen (Sandman)*.

NOVEMBER 10

Roland Emmerich born in Stuttgart.

NOVEMBER 16

Genschow's *Dornröschen (Sleeping Beauty)* with Angela von Leitner.

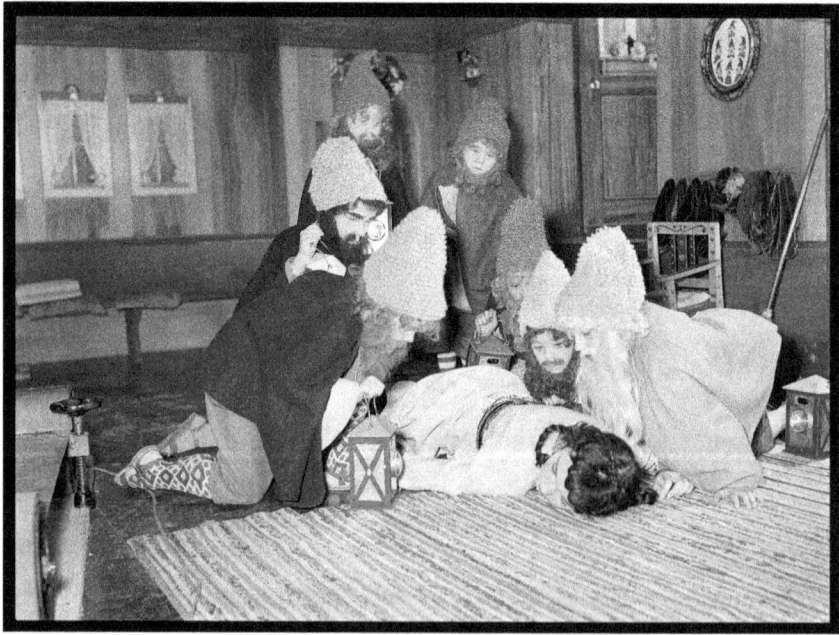

Schneewittchen und die sieben Zwerge (Snow White and the Seven Dwarfs)
Courtesy of Schongerfilm

NOVEMBER 20

Der Teufel mit den drei goldenen Haaren (The Devil with Three Golden Hairs), a Grimm fairy tale directed by Hans F. Wilhelm for Domo Film Munich, starring Alexander Golling as Devil, at the huge Lichtburg Cinema in Essen.

NOVEMBER 27

Hubert Schonger's Agfacolor film remake of his own *Schneewittchen und die sieben Zwerge (Snow White and the Seven Dwarfs)* directed by Erich Kobler at the Gloria Palace in Berlin (West). Elke Arendt as Snow White, Addi Adametz as the evil Queen and Niels Clausnitzer as the Prince. This time the dwarfs were not played by midgets but by children, members of the Children's Dance Group Suse Böhm. Actually, children were the role models for Grimm's fairy tale. The real dwarfs were child laborers working in the copper mines. Screenplay by Konrad Lustig and Walter Oehmichen.

1956

Federal Republic of Germany
Cinemas: 6438
Attendance figure: 817 million
120 feature films produced

German Democratic Republic
Cinemas: 1409
Attendance figure: 287 million
19 feature films produced

JANUARY 3

Official launch of Fernsehen der DDR (East-German television) located in Berlin Adlershof.

APRIL 7

Der Hexer (The Witcher/The Ringer), Franz Peter Wirth TV play based on Edgar Wallace.

MAY 18

Der kleine Häwelmann (The Little Haverman), DEFA puppet animation by Herbert K. Schulz and cameraman Erich Günther.

AUGUST 16

Johann Nestroy's magic play with Günther Lüders as evil ghost *Lumpazivagabundus*. Directed by Franz Antel.

Béla Lugosi, cured from drug addiction but still an alcoholic, died in Los Angeles.

SEPTEMBER 9

Fritz Genschow's *Tischlein deck dich (The Wishing Table)*.

SEPTEMBER 28

Das tapfere Schneiderlein (The Brave Little Tailor), a DEFA production directed by Helmut Spiess, premiered at the Babylon Cinema in Berlin (East). Kurt Schmidtchen in the title role as journeyman tailor who has disposed of seven flies at one go and, so far, feels fit to drive off the kingdom's worst enemies, two giants played by Wolf Kaiser and Gerhard Frei.

SEPTEMBER 30

Norbert Schultze, composer of *Lili Marleen* and Joseph Goebbels' last big propaganda film *Kolberg*, cast his sons Norbert Jr. and Kristian as Wilhelm Busch's *Max und Moritz (Max and Morris)*. Schultze's associate was **Francesco**

Stefani. Karl Vollbrecht, who had co-designed *Metropolis* for **Fritz Lang** and *Jew Suss* for Veit Harlan, built the sets.

OCTOBER 4

Liane, das Mädchen aus dem Urwald (Liane, Jungle Goddess): *This is Liane... a lost child who became savage queen of a black jungle!* Marion Michael ("Germany's answer to Brigitte Bardot") as female Tarzan, Hardy Krüger and Reggie Nalder. In the United States released by DCA (Distributors Corporation of America): *Beautiful...Proud...Untamed and more savage than the black jungle she ruled!*

1957

Federal Republic of Germany
Cinemas: 6577
Attendance figure: 801 million
111 feature films produced

German Democratic Republic
Cinemas: 1391
Attendance figure: 316 million
21 feature films produced

MARCH 7

Der ideale Untermieter (The Ideal Lodger/Too Young for Men) turns out to be a robot named Robsy. The movie was funded by filmmaker Wolf Schmidt, a film personality well-kown to German cinema goers and TV spectators as *Father Hesselbach* in a popular family series. *The Ideal Lodger* was released in Germany (on commission) by United Artists. In 1954 Schmidt had visited Hollywood including the set of Paramount's *The Naked Jungle* where he was photographed with his hosts, producer George Pal, director Byron Haskin and female star Eleanor Parker.

APRIL 26

Arthur Miller's 1953 drama *The Crucible* as French-East German co-production (Société Nouvelle Pathé Cinéma) made at DEFA Studios Babelsberg from a script by Jean-Paul Sartre: ***Die Hexen von Salem/Les sorcières de Salem (The Witches of Salem)*** featuring the French stars Yves Montand, Simone Signoret and Mylène Demongeot who at that time all sympathized with the French Communist Party. Music: Hanns Eisler. In Berlin (East) the movie was premiered at Babylon and Collosseum Cinemas. In the United States it was released in a subtitled version by Kinglsey-International Pictures.

MAY 28

At the same spot where once was Ufa's Zoo Palace Max Knapp built a new representative 1200-seat Zoo Palace.

AUGUST 27

Der Wolf und die sieben jungen Geisslein (The Wolf and the Seven Little Goats), an involuntarily funny Schongerfilm fairy tale with actors in animal costumes.

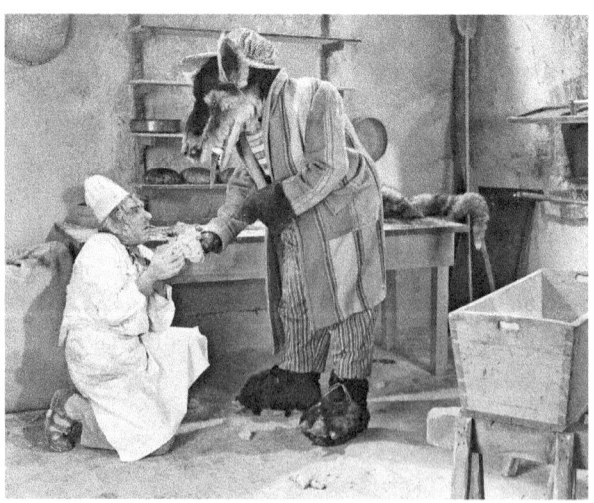

Der Wolf und die sieben jungen Geisslein (The Wolf and the Seven Little Goats) | Courtesy of Schongerfilm

SEPTEMBER 15

Aufruhr im Schlaraffenland (Trouble in the Land of Milk and Honey), a fairy tale produced by Alfred Förster and photographed in Agfacolor by Gerhard Huttula, premiered at Gloria Palace in Berlin (West).

OCTOBER 4

Sputnik 1 launched into an elliptical low Earth orbit.

OCTOBER 6

Schonger's best fairy tale entry *Rübezahl—Herr der Berge (Rübezahl: Ruler of the Mountains)* with Franz Essel at the Planie Cinema in Stuttgart. Cameraman Heinz Hölscher told that they experimented a lot to create the visuals for the story of the Silesian Giant of the Mountains who punishes the bad and rewards the good. Erich Kobler directed a cast that included Bobby Todd, Helmo Kindermann, Niels Clausnitzer, Paul Bös, Dietrich Thoms, Georg Lehn, Elke Arendt, Fritz Wepper, and Rolf von Nauckhoff.

Poster *Rübezahl—Herr der Berge (Rübezahl: Ruler of the Mountains)* | Courtesy of Schongerfilm

OCTOBER 11

The success of the first *Liane* Film instigated Arca producer Gero Wecker to immediately follow up with a sequel which confronts the white jungle goddess (Marion Michael) with her rich relatives in Hamburg: *Liane—die weisse Sklavin (Nature Girl and the Slaver)*.

DECEMBER 1

Die Gänsemagd (The Goose Girl) by **Fritz Genschow** at Gloria Palace in Berlin (West).

DECEMBER 13

Das singende, klingende Bäumchen (The Singing, Ringing Tree), another DEFA fairy tale favorite (directed by **Francesco Stefani**): To win the love of a beautiful but rather arrogant princess (Christel Bodenstein), a prince (Eckart Dux) sets out to find a magic tree but is transformed into a bear by an evil gnome (Richard Krüger).

1958

Federal Republic of Germany
Cinemas: 6789
Attendance figure: 750 million
109 feature films produced

German Democratic Republic
Cinemas: 1404
Attendance figure: 273 million
18 feature films produced

MAY 29

U.S. release of *Fiend Without a Face*, a British science fiction shocker (produced by Richard Gordon) with facehuggers animated in Munich by Flo Nordhoff and photographed by Karl Ludwig Ruppel. West German release date was May 20, 1959, titled *Ungeheuer ohne Gesicht*.

JULY 19

Die Geschichte vom armen Hassan (The Story of Poor Hassan), a Uygur fairy tale directed at DEFA Studios Babelsberg by Gerhard Klein: Hassan, a poor devil, ekes out a living in the stony desert. While he is literally dying of thirst, the fountains in the wealthy merchant Machmud's garden are brimming over. One day, Hassan's parrot perches on the edge of a fountain soon to be attacked by Machmud's watchdog. To rescue his erstwhile friend, Hassan is compelled to kill the dog. He is taken to court and sentenced by the qadi to be chained and to take on the watchdog's duties. And when he fails to prevent a horse being stolen, he has to carry out this animal's work as well. His only ray of hope is Fatima, a slave girl. But not even she can persuade him to escape. He believes his place on earth is predestined by Allah. Not until he happens to overhear the merchant and the qadi making deals, does he finally realize that the rich dictate the order of the world. The two villains go out riding, with Hassan taking on the part of one of the horses. He suddenly slips off his shackles and, with all his might, flings the carriage—and its passengers—against a rock. He goes back to open the merchant's garden to all who are thirsty.[44] Hassan is played by Ekkehard Schall, the rich merchant by Erwin Geschonneck.

AUGUST 18

Nosferatu cameraman **Fritz Arno Wagner** died after a fall from a camera car in Göttingen.

OCTOBER 25

Heinrich Holk died in Bremen Schwachhausen. In the early 1920s, as Heinrich Dieckmann, he was the business manager of Prana Film which produced

---

44 Synopsis according to Progress Film-Verleih, Berlin/GDR.

Nosferatu. The same year Waldemar Roger died who had transformed *Nosferatu* into the sound-on-disc film *Die zwölfte Stunde (The Twelfth Hour)* and Hamilton Deane, the creator of the British stage version of *Dracula* (which was remade by Hammer Films London in color).

OCTOBER 31

Das Stacheltier: Der junge Engländer by **Gottfried Kolditz** based on a fairy tale by Wilhelm Hauff.

DECEMBER 5

Not only was Ray Harryhausen's *The 7th Voyage of Sinbad* released in West Germany one week ahead of the United States *(Sindbads siebente Reise)*, but due to a musicians's strike in Hollywood the score by Bernard Herrmann had to be done with a film orchestra in Munich (Kurt Graunke).

DECEMBER 25

Der Teufel muss weg (The Devil Must Go), a 15-minute East German TV puppet film by Gerhard Behrendt (assisted by Peter Blümel).

1959

Federal Republic of Germany
Cinemas: 7085
Attendance figure: 671 million
107 feature films produced

German Democratic Republic
Cinemas: 1389
Attendance figure: 259 million
27 feature films produced

FEBRUARY

Pleased with the results of *Fiend Without a Face*, producer Richard Gordon again relied for special effects on the services of the Munich-based team of Flo Nordhoff (Baron Florenz von Fuchs-Nordhoff) and Karl Ludwig Ruppel for *First Man into Space*. The same month the animated short *Die Purpurlinie (The Purple Line)* by Ruppel and Nordhoff was shown at the Oberhausen Film Festival.

APRIL 24

Another highlight popular with East German audiences was Hans Christian Andersen's *Das Feuerzeug (Tinder—The Box)*: An old witch asks a poor soldier (Rolf Ludwig) to fetch her an old tinder box hidden in a hollow oak tree. He finds the tree filled with chests of treasure guarded by fearsome giant dogs (thanks to Ernst Kunstmann's mirror magic) and outwits the witch who tries to betray him. The magic lighter finally saves his life when he is sentenced to death. Finally, he is given the hand of a princess.

JULY 24

Horst Frank plays a mad doctor who considers himself a genius and amputates the head of his mentor so that he can watch him doing horrible experiments like giving a hunchbacked nurse the body of a stripper. Nazi film director Veit Harlan (*Jew Suss, Kolberg*) was aghast when West German producer Wolf C. Hartwig dared to offer him this horror film titled *Die Nackte und der Satan* (rerelease title: *Des Satans nackte Sklavin*) and turned him down flat. Russian-born Victor Trivas, who during his emigration in the United States had co-authored Orson Welles' *The Stranger*, wrote and directed while French character actor Michel Simon, partially paralyzed after having some tainted makeup applied on a previous picture (*Un certain Monsieur Jo*), had to accept the part of *The Head*—that's the title of the limited American release:

At the head of all masterpieces of horror that you've ever seen... you must place **The Head**.

Professor Abel has developed a detached point of view.
The body is gone… but the head lives on!
It just won't lie down and stay dead!

This sad film was destined to continue the great tradition of pre-war German horror flicks. **Hermann Warm** who co-designed the Expressionist sets for *The Cabinet of Dr. Caligari* was called in as supervising art director.

AUGUST 1

In Geiselgasteig near Munich Bavaria was reorganized by West-German TV (Westdeutscher Rundfunk: 50 %, Süddeutscher Rundfunk: 25 %) and the old Bavaria Filmkunst (25 %). First managing director was a former TV man: Helmut Jedele. More and more German producers while taking oaths of loyalty with the cinema were looking for a shoulder to shoulder with TV.

SEPTEMBER 4

With German talent produced in Danmark, Constantin Preben Philipsen launched an Edgar Wallace series revival with *Der Frosch mit der Maske (Face of the Frog)*. From a screenplay by Egon Eis (using the nom de plume Trygve Larsen) and J. Joachim Bartsch directed by **Dr. Harald Reinl**. With Joachim Fuchsberger, Siegfried Lowitz, Eddie Arent as comic relief, Karl Lange as the Executioner of London, and Jochen Brockmann as Frog.

Falk Harnack directed *Arzt ohne Gewissen (Doctor without Scruples)* with Ewald Balser as Professor Lund whose experiments in organ transplant make him a criminal.

SEPTEMBER 25

Schongerfilm and Jugendfilm premiered *Die Bremer Stadtmusikanten (The Bremen Town Musicians)* at U.T. Schwachhausen in Bremen.

Die Bremer Stadtmusikanten (The Bremen Town Musicians) | Courtesy of Schongerfilm

OCTOBER 14

Ein Mann geht durch die Wand (The Man Who Walked Through the Wall) with Heinz Rühmann as Mr. Buchsbaum, a little office clerk who suddenly discovers that he is able to walk through walls was premiered in Cologne. Directed by Ladislao Vajda. Photographic effects by Ernst Kunstmann and Karl Ludwig Ruppel.

OCTOBER 20

Werner Krauss died in Vienna.

NOVEMBER 22

Unser Sandmännchen (Our Sandman), a stop-motion character created by Gerhard Behrendt, became a favorite on East German TV.

DECEMBER 16

First part of **Fritz Genschow's** TV *Schneewittchen (Snow White)*.

DECEMBER 23

Second part of **Genschow's** TV *Schneewittchen*.

DECEMBER 25

A perennial German favorite (NWDR Nordwestdeutscher Rundfunk) for the first time on TV: *Peterchens Mondfahrt (Little Peter's Journey to the Moon)* based on a 1912 children's play by Gerdt von Bassewitz, imaginatively designed and co-written by Hein Heckroth. Two kids, Anneliese and Peter, travel with Sumsemann, a maybug, to the Moon to recover a leg Sumsemann has lost to the evil Man in the Moon.

1960

Federal Republic of Germany
Cinemas: 6950
Attendance figure: 605 million
98 feature films produced

German Democratic Republic
Cinemas: 1369
Attendance figure: 238 million
24 feature films produced

FEBRUARY 26

Der schweigende Stern (The Silent Star/Planet of the Dead), with production postponed for two years (after a deal with French producers fell through), was the first (East) German space travel picture after the war. Director Kurt Maetzig adapted it finally as GDR-Polish co-production from the novel *Astronauci* by Stanisław Lem who disliked this screen version in Agfacolor and Totalvision: When they enter the deserted surface of Venus in the future of the year 1970, Cosmonauts of various nations discover that the Venusians destroyed their own civilization when they attempted to attack Earth with atomic weapons.

The Venusian world of The Silent Star *has been described as "Daliesque". It is surreal. Glassy erectile structures which look like sponges or other marine life proliferate on the obsidian landscape. Weird colorful mists hover and dissipate. Strange screw-like pylons and ancient tunnels are found. One of the team members encounters bouncing metal "insects". The film lacks a monster but makes up for it with unusual compositions and art design* [by DEFA architect Alfred Hirschmeier]. [45]

Dr. Kurt Maetzig and the writers (Jan Fethke, Wolfgang Kohlhaase, Günter Reisch, Günther Rücker, Alexander Stenbock-Fermor) also introduced a small robot named Omega that was not part of Lem's book but became the most popular character in the movie. In the United States released by Crown International in a heavily chopped version as *First Spaceship on Venus* mostly to the drive-in market, it might have left an impact on Gene Roddenberry in designing *Star Trek* with its multinational crew that consisted of an American nuclear physicist, a German pilot, a Polish chief engineer, a Soviet cosmonaut, an Indian mathematician, a Chinese linguist, an African technican and Paris-born Japanese actress Yoko Tani remembering the atomic bombing of Hiroshima. The last film appearance of famed German actor Eduard von Winterstein (Freiherr von Wangenheim) who died in 1961 in East Berlin.

APRIL 14

Premiere in Hamburg: The first part of *Herrin der Welt (Mistress of the World)*, a title borrowed from **Joe May** and author Karl Figdor. The focus is on the invention of a huge magnetic pulse that knocks out all electricity and therefore has to be protected from Chinese agents. The international cast included Martha Hyer, Carlos Thompson, Micheline Presle, Wolfgang Preiss, Sabu, Gino Cervi and Lino Ventura. Wilhelm (William) Dieterle who had returned from Hollywood directed but left the project after a disagreement with the

---

45 https://monsterminions.wordpress.com/2011/08/22/the-silent-star-der-schweigende-stern-1960/.

production. Cameraman Richard Angst had to finish **Artur Brauner's** 2-part French-German-Italian co-production.

APRIL 16

Ein Toter hing im Netz (Horrors of Spider Island): With *Nackte und der Satan* obviously successful enough, Rapid Film producer Wolf C. Hartwig continued his horror film activities with a story written and directed by Fritz Böttger who had been trained as dancer, then worked as choreographer in films of the late 1930s and later went to direct TV. American prints renamed him Jaime Nolan. The members of an all-woman dance company who have survived a plane crash have to fight spiders on a remote island whose bite turn their manager (played by Egyptian Alexander D'Arcy) into a monster: *One bite from a giant spider turned him into the world's most hideous monster with a diabolical lust to kill! So terrifying and shocking you will be frightened out of your wits!* Locations were filmed in Yugoslavia which proved a cheap film country. Special make-up by Karl Hanoszek who had worked on *Nackte und der Satan* as did cinematographer Georg Krause. This movie was premiered at Bonbonniere Cinema in Berlin (West).

APRIL 26

Part 2: *Herrin der Welt (Mistress of the World)*.

JULY 29

Das Zaubermännchen (The Dwarf Magician), East German DEFA Studios' adaptation of *Rumpelstiltskin* with Siegfried Seibt.

AUGUST 19

Munich premiere of *I Aim at the Stars (Ich greife nach den Sternen),* an Anglo American-West German co-production between Morningside Charles H. Schneer and Fama Friedrich A. Mainz with Curd Jürgens hailed as **Wernher von Braun.**

SEPTEMBER 14

Die 1000 Augen des Dr. Mabuse (The 1,000 Eyes of Dr. Mabuse): West-Berlin based producer Artur Brauner who had purchased real estate in the Spandau district which formely served as a laboratory facility for poisoning agents got the idea to revive *Dr. Mabuse* as he had an agreement with émigré director Fritz Lang whom he had lured back to Germany. Lang interviewed by Peter Bogdanovich: *"I was back in the United States when I got a letter from him (Brauner): do I want to remake* **Die Nibelungen***? It's a ridiculous idea—there are many, many reasons why it shouldn't be done—and why should I repeat myself?"* Brauner wouldn't give up the idea of a *Nibelungen* remake and worked on it for several years but to please Lang he suggested the *Mabuse* property. Lang was reluctant too: *"I already killed that son-of-a-bitch! That's why I made* **The Last Will of Dr. Mabuse** *(1932). It's finished."* But he insisted, so it became a kind of *a challenge to me- and I had an idea that it might be interesting to show a similar criminal almost thirty years later and again say certain things about our time—the danger that our civilization can be blown up and that on its rubble some new realm of crime could be built up.* [46] Mabuse's heir (Wolfgang Preiss) who resides at Luxor hotel that, in true Nazi tradition, is crammed with surveillance equipment (the thousand eyes of the title) plans to steal nuclear technology from a visiting American industrialist (Peter van Eyck). Lang later regretted to have done the film. At least it reunited him with his old art director Erich Kettelhut. It was Lang's final directorial assignment.

SEPTEMBER 30

Faust: Movie version by Divina and Gloria Film of the famous Hamburg stage production of **Goethe's** play with Will Quadflieg as Faust, the alchemist, who calls the Devil for help: Gustaf Gründgens in his prime role as Mephistopheles.

---

46   Peter Bogdanovich, *Fritz Lang in America*. London: Studio Vista, 1967, pp. 115-116.

DECEMBER 15

Das Spukschloss im Spessart (The Haunted Castle): The friendly ghosts of once executed thieves from Spessart Forest (played by Paul Esser, Hans Richter, Georg Thomalla, Curt Bois and Hanne Wieder) help Liselotte Pulver as young Comtesse Charlotte von Sandau to save the castle she has inherited. Hein Heckroth who had designed *The Red Shoes* and was going to work with Alfred Hitchcock on *Torn Curtain* was the art director while Theo Nischwitz's optical department at Bavaria Studios supplied some simple but effective greenish superimpositions instead of more costly travelling mattes as suggested by Karl Ludwig Ruppel. The Spessart series was directed by Kurt Hoffmann, the son of cameraman Carl Hoffmann. **Rainer Erler** served as assistant director.

DECEMBER 26

Das tapfere Schneiderlein (The Brave Little Tailor), East German TV version on the stage of Theater der Freundschaft.

1961

Federal Republic of Germany
Cinemas: 6666
Attendance figure: 517 million
80 feature films produced

German Democratic Republic
Cinemas: 1327
Attendance figure: 219 million
25 feature films produced

JANUARY 24

Nastassja Kinski born in Berlin West.

MARCH 28

Die toten Augen von London (Dead Eyes of London): a moody German remake of **Béla Lugosi's** British Edgar Wallace thriller from 1939. The Lugosi part of the allegedly blind Reverend Paul Dearborn was played by Dieter Borsche. Wolfgang Lukschy was seen as his equally criminal brother. Joachim Fuchsberger was cast as Inspector Larry Holt. Former Austrian wrestler Ady Berber, fresh from a bit part in *Ben-Hur*, and **Klaus Kinski** added to the sinister atmosphere.

APRIL 12

Soviet Air Force pilot Yuri Alekseyevich Gagarin became the first human to journey into outer space.

MAY 13

Fairy tale producer **Alf Zengerling** died in Berlin.

JULY 3

Das Wunder des Malachias (The Miracle of Father Malachia) from a novel by Bruce Marshall: Horst Bollmann as Father Malachia whose prayers remove the huge Eden Bar from the neighborhood of his church to a lonely island in the North Sea. Director Bernhard Wicki received a Silver Bear, Berlin International Film Festival.

JULY 13

Die goldene Jurte (The Golden Yurt), a fairy tale directed by **Gottfried Kolditz** co-produced by East German DEFA and Mongolkino.

AUGUST 24

Almost thirty years after its ban Constantin Film Munich released **Fritz Lang's** original *The Last Will of Dr. Mabuse*.

SEPTEMBER 8

The first issue of a German science fiction pulp series was published: *Perry Rhodan* (Perry from Perry Mason, Rodan from a Japanese Kaiju) was created by Clark Darlton (i.e. Walter Ernsting) and Karl Herbert Scheer.

SEPTEMBER 21

Hubert Schonger purchased a package of American International Pictures for release in Germany and presented Roger Corman's *House of Usher* under the German title *Die Verfluchten (The Cursed)* via Gerhard Goldammer's Goldeck film distribution. Vincent Price was dubbed by Curt Ackermann.

OCTOBER 1

Der Mann mit dem Objektiv (Man with the Objective): A rocket pilot from the year 2222 played by East German star Rolf Ludwig lands thanks to a technical failure in the year 1960: Naked he walks out of a lake. The astronaut has the abililty to see inside people. Frank Vogel directed this DEFA film from a screenplay by Paul Wiens.

OCTOBER 13

Im Stahlnetz des Dr. Mabuse (The Return of Dr. Mabuse): Producer **Artur Brauner** continued his *Dr. Mabuse* series competing with Rialto Film Preben Philipsen's Edgar Wallace films. Instead of **Fritz Lang** who had had enough he turned to Leni Riefenstahl's erstwhile *Tiefland* assistant and Wallace director **Dr. Harald Reinl** to helm the project and imported from Italy a former American Tarzan, Lex Barker (a year later to star as German western hero Old Shatterhand), who played FBI agent Joe Como on the trail of Dr. Mabuse who is using brainwashed prison inmates to commit crimes for him. Barker's partners were Gert Fröbe as Inspector Lohman, Daliah Lavi from Israel and Wolfgang Preiss as Dr. Mabuse.

OCTOBER 15

Michael Ende's children's book *Jim Knopf und Lukas der Lokomotivführer (Jim Button and Luke the Engine Driver)* was turned into a successful marionette TV series created by Augsburger Puppenkiste and produced by Hessischer Rundfunk.

OCTOBER

German location shooting wrapped on MGM/Cinerama's *The Wonderful World of the Brothers Grimm* that included three fairy tales in a framework starring Laurence Harvey as Wilhelm and Karlheinz Böhm as Jacob Grimm. George Pal's crew filmed at Neuschwanstein Castle (the Royal Palace in *The Dancing Palace*), at Weikersheim Castle in Baden-Wuerttemberg (the Duke's Residence), in the Rhine Valley, and in Rothenburg ob der Tauber in Middle Franconia which falsely substituted as the Grimm's hometown. In the beginning, six fairy tales were planned but then Pal decided for three lesser known, including *The Singing Bone* which featured a wild boar in the original, a long-necked jewelled dragon animated by Jim Danforth (Project Unlimited) in the 3-strip Cinerama version.

In his memoirs Jim Danforth remembered a sequence originally planned for the German footage that didn't make it in the final cut: *Another planned sequence was to have occurred during the Grimm Brothers trip down the Rhine River. At one point they were to see a "Rhine Maiden" and "Siegfried" on a rock near the river, and at another point "Valkyries" were to be seen riding their horses through the sky. Originally these were to be stop-motion puppets composited with location scenes from Germany. I was very excited about doing these scenes and began drawing sketches of my ideas. Eventually it was decided to use cartoon animaton instead. Bill Brace suggested that he might use my costume ideas in his designs for the characters.*

Later someone other than Bill designed these scenes, which were animated in colored crayons. The character designs reminded me of the opera-parody characters seen singing the quartet from Verdi's **Rigoletto** *in a humorous, refreshment-counter ad which was shown in movie theaters in the 1950s. I couldn't believe that his* *completely inappropriate design concept had actually been approved and filmed in Cinerama. Fortunately, these scenes were deleted from the final version of the film.*[47]

OCTOBER 6

Schneewittchen (Snow White), the East German version of the fairy tale directed by **Gottfried Kolditz**.

NOVEMBER 12

Schongerfilm's cycle of German fairy tales ended with a new (Agfacolor) version of *Frau Holle (Mother Holly)* starring Lucie Englisch. The reason: FSK Freiwillige Selbstkontrolle der Filmwirtschaft, the Self-Regulatory Body of the West German movie industry, began to approve children's films with age restriction not under 6 years which meant that the main audience wasn't allowed to see such films in the cinemas.

DECEMBER 8

Produced with great expenditure, the 68-minute DEFA puppet film *Die seltsame Historia von den Schiltbürgern (The Strange Story of the Inhabitants of Schiltsburg)* tried to tell sort of an "original version" of the well-known German chapbook and at the same time indulged itself in innuendos on the (East-German) reality back then. "In a major effort of a three-year production schedule more than 100 puppets had to be built and animated, there were miniatures and sets in great number," recalled director Johannes (Jan) Hempel later. Yet the finished film wouldn't become the artistic and commercial success as hoped for.

DECEMBER 25

Director **Stefan Ruzowitzky (*Anatomy*)** born in Vienna.

---

47 Jim Danforth, *Dinosaurs, Dragons & Drama: The Odyssey of a Trickfilmmaker*. Vol. 1. Archive Editions: Los Angeles, 2015.

1962

Federal Republic of Germany
Cinemas: 6327
Attendance figure: 443 million
64 feature films produced

German Democratic Republic
Cinemas: 1277
Attendance figure: 191 million
25 feature films produced

FEBRUARY 16

Schongerfilm and Mercator Filmverleih (Bodo Gaus in Bielefeld) released Roger Corman's *A Bucket of Blood* in Germany under the title *Das Vermächtnis des Professor Bondi* and added a German-film prologue in which an unknown masked actor introduces himself as *Professor Bondi* and Dick Miller, Corman's "star", as his nephew. In German versions Vincent Price in *House of Wax* had become Professor Bondi and the German distributors tried to cash in.

FEBRUARY 28

8th Short Film Festival in Oberhausen: 26 young West German filmmakers signed the Oberhausen Manifesto claiming license to create a New German Cinema. The festival screened an animated short film *Die Gartenzwerge (The Garden Dwarves)* which was produced by three of the signatories: written by Boris von Borresholm and Peter Schamoni and animated by Wolfgang Urchs. The film *shows metaphorically—in a graphic style with simplified backgrounds, colors and movements—hardworking dwarfs constructing new houses on the ruins of war-torn buildings. Soon, however, they get caught up in the capitalist cycle and eventually degenerate into hedonistic bourgeoisie.*[48]

---

48   Franziska Bruckner, *The Graphic Films of Germany. Trends and Tendencies in the German Animated Films of the 1960s*. In: Kultur und Politik: Reflexion oder Aktion? Vienna: Facultas Verlags- und Buchhandels AG, 2016.

This year's big award, however, went to an abstract Zagreb short: *Don Kihot*. The creator, Vlado Kristl, seized the chance to get in touch with German filmmakers Alexander Kluge and Peter Schamoni and finally settled in the Federal Republic of Germany.

MARCH 30

Lex Barker is back as Joe Como chasing Dr. Mabuse's heir (Wolfgang Preiss) who kidnaps a scientist who has developed a device that makes all matter invisible: *Die unsichtbaren Krallen des Dr. Mabuse (The Invisible Dr. Mabuse/ The Invisible Horror)*. Produced by **Artur Brauner** and directed by **Harald Reinl**. Special sequences supervised by Karl Ludwig Ruppel, at that time Germany's leading Blue Screen expert.

MARCH/APRIL

Munich-based comic book editor Rolf Kauka published a series based on Ray Harryhausen's *Mysterious Island* (*Fix und Foxi* Nos. 323-335). Artist: Florian Julino.

JULY 11

Director **Robert Sigl** born in Günzburg.

JULY 13

A DEFA version of *Rotkäppchen (Little Red Riding Hood)* directed by Götz Friedrich, Walter Felsenstein's assistant at Komische Oper in East Berlin.

SEPTEMBER 7

While Constantin Film had released the original, **Artur Brauner** offered a fresh remake of *Das Testament des Dr. Mabuse (The Last Will of Dr. Mabuse)* with Gert Fröbe as Police Inspector Lohmann, Harald Juhnke and Wolfgang Preiss.

SEPTEMBER 18

Another TV version of Edgar Wallace's *Der Hexer (The Witcher/The Ringer)*, this one directed by Hans Knötzsch.

OCTOBER 2

Seelenwanderung (Transmigration of Souls), a TV play by **Rainer Erler** produced at Bavaria Studios. Axel (Hanns Lothar) convinces Bum (Wolfgang Reichmann) to put his soul into a box and sell it to a pawnbroker. 16mm prints were released by Matthias Film to churches et al.

OCTOBER 9

Ein Toter sucht seinen Mörder (The Brain): 3rd film adaptation of **Curt Siodmak**'s novel *Donovan's Brain* as German-British co-production by CCC Filmkunst (**Artur Brauner**) and Raymond Stross Productions, this one not made at Brauner's studios in Berlin Spandau but directed at Twickenham Studios by Freddie Francis. Siodmak disliked all three versions.

OCTOBER 29

In competition with the East German puppet character West German TV established its own stop-motion *Sandman* (animated by Herbert K. Schulz, a GDR refugee).

NOVEMBER 4

Jim Knopf und die Wilde 13 (Jim Button and the Wild 13), the sequel of **Michael Ende**'s popular book presented by Augsburger Puppenkiste and Hessischer Rundfunk TV.

NOVEMBER 30

Christopher Lee, Thorley Walters and director Terence Fisher had a bad time feeling like being in Foreign Legion when they came to CCC Studios in Berlin

Spandau to do *Sherlock Holmes und das Halsband des Todes (Sherlock Holmes and the Deadly Necklace/Valley of Fear)*, a new entry in a series (!) planned by producer **Artur Brauner** that never got off the ground. **Curt Siodmak** adapted from Arthur Conan Doyle.

1963

Federal Republic of Germany
Cinemas: 5964
Attendance figure: 366 million
58 feature films produced

German Democratic Republic
Cinemas: 1206
Attendance figure: 158 million
21 feature films produced

FEBRUARY 7

Unternehmen Proxima Centauri (Operation Proxima Centauri), a 19-minute East German puppet film.

FEBRUARY 19

Die Nashörner (Rhinoceros), cut-out animation by Jan Lenica based on the 1959 play by Eugène Ionesco, screened at the Oberhausen Short Film Festival.

MARCH 27

Harry Piel died, almost forgotten, in Munich.

APRIL 1

ZDF Zweites Deutsches Fernsehen (Second Channel of German Television Broadcasting) on the air.

APRIL 2

The commercial mascots of ZDF are the animated *Mainzelmännchen (Little Mainz Men)* created by Wolf Gerlach and in the beginning animated by Wolfgang Urchs.

APRIL 13

Captain Sindbad (Kapitän Sindbad)

The King Brothers (Frank, Maurice and Herman) had already worked at Bavaria Studios in the 1950s (*Carnival Story*). Now they decided to copy Ray Harryhausen's *7th Voyage of Sinbad* success with the technical resources of the Bavarians which turned out pretty poor according to director Byron Haskin: "Captain Sindbad *was filmed in the winter of 1962. It was extremely cold in Germany. Even in June, when our contract was to be up, there was snow two feet high on the curbstones in Munich. I was assured that there were all kind of facilities in the Bavaria Studios, everything we wanted. I got there and it was absolutely 'Mack Sennett, 1917.' Nothing there.*"[49]

Haskin was once in charge of one of the largest SFX departments ("Stage 5") in the world in the Burbank studios of Warner Bros. In Munich, so Haskin, they had no more than an old process projector and some optical equipment. Thus, many of the effects had to be done in-camera or by using mirrors to illustrate Sindbad's fight (Guy Williams, Disney's TV *Zorro*) against the evil ruler of Baristan, El-Carim (Pedro Armendariz) who cannot be killed as his heart is safely stored in a tower surrounded by dangers including a multi-headed dragon. (The idea of depositing a sorcerer's heart somewhere else was

---

49 Byron Haskin. Interview by Joe Adamson. A Director's Guild of America Oral History. Lanham, Maryland: Scarecrow Press, 1984.

straight from Stravinsky's ballet *Firebird*). Some mechanical SFX experts were imported from Hollywood (Lee Zavitz, Augie Lohman), optical effects outsourced to MGM British's VFX lab supervised by Tom Howard (who already had handled the Kings' monster-on-the-loose melodrama *Gorgo*). In cast and crew there were some German names (Heidi Brühl as Princess Jana, Helmuth Schneider, Rolf Wanka, Margaret Jahnen and imported from America Berlin-born **Henry Brandon** as El-Carim's henchman). Cinematographer **Eugen Schüfftan** (Eugene Shuftan) was dismissed after a few days of shooting and substituted by Günter Senftleben. Metro-Goldwyn-Mayer released worldwide, Bavaria Filmverleih in Germany. A planned *Sindbad* TV series fell through.

MAY 2

Raphael Nussbaum's *Der Unsichtbare (The Invisible Man/The Invisible Terror)* vastly purloined from Universal's *The Invisible Man Returns* premiered at Hanns Eckelkamp's Europa Palace in Duisburg.

JUNE 3

Von einem, der auszog, das Gruseln zu lernen (The Story of the Youth Who Went Forth to Learn What Fear Is), an East German TV film.

JUNE 29

Der Hexer (The Sorcerer/The Ringer), TV movie directed by **Rainer Erler** based on a play by Edgar Wallace.

JULY 5

Der schwarze Abt, another entry in Rialto and Constantin Film's endless series of Edgar Wallace pictures. This one, based on *The Black Abbott*, starred Joachim Fuchsberger, Dieter Borsche, Charles Regnier, Werner Peters, **Klaus Kinski** and Eddi Arent.

AUGUST 8

Part 1 of **Fritz Genschow's** fairy tale *Der vertauschte Prinz (The Reversed Prince)* on West German TV.

AUGUST 13

Part 2 of *Der vertauschte Prinz (The Reversed Prince)*.

SEPTEMBER 11

Richard Oswald died on a visit to Dusseldorf.

SEPTEMBER 20

Once more the evil spirit of Dr. Mabuse (by the grace of **Artur "Atze" Brauner**) absorbs the body of someone else, a scientist of course, to establish a criminal empire of his own: *Scotland Yard jagt Dr. Mabuse (Scotland Yard vs. Dr. Mabuse)* with Peter van Eyck, Dieter Borsche and **Klaus Kinski**. Working title: *Der Todesspiegel des Dr. Mabuse (Dr. Mabuse's Mirror of Death)*.

SEPTEMBER 27

Roger Corman's 1958 *War of the Satellites* that run only 66 minutes was released with additional German scenes as *Planet der toten Seelen (Planet of Dead Souls)*. The actors in those scenes are identified as Ursula Herwig, Klaus Kindler, Eberhard Mondry, Horst Naumann und Werner Uschkurat.

OCTOBER 13

East German version of *Frau Holle (Mother Holly)* directed by **Gottfried Kolditz**.

NOVEMBER 22

Der Henker von London (The Mad Executioners), produced from a mystery script by Robert Adolf Stemmle and Bryan Edgar Wallace (who only lent his name) by **Artur Brauner**. Edwin Zbonek directed. Hansjörg Felmy, Maria Perschy, Dieter Borsche and Rudolf Forster (sound film's first Mackie Messer) starred.

1964

Federal Republic of Germany
Cinemas: 5551
Attendance figure: 320 million
70 feature films produced

German Democratic Republic
Cinemas: 1024
Attendance figure: 141 million
15 feature films produced

JANUARY

Ufa sold what was left to Bertelsmann Publishing House in Gütersloh.

Parallel to the West German release of Columbia's *Jason and the Argonauts*, Rolf Kauka published a comic strip based on the movie on the Harryhausen movie (and drawn by Turkish artist Mehmet Gülergün) in *Fix und Foxi* Nos. 426-429.

FEBRUARY 14

A masked killer takes murderous revenge for a crime that happened years ago on board of a luxury yacht: *Das Phantom von Soho (The Phantom of Soho)*, adapted by Ladislas Fodor from an idea by Bryan Edgar Wallace and produced by **Artur Brauner**.

MARCH 6

Rolf Losansky recommended himself as director of children's fantasy films with DEFA's *Die Suche nach dem wunderbaren Vögelchen (Quest for the Bird of Many Colors)* based on a book by Franz Fühmann.

MARCH 23

Peter Lorre died in Hollywood.

APRIL 10

The vampires of a mad scientist (Wolfgang Preiss) terrorize a village: *Der Fluch der grünen Augen (The Curse of the Green Eyes)*. **Adrian Hoven** as Interpol Inspector Frank Dorin is going to do some research on the odd case. Richard Gordon bought the first genuine German vampire movie after the war for release in the United States under the title *Night of the Vampires*, the first in fact after *Nosferatu* and *Vampyr*.

APRIL 17

Kurt Weiler's DEFA puppet animation film *Das tapfere Schneiderlein (The Brave Little Tailor)* designed by Achim Freyer and photographed by Erich Günther.

APRIL 24

Der Chef wünscht keine Zeugen (The Chief Wants No Survivors/U.S.: *No Survivors, Please)*: Aliens, who prepare for an invasion, substitute humans they have eliminated with doppelgangers. Directed by producer Hans Albin and Peter Berneis.

APRIL 30

Die Gruft mit dem Rätselschloss (The Curse of the Hidden Vault): Edgar Wallace mystery directed by Franz Josef Gottlieb and produced by **Horst Wendlandt**. **Klaus Kinski** in a supporting role.

JULY 2

In *Das Ungeheuer von London City (The Monster of London City)* producer **Artur Brauner** (who had a contract with Bryan Edgar Wallace, the inept son of a better writer) invoked the spirit of Jack the Ripper in 1960s London.

AUGUST 21

Der Hexer (The Mysterious Magician), this version of Edgar Wallace's *The Ringer* produced for the cinema by **Horst Wendlandt**.

SEPTEMBER 6

Oscar Wilde's *Das Gespenst von Canterville (The Canterville Ghost)* directed for TV by Helmut Käutner.

SEPTEMBER 18

Die Todesstrahlen des Dr. Mabuse (The Death Ray of Dr. Mabuse) with Peter van Eyck, O.E. Hasse, Yvonne Furneaux and Walter Rilla announced as pathetic climax of **Artur Brauner's** *Dr. Mabuse* series.

OCTOBER 7

Bernhard Goetzke died in Berlin (West).

DECEMBER 11

Ray Harryhausen's *First Men in the Moon* was released in West Germany in 35mm and 70 mm (!) prints.

DECEMBER 25

Der fliegende Holländer (The Flying Dutchman), Richard Wagner's opera produced by DEFA.

Frau Luna: operetta by Paul Lincke on West German TV (ZDF).

Around the same time, at East Germany's DEFA Studios in Babelsberg, director Heiner Carow and scenarist Franz Fühmann began work on *Simplicius Simplicissimus*, the film adaptation of a 1668 picaresque novel by Hans Jakob Christoffel von Grimmelshausen, indeed the first German bestseller, inspired by the horrors of the Thirty Years' War. Carow fought the next ten years for this project but it would have been too expensive for East German resources, and so it was shelved and eventually abandoned.

The seventeenth century was a transition period, when the national consciousness was almost annihilated by the religious and political struggles which made Germany a cockpit for half the nations of Europe. The claim of Frederick the Elector Palatine to the throne of Bohemia was the initial episode of the Thirty Years' War, which began in 1618 as an internal conflict, developed into a European war and was only concluded in 1648 by the Treaty of Westphalia. The combination of religious, political and feudal quarrels, brought upon German soil, ill-disciplined hordes of French, Walloon, Italian, Spanish, Swedish, Danish, and Croat mercenaries, to say nothing of Scotch and Irish soldiers of fortune, who fought for the most part not for any particular cause, but for the master who paid them. In consequence there was little restraint put upon looting and violence, and the soldiers and citizens looked upon each other as natural enemies. The overrunning of the country with these foreign armies, and the degeneration of social life to the verge of barbarity, even to cannibalism, present a picture of utter national degradation, which lasted far beyond the conclusion of peace. The ruin to which the country was brought may be judged by the fact that the population of the Empire sank during the period from 16 million to 6 million, a diminution of about two-thirds.

The protagonist of Grimmelshausen's novel (and Carow's screenplay) was a foundling of noble birth from Spessart, a low mountain range in southern Hesse, named Simplicius or Simplex for his simple mindedness, raised by an illiterate peasant family, adopted by a forest hermit. At a young age he is conscripted into service and from there embarks on years of foraging, military triumph, wealth, disease, and countless adventures all over Europe,

Germany, France and Russia. In the end he says to himself: *Your life was nothing but death.*

One central dream sequence, designed by art director Alfred Hirschmeier, was to play during Walpurgis Night on Blocksberg:

A CAPTAIN'S WIFE tries to seduce SIMPLEX and throws him a can with a special ointment (also known as flying ointment, green ointment, magic salve and lycanthropic ointment). The ointment works like a drug. The effect is hallucinatory.

Everything in front of Simplex's eyes seems to be blurred while the captain's wife opens their gowns, his and her own.

CAPTAIN'S WIFE (O.S.)
Put on the lotion!

SIMPLEX
What's it?

CAPTAIN'S WIFE
We're gonna ride to the Blocksberg!
This lotion will help us go there!

Reluctantly Simplex puts on the lotion. All of a sudden, he sees the captain's wife sitting astride on the fireside bench.

FLIGHT TO BLOCKSBERG   (EFFECT OF DRUG)   EXT./NIGHT
The nightly kingdom of Blocksberg represents the contradiction between night and day. Both belong to human life. There is evil and good in both.

The Blocksberg or Brocken is the highest peak of the Harz mountain range. The peak above the tree line tends to have a snow cover from September to May, and mists and fogs shroud it up to 300 days of the year. The Brocken specter is a common phenomenon on this misty mountain, where climber's shadow cast upon fog creates eerie optical effects.

Skyward they fly to get there in time.

Shreds of fog.

CALLS
We come –
We come –
We come –

Wraithlike, in pale moonlight: Witches and sorcerers riding on broomsticks, pitchforks, baking trays, flying goats, cats, pigs.

A huge black massif in front, crowned by oak wood where someone is hanged.

CAPTAIN'S WIFE (to Simplex)
The Blocksberg!

They fly over the Blocksberg plateau that looks like the frustum of a cone.

Among the dancers are many old women. Some wear pearlies, others only shirts, some are naked. There are also men around: fashionably dressed officers, monks, clergymen, peasants.

Nose-diving. Bad landing.

BLOCKSBERG/PLATEAU/WITCHES' SABBATH (EFFECT OF DRUG) EXT./NIGHT
Everywhere fires. Dark creatures with torches. Ghost lights: ignis fatuus, will-o'-the-wisp. Simplex' green vest radiates like phosphor.

Seven circles of dancers have transformed into a spiral. In the center thrones a dark shape.

A CALF-LIKE CREATURE offers Simplex a lute:

CALF CREATURE
Take it! Play!

A FEMALE DANCER joins Simplex and links arms with him. She bites his ear.

The landscape has magically transformed: The Blocksberg resembles the ghostly, nightmarish forest that Simplex knows from his childhood.

At a fire TWO YOUNG WITCHES roast bats and snakes. A THIRD gnaws on a batwing and offers Simplex a piece.

Nearby a WOMAN arms a rutting donkey.

Eventually Simplex sees the captain's wife dancing along. He jumps to her but again he is carried away by the vortex of dancers.

SIMPLEX
Wait!

Now they dance and stomp as they did at Ramsay's feast.

The earth cracks, fire.

Dancers fall into a torture chamber that looks like the one where Simplex had been made a calf. Torturers are waiting for victims.

Above whooping and shouting for joy.

Down there: cracks of whips.

A white stallion races through the lines of dancers. The rider is a boy who resembles young Simplex.

Witches and sorcerers cheer as they see the stallion and run after it.

When a wine barrel is being opened a flood of wine pours out.

In the center of Blocksberg there is an enormous throne.

Sitting on it and presiding, without face, Satan himself.

His shape is glittering gold. His glance dazzles. Around the throne his court—twelve persons, among them the captain's wife.

Satan rises. His golden glitter fills the night. Everybody, Simplex included, looks bashfully at the ground.

A clap of thunder and on an altar a black goat appears, as huge as a monument. The captain's wife is sitting on the goat's back.

They all pay their tribute to Satan. Noblemen and foresters, generals and prelates, noblewomen and nuns. They all kiss the goat's anus.

Simplex wants to follow them and pay his homage too.

But suddenly the distorted face of a raped maidservant appears to warn him.

MAIDSERVANT (breathing heavily)
Run, boy, run. He's the Devil!

On the altar thrones a naked girl with a devil's mask in her lap. She seems to smile at him.

SIMPLEX
Who is it?

He is told that this is "Miss World": *You want to greet her?*

Miss World lifts the goat's tail and Simplex kisses the ass. [50]

This sequence certainly would have been the weirdest piece of film fantasy filmed in Germany up to that time.

1965

Federal Republic of Germany
Cinemas: 5209
Attendance figure: 294 million
56 feature films produced

German Democratic Republic
Cinemas: 973
Attendance figure: 119 million
17 feature films produced

FEBRUARY 17

VFX supervisor **Volker Engel** born in Bremerhaven.

FEBRUARY

Jan Lenica's cutout animation *A* (produced by Boris von Borresholm) at the Short Film Festival in Oberhausen: *…a man's home and freedom is invaded by the letter A. Over the course of the film the protagonist tries to get rid of his opponent with various measures: hiding, dismantling, blasting, conjuring away etc., however, A is indestructible and torments him in any form. Only when the man seems to be broken and dead A leaves, but as the protagonist recovers and starts to enjoy his freedom, the letter B emerges. Jan Lenica's famously stylized animations are influenced*

---

50 Translated by author with the permission of the script's owner, Hanns Eckelkamp.

by his work as a graphic designer. In **A** *the setting is reduced to black and white, with a woodcut-like background and a schematic figure i.e. typography.*[51]

MAY 23

Director **Tom Tykwer** born in Wuppertal.

MAY 25

Another TV adaptation of *Das Gespenst von Canterville (The Canterville Ghost)*, this one directed by Dieter Lemmel.

JUNE 4

Neues vom Hexer (Again the Ringer), the sequel to **Horst Wendlandt's** first *Hexer* production.

JUNE 22

Uwe Boll born in Wermelskirchen.

JULY 1

The Bertelsmann Publishing House acquired 60 % shares of Constantin Film.

AUGUST 6

In the 1960s British producer Harry Alan Towers was partially funded by Constantin Film and even maintained a flat on Kurfürstendamm in Berlin West. With Constantin's support and some German actors in tow (Joachim Fuchsberger, Karin Dor, Walter Rilla, Peter Mosbacher) Towers began a series

---

51 Franziska Bruckner, *The Graphic Films of Germany. Trends and Tendencies in the German Animated Films of the 1960s*. In: Kultur und Politik: Reflexion oder Aktion? Vienna: Facultas Verlags- und Buchhandels AG, 2016.

featuring Sax Rohmer's Fu Manchu to be played by Christopher Lee: *Ich, Dr. Fu Man Chu (The Face of Fu Manchu)*.

DECEMBER

Ztracená tvář (The Lost Face): This Czechoslovakian science fiction film about a modern "Dr. Frankenstein" was co-produced with support from German Democratic Republic. Based on a story by Josef Nesvadba.

DECEMBER 3

Lumpazivagabundus, an Austrian-German co-production with Helmut Qualtinger.

DECEMBER 17

Der unheimliche Mönch (The Sinister Monk) was based on Edgar Wallace's play *The Terror* made at CCC Studios in Berlin Spandau with locations shot in Hamelin, Hamburg, and London. **Harald Reinl** directed.

1966

Federal Republic of Germany
Cinemas: 4784
Attendance figure: 257 million
60 feature films produced

German Democratic Republic
Cinemas: 941
Attendance figure: 102 million
9 feature films produced

FEBRUARY 3

Friedrich Wilhelm Murnau Stiftung (Foundation) established in Wiesbaden. Bertelsmann sold the old Ufa films for 13,6 million Deutschmark.

MAY 8

Eric (Erich) Pommer died in Woodland Hills, California.

AUGUST 26

Der Bucklige von Soho (The Hunchback of Soho) was Rialto/Constantin's first Edgar Wallace film in color. Herbert Reinecker, a former member of the SS and acknowledged contributor to German TV crime series, adapted the yarn quite freely from a treatment by Harald G. Petersson. Richard Haller was cast as the hunchback.

SEPTEMBER 2

With German support (and actors Heinz Drache and Harald Leipnitz) Harry Alan Towers continued his Sax Rohmer/Christopher Lee series with *Die dreizehn Sklavinnen des Dr. Fu Man Chu (The Brides of Fu Manchu)*. The daughters of prominent scientists are kidnapped by the Oriental master criminal, chance enough to cast aspiring starlets.

SEPTEMBER 17

Raumpatrouille (Space Patrol): A seven-part science fiction TV series developed by TV writer Rolf Honold and produced at Bavaria Studios that came closest to *Star Trek* (both filmed around the same time but this one in black and white) and *Perry Rhodan*. Of course, Perry was not Perry but Commander Cliff Allister McLane (played by Dietmar Schönherr) who, together with the crew of spaceship Orion, fought the invasion of the alien Frogs, translucent, shimmering humanoids who attack in arrow-like spaceships and are able to blast whole planets. Theo Mezger, who directed along Michael Braun, told me that behind the curtains **Wernher von Braun** acted as consultant. The technical director of Bavaria knew von Braun from Peenemünde V2 days. He flew to America and got precious advice as well as special film stock. Rolf Zehetbauer and Werner Achmann designed the show, putting in irons and what else in the Orion bridge, Werner Hierl, a comic book artist and animation expert, designed the special effects with model shots supervised by department head Theo Nischwitz, an old Ufa stalwart: *The most complicated effect of that show was the takeoff of the Orion from its underwater base through a whirlpool. The whirlpool was produced by putting Alka-Seltzer tablets in a glass tank and photographing the result with a camera positioned upside-down. For the next shot, when the spaceship left the whirlpool, we used an experimental basin at the Technical University in Munich. Thanks to a Scope lens, I was able to extend the whirlpool's mouth. For the explosion of a planet, we filled up a miniature planet with a mix of coffee beans, raisins, seminola and other odds and ends, and then forced it out with compressed air and photographed the results at 120 frames per second.*

NOVEMBER 26

Siegfried Kracauer died in New York City.

DECEMBER 1

Die Nibelungen Part One: Siegfried von Xanten premiered at Mathäser Film Palace in Munich. In the years following **Fritz Lang's** turndown of a *Nibelungen* remake, in fact one of Hitler's favorites, **Artur Brauner**, survivor of Hitler's Holocaust, hadn't given up the idea of remaking it in color and scope. He ignored the warnings of film critics and contacted the Allensbach Institute for Public Opinion Research. The poll attested that at least every third federal citizen would like to watch such a remake. The following years Brauner toyed with a lot of casting ideas: Marianne Koch or Romy Schneider as Kriemhild; Dieter Borsche, Walter Reyer, Claus Holm or Will Quadflieg as her brother, Burgundians' King Gunther; Brunhild, Gunther's love affair, to be played by Barbara Rütting, Eva Bartok or Cuban (!) actress Chelo Alonso; the part of Siegfried's sworn enemy, grim Hagen Tronje, offered to Gert (*Goldfinger*) Fröbe and as Siegfried, the beefy blond hero, Jerome Courtland, who after some parts in the *Disneyland* series was stranded in Germany where Kirk Douglas' Bryna

Productions shot *Tales of the Vikings* in 1959. But the distributors protested: A German hero had to be played by a genuine German, an Aryan so to speak, and not an American. Brauner was desperate, "There is no Siegfried here anymore! Give me a German Siegfried and I will start." Years went by, and eventually Brauner found a Teutonic hero that finally pleased Germany's biggest distributor, Constantin Film that also released the Karl May westerns with Lex (ex-*Tarzan*) Barker and Pierre Brice. He was an ersatz-Johnny Weissmuller named Uwe Beyer, a tall (6'3") German track and field athlete and hammer thrower, who had enough muscle at his command but not enough brain to act out the demanding part. His father, Erich Beyer, by the way, had failed to qualify for Hitler's Olympic Games in 1936 as a shot putter. Nazi film-schooled Gerhard Menzel, who after the war wrote West Germany's first scandalous movie, *Die Sünderin (The Sinner)* that aroused the protest of the Catholic Church organized by Chaplain Carl Klinkhammer, was hired to write the screenplay, but Brauner was not satisfied because Menzel saw the dragon not larger than a lizard from the zoo! Alas (or fortunately?), Menzel passed away in 1966 and Brauner decided—a surefire way—to hire Karl May (and Nazi film) veteran Harald G. Petersson and with him two other May experts, director **Harald Reinl** and cinematographer Ernst Wilhelm Kalinke. The rest of the cast wasn't that spectacular anymore but at least more competent than the hammer thrower: Karin Dor, back then Reinl's wife, played Brunhild, Maria Marlow was seen as Kriemhild, Rolf Henniger as Gunther, Mario Girotti (a.k.a. Terence Hill) as Giselher and Herbert Lom as Etzel/Attila, King of the Huns, who fulfills the revenge of Kriemhild, widow of Siegfried slain by another Siegfried, in this case actor Siegfried Wischnewski who played the maligned Hagen. In 1966 and 1967, the two parts actually made their money—despite all the negative reviews. DER SPIEGEL, for instance, called the production *childish hero cinema: Siegfried demonstrates his muscles, a hydraulically operated dragon chuffs fire from its nozzles, ladies in glossy paper Gothic make faces and Burgundy's unloquacious veterans' association looks solemnly around.*[52]

The dragon was supposed to be the highlight of Part One but didn't work properly. A gruff Reinl had to shoot around, showing only details like head,

---

52   *Leichen unter Eichen.* In: DER SPIEGEL, 52/1966, December 19, 1966.

claws and tail but not the whole creature in all its gory "glory". Location shooting in Yugoslavia, Spain and Iceland (Brunhild's castle). At least composer Rolf Wilhelm produced an adequate, thundering score for almost no money because Brauner was known to be penny-cosncious.

1967

Federal Republic of Germany
Cinemas: 4518
Attendance figure: 216 million
72 feature films produced

German Democratic Republic
Cinemas: 924
Attendance figure: 99 million
16 feature films produced

JANUARY 31

Experimental and animation filmmaker **Oskar Fischinger** died in Hollywood. His last invention, the Lumigraph, played a major role in Ib Melchior's sci-fi picture *The Time Travelers*.

FEBRUARY 8

The second part of **Artur Brauner's** *Nibelungen* remake opened at the Mathäser Film Palace in Munich: *Kriemhilds Rache (Kriemhild's Revenge)* with Maria Marlow as Kriemhild, Herbert Lom as Etzel and Sam Burke as Etzel's brother Blo-Edin.

FEBRUARY 17

A Japanese *Godzilla* film produced by Toho *Kaiju Daisenso (Invasion of the Astro-Monster)* was released in Germany by Constantin Film Munich as "based on a novel by **Hans Dominik**", appropriately titled *Befehl aus dem Dunkel (Command from the Dark)* and dubbed by Manfred R. Köhler at Aventin Studios.

APRIL 5

Die Utopen, a 9-minute short film animated by Vlado Kristl at the Oberhausen Short Film Festival: The Utopes are double-faced creatures that are split by a uniformed man with a sabre.

APRIL 28

A homicidal maniac calling himself *The Blue Hand* starred in **Horst Wendlandt's** production of *Die blaue Hand* by Edgar Wallace adapted by screenwriter Alex Berg (a.k.a. Herbert Reinecker). Harald Leipnitz, **Klaus Kinski**, Carl Lange, and Ilse Steppat starred. In the United States released as *Creature with the Blue Hand* and in a recut version on video as *The Bloody Dead*.

JUNE 25

DEFA's *Frau Venus und ihr Teufel (Lady Venus and her Devil)* was written by Brigitte Kirsten and directed by her husband Ralf Kirsten. Lady Venus (Inge Keller) sends Hans Müller (played by Manfred Krug), an ordinary citizen of the German Democratic Republic, to the Middle Ages where he, disguised as Tannhäuser competing with a horde of minstrels, must learn the true meaning of love.

JULY 13

Producer Harry Alan Towers made *Jules Verne's Rocket to the Moon* partly with German money. Therefore, some German actors were included: Gert Fröbe, Joachim Teege, Renate von Holt. In America it was titled *Those Fantastic Flying Fools*, in Germany *Tolldreiste Kerle in rasselnden Raketen (Those Foolish Guys in their Rattling Rockets)* to capitalize on the success of *Those Magnificent Men in Their Flying Machines*.

JULY 21

The Spanish horror film *La Isla de la muerte (Das Geheimnis der Todesinsel/ Island of the Doomed)* with Cameron Mitchell as Baron von Weser, Kai Fischer and Rolf von Nauckhoff directed by Mel Welles, was co-produced by Ernst Ritter von Theumer's Munich-based Tefi Filmproduktion: *What was the terrifying secret of the vampire tree?*

AUGUST 11

A villainous *Monk with the Whip*: *Der Mönch mit der Peitsche* by the late Edgar Wallace and Herbert Reinecker.

SEPTEMBER 21

The ghosts from Spessart Forest go Outer Space: *Herrliche Zeiten im Spessart (Glorious Times in the Spessart)*. With Liselotte Pulver, Harald Leipnitz, Hubert von Meyerinck, Willy Millowitsch, Hannelore Elsner, Vivi Bach, Tatjana Sais, Hans Richter, Joachim Teege, Rudolf Rhomberg and Paul Esser.

OCTOBER 5

Die Schlangengrube und das Pendel (The Torture Chamber of Dr. Sadism) made at Bavaria Studios was Constantin Film's attempt at a horror film series shaped after Roger Corman's Poe *(The Pit and the Pendulum)* and Hammer's Dracula series that didn't work out. Under **Harald Reinl's** direction Lex Barker and Reinl's wife Karin Dor fell victim to Count Regula (played by Christopher Lee).

OCTOBER 27

There were several attempts to film *Perry Rhodan*. **Bernd Eichinger** later had an option, others had too—but only once one such try (almost) succeeded but didn't launch the pulp series Constantin Film was hoping for: *Perry Rhodan— SOS aus dem Weltall (Mission Stardust)* was produced by Ernst Ritter von Theumer in Rome, directed by Primo Zeglio. Canadian actor Lang Jeffries was cast as Perry Rhodan. *Perry Rhodan* co-author Karl Herbert Scheer was sent as consultant to Italy but SFX supervisor Antonio Margheriti wouldn't listen to him and used different spaceship designs. Only some of the actors displayed mild interest when they learned from *Rhodan's* co-creator that it was a series (and they might be used in the following entries).

DECEMBER 25

Peter Schlemihls wundersame Geschichte (Peter Schlemihl's Strange and Wonderful History), Peter Beauvais' TV adaptation of Adelbert von Chamisso's art fairy tale with Götz George in the title role, Rudolf Platte as the mysterious Grey One and Albert Lieven as Chamisso.

1968

Federal Republic of Germany
Cinemas: 4060
Attendance figure: 179 million
Feature films produced: 89

German Democratic Republic
Cinemas: 887
Attendance figure: 101 million
Feature films produced: 14

JANUARY 18

Der Hund von Blackwood Castle (The Monster of Blackwood Castle) was more *Hound of the Baskervilles* than Edgar Wallace.

Producer **Horst Wendlandt**, Preben Philipsen's Rialto Film partner, was awarded a *Goldene Leinwand (Golden Screen prize)* for 25 Edgar Wallace films.

APRIL 19

Aquila Film Enterprises based in Berlin (West) and **Adrian Hoven**, the male star, were the producers of *Necronomicon—Geträumte Sünden* (*Succubus*, directed by Jesús Franco Manera) that was premiered at the Astor Cinema on Kurfürstendamm in Berlin (West).

APRIL 26

Im Banne des Unheimlichen (The Zombie Walks) inspired by the writings of Edgar Wallace premiered in Oberhausen at Europa Cinema: Joachim Fuchsberger as Inspector Higgins versus a criminal calling himself *The Laughing Corpse* whose mask resembles that of the *Crimson Ghost* from Republic serials.

JULY 26

Im Schloss der blutigen Begierde (Castle of Bloody Lust/Castle of the Creeping Flesh) written and directed by Percy G. Parker (a.k.a. **Adrian Hoven**): A mad scientist (Howard Vernon) in need of body parts to succeed in reviving his dead daughter welcomes a group of drunken party-goers to his castle. Filmed at Castle Kreuzenstein, Leobendorf, Lower Austria.

AUGUST 23

Der Todeskuss des Dr. Fu Man Chu (The Blood of Fu Manchu) with Christopher Lee, Götz George, and Viennese-born Maria Rohm, in private life Mrs. Harry Alan Towers. Towers had joined forces with Spanish director Jess Franco (i.e., Jesús Franco Manera).

SEPTEMBER 27

Der Gorilla von Soho (The Gorilla Gang): A killer in a gorilla costume sneaks through London. Director Alfred Vohrer and producer **Horst Wendlandt** adapted the story freely (under the pen name Freddy Gregor) from Edgar Wallace.

OCTOBER 10

Adam II, feature-length Kafkaesque experimental animation by Jan Lenica (produced by Boris von Borresholm, Lux Film Munich) shown at the International Film Festival in Mannheim, expresses the desire to renounce from any notion of control by bureaucracy in the era of technology.

OCTOBER 21

Production on American International Pictures' high-budgeted *De Sade* project started in Germany. Originally scheduled with Atlas International (Dieter Menz) for shooting at Bavaria Studios in Munich *De Sade* then changed locals for Berlin Spandau as **Artur Brauner's** CCC Studios became the new co-producers. Richard Matheson had penned the screenplay, but Cyril Endfield seemed to have trouble to direct some nightmarish orgy scenes and had to be hospitalized. Roger Corman was sent to Germany to direct in the meantime. Keir Dullea starred in the title role with Senta Berger, Lilli Palmer, Sonja Ziemann, Anna Massey, Uta Levka and John Huston in supporting parts.

DECEMBER 11

German release date of Stanley Kubrick's *2001: A Space Odyssey*. At the end of the prologue a victorious ape-man throws a bone into the air that transforms into a nuclear satellite. The original 2D element of the satellite has a (West) German emblem.

DECEMBER 13

German release of Disney's *The Jungle Book* (German title: *Das Dschungelbuch*) developed into a major hit thanks to German dubbing expertise handled by Simoton Film Berlin and Heinrich Riethmüller:

Das Dschungelbuch was Heinrich Riethmüller's first solo effort. He brilliantly accepted the challenge to write and arrange the German versions of the Sherman Brothers' songs. Riethmüller cast Siegfried Schürenberg, Clark Gable's German voice, as Shere Khan, Klaus Havenstein as King Louie, Edgar Ott as

Baloo, Joachim Cadenbach as Baghira and Erich Kestin, a Disney dubbing veteran, as Kaa. Kestin, who also voiced Winnie the Pooh, died in 1969.

Edgar Ott sang *Probier's mal mit Gemütlichkeit (Try Taking It Easy=The Bare Necessities)*. Erich Kestin whispered *Hör auf mich (Trust In Me)*. Klaus Havenstein did a top job interpreting *Ich wär so gern wie du (I Wan'na Be Like You)*.

The film's amazing Teutonic success story is attributable to talent and lucky timing, and of a group of irreverent German musicians and cabaret artists who freely adapted the original Disney songs to suit their generation. [...]

I don't tend to like dubbed versions, I prefer the originals, but in this case, the German version is better," says Daniel Kothenschulte, film critic for the Frankfurter Rundschau *and one of the leading experts on animation film in Germany. "Riethmüller makes the song lyrics to* The Jungle Book *better than they actually were."*

Take, for example, Baloo's signature song: "The Bare Necessities." Riethmüller's German version, "Probiers mal mit Gemütlichkeit" (or, roughly translated, Try Taking it Easy), changes the original meaning, from "be satisfied with the simple things in life" to "chill out and you'll be happy."

"The original version, by the American folk singer Terry Gilksyon, has a pretty conservative message, when you think of it, of making due with less," says Kothenschulte. "Riethmüller's lyrics are more liberal and positive, they promise both freedom and comfort, the jungle as a sort of boundless utopia." [53]

DECEMBER 20

Stunde des Skorpions (Hour of the Scorpion), an East German TV miniseries set in the 21st century: Socialism has been victorious, but the few remaining capitalist states get hold of an alien energy source and turn it into a super-weapon.

---

53 *Why Disney's Original 'Jungle Book' Is Germany's Biggest Film of All Time*. In: The Hollywood Reporter. April 22, 2016.

DECEMBER 21

Hilfe, Hilfe, die Globolinks, a science-fiction opera for children that dealt with an invasion of aliens, the Globolinks that are defeated by music, premiered at Hamburgische Staatsoper. Music: Gian Carlo Menotti. The play was recorded for television.

In addition:

Hans Joachim Alpers began editing *Science Fiction Times.*

1969

Federal Republic of Germany
Cinemas: 3739
Attendance figure: 172 million
110 feature films produced

German Democratic Republic
Cinemas: 864
Attendance figure: 93 million
14 feature films produced

APRIL 3

Sieben Tage Frist (Seven Days Grace/School of Fear): ...*an education in Terror!* Mystery thriller set at a boarding school for boys in Northern Germany. Adapted by Manfred Purzer from a novel by Paul Hendriks and directed by Edgar Wallace film veteran Alfred Vohrer. Joachim Fuchsberger was cast in the lead.

MAY 3

Karl Freund died in Hollywood.

MAY 18

Dr. Ludwig Berger died in Schlangenbad.

JULY 8

Das Rätsel von Piskov (The Piskov Mystery), a TV film loosely based on H. G. Wells' *Time Machine*, adapted by Czech dramaturge Zdenek Bláha and directed by Karl Peter Biltz: A female from the future (Year 523 A.G. Ante de *Gagarin!*) enters Piskov, a small Czech town, and contacts Dr. Pavelka (Wolfgang Büttner), an archeologist. Two journalists (played by Hellmuth Lange and Hannelore Elsner).

AUGUST 29

Grimms Märchen von lüsternen Pärchen (Grimm's Fairy Tales for Adults): Rolf Thiele's sexist retelling of classic fairy tales *Snow White* (Marie Liljedahl), *Cinderella* (Eva Reuber-Staier) and *Sleeping Beauty* (Gaby Fuchs).

Edgar Reitz filmed **E. T. A. Hoffmann's** *Das Fräulein von Scuderi (The Young Woman of Scuderi)* under the title *Cardillac* with Hans-Christian Blech as goldsmith who murders his customers.

DECEMBER 13

Inspired by the box-office success of the German-dubbed version of Disney's *Jungle Book*, Budweis-born Curt Linda who had become interested in animation while in Yugoslavia joined forces with distribution company Gloria Film and had Erich Kästner's anti-war fable *Konferenz der Tiere (Conference of Animals)* animated. Kästner would have preferred if Disney had transformed his *Conference of the Animals* (published in 1949) into an animated feature film. Erich Kästner's idea of a worldwide animals' conference-of animals united to ban war, the scourge for mankind, forever, got a new meaning during the Cold War. Maybe that was the reason that Disney who had produced two live-action movies from Kästner's books (*The Parent Trap* and *Emil and the Detectives*) wouldn't buy this topic.

As Linda didn't have much spending power, he tried to break away from the costly style of the American by hiring an artist from Serbia: Boris Šajtinac's art was completely different from Disney's. For a brief time, they were negotiating to have the DEFA Studio for Animated Films on board. But eventually the "bourgeois pacifist position" of the project looked suspicious to the political authorities of GDR.

1970

Federal Republic of Germany
Cinemas: 3446
Attendance figure: 160 million
105 feature films produced

German Democratic Republic
Cinemas: 858
Attendance figure: 91 million
13 feature films produced

FEBRUARY 19

Michael Reeves' *Witchfinder General* imported by Rob Houwer became that successful at German box offices that **Adrian Hoven** produced his own version of witch-hunt (directed by Michael Armstrong): *Hexen bis aufs Blut gequält (Mark of the Devil)* starring Herbert Lom, **Udo Kier**, Reggie Nalder and Herbert Fux.

FEBRUARY 20

Hänsel und Gretel verliefen sich im Wald (Lass uns knuspern, Mäuschen/The Naked Wytche/The Erotic Adventures of Hansel and Gretel), sex film version of the Grimm fairy tale directed by Franz Josef Gottlieb and produced by Hans-jürgen Pohland. Karl Dall and Herbert Fux in supporting roles.

MAY 15

Jonathan by Hans W. Geissendörfer was a New German vampire movie with dialogue straight from Bram Stoker's *Dracula* novel. Jürgen Jung played the title character who is going to track down the leader of the undead (Paul Albert Krumm).

JUNE

Ein grosser graublauer Vogel (A Big Grey-Blue Bird) centers around a formula that is encoded in a poem (by Arthur Rimbaud). Thomas Schamoni directed from a screen story by Uwe Brandner, Max Zihlmann and Hans Noever. Premiered at Berlin International Film Festival.

AUGUST

Die Bremer Stadtmusikanten (The Bremen Town Musicians) was the last puppet film produced by the **Diehl Brothers**.

SEPTEMBER 1

Rote Sonne (Red Sun) by Rudolf Thome: dada style acting and pantomime violence set in a bizarre environment.

SEPTEMBER 9

Walter Kohut as reporter Will Roczinski who attends an actual UFO congress in Mainz that was featured in **Rainer Erler's** TV movie *Die Delegation (The Delegation)*. Among the "authentic" UFO guests are Karl L. Veit, Hermann Oberth and American Donald E. Keyhoe who, in 1956, was mentioned in connection with the movie **Earth vs. the Flying Saucers**.

OCTOBER 18

Das Millionenspiel (The Game of Millions) produced by Peter Märthesheimer and directed by Tom Toelle from Robert Sheckley's novel *The Seventh Victim* (adapted by Wolfgang Menge) as a TV show hosted by Dieter Thomas Heck: To win the grand prize of one million marks, a candidate has to survive seven days on the run while being hunted by Dieter Hallervorden and his gang.

DECEMBER 11

East German *Hoffmanns Erzählungen (The Tales of Hoffmann)* directed by Walter Felsenstein.

DECEMBER 17

Signale—Ein Weltraumabenteuer (Signals: An Adventure in Space) by **Gottfried Kolditz**, a director of musicals and fairy tales, as a 70mm East German/Polish co-production about a rescue mission in outer space loosely based on a science-fiction novel (*Asteroidenjäger/Asteroid Hunters*) by Carlos Rasch. The movie starred Gojko Mitić, DEFA's chief Indian.

Signals *starts when The Icarus—a research ship searching for signs of intelligent life in the universe—is destroyed by meteorites near Jupiter. When no signals are received from the Icarus, it is presumed lost, and attempts to retrieve it are abandoned. This doesn't sit well with everyone, particularly Commander Veikko of the Laika and Pawel (Yevgeni Zharikov), a young pilot whose sweetheart is among the missing. While repairing unmanned space stations, the crew of the Laika continues to search for the missing Icarus, in spite of the official edict that the ship is lost.* [...]

According to Sonja Fritzsche in an article for German Studies Review, Kolditz fell ill during production and the project was taken over by its cinematographer, Otto Hanisch. This would explain a lot. The film lacks Kolditz's usual pizazz and seems more interested in the technical aspects of the special effects than the story. No doubt Hanisch was anxious to explore Kubrick's film techniques for portaying rockets and zero gravity, nut, unlike **2001**, **Signals** *at least attempts to create back stories for the main characters (a common beef about the Kubrick film).*[54]

---

54 Jim Morton, *Signals*. August 26, 2011. Eastgermancinema.com/2011/08/26/signals/

DEFA's leading VFX cameraman Kurt Marks confirmed to this writer that during production they indeed went to West Berlin to see, study and "copy" Kubrick's space opera.

In addition:

Merkwürdige Geschichten: TV mystery series.

1971

Federal Republic of Germany
Cinemas: 3314
Attendance figure: 152 million
112 feature films produced

German Democratic Republic
Cinemas: 849
Attendance figure: 83 million
16 feature films produced

MARCH 16

Rudolf Thome's TV *Supergirl Das Mädchen von den Sternen (The Girl from the Stars)* featured Iris Berben as Francesca Farnese who claims to have come from another planet. As guests: **Rainer Werner Fassbinder** and Eddie Constantine.

MARCH 26

DEFA Studios' *Dornröschen (Sleeping Beauty)* with Juliane Korén directed by Walter Beck.

APRIL 8

Adult version of *The Nibelungs* produced by **Adrian Hoven**: *Siegfried und das sagenhafte Liebesleben der Nibelungen (The Long Swift Sword of Siegfried/The Lustful Barbarian)* with Raimund Harmstorf as Siegfried and Sybil Danning as Kriemhild.

MAY 17

Fata Morgana: The story of mankind (Creation, Paradise, Golden Age) according to **Werner Herzog**. Shown at the Film Festival in Cannes. F. W. **Murnau** biographer **Lotte H. Eisner** narrated.

MAY 28

Les lèvres rouges/Blut an den Lippen (Daughters of Darkness) by Belgian director Harry Kümel shown in New York City. The picture was co-produced by Munich-based Roxy Film (Luggi Waldleitner). Besides Delphine Seyrig as Vampire Countess Erzsébet Báthory two German actors were cast: Andrea Rau and Paul Esser. Manfred R. Köhler supervised the German-language dubbing.

MAY 31

Wolfgang Liebeneiner's TV version of Gore Vidal's *Visit to a Small Planet (Besuch auf einem kleinen Planeten)* with Peter Fricke as Kreton.

JUNE 4

Gebissen wird nur nachts—das Happening der Vampire (The Vampire Happening) directed by Freddie Francis and produced by Aquila Enterprises Berlin (West): An American actress (Pia Degermark) inherits a castle in Transylvania. **Ferdy Mayne** repeats his vampire role from Polanski's *Dance of the Vampires*. Mayne was born in Mainz and got to England when the Nazis came to power. Castle Kreuzenstein in Lower Austria served as filming location.

JUNE 13

Albin Grau who had designed *Nosferatu* spent his final years in Bayrischzell and died in Hausham, Bavaria.

JUNE 18

Since 1966 East German animators under the supervision of Lothar Barke and Helmut Barkowsky worked on the feature-length Grimm fairy tale *Der arme Müllersbursch und das Kätzchen (The Poor Miller's Boy and the Kitten)*: Lothar Barke was considered an experienced director and brilliant animator whose films were always a guarantor for unanimous and longstanding audience success. Barke, however, refused to finish the directorial commitment because he wouldn't declare his agreement with the official politics of GDR at the time of The Prague Spring in 1968. Helmut Barkowsky was called in to replace him, but the models weren't lip-sync. This resulted in a certain artistic breach in the narrative style that is noticeable even today.

JUNE 27

Uwe Brandner's *Ich liebe dich, ich töte dich (I Love You, I Kill You)* is set in the near future in a Bavarian village that is populated by emotionless citizens, kept in place with pills and pleasures while wealthy persons arrive to hunt in the nearby area. Premiere at Berlin International Film Festival.

JUNE 30

Alexander Kluge's attempt at science fiction *Der grosse Verhau (The Big Mess)* screened at Berlin International Film Festival. In the year 2034 two astronauts make their way with shady dealings, smuggling and spaceship wrecking, but whenever they get anywhere, they find they've been beaten to it by monopolist enterprises.

Based on a book by Russian-born Paul Alexander Baran.

JULY 15

Vampyros Lesbos by Jess Franco produced by CCC Telecine (**Artur Brauner**).

OCTOBER 21

Dreht euch nicht um, der Golem geht rum oder Das Zeitalter der Musse (Don't Turn Around, the Golem Walks or: The Era of Vacancy): Part 1 of a dystopian TV film by Peter Beauvais set in Cologne of the year 2300.

OCTOBER 24

Part 2 of *Dreht euch nicht um, der Golem geht rum* on First Channel TV.

Der Flaschenteufel (The Bottle Imp) based on Robert Louis Stevenson and directed by Frank Guthke for ZDF TV.

DECEMBER 8

Grischa Huber as female bloodsucker who celebrates occult rites is joined by a hunchback (Louis Waldon), a sorceress and a werewolf in **George Moorse's** TV movie *Vampira*.

DECEMBER 10

Jess Franco's *Sie tötete in Ekstase (She Killed in Ecasty)* was made in Spain but again funded by **Artur Brauner's** CCC Telecine.

In addition:

Falscher Verdacht Haytabo: **Ulli Lommel** moved between **Rainer Werner Fassbinder** and cheap American horror pictures (*Boogeyman*). The story of a biochemistry professor (played by Eddie Constantine) who disvovers a mysterious manuscript from the 19th century with an uncomplete formula of an immortality drug. Rainer Langhans, a former member of Kommune I in Berlin (West), co-wrote and acted besides Uschi Obermaier, his love affair, and Fassbinder. It is not known when the movie was screened. TV premiere: August 16, 1990.

1972

Federal Republic of Germany
Cinemas: 3171
Attendance figure: 150
108 feature films produced

German Democratic Republic
Cinemas: 838
Attendance figure: 82 million
17 feature films produced

JANUARY 11

The story of Jason, the Argonauts and the Golden Fleece played by children: *Das goldene Ding (The Golden Thing)* was produced by Edgar Reitz Film.

JANUARY 19

Dr. Alexander Kluge, one of the thought-leaders of New German Cinema, tried several times (unsuccessfully) to link with a big audience. This is another attempt to enter the field of science fiction: *Willi Tobler und der Untergang der 6. Flotte (Willi Tobler and the Decline of the 6th Fleet)*. The underbudgeted movie was produced in 1969 and televised by ZDF Zweites Deutsches Fernsehen.

In **Willi Tobler and the Decline of the 6th Fleet,** *Willi (Alfred Edel) endeavours to survive in a world where annihilistic galatic battles rage, by taking a job at the centre of power. But it's the wrong side that he takes in this civil war.*[55]

---

55 Filmmuseum Munich.

MAY 27

Mario Bava's *Gli orrori del castello di Norimberga (Baron Blood)* was filmed at Castle Kreuzenstein in Leobendorf, Lower Austria, and cast with Elke Sommer who starred besides Joseph Cotten (as Baron von Kleist). The film was co-produced by Dieter Geissler.

AUGUST 18

At East-German DEFA Studios director Rainer Simon adapted Grimm's *Sechse kommen durch die ganze Welt (How Six Men Got on in the World)*.

Richard Burton as ladykiller in Edward Dmytryk's *Bluebeard (Blaubart)*, a German co-production made in Budapest. Burton's co-stars were Raquel Welch, Virna Lisi and Nathalie Delon with some German actors in supporting roles (Erica Schramm, Karl-Otto Alberty, Kurt Grosskurth).

SEPTEMBER 21

Eolomea was an East-German science fiction film co-produced with the support of Mosfilm based on a book by Bulgarian writer Angel Vagenshtain (a.k.a. Angel Wagenstein). that was shot with 70mm technology, same as the previous DEFA sci-fi entry *Signale*. Alas, the visual impact was minimal, the movie itself rather slow-paced. Director **Herrmann Zschoche** was more interested in the human conflicts on orbital space station "Margot" where they try to find out more about the disappearance of eight spaceships that followed a mysterious light signal years ago.

The story centers around two people: Maria Scholl (Cox Habbema), a science professor and one of the big-wigs at the space authority; and Dan Lagny (Ivan Andonov), a bored and aimless cosmonaut. The story is told in a non-linear fashion, hopping back and forth through time and space, allowing the story to unfold slowly. Most of the film centers around Cosmonaut Lagny, who is on Earth in one scene, and in space in the next. The space sets have the cold metallic look common to space movies at the time, but with a slightly more lived in look than most. The obligatory robot ios nicely funky-looking, falling somewhere between the **Lost in Space** *robot, C3PO of* **Star Wars**, *and a reel-to-reel tape deck.*[56]

OCTOBER

The first issue of *Vampir*, a semiprofessional magazine devoted to Science Fiction and Horror Films, edited by Manfred Knorr, Nuremberg.

NOVEMBER 28

Nachtschatten (Nightshade) by Niklaus Schilling with Elke Haltaufderheide and John Van Dreelen, sort of a homage to Dreyer's *Vampyr*.

1973

Federal Republic of Germany
Cinemas: 3107
Attendance figure: 144 million
82 feature films produced

German Democratic Republic
Cinemas: 833
Attendance figure: 84 million
13 feature films produced

JANUARY 26

Adrian Hoven continued his witchfinder series with *Hexen geschändet und zu Tode gequält (Mark of the Devil II)*.

---

56 Jim Morton, *Eolomea*. December 14, 2010. Eastgermancinema.com/2010/12/14/eolomea/

FEBRUARY 18

Max Mack, director of *Der Andere*, died in London.

MARCH

ZDF TV canceled *Schweinchen Dick (Porky Pig)* cartoons due to protests of politicians who claimed to be concerned about the very young audience and the graphic violence they were exposed to.

APRIL 15

Smog, an acclaimed TV movie conceived by Wolfgang Menge and directed by young **Wolfgang Petersen**, fresh from film school, dealt with the events of smog warning.

MAY 9

Mario Bava's *Lisa e il diavolo (Lisa and the Devil/Lisa und der Teufel)* with Telly Savalas and Elke Sommer was co-produced by Roxy Film Munich, presented at the Cannes Film Market and released in the United States by Allied Artists.

JULY 12

Rainer Werner Fassbinder entrusted **Ulli Lommel** with the direction of *Die Zärtlichkeit der Wölfe (Tenderness of the Wolves)* shot in Gelsenkirchen, North Rhine-Westphalia. Written by and starring Kurt Raab, a poor man's **Peter Lorre**, as gay serial killer.

The Tenderness of the Wolves *is not an enjoyable film but a grisly depiction of depravity. This collaboration between Fassbinder, Lommel and Raab created a seedy and often gruesome melodrama telling the true and horrific tale of the "Butcher of Hanover" aka Fritz Haarmann. And as producer and editor (and actor), Fassbinder gives full throttle to his macabre sense of humour in his vibrant 1940s styling that explores, in often explicit detail, the 1920s life and times of the gay serial killer and his dystopian world of cannibalism with a sideline as a vampire.*

Fassbinder was too busy with **The Bitter Tears of Petra von Kant** *and* **Fear Eats the Soul** *to directed so he enlisted the help of his protégé Ulli Lommel, who had a few films under his belt and went on to make the* **Boogeyman** *hits. Kurt Raab wrote the script and takes the part of Haarmann, looking seriously wan and ungemütlich wild with his pallid, shaved head adding to his scary appearance, unlike that of Klaus Kinski in* **Nosferatu.**

Zärtlichkeit der Wölfe was the opening film of Berlinale 1973.

JULY 13

The first issue of new horror pulp series *John Sinclair: Die Nacht des Hexers (The Night of the Warlock)* published by Bastei-Lübbe. The character of the modern-day witch hunter was created by Helmut Rellergerd who signed as Jason Dark.

AUGUST 16

Susanne und der Zauberring (Susanne and the Magic Ring) by East German director Erwin Stranka: 12-year-old Susanne is a dreamer and feels excluded from her classmates. When she tells an older lockkeeper about her problems, he understands her immediately and presents her with a magic ring that is supposed to help her. At the end, Susanne knows that one must believe in oneself.

SEPTEMBER 26

Einladung zur Enthauptung (Invitation to a Beheading), Horst Flick's TV version of Vladimir Nabokov's Kafkaesque novel: Cincinnatus C. is sentenced to be executed for the (nonsensical) crime of "gnostical turpitude".

OCTOBER 14

Impressed by Daniel Francis Galouye's science-fiction novel *Simulacron 3* that dealt with a parallel society unconscious about the fact that it is virtual, TV editor and producer Peter Märthesheimer (WDR Cologne) asked **Rainer Werner Fassbinder** to direct a two-part mini-series *Welt am Draht (World on a Wire)*. Fassbinder cast Klaus Löwitsch, Babara Valentin, Mascha Rabben, Günter Lamprecht, **Ulli Lommel**, Joachim Hansen Kurt Raab, Margit Carstensen, Ingrid Caven, Gottfried John, Werner Schroeter, Christine Kaufmann, Peter Kern, Elma Karlowa and his mother, Lilo Pempeit.

Löwitsch is seen as Fred Stiller, a cybernetics engineer who uncovers a massive corporate conspiracy concerning virtual reality.

NOVEMBER 2

Pan by **George Moorse** with Louis Waldon in the title role. The ancient Greek god is transferred into Celtic mythology. **Udo Kier** was cast as a Pilgrim of Death.

NOVEMBER 15

In *Traumstadt (Dream City)* director Johannes Schaaf outlined a utopian town that seems to grant absolute freedom but behind the surface perversion and violence are spreading. Adapted from a novel by Bohemian artist Alfred Kubin (1877-1959).

NOVEMBER 30

Udo Kier appeared on German screens as *Andy Warhol's Frankenstein (Flesh for Frankenstein)* directed by Paul Morrissey.

DECEMBER 12

Maria d'Oro and Bello Blue (Once Upon a Time), the first (and due to disappointing box-office results final) feature-length animation produced by comic book editor Rolf Kauka, interestingly not done by Kauka's regular Munich-based artists but by Italian animation studio Gamma Film (Roberto and Gino Gavioli).

1974

Federal Republic of Germany
Cinemas: 3114
Attendance figure: 136 million
77 feature films produced

German Democratic Republic
Cinemas: 831
Attendance figure: 79 million
19 feature films produced

FEBRUARY 5

Die letzten Tage von Gomorrha (The Last Days of Gomorrha) directed for TV by Helma Sanders Brahms (a former TV announcer) and featuring Mascha Rabben as a young woman who plans a revolt against modern mass media when her life partner crawls away into TV entertainment.

MARCH 1

Udo Kier as *Andy Warhol's Dracula (Sangue per Dracula)* directed by Paul Morrissey.

MARCH 8

Fulfilling a special request of his granddaughter, Gert (*Goldfinger*) Fröbe starred as *Räuber Hotzenplotz (Hotzenplotz the Robber)*, a well-known children's book character created by Otfried Preussler, under the direction of Gustav Ehmck. Josef Meinrad joined him as Petrosilius Zwackelmann, a mad magician.

MAY 9

Undine 74, a German-Austrian co-production directed by Rolf Thiele, a modern version of the mermaid tale written by Friedrich de la Motte Fouqué. Angela von Radloff as Undine and Elisabeth Flickenschildt as Aja, the old nixie.

MAY 22

Science fiction TV *Die phantastische Welt des Matthew Madson (The Fantastic World of Matthew Madson)* by Cinegrafik's **Helmut Herbst** (co-written with Klaus Wyborny) who was going to instruct his students at the West Berlin Academy for Film and Television in special effects techniques: A group of astronauts tries to rescue a man from another era who has gotten stranded on a certain planet. After a while, the astronauts realize that they need rescuing themselves.

Magdalena, vom Teufel besessen (Magdalena: Possessed by the Devil): Dagmar Hedrich as Magdalena Winter who attends a boarding school is possessed by a demon. The casting of Rudolf Schündler who had a supporting part in *The Exorcist* refers to the main influence of this picture that was directed by Walter Boos, an editor-turned-director, and produced by TV 13 (Horst Hächler).

JULY 5

Hans Röckle und der Teufel (Hans Röckle and the Devil), a DEFA Studios fairy tale about a pact that Master Hans Röckle (Rolf Hoppe as Jack Coat), an ingenious puppeteer, enters with Flammfuss (Flame-Foot), the Devil (Peter Aust). Hans Kratzert directed.

JULY 10

Telerop 2009—Es ist noch was zu retten: TV series that sees Earth destroyed by pesticides and pollution in 2009. Telerop is a fictitious television channel which reports from German disaster zones. Written by Jürgen Voigt and Karl Wittlinger. Michael Kehlmann (12 episodes) and Eberhard Itzenplitz

(1 episode) directed a cast that consisted of Ingrid Resch, Fred Maire, Antje Hagen, Gisela Fischer, Günter Strack, Charlotte Kerr, Walter Kohut, Walter Ladengast, Rose Renée Roth, Rosemarie Fendel, Dagmar Heller, Bruni Löbel, Karl Maria Schley and Jörg Pleva. Rolf Wilhelm composed the score.

OCTOBER 10

Rolf Losansky's *Blumen für den Mann im Mond (Flowers for the Man in the Moon)* made at DEFA Studios: The Moon tells Adam Ledermann (Sven Grothe), a boy with a vivid imagination, how wonderful it would be if flowers would grow on her vast, bleak landscape.

OCTOBER 15

Start of a Bavaria-produced pre-evening TV series directed by **Rainer Erler**: *Das blaue Palais (The Blue Palace)*.

A group of progressive, independent scientists gather in the Blue Palace to inquire into the different aspects of our future crossing ethnic and moral borders. Their topics are transfer of memory, laser light and antimatter, parapsychology and telepathy, elimination of our aging gene, and synthetic material to replace steel.

Series run until 1976 and was awarded with the Adolf Grimme Prize in Gold.

In addition:

Alpha und Asphalt (Alpha and Asphalt) directed for ZDF-TV by Frank Guthke: Christiane Krüger as genetically programmed math professor and a prostitute (in her secret life).

1975

Federal Republic of Germany
Cinemas: 3094
Attendance figure: 128 million
55 feature films produced

German Democratic Republic
Cinemas: 833
Attendance figure: 77 million
15 feature films produced

H. P. Lovecraft: Schatten aus der Zeit (The Shadow Out of Time), German TV movie directed by **George Moorse** and starring Anton Diffring and Ingrid Resch.

APRIL 2

La casa dell'esorcismo (The House of Exorcism/Der Teuflische), a re-edit of *Lisa und der Teufel* in the wake of the *Exorcist*. Co-produced by Roxy Film Munich.

MAY 2

West German-Austrian co-production *Parapsycho—Spektrum der Angst (Parapsycho: Spectrum of Fear)* consisting of three horror episodes by Viennese director Peter Patzak with Marisa Mell, Mascha Gonska, Matthieu Carrière, William Berger, Leon Askin and Helmut Förnbacher.

MAY 15

Konzert für Bratpfanne und Orchester (Concerto for Frying-Pan and Orchestra), a DEFA children's film that contains a lovely stop-motion sequence with a dancing coffee pot.

JULY 5

Synthetischer Film oder Wie das Monster KING KONG von Fantasy und Präzision gezeugt wurde (Synthetic Film or: How the Monster KING KONG was created by Imagination and Precision): **Helmut Herbst** documentary (16mm) about special effects techniques and the movie *King Kong* screened at the film market of Berlin International Film Festival.

JULY 11

Abenteuer mit Blasius (Adventures with Blasius): Two boys encounter a strange person who turns out to be a robot.

SEPTEMBER 22

Die Halde (The Rubbish Tip), a bizarre "Apocalyptic Comedy" about a young man who follows a girl to an idyllic weekend colony which gets buried under a giant rubbish tip. Water, air, vegetables—all poisoned from the rubbish. Written, produced and directed by **Rainer Erler** for ZDF TV.

OCTOBER 30

Die Verwandlung (The Transformation): Jan Nemec's TV adaptation of Franz Kafka's strange case of Gregor Samsa who mutated into a repulsive insect.

NOVEMBER 11

Die Insel der Krebse (Crabs on the Island), TV movie produced for Second Channel TV from a story by Anatolij Dnjeprow. Directed by Gerhard Schmidt.

NOVEMBER 14

Paranormal phenomena explored by Rolf Olsen: *Reise ins Jenseits—Die Welt des Übernatürlichen*: *Is there life after death?* American release version *Journey into the Beyond* narrated by John Carradine ("your guide through *the world of the supernatural*): *In this film we show only the facts. We have not censored anything, however,* You *may need to. There are scenes in the film of para-normal acts which are gruesome and bloody.*

DECEMBER 25

Die schwarze Mühle (The Black Mill): Krabat works in a mill for the Black Miller, a sorcerer who keeps his slaves like concentration camp victims. The Miller guards an iron chest with seven locks on it. It keeps the Book of Knowledge hidden. Whoever finds it, will be able to solve all riddles. Directed by Celino Bleiweiss for East-German TV at DEFA Studios in Babelsberg.

1976

Federal Republic of Germany
Cinemas: 3092
Attendance figure: 115 million
60 feature films produced

German Democratic Republic
Cinemas: 833
Attendance figure: 80 million
14 feature films produced

FEBRUARY 12

Black Moon, a Franco-German co-production (Nouvelle Éditions de Films and Bioskop Film) by Louis Malle: A girl tries to escape a future war between genders and seek refuge in the country side. The last film of Brecht actress Therese Giehse.

MARCH 14

Das blaue Licht (The Blue Light), a DEFA production directed by Iris Gusner from a Grimm fairy tale (that also was adapted by Hans Christian Andersen and filmed by DEFA 17 years ago): A mean king cheats Jack (Hans played by Viktor Semyonov, a Russian actor), a soldier, who has served for him in war out of his pay. On his way home, Jack is asked by a witch to retrieve a blue light which she has accidentally dropped into a well. While in the well he discovers that the light has magic powers. A dwarf (played by Fred Delmare) appears who must always serve and obey whoever is in possession of the blue light.

The Blue Light *is loosely based on a Grimms fairytale, although it's really a complete reboot of the original fairytale. It takes the story and stands it on its head, changing the message and the priorities of the characters to better suit a socialist perspective.* [...]

In the original story, the soldier eventually marries the princess, but no one would want to marry the princess in this movie, she's a spoiled child-woman who pouts and sucks her thumb and is dumb as a bag of hammers. Romantic interest is provided, instead, by Anne, who works at the local inn. This is, after all, an East German film, and being born in a royal family doesn't make a person better; only more likely to be corrupt. [57]

MAY 17

Art Director **Hermann Warm** (*Caligari, Vampyr*) died in Berlin West.

MAY 20

Michael Carreras and Hammer, on their way down, tried their hands on another novel by Dennis Wheatley. They cast unhappy American Richard Widmark (who called this a Mickey Mouse production), Christopher Lee as leader of a group of satanists and (asked so by German co-producer Terra Filmkunst) **Nastassja Kinski** as victim of the Satanists in *To the Devil... a Daughter*. In Germany released as *Die Braut des Satans (The Bride of Satan)* by Terra's distributor Constantin Film.

---

57 Jim Morton, *The Blue Light*. July 13, 2019. Eastgermancinema.com.

JULY 1

Im Staub der Sterne (In the Dust of the Stars), DEFA science fiction (co-produced with Buftea Film Studios near Bucharest) written and directed by **Gottfried Kolditz**:

Sometimes referred to as the "East German Barbarella,*"* **In the Dust of the Stars** **(Im Staub der Sterne)** *is one of the strangest films to grace the movie screens of the GDR; or anywhere else for that matter. Featuring a cast that heralded from a number of different eastern European countries,* **In the Dust of the Stars** *is the story of a space team sent from the Planet Cyrno in response to a distress call on TEM 4, a desolate planet on the outskirts of inhabited space. When they arrive, they are whisked off to an extravagant compound belonging to a man known only as the "Chief"—a decadent despot who has enslaved the indigenous people of TEM 4 for his own profit and enjoyment. The team is invited to a party that features dancing maidens in an art park, boa constrictors on the hors d'ouevre table, and a screaming woman on a trampoline. At the party, the team is brainwashed into assuming that nothing is wrong on the planet, but the one crew member that skipped the party remains sceptical.* [58]

The cosmonauts find out that the members of the working class, the Turi, the native population, are enslaved to do compulsory labor for the "Chief" (played by Ekkehard Schall) and work in a mine. A revolution is at stake against the Turis' oppressors.

AUGUST 2

Fritz Lang died in Beverly Hills.

SEPTEMBER 23

Swiss-German co-production *Jack the Ripper: Der Dirnenmörder von London* directed by Jess Franco on location in Zurich (the home of producer **Erwin C.**

---

58 Jim Morton, *In the Dust of the Stars*. March 14, 2001. Eastgermancinema.com/2011/03/14/in-the-dust-of-the-stars/

Dietrich) plus a few stock shots of London for "authenticity". Starring **Klaus Kinski** as Dr. Dennis Orloff who is supposed to be the Ripper.

OCTOBER 5

Hans im Glück (Hans in Luck), a TV movie by **Wolfgang Petersen** for Sender Freies Berlin and ORF (Austrian TV), is based on the fairy tale by the Grimm Brothers. Jürgen Prochnow, at that time Petersen's favorite actor, was cast as Hans Schmidtke.

NOVEMBER 4

After drinking from the *The Devil's Elixirs*, a Capuchin monk (played by Dieter Laser) is confronted with sensual desires previously unknown to him: Manfred Purzer adapted **E. T. A. Hoffmann's** Gothic novel *Die Elixiere des Teufels* (inspired by Matthew Gregory Lewis' *The Monk*) for what in those days was called an "amphibian film", a co-venture between TV (Bayerischer Rundfunk) and cinema (Divina and Luggi Waldleitner's Roxy Film).

NOVEMBER 30

Fritz Rasp died in Gräfelfing near Munich. According to an interview, at one time he was considered as replacement for the late Lon Chaney.

DECEMBER 25

Andreas (Ingolf Gorges) and Maren (Brigitte Heinrich), a young couple, are going to wake up *The Rainmaiden* (Cox Habbema, an actress from Amsterdam) who has fallen asleep: *Die Regentrude*, made from a novel by Theodor Storm for East German TV at DEFA Studios.

1977

Federal Republic of Germany
Cinemas: 3072
Attendance figure: 124 million
52 feature films produced

German Democratic Republic
Cinemas: 837
Attendance figure: 84 million
15 feature films produced

FEBRUARY 4

East-German children's film directed by Erwin Stranka: *Der kleine Zauberer und die große 5 (The Little Magician and the Big Bad Mark)*: A boy tries to remove his bad school note with the help of magic. Based on a tale by Uwe Kant.

FEBRUARY 9

Twilight's Last Gleaming (Das Ultimatum), one of the depreciation projects of Munich-based Geria Company, starred Burt Lancaster as renegade U.S. Air Force General Lawrence Dell who is going to follow the example of Stanley Kubrick's Jack D. Ripper by threatening to start WW3—unless President Stevens reveals details of a secret meeting between Dell and the President's advisors at the beginning of the Vietnam War. Lancaster's co-stars were Roscoe Lee Browne, Joseph Cotten, Melvyn Douglas, Charles Durning and Richard Widmark. Robert Aldrich directed the project on the lot of Munich's Bavaria Studios. Released in the United States by Allied Artists.

JUNE 9

Prosperos Traum (Prospero's Dream): ZDF TV movie by **George Moorse** with characters from Shakespeare's play *The Tempest* portrayed by Peter Lühr

(Prospero), Miriam Mahler (Miranda), Sebastian Baur (Ariel) and Vadim Glowna (Caliban).

JUNE 16

Wernher von Braun passed away in Alexandria, Virginia.

JUNE 21

Fritz Genschow died in Berlin.

SEPTEMBER 3

Another DEFA children's film directed by **Rolf Losansky**: *Ein Schneemann für Afrika (A Snowman for Africa)*: A little African girl named Asina is waiting for her new friend Karli, a sailor from East German port city Rostock, to bring her a snowman that finds shelter in a cooling chamber of the ship. The snowman comes to life thanks to stop motion photography by Kurt Weiler, Erich Günther, Heiko Ebert and Tony Loeser.

SEPTEMBER 6

Eugen Schüfftan died in New York City.

OCTOBER 24

After filing for bankruptcy, the ruins of Constantin Film, once the flagship of the German film industry, were transformed into Neue Constantin Film (New Constantin).

OCTOBER 28

Das Schlangenei (The Serpent's Egg) directed by Ingmar Bergman: *The kind of terror that could never be… until now… until Bergman!* Producer Dino De

Laurentiis arranged with his German colleague **Horst Wendlandt** a shooting at Bavaria Studios in Munich.

One rainy night in Weimar Berlin, Jewish American circus performer Abel Rosenberg (David Carradine) discovers that his brother Max, his trapeze-act partner, has killed himself. What follows is one of Bergman's darkest and most fearful visions, as the drowned-in-drink Abel and Max's ex-wife, cabaret singer Manuela (Liv Ullmann), feel increasingly unwelcome in a menacing and destitute city, eyed by the police as well as a scientist with diabolical intentions. The director's sole big-budget Hollywood production, for which he created a surreal and atmospheric Berlin on a Munich soundstage, The Serpent's Egg *conjures a Kafkaesque nightmare about the decaying society that gave rise to the horrors of Nazism.* [59]

NOVEMBER 5

London premiere of Hans Jürgen Syberberg's *Hitler, ein Film aus Deutschland (Hitler: A Film from Germany)*, a bizarre seven-hour Third Reich mix with puppetry, background (front) projection and Wagnerian score.

DECEMBER 2

Wer reisst denn gleich vor'm Teufel aus? (Who's Afraid of the Devil?): DEFA's remake of Grimm Brothers' *Devil with Three Golden Hairs*.

DECEMBER 6

Der Heiligenschein (The Halo), a West-Berlin TV production (by Sender Freies Berlin), was adapted from **Curt Siodmak's** original story by director Heinz Schirk and starred Horst Frank as a man who can't get rid of his halo.

DECEMBER 11

Rainer Erler's *Operation Ganymed* on Second Channel TV: The crew of a

---

[59] www.criterion.com.

spaceship, one of three left from a tragic mission on the Jupiter Moon Ganymede, has to find out what had happened on Earth during their flight. Their return turns out to be a horror trip. Nobody is waiting for them; they gave been written off. After two and a half years of radio silence, they are no longer expected. They have to make an emergency landing on a God-forsaken spot on the Pacific coast of Mexico followed by a hopeless march through desolate deserts. The first village which they reach is deserted and in ruins. Until their return to earth, crammed into a small spaceship, the crew was a functioning unit. Now, in the endless desert, it loses its feeling of coherence and breaks up. The five astronauts suffer from the torture of thirst and hunger, from spells of weakness and hallucinations. Aggressions build up and lead to violence and murder. Only one survivor manages to reach the next inhabited place. Post-doomsday apocalypse with Horst Frank, Jürgen Prochnow, Uwe Friedrichsen, Claus-Theo Gärtner and Dieter Laser.

DECEMBER 24

Die zertanzten Schuhe (The Shoes that Were Danced to Pieces), Grimm's fairy tale broadcast by East German TV.

This year East German TV presented a play based on a story by Stanisław Lem: *Der getreue Roboter (The Faithful Robot)*.

1978

Federal Republic of Germany
Cinemas: 3110
Attendance figure: 136 million
57 feature films produced

German Democratic Republic
Cinemas: 839
Attendance figure: 80 million
17 feature films produced

JANUARY 1

Klaus Piontek as *Der Meisterdieb (The Master Thief)* in a Grimm fairy tale adaptation on East German TV.

FEBRUARY 9

German release of *Star Wars (Krieg der Sterne)* by George Lucas.

"Episode IV" in its original packing was nothing else than WW2 in Outer Space. Many of the X-winged VFX elements seen on the screen were modeled frame by frame copying footage from dogfights taken from newsreels and from *The Dam Busters*, a 1955 British war film that described an air raid of Avro Lancaster Bombers against a dam which contained the Möhnesee (May 16/17, 1943). ...*one of the key visions I had of the film when I started,* Lucas said, *was of a dogfight in outer space with spaceships—two ships flying through space shooting at each other. That was my original idea.*

To a World War II history buff, the iconic Millennium Falcon from **Star Wars** *resembles one of the best-known bombers of all time.*

The greenhouse cockpit configuration, along with the gun turrets, aboard the ship was lifted straight out of the blueprints for the Boeing B-29 Superfortress.

The Superfortress was a workhorse of the US Army Air Forces that was best known for dropping atomic bombs on the Japanese cities of Hiroshima and Nagasaki.

Star Wars *creator George Lucas is known to have studied 20 to 25 hours of footage from World War II dogfights while doing research for the film.* [...]

According to a 1997 interview with Willard Huyck, a screenwriter who is a friend of Lucas, footage of World War II dogfights was used as a placeholder before the special effects were edited into the original film. [60]

---

60   Alex Lockie, https://www.businessinsider.com/star-wars-world-war-ii-dogfights-2-ww2-2015-12. December 18, 2015.

FEBRUARY 10

Evelyne Kraft as *Lady Dracula* bitten by Count Dracula (played by Stephen Boyd who had arrived at the bottom of his career) 100 years ago in an Austrian-German comedy directed by Franz Josef Gottlieb that also featured Theo Lingen, Eddi Arent, Walter Giller, Roberto Blanco, Herbert Fux, Heinz Reincke and Rinaldo Talamonti.

MARCH 3

Tabea Blumenschein aboard a lesbian pirate ship: *Madame X* co-directed by Ulrike Ottinger.

MARCH 9

Neues vom Räuber Hotzenplotz (The Latest on Robber Hotzenplotz), Gustav Ehmck's sequel with Gert Fröbe replaced by a less impressive, rather feminine Peter Kern in the title role.

JUNE 9

Gloria Film Distributors, sold by Ilse Kubaschewski a few years ago to U.S. company Project Seven Inc., went bankrupt.

JULY 11

Eurydike—Die Braut aus dem Jenseits (Eurydike oder Das Mädchen von Nirgendwo/Euyridice, the Bride from the Netherworld/Eurydice or The Girl from Nowhere): A nuclear scientist establishes paranormal contact with victims of the atomic bomb of Hiroshima who were transferred to another dimension. TV movie written and directed by Jochen Richter.

OCTOBER 22

1982: Gutenbach, a TV movie by Michael Verhoeven.

OCTOBER 30

Der Nachlass (The Legacy), an East German TV movie: Two physicians try to get hold of the invention of their late professor.

DECEMBER 22

Rochus Gliese, a close collaborator of **Paul Wegener,** died in Berlin West.

DECEMBER 30

Zwerg Nase (Nose the Dwarf), East German TV movie adapted from Wilhelm Hauff.

Die Quelle (The Source) by **Rainer Erler:** A young adventurer ends up on a remote island where water is more precious than gold.

Plutonium, enough for five bombs of the Hiroshima type, in the false hands. Camouflaged as political suspense documentary by **Rainer Erler.**

1979

Federal Republic of Germany
Cinemas: 3196
Attendance figure: 142 million
65 feature films produced

German Democratic Republic
Cinemas: 837
Attendance figure: 81 million
19 feature films produced

JANUARY 1

Günter Meyer entered the field of supernatural ghost family TV with *Spuk unterm Riesenrad (Spooky under the Ferris Wheel)*, a 7-part series for Television of German Democratic Republic, created in cooperation with writer C. U. Wiesner. Accidentally, three kids bring a trio of specters to life: a witch (Katja Paryla), a giant (Stefan Lisewski), and Rumpelstiltskin (Siegfried Seibt). A feature film version of the series was also shown theatrically.

FEBRUARY 25

Nosferatu Phantom der Nacht (Nosferatu the Vampyre), a Franco-German co-production, entered the International Film Festival Berlin. Director **Werner Herzog** liked the idea of a *Nosferatu* remake (later he insisted to call it only a homage) and studied the film books written by German émigré **Lotte H. Eisner**. A friendship with the Grande Dame of film history was built and Herzog was reminded that, before the Third Reich and before Federal Germany postwar cinema, there was a thing called Expressionist Cinema that was lost but artistically worthwhile enough to dig out. He left Eisner an illuminated man: **Nosferatu** *in my opinion is the most important film ever made in Germany. So, this is a challenge. And it establishes some sort of a link between the great Expressionist Cinema that we had in Germany and our film renaissance now. It is a film that is beyond my own private person.* Herzog felt that it was necessary to have *a continuity in film history.* He gave the characters the names they had in Bram Stoker's novel: Count Orlok became Count Dracula (played by **Klaus Kinski**), Thomas Hutter became Jonathan Harker (Bruno Ganz), his wife Ellen Lucy Harker (Isabelle Adjani) and Professor Bulwer Dr. Van Helsing (Walter Ladengast).

Klaus Kinski about his part in *Nosferatu*: *It's me. It's me because I am Nosferatu in a* **Nosferatu** *picture, so my answer is: Nosferatu is me. It's real. If you are something you ... I mean, of course, you automatically believe in it. You haven't to point it out so much that you believe in it. I would have never accepted it if it wouldn't be in me if I couldn't feel the metamorphosis. I look as I have to look.* [61]

---

61   TV interview given during the shooting of the film.

A little bit more coherently Kinski described his work in another interview: *Nosferatu for Twentieth Century Fox. In Holland and Czechoslovakia and all the way to the Mountains on the Czech-Polish border. The departure point is Munich. Four weeks before shooting starts, I have to fly there for costuming. And this is where I shave my skull for the first time. I feel exposed, vulnerable, defenseless. Not just physically (my bare head becomes as hypersensitive as an open wound) but chiefly in my emotions and my nerves. I feel as if I have no scalp, as if my protective envelope has been removed and my soul can't live without it. As if my soul had been flayed.*

At first, I go outdoors only when it's dark (I've been through that with **The Idiot***, but this is much, much worse). Besides, I wear a wool cap all the time even though it's spring. You may think, "So what? Some guys are bald." But the two have absolutely nothing to do with one another. What I mean is the simultaneous metamorphosis into a vampire. That nonhuman, nonanimal being. That undead thing. That unspeakable creature, which suffers in full awareness of its existence. […]*

There must be some significance (even though I don't give a fuck) in the fact that I play parts involving what I have to experience myself but can barely endure. Or do I have to experience it personally after playing the part? Is it a warning or a repetition? Is it a chain reaction? Does one detonate the other? Or do both happen simultaneously—my life, and the part I have to play? Do I transfer other people's bells to my own life, or do I transfer my own life to the character I have to play? Does the event in question occur in my own life through mystical force, so that I may suffer more deeply when I have to play the part? No one can answer these questions. In any case, it's part of the curse of being—as they put it—'the ultimate actor'. Which, however, has nothing to do with this hummy bullshit.

Kinski as always behaved extravagantly and revealed himself as the eccentric everybody expected:

When we move from Holland to Czechoslovakia […] I demand a trailer that I pick myself so I can live in it, sleep in it, cook, and do my laundry. I don't want to be billeted in some shitty Czech hotel, where you run into the whole motley crew after shooting. [62]

Klaus Kinski's *Nosferatu* | Limited edition by Don Post Studios
Courtesy of Rolf Giesen Collection/Deutsche Kinemathek

While he was performing in *Nosferatu Phantom der Nacht*, Kinski's third wife Minhoi [Loanic], a Vietnamese, was about to divorce him. She also was going to take their son, Nanhoi, better known as Nikolai. This was the reason he felt even more vulnerable.

62 www.guido-boehm.info

MARCH 13

Art Director **Erich Kettelhut** (*Dr. Mabuse, Nibelungen, Metropolis*) died in Hamburg.

MAY 21

Fleisch (Spare Parts), TV movie by **Rainer Erler** dealing with an ambulance on the search for human organ parts. Honeymooning couple Monica and Mike that has checked into a motel in New Mexico becomes its easy prey.

JULY 6

Schneeweisschen und Rosenrot (Snow White and Red Rose), another version of the Grimm faiy tale, this time produced by DEFA in Babelsberg. Two girls versus evil mountain goblin "Moldy Beard" (played by Hans-Peter Minetti).

JULY 19

Das Ding im Schloss (The Thing in the Castle): Erwin Geschonneck as senior professor who is kidnapped by residents of a veterans' home who ask him to invent a "rejuvenating machine". Written and directed by **Gottfried Kolditz**.

JULY 23

Aktion Abendsonne (Campaign Evening Sun): A TV show in the near future presents four old lonely people in need for a new family. They are asked to prove what they are able to do. ZDF TV movie written and directed by Diethard Klante.

SEPTEMBER 6

The first German doctoral thesis in order to obtain a PhD. at Freie Universität Berlin was *Der phantastische Film. Zur Soziologie von Horror, Science-Fiction und Fantasy im Kino* by Rolf Giesen.

OCTOBER 12

Graf Dracula (beisst jetzt) in Oberbayern (Dracula Blows his Cool), a sex comedy by Carl Schenkel with Gianni Garko as Count Stanislaus, Bea Fiedler as Mausi and Ralf Wolter as the vampire's loyal servant Boris. Produced by German-Austrian Lisa Film (Karl Spiehs) at Castle Moosham, Salzburg, Austria.

NOVEMBER 22

Peter Fleischmann's *Die Hamburger Krankheit (The Hamburg Plague/The Hamburg Syndrome)* deals with a mysterious, deadly plague that befalls West Germany. A group from Hamburg tries to escape to the Bavarian mountains and heads for an odyssey through the country searching for other survivors and salvation. Cast includes Helmut Griem, Fernando Arrabal, Tilo Prückner, Ulrich Wildgruber, Rainer Langhans and Rosel Zech.

DECEMBER 22

Die Gänsehirtin am Brunnen (The Goose-Girl at the Well), an East German TV movie based on a fairy tale by the Grimm Brothers.

1980

Federal Republic of Germany
Cinemas: 3354
Attendance figure: 144 million
49 feature films produced

German Democratic Republic
Cinemas: 826
Attendance figure: 79 million
15 feature films produced

JANUARY 23

Lil Dagover (*Caligari*) died in Geiselgasteig.

APRIL 18

Warum die Ufos unseren Salat klauen (Why the UFOs Steal Our Lettuce), a very strange, totally silly science fiction comedy produced and directed by Hans Jürgen Pohland (one of the founders of New German Cinema who signed the Oberhausen Manifesto in 1962) about Berlin hobby biologist Peter McDonald (Tommy Piper) who accidentally disovers the secret of the extraterrestrials' spacecraft power: lettuce! Peter's mother is played by Hildegard Knef, the leader of the extraterrestrials by Curd Jürgens. Working title: *Berlin Ballad II*. Released on video as *Checkpoint Charly*.

APRIL 24

Geburt der Hexe (Birth of the Witch) by Wilfried Minks, a co-production between German (ZDF) and Swiss (SF DRS) TV at the Oberhausen Film Festival. Peasants led by a witch (played by Ulla Berkévicz) rebel against a feudal landlord who rules with cruelty.

MAY 9

Der gekaufte Tod (Death Watch): A morbid, voyeuristic TV show of a future where death of illness is rare monitors a terminally ill woman with camera implants. Bertrand Tavernier directed Romy Schneider as Katherine Mortenhoe, Harvey Keitel, Harry Dean Stanton, Max von Sydow and Bernhard Wicki. Based on the novel *The Unsleeping Eye* by David G. Compton. Co-produced by German TV 13 Filmproduktion.

NOVEMBER 21

U.S. start of Menahem Golan's sci-fi musical *The Apple* produced in Berlin (West) including interiors in **Artur Brauner's** CCC Studios. Brauner also provided some German artists to work on that movie including art director

Hans Jürgen Kiebach, costume designer Ingrid Zoré and special effects technician Richard Richtsfeld. Funded by NF Geria II Filmgesellschaft.

NOVEMBER 28

Mia May, wife of director **Joe May**, died in Hollywood.

DECEMBER 8

Ein Guru kommt (Here Comes the Guru): Satirical TV film by **Rainer Erler** with Wolfgang Reichmann as failed opera singer who rises to the Baghwan-like leader of a religious sect.

DECEMBER 28

Gevatter Tod (Godfather Death), a Grimm adaptation for East German TV. Death is played by Dieter Franke.

1981

Federal Republic of Germany
Cinemas: 3486
Attendance figure: 141 million
76 feature films produced

German Democratic Republic
Cinemas: 832
Attendance figure: 76 million
17 feature films produced

MARCH 27

Jess Franco's *Die Säge des Todes (The Saw of Death/Bloody Moon)* was put into action by German funding (co-produced by Lisa, Metro and Rapid Film).

APRIL 6

Günter Rätz had worked since 1978 on the stop-motion animation of the feature-length East German puppet film *Die fliegende Windmühle (The Flying Windmill)* produced at DEFA Studio für Trickfilme in Dresden: Young girl Olli, Pinkus the dog and Alexander the horse seek refuge from a storm in an old mill which happens to be the hidden laboratory of a professor and his crocodile Susi. When Olli inadvertently presses a button, the windmill moves and starts to outer space.

The Flying Windmill was reviewed by the DEFA Trickfilm Studio brass downright euphorically: "We are happy to have this film. We are glad that there is such a director and such a collective." Thanks to the bizarre puppets created by Horst Tappert and the pointed dialogue by Günter Rätz, the story of cheeky little Olli who had run away because of her lousy school certificate later enjoyed "cult status".

MAY 18

Adrian Hoven died in Tegernsee, Bavaria.

MAY 25

Inhuman ecstasy fulfilled. She created a monster as her secret lover—a green-eyed ogre: Andrzej Zulawski's psychological horror drama *Possession* won Isabelle Adjani a Best Actress Award at the Cannes Film Festival. Adjani's co-stars were Sam Neill, Margit Carstensen and Heinz Bennent. The French production was shot in Berlin, mainly in the Kreuzberg district near the Berlin Wall. German co-production partner was Soma Film company. One year later it was shown at a Berlin film festival, the 1st Fantastival.

APRIL 10

Die Todesgöttin des Liebescamps (Love Camp): Sexploitation produced, directed by and starring German singer Christian Anders versus the Goddess of a camp of free loving hippies, played by Java-born *Black Emanuelle* Laura Gemser. Theatrically released by Avis Film Josef Koschella.

JUNE 19

Lotte Reiniger died in Dettenhausen near Tübingen.

AUGUST 1

Bavaria opened a studio tour on its lot in Geiselgasteig.

OCTOBER 4

TV start of a 13-part Czech fantasy series *Die Märchenbraut (Arabela)* that was co-funded by Gert K. Müntefering (Westdeutscher Rundfunk Cologne): Arabela, the daughter of the King of Fairy Tales, escapes the revenge of Rumburak the Magician and creates turmoil and havoc in our world.

NOVEMBER 6

Freak Orlando by Ulrike Ottinger.

DECEMBER 25

Das tapfere Schneiderlein (The Brave Little Tailor) on East German TV.

1982

Federal Republic of Germany
Cinemas: 3598
Attendance figure: 125 million
70 feature films produced

German Democratic Republic
Cinemas: 832
Attendance figure: 72 million
14 feature films produced

JANUARY 11

Wir (We): Dystopian TV movie by Voytech Jasný based on a novel that was written, long before Aldous Huxley and George Orwell, in 1920 by Yevgeny Zamyatin: *A Vision of a United Totalitarian State*. This world of quadratic harmony and blue-grey comformity is the product of a Hundred Years' War and lasts already for thousand years. It is ruled by the Great Benefactor.

APRIL 2

Meister Eder und sein Pumuckl: A cabinet maker (Gustl Bayrhammer) begins to see a red-haired goblin. Live action was recorded in Munich, 2D animation executed by Pannónia Studios in Budapest. Released theatrically and as TV series. Voice of Pumuckl supplied by Hans Clarin.

APRIL 4

Unheimliche Geschichten: 13-part TV mystery series produced for First Channel TV.

APRIL 22

Jess Franco had not only some German funding for his *La tumba de los muertos vivientes* (*Der Abgrund der lebenden Toten/Oase der Zombies/The Treasure of the Licing Dead*) but also *Bloodsucking Nazi Zombies* (video title) on the screen.

JUNE 2

Amphitryon, TV version directed by Jürgen Flimm.

JUNE 4

Der Fan (The Fan): *Neue Deutsche Welle* with a cannibalistic twist. Désirée Nosbusch as blood groupie.

JUNE 10

Drug-addicted **Rainer Werner Fassbinder** died in Munich.

JUNE 15

East German director **Gottfried Kolditz** died in Ljubljana, Slovenia.

JULY 13

Der lange Ritt zur Schule (The Long Ride to School) by **Rolf Losansky** has a boy watching secretly a western on TV become part of the action.

JULY 15

Shalom Pharaoh, the biblical story of Joseph and his Brethren animated by Curt Linda.

JULY 16

A homicide detective (played by **Rainer Werner Fassbinder** in leopard tard, released posthumously) investigates bombings in the totalitarian future of the late 1980s: Wolf Gremm's *Kamikaze 1989* was based on a crime novel by Swedish writer Per Wahlöö.

SEPTEMBER 16

Doktor Faustus adapted from Thomas Mann's novel by Franz Seitz with Jon Finch as Adrian Leverkühn, a musician, who believes to have been a tacit pact with Satan (played by Austrian enfant terrible André Heller).

Der Hase und der Igel (The Hare and the Hedgehog) on East German TV.

OCTOBER 30

Life-size figure of Christ on tour through Bavaria: *Das Gespenst (The Ghost)* written, produced, directed by (and starring) Herbert Achternbusch.

NOVEMBER 12

Zeichen und Wunder (Signs and Miracles) by Niklaus Schilling: a fictitious report about an accident in the European Patent Office in Munich.

NOVEMBER 28

Der Prinz hinter den sieben Meeren (The Prince Beyond the Seven Seas), a DEFA-produced fairy tale by Walter Beck.

DECEMBER 20

Wuk der Fuchs (Vuk), animated feature film coproduced by Pannónia Studios in Hungary and Munich-based Infafilm Manfred Korytowski.

In addition:

East-German TV brought Günter Meyer's *Spuk im Hochhaus (Spooky in a Skyscraper)* with two ghosts spooking in a tower building which is located where their tavern once was.

1983

Federal Republic of Germany
Cinemas: 3664
Attendance figure: 125 million
Feature films produced: 77

German Democratic Republic
Cinemas: 824
Attendance figure: 73 million
Feature films produced: 15

APRIL 21

In two West Berlin cinemas (Filmkunst 66 and Hollywood) the *Fantastival—2nd International Festival of Fantastic Films* (organized by Rolf Giesen) opened. Guests of honor were Ray Harryhausen and Jean-Pierre Mocky.

MAY 19

Der Preis (The Prize/Soft Error), an experimental TV movie by Lutz Heering, set in a state of the future populated by bald-headed robots and uniformed display dummies modeled after Orwell's *1984*.

MAY 22

Die Schöne und das Tier (Beauty and the Beast), an East German TV movie by Rainer Bär.

JUNE 17

East German *Automärchen (Motoring Tales)*: Strange incidents concerning cars.

AUGUST 1

Amadeus August as a sect leader by the name of Gottfried Hofer who slightly resembles Adolf Hitler and establishes his bizarre followership in the fictitious town of Hochheim: *Der grüne Stern (The Green Star)*. The ZDF TV movie was based on a novel by Hans Weigel and directed by Heide Pils.

NOVEMBER 25

Murnau biographer **Lotte H. Eisner** died in Paris.

NOVEMBER 27

Die Zaubergräte, an East German TV film based on Charles Dickens' *The Magic Fishbone.*

DECEMBER 2

Moritz in der Litfasssäule (Moritz in the Advertising Pillar), a children's film directed by **Rolf Losansky** at DEFA Studios Babelsberg: Nine-year old Moritz Zack runs away from home and makes the acquaintance of a (stop-motion animated) cat that likes drinking beer.

Das schöne Ende dieser Welt (The Beautiful End of this World) by **Rainer Erler**: On behalf of a German concern a chemist travels to Western Australia. Pretending to be a private investor he purchases industrial real estate for a pesticide factory.

Neue Constantin Film announced a sci-fi comedy with popular German comedian Otto Waalkes: *Invasion der Spaghetti-Monster (Invasion of the Spaghetti Monsters)* modeled after *Attack of the Killer Tomatoes* that got a limited release in W. Germany thanks to the activities of Rolf Giesen. But Otto gave **Bernd Eichinger** and his deputy Herman Weigel the cold shoulder and signed with **Horst Wendlandt** who would offer the fastest with the mostest. The Constantin project was abandoned.

1984

Federal Republic of Germany
Cinemas: 3611
Attendance figure: 112 million
Feature films produced: 75

German Democratic Republic
Cinemas: 830
Attendance figure: 73 million
Feature films produced: 15

JANUARY 13

Gábor Altorjay's (West German TV) vision of future East Berlin (in 1995) turned into a madhouse: *Pankow '95* with **Udo Kier**, Christine Kaufmann and Dieter Thomas Heck.

FEBRUARY 19

Decoder was a low-budget movie by Jürgen Muschalek (featuring as Muscha) who was brought up in the punk scene of Dusseldorf: A burger shop employee discovers that by changing the background music from pleasantly calming to industrial "noise", he is capable to incite a revolution against the ruling system.

West Berlin premiere of *Schneeweisschen und Rosenrot (Snow White and Rose Red)*, directed by Rita-Maria Nowotny-Genschow who had co-written the fairy tale screenplay years ago with her husband, **Fritz Genschow** who passed away in 1977, and with her daughter Marina Geschow who was cast as Schneeweisschen while Madeleine Stolze played Rosenrot. Son Gabriel Genschow photographed the show.

FEBRUARY 22

Roland Emmerich's first movie *Das Arche Noah Prinzip (The Noah's Ark Principle)* finished at Hochschule für Film und Fernsehen in Munich and screened at Berlin International Film Festival. Emmerich was already hailed as master of special effects although there was no more than a single spaceship on screen.

MARCH 9

Dorian Gray im Spiegel der Boulevardpresse (Dorian Gray in the Mirror of the Yellow Press) by Ulrike Ottinger. Veruschka von Lehndorff as Dorian Gray and Delphine Seyrig as Frau Dr. Mabuse.

APRIL 6

Premiere of *Die unendliche Geschichte (The NeverEnding Story)* made from the bestsellimng fantasy novel by **Michael Ende**. A boy reading a magicbook saves the realm of imagination known as Phantasia from the forces of Nothing. Former actor and producer Dieter Geissler had found the right person to talk Ende into signing a film contract, then went to **Bernd Eichinger** (Neue Constantin Film) and Mark Damon (Producers Sales Organization) for funding. **Wolfgang Petersen** who previously had done Germany's most successful post-war movie *Das Boot (The Boat)* directed at Bavaria Studios in Munich. Twice-Academy Award winner Brian Johnson and his team were brought over from England to handle the complex special and visual effects and sold the naïve Germans the largest Blue Screen in the world (which wasn't necessary that way). Everything became more and more expensive and when the books were checked later, they found out that the movie was more costly then announced to the press: instead of 50 it cost 70 million mark. Ende was very unhappy with the result. He had hoped the producers would hire a real artist director like Akira Kurosawa or Andrzej Wajda.

MAY 11

Super by Adolf Winkelmann was a doomsday story about a dying earth with German rock stars Udo Lindenberg and Inga Humpe.

MAY 13

Die vertauschte Königin (The Reversed Queen), another entry in the series of East-German fairy tales.

SEPTEMBER 30

Dr. Erasmus Beilowski (Klaus Schwarzkopf), an internist, his brother-in-law psychiatrist Dr. Robert Risolani (Peter Pasetti), Professer Danzke (Siegfried Wischnewski), a politician, and engineer Erwin Pfeil (Frank Hoffmann) have a discussion on how to use a time machine that they found in a Berlin antique store in 1925 and identified as the device described by H. G. Wells in his novel: *Die Rückkehr der Zeitmaschine (The Return of the Time Machine)*. The TV movie was made by two GDR émigrés, writer Günther Kunert and director Jürgen Klauss.

During the production of *Joey* (U.S.: *Making Contact*) in Magstadt near his hometown Sindelfingen, director **Roland Emmerich** outlined a science fiction project tentatively titled *Necropolis* which a decade later mutated into *Stargate*.

In addition:

Meanwhile young fan Jörg Buttgereit finished a 16mm short film titled *Horror Heaven*. Over the years he established an underground cult of worshippers. These cults supported by dubious "genre film" theories work like savage tribes who fiercely protect and defend their cult objects against any criticism.

1985

Federal Republic of Germany
Cinemas: 3418
Attendance figure: 104 million
Feature films produced: 64

German Democratic Republic
Cinemas: 819
Attendance figure: 71 million
Feature films produced: 15

FEBRUARY

A huge *Special Effects* Retrospective at the Berlin International Film Festival was accompanied by an exhibition at Kaufhaus Wertheim, a department store on Kurfürstendamm. The event was curated by Dr. Rolf Giesen and showed works of Georges Méliès, **Lotte Reiniger**, Ray Harryhausen, George Pal et al. Among the guests of honor, besides Harryhausen: Forrest J Ackerman, **Curt Siodmak, Ferdinand Diehl**, Albert Whitlock, Dennis Muren, and Lorne Peterson (ILM).

FEBRUARY 9

Die Geschichte vom goldenen Taler (The Fairy Tale of the Golden Thaler), an East-German TV movie by Bodo Fürneisen based on a fairy tale by Hans Fallada (born Rudolf Wilhelm Friedrich Ditzen) featured some interesting mirror shots of an enchanted tiny man who helps a poor girl confined by a bizarre character named Hans Geiz [Jack Greed]. Produced at DEFA Studios in Babelsberg. Effects photography by Kurt Marks and Erich Günther.

MARCH 7

Gritta von Rattenzuhausbeiuns (Gritta of the Rat's Castle), a children's film from East German DEFA Studios directed by Jürgen Brauer: Thirteen-year-old Gritta, the Grand Countess of Rattenzuhausbeiuns, lives with her father who has invented a throne-saving machine in a castle—until her new stepmother tries to put her away in a convent.

APRIL 26

When Rolf Giesen published a fictitious April Fool's Day short story in Berlin's tip magazine about Bodo Wawerka, a German filmmaker lost somewhere in the jungle who was said to have anonymously worked on *King Kong*, he couldn't know that Munich filmmaker Heiner Stadler would take the idea and make a semi-documentary titled *King Kongs Faust (King Kong's Fist)* without asking him. An agreement was reached later with producer Katrin Seybold. Among the featured players were Wim Wenders, **Bernd Eichinger**, Werner Grassmann and one of the surviving sfx cameramen of the original *Kong*, Bert Willis (erroneously credited Burt Willis).

JUNE 28

Loft—Die neue Saat der Gewalt: Set in a post-doomsday world. Young anarchists torture high society guests in their loft flat.

SEPTEMBER 5

Clemens Klopfenstein's rather experimental witches' brew *Der Ruf der Sibylla (The Call of Sibylla)* was co-financed by Swiss and German TV.

OCTOBER 10

A time traveler from the 22nd century visits the 19th century to buy some paintings by Vincent Van Gogh before he will be famous: *Besuch bei Van Gogh (Visit with Van Gogh)*.

OCTOBER 24

Giulietta Masina as Feather Fairy *Perinbaba (Frau Holle/Mother Holly)* in a Czech-German-Austrian co-production. Omnia Film Munich and Second Channel TV ZDF Mainz were the German co-producers.

Gespenstergeschichten (Ghost Stories): TV series (each episode 30 minutes) directed by **George Moorse** and Wolfgang Panzer with Wolfgang Büttner,

Peer Augustinski, Gabriel Barylli, Ilse Biberti, Ruth-Maria Kubitschek and **Udo Kier**. Writers: **Rainer Erler**, E. F. Benson, Elizabeth Bowen, Amelia Edwards, Amelia Jacobs, W. W. Jacobs, Marie Luise Kaschnitz, John MacLaughlin, Oliver Storz.

NOVEMBER 21

Joey: Following the death of his father, nine-year-old telekinetic Joey is plagued by a sinister ventriloquist's dummy. A sequence in which the owner, the ventriloquist himself who didn't realize that he is dead, comes to ghostly life again get lost on the cutting room floor so that the story appeared a little bit uncomprehensible until all hell broke loose, including a lot of *Star Wars* merchandise and a cheeseburger monster. *Joey* was put together from bits and parts of *Poltergeist*, *E.T.*, *Goonies* and other American movies by young **Roland Emmerich** in a factory hall in Magdstadt near his hometown Sindelfingen. The music (by Hubert Bartholomae) went all John Williams. Released in a cut version in the United States as *Making Contact* by New World Pictures.

DECEMBER 12

When director Richard Loncraine failed to settle the extraterrestrial world of Fyrine IV on a remote volcanic island off the coast of Iceland, Twentieth Century Fox turned to German director **Wolfgang Petersen** who insisted on shooting *Enemy Mine*, sort of an unauthorized remake of *Robinson Crusoe on Mars*, the meeting of an Astronaut and a Drac, similar to Defoe's Robinson and Friday, on Bavaria stages in Munich.

In addition:

Cuban animated feature *¡Vampiros En La Habana!* by Juan Padrón was co-produced with German participation (Manfred Durniok) and released in this country as *Krieg der Vampire* (*War of the Vampires*).

1986

Federal Republic of Germany
Cinemas: 3262
Attendance figure: 105 million
Feature films produced: 60

German Democratic Republic
Cinemas: 823
Attendance figure: 71 million
Feature films produced: 15

JANUARY 19

Der Bärenhäuter (The Bear-Skinned Man): DEFA fairy tale directed by Walter Beck.

FEBRUARY

Exhibition *Asterix, Mickey Mouse & Co.* opened in Berlin (West).

JUNE 19

Der Sommer des Samurai (The Summer of the Samurai) by Hans-Christoph Blumenberg with Hans Peter Hallwachs as "Japan Phantom", a mysterious, black-robed burglar, and Nadja Tiller as Dr. Feuillade. Blumenberg, a former film critic and film historian, borrowed the name Feuillade from French serial pioneer Louis Feuillade.

JULY

Video premiere of the German-Czech co-production *Die Galoschen des Glücks (The Magic Shoes)*.

JULY 17

Michael Ende's 1973 parable *Momo* about grey men who come and create accounts to collect time and therefore evoke stress among the once peaceful community. Directed by Johannes Schaaf with Radost Bokel as young girl Momo, Armin Müller-Stahl as leader of the grey men and John Huston as Master Hora. Co-produced by Rialto (**Horst Wendlandt**) and Iduna Film (Leo Kirch) in Rome at Cinecittà Studios. The project had been put in a waiting position for some time, because Ende wasn't pleased with the original screenplay. Eventually he agreed with Schaaf's concept.

JULY 30

Orchideen des Wahnsinns (Orchids of Madness) by Nikolai Müllerschön: A nightmarish stay in a castle. Somebody has killed Vera's father and now wants to kill the sole heiress.

OCTOBER 9

Once-successful director **Dr. Harald Reinl** was stabbed by his third wife, Czech starlet Daniela Maria Delis, an alcoholic, in their apartment in Pueto de la Cruz, Teneriffa.

OCTOBER 30

An alien (played by Carlos Pavlidis) lands in rural Bavaria but everybody takes him for a tourist, including young Xaver: *Xaver und sein ausserirdischer Freund (Xaver and his Extra-Terrestrial Friend)*. Directed by Werner Possardt and obviously inspired by *E.T.*

*NEWS—Bericht über eine Reise in eine strahlende Zukunft (Journey to a Glowing Future/*U.S.: *The Nuclear Conspiracy)* by **Rainer Erler** dealing with the nuclear waste of European and Japanese power plants which represents a desirable target for ruthless profiteers. Concentrated death, in the wrong hands, is profitable merchandise. The owners believe that the consignment is bound for a high-tech recycling plant in Australia but David, a freelance journalist with the London-based News agency, is suspicious. He is hot on the trail hoping to make a scoop with the scandal of the century. But the crooks are already after him…

In addition:

A concept for a series *Die Murks (The Goofs)* conceived by Rolf Giesen was canceled shortly before signing of contracts between FuturEffects Berlin and WDR Television Cologne: Hans Bacher and Harald Siepermann, later with Disney, had designed a surefire trio of mischievous (animated) gremlin-like characters that were walled in the cathedral of Cologne but revived in present-day Cologne. The Bläck Fööss, a well-known music group, had already recorded a title song. Ten years later Disney used a similar concept for three gargoyles in *The Hunchback of Notre Dame* but that's just a coincidence.

Original model sheet *Die Murks (The Goofs)* | Authors' collection

Originally, Hans Bacher was supposed to design an animated TV feature *Die grosse Käseverschwörung (The Great Cheese Conspiracy)*, but Gert K. Müntefering (WDR TV in Cologne) decided to have the movie produced in Prague.

Václav Bedřich directed, Gene Deitch, an American working in Czechoslovakia, assisted the director in designing the characters.

1987

Federal Republic of Germany
Cinemas: 3252
Attendance figure: 108 million
Feature films produced: 65

German Democratic Republic
Cinemas: 821
Attendance figure: 69 million
Feature films produced: 15

FEBRUARY 26

With *Hatschipuh* producers Matthias Deyle, Martin Moszkowicz and Leon Pulwer tried to cash in on the *Pumuckl* formula of mixing 2D-animated gnomes with live action about a farm that has to be saved.

JUNE 25

Roland Emmerich's *Hollywood Monster (Ghost Chase)* with a ghost butler who looks like E.T.'s uncle.

Magic Sticks by Peter Keglevic: A down-and-out drummer (played by George Kranz) obtains a pair of magic drumsticks from a street vendor.

JULY 3

Rolf Losansky's DEFA children's film *Das Schulgespenst (The School Ghost)* featured Carola Huflattich (Nicole Lichtenheldt who was cast in Frankfurt/Oder) who is full of mischief and likes fooling around at school. One day

Carola has a brainwave. She invents an "International Ghost's Day" and draws the matching ghost called "Buh" (Boo!) on the blackboard. "Buh" immediately is alive, thanks to cut-out animation by Heiko Ebert, Tony Loeser and cameraman Erich Günther.

AUGUST

A **Fantasy Film Fest** was founded in Hamburg that expanded over the years and toured through Germany.

OCTOBER 29

Wim Wenders' *Der Himmel über Berlin (The Sky Over Berlin/Wings of Desire)* has Bruno Ganz as Damiel and Otto Sander as Cassiel, two angels, wander around West Berlin. Peter Handke co-wrote the screenplay. Photography by Henri Alékan.

DECEMBER 13

DEFA's *Hasenherz (The Coward)* tells of a 13-year-old girl named Janni (Bettina Hohensee). Janni is grief-stricken because she isn't taken seriously as a girl by her classmates. One day, a film director, taking her for a boy, casts her in the role of a prince in a fairy tale film.

DECEMBER 17

Das Mädchen mit den Feuerzeugen (Cripples Go Christmas): Four disabled persons receive the gift of three wishes. Co-written and directed by Ralf Huettner.

DECEMBER 19

Günter Meyer's East-German TV Spook series was continued with *Spuk von draussen (Spook from Outside)* featuring nine 30-minute episodes.

In addition:

This year young fan Jörg Buttgereit made a 16mm underground splatter film titled *NEKRomantik*.

1988

Federal Republic of Germany
Cinemas: 3246
Attendance figure: 109 million
Feature films produced: 57

German Democratic Republic
Cinemas: 808
Attendance figure: 69 million
Feature films produced: 15

MARCH 16

Hollywood talent agent (and former Universal producer) **Paul Kohner** died in Los Angeles.

MARCH 24

In der Arche ist der Wurm drin (Stowaways on the Ark): Feature-length animation by Wolfgang Urchs about a woodworm named Willie who is accused to be responsible for a leak in Noah's Ark, but the real culprits are termites that must be stopped. With this only mildly successful movie Dr. Michael Schoemann tried to establish himself as Germany's leading animation producer.

JUNE 30

Zärtliche Chaoten II (Lovable Zanies II): Begins in Year 2038. Two clearks working at the patent office use a time machine to travel 50 years backwards and prevent the birth of their mean boss. Produced by Munich-based Roxy Film Luggi Waldleitner and Karl Spiehs with the support of Second Channel TV. Directed by TV star Thomas Gottschalk and Holm Dressler. David Hasselhoff seen in a supporting role.

JULY 1

DEFA's *Froschkönig (The Frog Prince)*: Walter Beck's ill-fated version of the fairy tale that seemed to be more inspired by Socialist Realism than Grimm, with a fat, almost immobile stop-motion frog.

AUGUST 5

Felix und der Wolf (Felix and the Wolf), a DEFA children's film.

SEPTEMBER 25

Der Eisenhans (Iron John), a DEFA fairy tale: Iron Jack guards over forests and animals and is therefore always opposed to the king who is asking for animals slaim for his opulent banquets. The king commissions the Black Hunter to arrest him, but Prince Joachim, the king's son, defies his father's demands and flees with Jack into the woods.

OCTOBER 27

Faust—Vom Himmel durch die Welt zur Hölle (Faust: The Movie) directed by Dieter Dorn at Bavaria Studios: Helmut Griem as Faust, Romuald Pekny as Mephistopheles and Cornelia Froboess as Marthe Schwerdtlein.

DECEMBER 1

Der Fluch (The Curse) by Ralf Huettner: Vacationers in distress when 8-year-old Melanie finds the corpse of a girl in the mountains that looks like a doppelganger.

DECEMBER 8

German premiere of *The Adventures of Baron Munchausen (Die Abenteuer des Baron Münchhausen)*: By invitation of the film's producer, I visited the set at Cinecittà in Rome watching the shooting of Munchausen's ride on a cannonball in a newly erected blue screen stage. Gilliam claimed to have been inspired by Karel Zeman's Czech fantasy film *Baron Prášil (Baron Münchhausen)*, but to me it was pretty much like the Ufa *Münchhausen* of 1943. I only learned later from director Terry Gilliam that the project started with the idea of showing the baron riding half a horse. They couldn't figure, however, how to solve that shot in pre-digital days. Everything went wrong during production—including the appearance of a German producer. The picture proved a disaster to the European completion bond system.

DECEMBER 26

At the end of the year, as usual, a fairy tale on East German TV: *Rapunzel oder Der Zauber der Tränen (Rapunzel or: The Magic of Tears)* with Sylvia Wolff. Directed by Ursula Schmenger at DEFA Studio für Spielfilme in Babelsberg.

In addition:

Ferdinand Raimund's play *Das Mädchen aus der Feenwelt oder Der Bauer als Millionär (The Peasant as Millionaire)* directed by Jürgen Flimm and recorded for TV.

1989

Federal Republic of Germany
Cinemas: 3216
Attendance figure: 102 million
Feature films produced: 68

German Democratic Republic
Cinemas: 805
Attendance figure: 65 million
Feature films produced: 14

APRIL

Todesvisionen—Geisterstunde (Deadly Visions—Witching Hour), another low-budget horror video: *Four mysterious stories—four deradly secrets—four gruesome murders.*

Macao oder die Rückseite des Meeres: Writer/Director Clemens Klopfenstein's beautiful and profound movie **Macao** *focuses on a married couple, Swiss linguists, who hike the Alps searching for rare words still uttered by rural populations. When on his way to a conference, the husband's plane goes down over the ocean. The wife is advised to give up hope of ever seeing him alive, but her heart tells her otherwise. When he comes ashore on a tropical island—warm blue water, sun on white sands, palm trees—he and the other survivor, the plane's pilot, are greeted by the smiling dark-skinned native speaking the island's language. Back home, she waits to hear word from the search team; on the island, he learns a few words of the native language while he awaits rescue. [...]* **Macao** *reminds us that we, like a film, are shadows on screen, briefly flickering, imprinted in the memory of those who loved us.* [63] Co-financed by Swiss and German TV.

OCTOBER 7

Zucker—Eine wirklich süsse Katastrophe (Sugar) by **Rainer Erler** premiered at the Festival of Fantastic Films in Munich: Genetically modified microbes that turn all paper to sugar escape from a laboratory.

---

63 Clemens Klopfenstein's Website.

OCTOBER 12

Asterix, the Gaul comic book character, this time not only French but German-French co-produced: *Asterix Operation Hinkelstein (Le Coup du Menhir/ Asterix and the Big Fight)* was based on two Asterix comic books—the very good *Asterix and the Big Fight*, from which it took only the premise, and a lesser one, *The Seer*.

NOVEMBER 9-10

Opening of the Berlin Wall and the border that separated East from West Germany.

Reineke Fuchs (Reynard the Fox) co-produced by Manfred Durniok Produktion für Film & Fernsehen, Berlin and Zweites Deutsches Fernsehen ZDF with Oriental Communications and Shanghai Animation Film Studio. Directors: He Yumen and Zhuang Minjin.

Johann Wolfgang von Goethe's poem (1793/94) in 2D animation. Manfred Durniok (1934-2003), the Berlin-based producer of István Szabó's *Mephisto* and *Oberst Redl*, had not only the dream to become a German Walt Disney. His second ambition: to produce animation cheaply. Durniok was Honorary Citizen of Beijing and fondly remembered by old members of the Chinese animation community. *Manfred Durniok was always drawn to distant places. A traveler in many continents, it was specially Asia which attracted him most. As one of the pioneers who brought Asian films to the attention of Western audiences, he promoted at the same time through co-productions the cultural encounters between East and West in films.* His work included Japan, Thailand and eventually China: *Manfred Durniok's first visit to China was in 1971. Shortly after, he made his first documentary for German television there in the People's Republic of China, followed by many other documentaries. It was during this time, in the beginning of the 70s, when Chinese films were nearly unknown outside China, that Manfred Durniok began to screen and select Chinese films in order to introduce them to German audiences.* [64]

---

64 www.durniok.com

NOVEMBER 11

Francesco Stefani died in Munich. In the 1960s the director of fairy tales had worked as editorial manager for Bayerischer Rundfunk.

In addition:

Thanks to video, more and more film amateurs got on the bandwagon: 20-year-old Olaf Ittenbach's first splatter movie *Black Past* was produced with the miniscule budget of 10,000 Deutschmark (and this is the highest estimate). Ittenbach played a character named Tommy who finds himself in front of a cursed mirror.

Another entry in this endless series of trash was *Violent Shit* with Andreas Schnaas as Karl the Butcher, a cannibalistic killer. Hamburg-born Schnaas was inspired by Lucio Fulci, Joe D'Amato and similar auteurs and got this project off the ground by saving 5000 Deutschmarks. Warning: We are going to cover these amateur efforts in this book not completely. They need stronger stomachs than mine.

More sincere was the following entry:

NOVEMBER 30

Laurin by **Robert Sigl**, a graduate of the Munich Hochschule für Film und Fernsehen. *Laurin* is a fairy-tale-like horror film set in 1900: In a sinister town located by the sea a little girl, Laurin, aged 12, hears a cry of help. From her window she sees a boy being kidnapped by an adult. At the same night, Flora, Laurin's mother, encounters the culprit on a bridge. The next day her body is found at the bottom of the bridge. A killer is prowling around the location. Finally, Laurin gifted with psychic powers unmasks the local schoolteacher as child murderer.

Laurin is nothing short than a "true masterpiece, a fantastic tale whose atmosphere evokes the stories of Perrault or the Grimm Brothers". [65]

The movie produced in Hungary won the Bavarian Film Award for Best Direction by a Newcomer.

1990

Federal Republic of Germany
Cinemas: 3754
Attendance figure: 103 million
Feature films produced: 48 (West Germany) and 21 (East Germany)

JANUARY 25

Es ist nicht leicht, ein Gott zu sein (Hard to Be a God), a West German-Soviet co-production directed by Peter Fleischmann, based on a dystopian science fiction novel by Boris and Arkady Strugatsky: A group of scientists from Earth study the middle-ages on a planet with living quite similar.

Der Todesking (The Death King): 7 episodes of violent death conceived by Jörg Buttgereit.

FEBRUARY 15

Actor **Henry Brandon** died in Los Angeles.

Die Geschichte der Dienerin (The Handmaid's Tale): U.S.-German co-production directed by Volker Schlöndorff: A young woman (Natasha Richardson) is put in sexual slavery in the right wing, totalitarian, religious tyranny of a polluted future in New England. Harold Pinter adapted the dystopian novel by Margaret Atwood.

---

65 Rüdiger Suchsland.

When his sci-fi movie about a helicopter defense force of criminals assigned to protect a mining station on remote *Moon 44* was mocked at a press screening in Berlin's *Hollywood* Cinema it was the last straw for director **Roland Emmerich**. He decided to leave Germany and try his luck elsewhere.

MARCH 26

Academy Award for German animation short *Balance* by brothers Wolfgang and Christoph Lauenstein.

APRIL 8

Der Drache Daniel (Daniel the Dragon), a modern DEFA fairy tale by Hans Kratzert: Eight-year-old Daniel mutates into a humanoid dragon.

MAY 24

Dr. M: In the not-too-distant future, West Berlin is shocked by a series of suicides that spreads like a virus. the people of West Berlin fall victim to a virus. A policeman's investigations lead to the sinister plot of a master criminal. Alan Bates as Mabuse-like criminal in a film directed by Claude Chabrol.

OCTOBER 3

German reunification. GDR officially joined the Federal Republic of Germany.

OCTOBER 13

A TV animation series with the duck character *Alfred J. Kwak* co-produced by the Netherlands, Spain, Japan and Germany.

OCTOBER 18

Wenn du gross bist, lieber Adam (When You Grow Up, Dear Adam): Egon Günther's fantasy was canceled by GDR politics in 1966 but could be reconstructed by the director in 1989/90 and finally shown. The title character, a boy named Adam (Stephan Jahnke), receives a flashlight from a white swan in a tram. This flashlight has special powers that lift every liar into the air. Adam and his father Sepp (Gerry Wolff) decide to produce it in series, but nobody is going for it.

OCTOBER 25

While author **Michael Ende** denied Part One of the film adaptation of his novel *The NeverEnding Story* he appeared on stage at the Berlin Zoo Palace premiere of the second part *Die unendliche Geschichte 2: Auf der Suche nach Phantásien (The NeverEnding Story II: The Next Chapter)* that was ineptly screenwritten by an inexperienced Karin Howard and ill-cast with Jonathan Brandis (who committed suicide at age 27 in 2003) as Bastian Balthasar Bux who again enters the pages of the magic book and returns to Fantasia to fight evil sorceress Xayide and her monstrous henchmen. Derek Meddings supervised the model shots of Bavaria Studios. Albert Whitlock came out of retirement in Santa Barbara to Munich to supervise the matte shots on behalf of Illusion Arts. The George Miller who is credited as director is not identical with the George Miller of *Mad Max* fame. He was born in Edinburgh, Scotland and mainly working in TV.

NOVEMBER 29

"Enfant terrible" Christof Schlingensief created a satirical German Chainsaw Massacre: *Das deutsche Kettensägenmassaker* (U.S. title: *Blackest Heart*). 16 million East Germans on their way to the West. 4 % never got there— but ended in the arms of a household of butchers. Actor Reinald Schnell (as Kurti): *Today we have sausages on offer.*

The German Chainsaw Massacre *is the second chapter of Schlingensief's German Trilogy. It's a genuine horror movie, but so over-the-top that you can't take it seriously. It's actually very funny, in a disgusting sort of way, mimicking American slasher movies while also satirizing German fears of reunification. (I think it's also a comment on how ordinary people in the East were treated like pack animals—or sausages!—to feed the hungry West German labour market.)* [66]

A big success in German cinemas (appox. 4,8 million admissions) was a live action/animation mix based on Brösel's (=Rötger Feldmann's) comic strip character *Werner—Beinhart!* The artist as himself desperately trying to find ideas for his (animated) cartoon character Werner. Live action directed by Niki List, animation by Gerhard Hahn.

Wolfgang Urchs' 2D animated version of Gerdt von Bassewitz' *Peterchens Mondfahrt (Peter in Magicland)*: Two kids join a beetle to retrieve his lost arm from the Man in the Moon.

Theo Kerp's 2D-animated version of Antoine de Saint-Exupéry's *Der kleine Prinz (The Little Prince)* commissioned by German Second Channel TV.

König Phantasielos: the last East-German produced TV fairy tale.

1991

Cinemas: 3686
Attendance figure: 120 million
72 feature films produced

FEBRUARY 9

The Phantom of the Opera, mini-series with Burt Lancaster, co-produced by Leo Kirch's Munich-based Beta Film, shown at the Monte-Carlo Television Festival.

---

66   Daniel Garber, *Christoph Schlingensief: Approach those you fear.* https://danielgarber.wordpress.com/tag/cheristof-schlingensief-art-without-borders/

FEBRUARY 11

Olle Hexe (Ole Witch): The last fairy tale produced by DEFA was directed by Günter Meyer. The company went into receivership after the fall of GDR. The Babelsberg Studios operated by DEFA were privatized. Two children and a blind horse are entering the castle of the old witch. Among the relics in the castle (only seen when you entered the original set) was a Karl Marx bust.

FEBRUARY 16

Hamburg-based Swiss-German filmmaker Michel Bergman cast entertainer Silvio Francesco, better known as brother of German singer Caterina Valente, as Maximilian, as aging silent film actor, who is stuck in a movie theater and wants to return to his film. Bergman made the acquaintance of Forrest J Ackerman and added him and some of his cohorts (Bobbie and Frank Bresee, **Ferdy Mayne**, Sara Karloff, Mike Jittlov, Ann Robinson, Brinke Stevens, John Baxter, and Bill Warren). *My Lovely Monster* was first shown at the Berlin International Film Festival.

MARCH 6

Die Kaltenbach Papiere (The Kaltenbach Papers), a two-part mini-series written and directed by **Rainer Erler**: Three nuclear warheads on their way to their final destination in North Africa. Two journalists and the daughter of weapon dealer Kaltenbach try to stop the deadly cargo. With Mario Adorf and Gudrun Landgrebe.

MARCH 21

Lippels Traum (Lippel's Dream) based on a novel by Paul Maar.

JUNE

NEKRomantik 2: Die Rückkehr der lebenden Toten (The Return of the Living Dead): Jörg Buttgereit's sequel amateur movie devoted to necrophilia.

A direct response to the West German government's cracking down on graphic horror films in the wake of the so-called British "video nasties panic" during the early eighties, **NekRomantik 2**—*much like its 1987 predecessor* **NekRomantik**—*probes the limits of artistic expression through a no-holds-barred engagement with the extreme taboo of necrophilia. At the same time, however, the sequel plays with the expectations of the ever-watchful German authorities, anticipating the cuts that would presumably be imposed by the regulatory bodies in order to allow for an official release. In* **NekRomantik 2** *the fault lines—so to speak—are located between long stretches of art-house* ennui *as eruptions of strong violence and deviant sexuality, creating a formal frame that separates the graphic moments from the rather mundane rest and crafting a highly symmetrical text. The result is a fierce attack on the stigmatization of violent art that results from a blanket condemnation of the horror genre as an inferior and emotionally scarring form of debased entertainment.*[67]

SEPTEMBER 12

Bis ans Ende der Welt (Until the End of the World): The future of 1999 according to Wim Wenders who called special effects in a TV show in February 1985 special defects but had to use them now while shooting interiors in Babelsberg, including the model of a space station, glass paintings and robots.

In the year 1999, the world is on the edge of a knife as a rogue nuclear satellite is going to crash. But Wenders wouldn't be Wenders if he would have made a disaster movie:

Conceived as the ultimate road movie, this decades-in-the-making science-fiction epic from Wim Wenders follows the restless Claire Tourneur (Solveig Dommartin) across continents as she pursues a mysterious stranger (William Hurt) in possession of a device that can make the blind see and bring dream images to waking life. With an eclectic soundtrack that gathers a host of the director's favorite musicians, along with gorgeous cinematography by Robby Müller, this breathless adventure in the

---

67 Kai-Uwe Werbeck, *The State vs. Buttgereit and Ittenbach: Censorship and Subversion in German No-Budget Horror Film*. In: Journal of the Fantastic in the Arts. Vol. 27, No. 3 (2016).

shadow of Armageddon takes its heroes to the ends of the earth and into the oneiric depths of their own souls. [68]

SEPTEMBER 13

Der Hausgeist (The Household Ghost): 21 episodes of a ZDF TV series with Susanne Uhlen as Henriette von Sydeck, a ghost on the track of Barbara Eden as *Jeannie*.

NOVEMBER 23

Klaus Kinski died in Lagunita near San Francisco.

NOVEMBER 28

German co-producers joined the Swedish-Norwegian-French fantasy *Kvitebjørn Kong Valemon (Der Eisbärkönig)*: the story of a princess and a prince who is transformed into a polar bear by the forces of black magic.

In addition:

I Know the Way to the Hofbräuhaus: a confused Super 8 silent by Herbert Achternbusch in which the dead mix with the living, including the protagonist (Achternbusch himself) falling in love with a mummy.

Zombie '90: Extreme Pestilence by Andreas Schnaas: Another (75 minute) low budget epidemic of zombieism announced as the *Ultimate Gore Film* but definitely amateurish.

The Butcher, 58-minute video (complete with obligatory chainsaw): *A Nightmare of Blood and Violence!*

---

68 www.criterion.com.

1992

Cinemas: 3630
Attendance figure: 106 million
63 feature films produced

FEBRUARY 14

*Die Abenteuer von Pico und Columbus (The Adventures of Pico and Columbus/*U.S.: *The Magic Voyage)*: Although *Stowaways on the Ark* was only mildly successful, producer Michael Schoemann decided to continue his worm stories with a smart wood worm who accompanies Christopher Columbus on his voyage to the new world. The movie turned out one of the biggest failures in German animation film history. It was released in the United States by Hemdale (with Dom DeLuise dubbing Columbus and Mickey Rooney as narrator) but due to problems with that company no dollars returned from America.

MAY 10

Babelsberg-produced TV series (8 episodes) *Sherlock Holmes und die sieben Zwerge (Sherlock Holmes and the Seven Dwarfs)* directed by Günter Meyer: Retired police chief Hans Holms (played by Hans Müller) is called out of retirement when the seven dwarfs turn up and tell that Snow White has been kidnapped.

MAY 13

At the Cannes Film Festival Austrian director Michael Haneke's shocking film *Bennys Video* was shown: A 14-year-old rather apathetic video enthusiast is caught in his makeshift world of violent imagery, a dilemma that ensnares the whole family. Some German actors were cast: Angela Winkler and Ulrich Mühe.

MAY 21

Natja Brunckhorst (*Christiane F.*) sinks into a nightmare of fright after becoming pregnant as the result of a one-night stand: Ralf Huettner's *Babylon—Im Bett mit dem Teufel (Babylon: In Bed with the Devil)*.

JUNE 6

Out of all places, Munich-based Bavaria opened a new film park in far-away Bottrop Kirchhellen located on the former site of Traumland Park (which, economically, proved the wrong choice and had to be closed after only two seasons). Part of the attractions were *Spaceship Orion* and an *FX Stage* arranged by Rolf Giesen (in association with Deutsche Kinemathek Berlin) and designed by Rolf Zehetbauer. The Stage presented original items from *Dr. Caligari*, F. W. Murnau's *Faust*, *The NeverEnding Story* and stop-motion artifacts created by Ray Harryhausen who, accompanied by his wife Diana, attended the opening as guest of honor.

JUNE 27

Das kleine Gespenst (The Little Ghost): Curt Linda's 2D-animated version of Otfried Preussler's ghost tale at the Munich Film Festival.

AUGUST 27

Puppet film producer **Ferdinand Diehl** died in Gräfelfing near Munich.

OCTOBER 30

Christof Schlingensief's *Terror 2000—Intensivstation Deutschland (Terror 2000: Intensive Care Unit Germany)*, co-written by Oskar Roehler, is another re-unification horror: *Springtime for Hitler... Again?* Margit Carstensen, Peter Kern and **Udo Kier** were in the cast.

NOVEMBER 5

Schneewittchen und das Geheimnis der Zwerge (Snow White and the Secret of the Dwarfs): Czech-German co-production with Natalie Minko as Snow White, Gudrun Landgrebe as evil queen and Dietmar Schönherr as King.

NOVEMBER 21

Sommer der Liebe (Summer of Love): Bizarre low-budget fantasy about a travelling Hippie Messias calling himself Oleander, directed by Braunschweig-born Wenzel Storch who at the time of the making was turning to LSD.

DECEMBER 25

TV mini-series of *Little Peter's Journey to the Moon: Peterchens Mondfahrt* produced by Iduna for ZDF.

In addition:

The Burning Moon: Olaf Ittenbach linked two short horror films with a drug-addicted character who reads these two "bedtime" stories to his little sister. *Dieser Film überschreitet alle Grenzen—This film exceeds all limits.*

Violent Shit II "starring" director Andreas Schnaas as Karl 'The Butcher' Junior who continues where his father left off.

Urban Scumbags vs. Countryside Zombies by Sebastian Panneck and Patrick Hollmann.

1993

Cinemas: 3735
Attendance figure: 131 million
67 feature films produced

FEBRUARY

Celebrating *King Kong's* 60th birthday, Berlin International Film Festival, Sat.1 and Kirch Group presented a huge statue of Kong (designed by Ray Harryhausen and made at the workshops of Bavaria Studios Munich) atop the Zoo Palace.

MAY 18

The Cannes Film Festival presented Wim Wenders' sequel to *Himmel über Berlin*: *In weiter Ferne, so nah! (Faraway, So Close)*. Besides Otto Sander and Bruno Ganz as angels Cassiel and Damiel the cast included Peter Falk, Horst Buchholz, Mikhail Gorbachev (!), **Nastassja Kinski**, Willem Dafoe and Heinz Rühmann.

Jörg Buttgereit continued his amateur film career with the bloody memories of serial killer *Schramm* played by Florian Koerner von Gustorf.

JULY 1

Der Sandmann (The Sandman) based on **E. T. A. Hoffmann**.

NOVEMBER 11

Zirri—Das Wolkenschaf (Cirry, the Cloud Lamb), **Rolf Losansky**'s final film for the recently defunct DEFA with a partly animated title animal, a white cloud sheep that was kicked out of the sky by evil black clouds. Based on a children's book by Fred Rodrian and Werner Klemke.

Seven years Lutz Dammbeck had worked on a 45-minute animation project titled *Herzog Ernst (Duke Ernest)*: Young Duke Ernest wants to become a good knight, but the circumstances are against him. The emperor who wants to claim the Duke's castle and marry his mother has Ernest wrongfully accused of murder and thrown him in the dungeon. Ernest's only chance to escape the death penalty is to join the army and go to the Orient in search of the legendary Carbuncle Stone.

DECEMBER 9

Donald Sutherland as Jonathan Younger who lives in a reality of his own in Percy Adlon's fantasy drama *Younger and Younger*.

DECEMBER 16

The legacy of the defunct DEFA Studio für Trickfilme in Dresden was transformed into a German Institute for Animated Films: Deutsches Institut für Animationsfilm.

DECEMBER

Rolf Giesen and Friedhelm Schatz moved the attractions of the former Bavaria Film Park's *FX Stage* from Bottrop Kirchhellen to the Babelsberg Film Park. Highlight was again the collection of Ray Harryhausen stop-motion memorabilia.

1994

Cinemas: 3795
Attendance figure: 133 million
60 feature films produced

FEBRUARY 3

Amoklauf by **Uwe Boll**: A waiter goes on a killing *rampage*.

MARCH 24

Pumuckl und der blaue Klabauter (Pumuckl and the Blue Ship's Kobold) added a second animated hobgoblin onboard of a steamboat on the Blue Danube to the *Pumuckl* series.

JUNE 2

Roland Emmerich became the mentor of Munich film students Klaus Knoesel and Holger Neuhäuser who mixed sci-fi and Monty Pythonesque medieval knights (led by John Rhys-Davies) who are entering an alien spaceship to conquer the Holy Land in *The High Crusade*. Former sex actor Rinaldo Talamonti as the Alien Chief. Based on a book by Poul Anderson. Motion Control and model shots by Karl-Heinz Christmann.

Karl-Heinz Christmann preparing model shoot and rigging motion control for *The High Crusade*
Courtesy of Karl-Heinz Christmann (KC Filmeffects), Kaiserslautern

OCTOBER 4

At the Ghent Film Festival: a Franco-Belgian/German/Hungarian/British/American co-production to promote Bibo Films'Toccata VFX/animation system was shown depicting the totalitarian, anti-machine world of *Taxandria*. *Taxandria* was the brainchild of Belgian director Raoul Servais, years in the planning (and postproduction), and starred Armin Mueller-Stahl.

Servais was heavily inspired by the Belgian surrealists, including Magritte, Ensor and Paul Delvaux and brought their paintings to life in Taxandria. *The film perfected his technique of "Servaisgraphy", a mixing of his own animation, as well as live images and actors. [...]*

The plot of the film is rather dizzying: an eccentric lighthouse keeper shows a curious young prince the way to the kingdom of "Taxandria", where everyone lives in a state of the "eternal present", wherein no technological progress can be made as per the local dictator's decree. They have no past or present, women are kept away from men and everything is stifled by a bloated absurd, Kafkaesque bureaucracy. The Prince meets an inventor named Aimé who dreams of flying away, making new inventions and yearns to learn about his country's past. Love, time, the black humour of endless bureaucracy—they're all fodder to be picked apart through Servais' gaze... [69]

OCTOBER 27

Suggested by this writer, producer Dieter Geissler moved his production activities from Bavaria Munich to the Babelsberg Studios and continued his **Michael Ende** film series with *Die unendliche Geschichte III: Rettung aus Phantásien (The NeverEnding Story III: Return to Fantasia)* directed by Peter MacDonald (who wasn't allowed to cut the movie which was trimmed by the producer himself). Part III turned out the worst of the series: A group of Nasties (no, not the Nazis) steal the magic book, the entry to a world of imagination, and enter the portal to Fantasia. Jason James Richter, known from *Free*

---

[69] Francky Knapp, *Where has the Dystopian Wonderland of Taxandria been Hiding all Our Lives?* June 28, 2019. https://www.messynessychic.com/2019/06/28/where-has-the-dystopian-wonderland-of-taxandria-been-hiding-all-our-lives/

Willy, as Bastian Balthasar Bux. Jack Black, in one of his first movie roles, is seen as Slip, the gang leader of the Nasties. User review on IMDb: *This movie does belong in a class by itself: Even worse than utterly terrible.* Geissler tried to save his operations by co-producing an animated TV series *The NeverEnding Story* with Nelvana Canda and installing a revolving production fund with Nordstern, an insurance group, but a few years later had to face bankruptcy.

NOVEMBER 3

A cat investigates brutal muders: *Felidae* animated under the supervision of Michael Schaack. Akif Pirinçci, who wrote the feline crime novel this animated feature film was based on, later sided with right-wing populists.

Curt Linda finished the 2D animation of *Harold und die Geister (Harold and the Ghosts)* for producer Franz J. Stockmann: Harold Mortimer Franklin McKelly is the last of a formerly wealthy Scottish Clan. All that is left to him is a decaying castle filled with his spooky ancestors. In his anger and despair, Harold decides to get rid of his ghostly ancestry once and for all. He gets his gun amnd chases the ghosts back to the graveyard. There he meets Paulo, a Spaniard, who earns his pay as a gardener. The two quickly become friends and share their problems. Harold tells of his castle and the ghosts and Paulo tells him of his beloved, sunny Spain and how much he would like to return there. Since nothing is keeping them in cold, gray Scotland they decide to travel to Spain together. Over the years, Paulo has built a boat—but how can they get it to the sea? This is when Harold remembers the old story of an enchanted fairy, who was imprisoned by an evil spell in a vase on the cemetery. It is said that if a man with a pure heart frees the fairy from her prison, a great flood will come. With his flood they could free the boat and get it to the sea…

DECEMBER 23

Weihnachten mit Willy Wuff (Christmas with Willy Wuff): Family TV with a speaking dog.

DECEMBER 25

Stella Stellaris: Miniseries directed by **Robert Sigl** about an extraterrestrial by the name of Stella (Sissi Perlinger) who comes from the planet Stellaris to study the feelings and emotions of human beings. Her supernatural powers soon create havoc...

In addition:

FuturEffects pitched a film script titled *Kein Blut für Erich* (*No Blood for Erich*). Matthias Wendlandt, son of Rialto Films' **Horst Wendlandt**, seemed interested in producing a story of vampirism in East Germany, the former German Democratic Republic, but nothing came out of it.

1995

JANUARY 3

A feature film version of the TV series *Sherlock Holmes und die sieben Zwerge (Sherlock Holmes and the Seven Dwarfs)*.

MAY

La Cité de Enfants Perdus (Die Stadt der verlorenen Kinder/The City of Lost Children) at the Cannes Film Festival: A weird scientist named Krank (Daniel Emilfork) kidnaps children in order to steal their dreams and by that slow his own aging process. A former circus strongman (Ron Perlman) whose brother had been kidnapped too sets out on a journey to Krank's nightmarish laboratory. Directed by Jean-Pierre Jeunet and Marc Caro, the creators of *Delicatessen*. Tele München Group joined the French partners in funding.

AUGUST 28

Michael Ende died in Filderstadt.

AUGUST 31

Rainer Matsutani's *Nur über meine Leiche (Over My Dead Body)*: Shot dead by a killer (**Udo Kier**, commissioned by his betrayed wife), Fred (Christoph M. Ohrt) manages to persuade Death to make a deal: He'll receive his old life back—provided he frees three women whose hearts he had broken from misery.

SEPTEMBER

Götz George won Coppa Volpi as Best Actor at the Venice Film Festival for his portrayal of Fritz Haarmann in Thomas Schühly's production *Der Totmacher (The Deathmaker)* directed by Romuald Karmakar:

Practically a documentary about a German serial killer of the 1920s turned into one-room theater, **The Deathmaker** *is repulsive and fascinating in equal measure. Auds are likely to be sharply divided in their reactions to the gleefully graphic descriptions of dismemberment, while others will tune out on pic's closed room, all-dialogue format.* [...]

Karmakar's documentary apprenticeship is apparent in his first film with actors. Pic's dialogue is lifted verbatim from a stenographer's record of the meetings between Fritz Haarman [...], a salesman who has confessed to murdering 24 young men, and Professor Ernst Schultze (Jurgen Hentsch), who was brought in by the court to determine Haarman's sanity. Film unfolds entirely in a claustrophobic examination room in mental asylum in 1924.[70]

OCTOBER 20

Götz George as Harry Kupfer, a well-known author who is suspected to be a serial killer: TV's *Der Sandmann (The Sandman)* was written by Matthias Seelig and directed by Nico Hofmann.

---

70   Deborah Young, *The Deathmaker*. In: Variety, September 18, 1995.

DECEMBER 3

Weihnachten mit Willy Wuff 2—Eine Mama für Lieschen (Christmas with Willy Wuff 2: A Mom for Lieschen) on TV.

DECEMBER 14

Die Sturzflieger (The Crash Pilots) written by Matthias Seelig and directed by Peter F. Bringmann, the team that gave Germany two successful *Theo* comedies with Marius Müller-Westernhagen and now turned to high-budget sci-fi starring Ingo Naujoks as rebellious space pilot Rio Kowalski and Götz (*Deathmaker*) George as stuttering android was a turkey (most likely the worst part of George's career). Shot at Bavaria Studios and on the lot of a former factory in Duisburg, with special effects supplied from providers in Oberhausen and Babelsberg, the movie's quality was so low that even the distributor (Senator Film Verleih Berlin) refused to have its name connected with the ill-fated production. The people at the effects company, however, were so enthusiastic that they paid money just to be part of the disaster.

In addition:

Berlin Snuff, a 33-minute horror short by Thomas Wind: A TV Action News team in need of audience ratings gives bloody images a little boost.

1996

FEBRUARY 22

United Trash (The Slit) by Christoph Schlingensief (co-written with Oskar Roehler): **Udo Kier** as General Brenner on a U.N. mission in Africa when his virgin wife (Kitten Natividad, a former nude model who had worked with Russ Meyer) suddenly gives birth to a child, like the Virgin Mary.

JUNE 11

Brigitte Helm died in Ascona, Switzerland.

AUGUST 29

Kondom des Grauens (Killer Condom) based on comic books by Ralf König. It looks like an ordinary condom, it feels like a condom, it fits like a condom—but in fact it's rather deadly: one Jaws-like condom. Udo Samel as gay detective Luigi Mackeroni is going to investigate the bloody track of the killer condom. Effects work supervised by Jörg Buttgereit and photographed by Erich Günther. Produced by **Erwin C. Dietrich**.

SEPTEMBER 23

Das Zauberbuch (The Magic Book), German-Czech co-production directed by Vaclav Vorlicek (who did the cult favorite *Drei Haselnüsse für Aschenbrödel/ Three Wishes for Cinderella)*. Tina Ruland as Princess Blanka confronts a witch (played by Mahulena Bocanová).

SEPTEMBER 19

Roland Emmerich returned to Germany in triumph with his Hollywood success *Independence Day*. All former critics fell silent. Highlight was the explosion of the White House by an alien invasion fleet. The blueprint was a movie **Curt Siodmak** had written for Charles H. Schneer and Ray Harryhausen in 1955-56: *Earth vs. the Flying Saucers*. In both films a U.F.O. armada attacks Washington D.C., but while Harryhausen and Schneer have it only landing in front of the White House, Emmerich actually had it destroyed by the spaceship. No American filmmaker would have dared. Nope, they were too patriotic to commit such kind of "blasphemy". For this job a German was needed. Roland Emmerich had the guts to blow a scale model of the White House to pieces.

German special effects people were at hand to design and film the disaster and won an Academy Award for it. VFX supervisor **Volker Engel** worked closely with cinematographers Anna Foester and Philipp Timme. Timme: *The schedule for* **Independence Day** *provided for two takes for each scene that involved explosives. Consequently, two models were built for each of these scenes [as safety factor]—including the White House. […]*

To capture the explosion from all conceivable angles we installed seven cameras with a frame rate between 300 and 120 frames per second. Except for the main camera, all other angles were planned in a way that no further postprocessing was necessary but that they could be used as plain in-camera effects. […] The lighting was finished the day before and when all cameras were ready for shooting, everything went by quite fast. The explosion lasted a few seconds and checking the image on the video monitors the result looked quite spectacular so that the whole set could be wrapped the same night. [71]

OCTOBER

Goblet of Gore, a mystical Viking chalice that brings death and destruction, travels from Iceland to New York. In story construction inspired by Robert Louis Stevenson's *Bottle Imp*. An Andreas Schnaas Film.

In addition:

Schneewittchen und die sieben Zwerge (Snow White and the Seven Dwarfs) co-produced by Manfred Durniok Produktion für Film & Fernsehen, Berlin and Shanghai Animation Film Studio. Grimm Brothers fairy tale made in China. Animation director: Qian Yunda.

1997

JANUARY 2

Heinrich Schafmeister as alien tourist *Harald*.

---

71   Lecture given in Cologne, November 28, 1997.

MARCH 24

Academy Award for Best Animated Short: *Quest,* an experimental stop-motion film by Tyron Montgomery and Thomas Stellmach, Kunsthochschule Kassel.

MARCH 27

A rat world located in the sewers of Manhattan (fighting a new lethal spray that is supposed to kill all rodents) as marionette show of Augsburger Puppenkiste: *Die Story von Monty Spinnerratz (A Rat's Tale).* Shot in a highly funded but ill-fated Would-Be-Hollywood in Oberhausen.

APRIL 10

Jürgen Brauer's *Lorenz im Land der Lügner (Lorenz in the Land of Liars)* filmed in Luxembourg featured a 2D-animated cat provided by Dieter Geissler's Babelsberg-based Cinemagic Studio. Wolfgang Urchs designed a lovely cat that was rejected by animation director Per Lygum who voted for a simple caricature of a cat easier to animate.

APRIL 13

RTL TV feature starring Florian Fitz as *Geisterjäger John Sinclair,* a British investigator for supernatural phenomena fighting a demon who wants to sacrifice a girl in the cathedral of Cologne where John de Mol's production company Endemol was located: *Die Dämonenhochzeit (The Demons' Wedding).* *John Sinclair* was based on the long-running pulp series created by Jason Dark (a.k.a. Helmut Rellergerd). Rellergerd dreamed that somebody like Steven Spielberg would film the series but in the end the TV people hired less expensive Klaus Knoesel.

MAY 11

Kerabans phantastische Reise (Jue jiang de Kailaban/Keraban's Fantastic Voyage): Keraban, a Turk, whom they call Die-Hard, doesn't want to pay the new taxes for passing the Bosporus from Constantinople to Skutari. Instead, he travels round the Black Sea and has many adventures. Jules Verne puppet animation adventure produced with German TV funding by Manfred Durniok in Shanghai. Directecd by Hong Hu Zhao.

JULY 24

Hal Foster's *Prince Valiant (Prinz Eisenherz)* produced by Constantin Film at Babelsberg Studios with Stephen Moyer in the title role, Thomas Kretschmann as Thagnar, Edward Fox as King Arthur and **Udo Kier** as the evil usurper Sligon. One of the sets later served as medieval restaurant at Babelsberg Studios Tour which was cleverly set up by Friedhelm Schatz.

OCTOBER 2

Die furchtlosen Vier (The Fearless Four): Updated animated version of the tale of the Bremen Town Musicians, produced by Eberhard Junkersdorf (mainly active in feature films) with the assistance of Michael Coldewey. Easygoing bloodhound Buster, woeful donkey Fred, graceful Siamese cat Gwendolyn and self-assured rooster Tortellini intend to go to Paris but end as street performers in Bremen and sign with dubious Mix Max Sausages.

DECEMBER 4

Benjamin Blümchen—Seine schönsten Abenteuer: Feature film compilation of Gerhard Hahn-produced direct-to-video cartoons starring an anthropomorphic *Benjamin the Elphant* created by Elfie Donnelly.

DECEMBER 21

Weihnachten mit Willy Wuff 3 (Christmas with Willy Wuff 3).

In addition:

Lexx: The Dark Zone was a weird TV sci-fi series created by Canadians Jeffrey Hirschfield and Halifax-native Paul Donovan. Three fugitives find themselves at the controls of a powerful spaceship called LEXX. Donovan's statements were corresponding with his freakhish mindset: "I think humans are a flawed species, and our characters will reflect that. *Star Trek* tells us that honorable deeds and pure thoughts will make the world a better place. I find that hard to relate to and very boring. Whereas I can identify with someone who runs when they're shot at. They just don't want to die. They have reluctant morality." Even some of the actors found that project a little stupid but Donovan was able to secure some German funding from producer Wolfram Tichy and shot parts of the series (green-screen) at Babelsberg Studios and some of the CGI in a nearby FX house. German directors were Rainer Matsutani and **Robert Sigl**.

Premutos, one of the fallen angels who have ambitions to rule the world, in a video written and directed by Olaf Ittenbach.

1998

JANUARY 8

Die kleine Zauberflöte: Curt Linda's 2D animated children's version of Wolfgang Amadeus Mozart's *The Magic Flute* using the libretto of Emanuel Schikaneder.

JANUARY 30

Actor **Ferdy Mayne** passed away in London.

MAY 21

Sieben Monde (Seven Moons), a werewolf thriller by Peter Fratzscher. Years before his Hollywood career Christoph Waltz is seen in a supporting part.

MAY 31

Kiss My Blood by David Jazay: An East Berlin housewife and a Vampyress in love are chased by a mysterious vampire killer.

AUGUST 8

Zombie: The Resurrection, a German horror video by Holger Breiner and Torsten Lakomy (special effects).

AUGUST 20

Tom Tykwer's 1998 film **Run Lola Run** *(***Lola rennt**, *in German) is often read by film theorists as a "video game" movie. Many aspects of the film are reminiscent of video game elements, including the editing, mise-en-scene, and narrative. Most notably, the 'three run structure' of the narrative is atypical of a film, but commonplace in video games. Video games allow one tov 'restart' following a death ot blunder, just as Lola is able to perform her run three times to get a different outcome.* [...]

Each time Lola does her run, she makes slight changes which in turn cause a different outcome. At the same time, the outcomes still seem fated to happen. [72]

SEPTEMBER 30

Spuk aus der Gruft (Spooky Crypt) by Günter Meyer, sort of a sequel to GDR TV's spooky series *Spuk im Hochhaus*.

OCTOBER 2

HeliCops—Einsatz über Berlin: TV series about an elite unit of the Berlin police using a high-tech prototype helicopter.

---

72   Fiona Merullo, Clothes-Minded: Costumes and Chaos Theory in Run Lola Run. July 21, 2016. https://medium.com/@fionamerullo/clothes-minded-costumes-and-chaos-theory-in-run-lola-run-161f1f7064bd.

NOVEMBER 6

Captain Cosmotic: direct-to-video release "starring" Jan-Hendrik Meyer versus four stupid aliens who set out to steal the earth's core.

NOVEMBER 8

Die Reise um die Erde in 80 Tagen (Around the World in 80 Days), Manfred Durniok's Shanghai-produced puppet film version of Jules Verne's novel.

NOVEMBER 19

After many years that included the deaths of the original producer, Eugen Alexandrow, and scheduled director Per Lygum, with most of the money lost, a cheaply animated version of *Hänsel und Gretel im Zauberwald (The Magic Forest)* was finally finished at Babelsberg Studios by producers Hanns Eckelkamp (Atlas Film), Dieter Geissler (CineVox), Rolf Giesen, Tony Loeser, Fama Film and Iris Productions. Geissler (*The NeverEnding Story*) went bankrupt during production.

1999

JANUARY 31

TV movie *Das Biest im Bodensee (The Beast in the Lake)* co-produced by RTL and Bavaria with a 3D digitized monster terrorizing the Lake of Constanz.

FEBRUARY 18

The son of a man who was killed by a drunk driver takes revenge in a video by Heiko Fipper: *Das komabrutale Duell (The Coma-Brutal Duel)*.

MARCH 21

Violent Shit III: Infantry of Doom by Andreas Schnaas.

APRIL 1

Hot Dogs: Wau—wir sind reich (Millionaire Dogs), an animated feature film written by the couple Karin Howard and Joe Steuben (who was basically a camera operator and passed away the very same year) for producer Michael Schoemann, very similar to Disney's *Aristocats.*

Hans im Glück (Hans in Luck), fairy tale directed by **Rolf Losansky**, produced by Gabriel Genschow.

APRIL 9

A remake of Lucio Fulci's *Man Eater* by his loyal fan Andreas Schnaas: *Anthropophagous 2000.*

JULY

Video special *Die Digedags in grauer Vorzeit (Prehistoric Digedags/The Digedags in the Dim and Distant Past),* a stop motion/2D digital animation special written by Rolf Giesen based on a comic-book series by Hannes Hegen [Hegenbarth] that was quite popular in GDR since 1955. Photographed by Erich Günther on the old SFX stage at Babelsberg Studios. A planned series never materialized, at least not at that time.

JULY 30

George Moorse died in Cologne (working as series director on German TV's *Lindenstrasse*).

AUGUST 9

Das Tal der Schatten (The Valley of Shadows) by Nathaniel Gutmann: Nathalia Wörner as a woman under the spell of an ancient heart develops into a killer.

SEPTEMBER 30

Animation producer Thilo Rothkirch convinced his friend, the new German Warner Bros. head Willi Geike, to co-produce an animated feature film based on his children's TV show *Tobias Totz und sein Löwe (Tobias Totz and his Lion)*. Tobias Totz is a zookeeper who is traveling to Africa to find a girlfriend for his favorite lion. From then on commercial German animation became definitely pre-school oriented. Belgian co-director Piet De Rycker:

By trying to be parent proof, as they do in Germany, educationally and politically correct, a lot of potential is cut already out before one starts a project. It means that there is a stop towards high adventure, not only by the false idea of not having the money to visualize it but just because there is a certain fear to impress, to excel in entertaining filmmaking. This idea of social rightness I see as a self limitation. In Germany there seems to be an unwritten law that says we need to protect future generations from crazy irrational behavior. So we will educate them well, and if things would go out of hand nobody can blame us. This doesn't mean that German movies can't be successful. On the contrary, they might be very popular, on the home market. But elsewhere, they will be hard to sell.

OCTOBER 4

13-episode sci-fi parody *Star Tresh—The De-Generation* (each episode 7 minutes) broadcast by Open Channel Kassel and one year later edited on VHS by Astro Film. An inept alcoholic starship captain named Jean-Luc Godard (!) is given the command of Starship Enterprise *to go where others had been already to see if they are still there*. Directed by Wolfgang Sieber.

NOVEMBER 25

Schrei—denn ich werde dich töten! (Scream—For I Will Kill You), RTL TV movie (shot on 16mm rather than 35mm) written by Kai Meyer and directed by **Robert Sigl**: a *teen giallo* mixing elements from Italian horror films and American slashers with motives of Polanski's *Repulsion* and *The Tenant*.

A brutal killer begins stalking and slashing a group of recently graduated high school students who are trying to leave their mark on the school. One-by-one they are killed until only two are left with a teacher.

Fango Video released it in the United States titled *School's Out*.

"The worldwide success of **Scream** *played a key role in the genesis of* **School's Out**,*" Sigl says. "We were lucky enough that Kai knew this producer, Jan Kromschroeder, who became head of the TV movie department at the German commercial network RTL. He wanted to do a genre project and approached Kai to write it."*

"Actually, he wanted to option my novel **Hex**,*" adds Meyer. "But since that had already been optioned, we decided to work on a new concept. I had wanted to write an original screenplay for a horror film ever since I was a teenager. I had several ideas, but I was pretty sure they wouldn't like any of them because German networks are all about recycling hit concepts from the U.S. But then* **Scream** *was released in Germany and became a huge success, and I told them, 'Look, here's this horror movie that everybody wants to see. How about doing something in the same vein but giving it a more European spin? Even then, it took some time to convince them, but finally RTL, Europe's biggest TV network, greenlighted the project."*

Robert Sigl entered the project after the third draft of the script was written.

"Most critics tried to ditch it because they hated the violence," says Sigl. *"Plus, they're only willing to accept horror films from foreign countries. They treat their own like bastards that didn't deserve to be born. But the audience liked it a lot and it got very high ratings; it was one of the highest-rated TV movies of 1999."* [73]

German premiere of the **Roland Emmerich** exec-produced ill-fated version of Daniel Francis Galouye's novel: *The Thirteenth Floor*. As there was some money offered some minor parts of the VFX were executed in an effects house in Oberhausen.

---

73 Jan Doense, *School's out: Cutting the Class*. In: Fangoria #196.

DECEMBER 4

De apparatspott: Star Trek parody made by Martin Hermann in Sulingen, Lower Saxony.

DECEMBER 9

Vaclav Vorlicek's Czech-German *Die Seekönigin (Queen of the Lake)*.

DECEMBER 16

Käpt'n Blaubär—Der Film (Captain Bluebear: The Movie): Feature-length cinema version with a comic and (since 1990) TV favorite created by Walter Moers. Bluebear tells a lot of nautical yarn.

A short film by Rolf Teigler and Chemnitzer Filmwerkstatt: *Wann ist der Mond eigentlich rund?*

DECEMBER 31

Ray Harryhausen called from London to cancel his involvement in a Babelsberg-planned series *Ray Harryhausen's World of Myth and Legend* after his introduction was already filmed. The intention was to have Ray Harryhausen introduce legends from of all over the world, from Greek mythology to *Ilya Muromets* up to Japanese ghost stories and illustrate the narration with puppet films. After a while of giving it a thought, Harryhausen refused to continue that way and said it had to be *Dynamation* topics, models composited with live-action, not 100 per cent puppet animation. He never thought of his films as puppet films but as VFX productions. "This is what we are identified with," he said and defined it as his trademark. This meant that the puppet film approach was out and VFX were in, but eventually the project was killed not about the quality of VFX but concerning the animation of a *Sinbad* test with a cyclops roasting a sailor and two cyclopes fighting over the victim.

2000

JANUARY 6

Start of a TV series *Geisterjäger John Sinclair (Ghosthunter John Sinclair)* produced at Barrandov Studios in Prague by Endemol for RTL TV. The horrific adventures of pulp series' Scotland Yard inspector who is in permanent combat with the forces of evil and darkness.

Kai Maertens starred in the pilot *Ich töte jeden Sinclair (I Kill Every Sinclair)*. Directed by Daniel Anderson (4 episodes), **Robert Sigl** (3 episodes), John van de Rest and cameraman Bernd Fiedler.

Series was abruptly stopped after eight episodes each running 45 minutes: *Das Horrorkabinett, Der Hexenclub, Anruf aus dem Jenseits, Der Sensenmann als Hochzeitsgast, Engelsgrab, Todeskarussell, Die Rattenkönigin, Der Gerechte.*

FEBRUARY 3

Stefan Ruzowitzky's horror thriller *Anatomie (Anatomy)* turned out fairly well for the German division of Columbia Pictures (at that time still headed by Jürgen Schau until NY decided to fire him):

Around 1998 in order to take advantage of industry and market transformations Columbia Tristar established a German subsidiary, Deutsche Columbia. Deutsche Columbia entered into an agreement with the production company of Claussen & Wöbke to bring out a big-budget horror film as a way of capitalizing on untapped markets and genres. The general success of **Silence of the Lambs** *(Demme, 1991) and* **Scream** *(Craven, 1996) had proved that there was indeed a mainstream market for horror films. [...] Both production companies agreed the time was ripe. [...]*

From this starting point, the film quickly took omn a transnational orientation. They signed on Ruzowitzky, an Austrian director, who had proven himself adept at innovating genre films through his socially critical Heimatfilm, **Die Siebtelbauern.** *They hoped he would bring the same energy to bear on the horror genre.* [74]

---

74 Randall Halle, *Chainsaws and Neo-Nazis: Contemporary German Horror Film Production.*

A secret Nazi Anti-Hippocratic Society performs gruesome experiments on living people. Paula Henning wins a place at an exclusive Heidelberg medical school. When the body of a young man she met on the train turns up on her dissection table, she begins to investigate the mysterious circumstances and the conspiracy surrounding his death. Franka Potente and Benno Fürmann starred. The props, created by Birger Laube, drew on the placticized cadavers of Gunther von Hagens.

FEBRUARY 27

Holgi is called by the filmmakers *Der böseste Junge der Welt (The Most Meanest Boy in the World)*. Screened at the Fantasporto Festival Internacional de Cinema do Porto in Portugal.

MARCH 23

Spuk im Reich der Schatten (Spooky in the Realm of Shadows), another entry in Günter Meyer's spooky TV movies.

APRIL 6

Flashback—Mörderische Ferien (Flashback/Murderous Vacation), a desperate, hopeless try to imitate American slasher movies, flopped at the box office. Elke Sommer in a supporting role.

MAY 15

Shadow of the Vampire, premiered at the Cannes Film Festival:

Was Max Schreck a real vampire? Did the star of **Nosferatu***, the 1922 horror classic, strike a bargain with its director FW Murnau—to appear in his movie in return for being allowed to drain the entire cast and crew of their blood afterwards? E. Elias Merhige's semi-serious comedy* **Shadow of the Vampire***, starring Willem Dafoe as Schreck, takes this much-mooted fantasy and runs with it to remarkably silly effect.* […]

John Malkovich plays Murnau as a Teutonic professor running amok in a lab coat and goggles. Ready to sacrifice life, limb and cast members to get "the shot", he's a stereotypical director-as-dictator, convinced that since art (and movies) last more or less forever and people don't, then one is expendable in the service of the other. [75]

Shadow of the Vampire didn't bear much truth, neither to the background of the original production nor to the characters involved: a huge team, more people than Murnau had seen on his original production, sets, costumes and makeup perfect, a great cast with Willem Dafoe even nominated for an Academy Award, but a hopeless screenplay that was based on a single idea: that Herr Schreck was a real vampire, but on almost no or, if at all, rather superficial research.

Steven Katz in fact had written it [the screenplay] more than a decade ago, and it circulated widely before winding up with actor Nicholas Cage, who had established a production company in 1996 to bankroll independent pictures. And it was Cage, who had seen and loved [director] Merhige's debut "Begotten", who contacted him about doing "Vampire". [...]

One of the reasons [for Merhige's involvement] was his admiration for Murnau and the 1922 "Nosferatu". "It is one of my favorite films," Merhige said. "It's a film I saw first when I was eleven years old, and it scared the hell out of me, and it still terrifies me. The way that Schreck moves, he seems deliberate and yet dangerous, he's almost like a shadow." [...]

Merhige's enthusiasm for Katz's screenplay was tempered, however, and so he worked with the writer to refine it. "The script was like an unfinished sculpture," he observed. "I just worked to hone it and bring certain things out and diminish certain other things. There was a certain danger of campiness in the script that I wanted to sort of extinguish and move into a more serious direction with it, and at the same time maintain the humor as a vehicle to express those serious ideas." One of the notions that he was at pains to include in the script was an analogy between filmmaking and vampirism: "I wanted to establish the motion picture camera itself

---

75   Michael Atkinson, *A Bloody Disgrace*. In: The Guardian, Friday, 25 January 2001.

as a vampire... As the camera fixes its gaze on the subject, it drains it of its flesh and blood and reduces it to a sort of shadow. And the shadow outlives the subject. It's a pretty creepy idea, [but it was] stylistically imperative and important and critical that that was shown and expressed." [76]

The budget was roughly 8 Million, the box-office receipts in the United States not much more. The movie entered lots of festivals but turned out a dismal failure.

MAY 21

Five friends lost in the woods (and in a horror video by Oliver Hummell). *The Dark Area*, a poor man's *Blair Witch Project*.

AUGUST 2

Hollow Man was produced with German money (Global Entertainment Productions GmbH & Company Medien KG).

AUGUST 11

Bless the Child (Die Prophezeiung) with Kim Basinger co-financed by Munich Film Partners & Company.

AUGUST 17

The Cell with Jennifer Lopez co-financed by Katira Produktions GmbH & Co. KG.

SEPTEMBER 26

Opening of the Filmmuseum Berlin located in the center of the German capital at Potsdamer Platz. Besides Marlene Dietrich, Ray Harryhausen's lifetime

---

76 E. Elias Merhige on *"Shadow of the Vampire"*. December 23, 2000. www.oneguysopinion.com

collection was on display in a special section *Artificial Worlds* (that also included a science-fiction section with artifacts from *Master of the World, Close Encounters of the Third Kind, Jurassic Park, Star Trek IV, Spider-Man* and *Independence Day*) for the next 8 years. The exhibition was arranged by Rolf Giesen for Deutsche Kinemathek. The dioramas were built by Holger Delfs and his team.

Ray Harryhausen meets Paul Hubschmid [a.k.a. Paul Christian], the star of his *Beast from 20,000 Fathoms* (1953), shortly before Hubschmid's death, at the opening of Filmmuseum Berlin

Courtesy of Stefan Birckmann

Ray Harryhausen and the author visit the village church of Harriehausen not far from Hanover

Courtesy of Stefan Birckmann

Dioramas under construction for Ray Harryhausen's *Artificial Worlds* exhibition in Berlin

Courtesy of Holger Delfs

SEPTEMBER 28

Der kleine Vampir (The Little Vampire) a.k.a. Rudolph Sackville-Bagg (Rollo Weeks) becomes the best friend of lonely American boy Tony Thompson (Jonathan Lipnicki) who lives in Scotland. Based on a novel by Angela Sommer-Bodenburg and directed by Uli Edel.

DECEMBER 12

Zwei vom Blitz getroffen (Two Striked by Thunderbolt), a SAT.1 TV movie with Mariele Millowitsch and Doris Kunstmann.

DECEMBER 17

Die Unbesiegbaren (The Unconquered), an RTL TV movie with Wotan Wilke Möhring.

DECEMBER 26

Küss mich, Frosch (Kiss Me, Frog), a modern-day TV version of *The Frog Prince*. Anna prefers to find her own path in life first before some guy will appear and turn everything upside down. But then her brother Raoul comes home with a frog. Before Raoul can torment the little creature to death, Anna rescues the frog from his clutches remembering the old fairy tale. In a light-hearted mood, she picks up the frog and kisses it and it really transforms into a Prince: Dietbert von Tuempelberg, a 1000-year-old Frog Prince. Directed by Dagmar Hirtz from a screenplay by Thomas Brueckner. Rita Russek's partners are Matthias Schweighöfer and Rufus Beck.

In addition:

This year also saw the release of *Die Insel der Angst (The Island of Fear)*, sort of a sequel to *School's Out* by **Robert Sigl**: The heroine from Sigl's previous slasher entry (played again by Katharina Wackernagel) is trying to recover from her traumatic experiences in a sanitarium on a remote island in Brittany. Turns out to be a very bad idea since the premises are stalked by a murderous man.

2001

JANUARY 30

A postman-turned love angel: TV movie *Dich schickt der Himmel (You Are Heaven Sent)* produced by Endemol.

MARCH 10

Staplerfahrer Klaus—Der erste Arbeitstag (Forklift Driver Klaus: The First Day on the Job), a mockumentary showing a chain reaction of bloody accidents, premiered at Filmschau Niedersachsen (Film Festival of Lower Saxony).

APRIL 12

Hilfe! Ich bin ein Fisch (Hjælp! Jeg er en fisk/Help! I'm a Fish), a German-Danish-Irish feature-length animated film budgeted at 18 million, turned three kids who have drunk a potion developed in the laboratory of an eccentric researcher into fish.

APRIL 19

Ein göttlicher Job (A Goddamn Job), produced by Wüste Film and Norddeutscher Rundfunk and distributed by the German branch of Buena Vista, was an incredibly bad fantasy comedy. Written and directed by Thorsten Wettcke. A sub-God selects comic book artist Niklas (played by Oliver Korittke) to be his successor, but Niklas isn't willing to leave Earth as he has fallen in love with a pizza delivery woman. With Heike Makatsch, Martin Semmelrogge, Fatih Akin, Anna Loos, Bela B. Felsenheimer (who named himself after **Béla Lugosi**) and Wotan Wilke Wöhring.

JULY 12

Die grüne Wolke (The Green Cloud/The Last Man Alive): Only a few children and two adults survive a green cloud that turns all mankind into stone. Directed by Claus Strigel from his own book.

JULY 20

Jeepers Creepers: American Zoetrope horror movie co-financed by Cinerenta Medienbeteiligungs KG. premiered at the Munich Fantasy Filmfest.

AUGUST 6

After killing a man Hardy Krüger Jr. is sent to the *Vortex*, a new kind of prison established by a future government. Here the delinquents must commit their crimes over and over again. Written and directed by Michael Pohl.

AUGUST 9

Olaf Ittenbach's *Legion of the Dead* at the Fantasy Filmfest.

AUGUST 25

Demonium (shot in English language in Italy by Andreas Schnaas) at the London FrightFest Film Festival. When family and friends of a murdered scientist arrive at the dead man's castle to listen to his last will, a series of slaying occurs.

SEPTEMBER

Before 9/11 a competition was set up by Hanns Eckelkamp for a new *Dr. Mabuse* film. Eckelkamp had purchased an option on the series from his colleague **Artur Brauner**. Among the participants were **Stefan Ruzowitzky** and Peter Märthesheimer.

Two days before 9/11, German TV was going to broadcast a commercial that had to be withdrawn from circulation immediately. The spot opened in a sidewalk cafe in Manhattan. Above it, we recognize a skyscraper that resembles, with some imagination, a tower of the World Trade Center. A young couple is served red whine and coffee when the table begins to vibrate. Aircraft engines are roaring. Horrified, the guests look up. They see a passenger airplane crashing in broad daylight into the tower above them. People flee screaming while—cut—the passengers aboard the airplane are given a good shake. The plane penetrates the building like a gigantic arrow and we see a huge billboard with the phone number of the client. Everybody has a good laugh. No catastrophe, nobody is harmed or injured, no victims, no dead, just a spectacular special effect for entertainment's sake.

In charge of the model work was SFX supervisor Joachim Grüninger, CEO of the Munich-based Magicon GmbH. Since the early days, Grüninger worked repeatedly with his friend **Roland Emmerich** (although he was not involved in *Independence Day*). The spot was the brainchild of a Hamburg advertising agency that was commissioned by Telegate AG, a communication service provider founded in August 1996 by Dr. Klaus Harisch and Peter Wünsch. Anja Meyer, in charge of Telegate's public relations, was aghast when she saw the *real* events of 9/11. She stormed into the office of her bosses, "I don't believe this. Turn on the TV. In New York somebody tries to imitate our spot." Harisch and Wünsch watched the terrorist attacks with unbelieving eyes. Harisch's first thought: "Damn, we have to stop our spot! Immediately!!" No thought wasted on the victims and casualties, only damage control.

SEPTEMBER 20

Kommando Störtebeker (Störtebeker the Command), an animated feature film based on characters designed by comedian Otto Waalkes.

OCTOBER 4

Der kleine Eisbär—Der Kinofilm (Little Polar Bear), a German children's book and TV animation favorite in his first feature film: Lars, the little Polar Bear cub (*Lars de kleine ijsbeer*) created by Dutch author Hans de Beer, co-produced by Cartoon Film (Thilo Rothkirch) and Warner Bros. Germany (Willi Geike). The feature had no continuous plot but consisted of three segments, one aboard a Black Ship, sort of an automatic fish factory.

OCTOBER 8

Olaf Ittenbach's Backwood thriller *Riverplay* seems to have been inspired by John Boorman's *Deliverance*.

OCTOBER 25

Die Abrafaxe—Unter schwarzer Flagge (The Abrafaxe: Under the Black Flag): 3D-animated feature film with three youthful East German comic book heroes (Abrax, Brabax and Califax) meeting Anne Bonny and Captain Blackbeard. Part of the animation was outsourced to producer Gerhard Hahn's studio in Saigon, Vietnam.

NOVEMBER 17

Planet der Kannibalen (Planet of the Cannibals) directed by former film critic Hans-Christoph Blumenberg is set in Germany 2020 which has turned into a police state. Two TV companies, Alphaplus and Eurolux, are in competition for viewers. Eurolox offers *Cannibal Talk* starring a Hannibal Lecter-like serial killer while Alphaplus is on the track of extraterrestrial cannibals. Emma Trost who heads up the trend management at Alphaplus, is told by her boss that these aliens have landed somewhere in Europe—but before he can come up with details, he is murdered, apparently by Emma, or by her double. Produced by Rotwang Film Hamburg in association with ARTE TV.

NOVEMBER 18

Lenya—Die grösste Kriegerin aller Zeiten (Lenya, the Greatest Warrior of All Time): Teutonic heroic fantasy written by Peter Freund who was associated with Phönix Film, the production company, and later created the books around *Laura Leander*, a German pendant of Harry Potter. A peasant girl is chosen by the Nordic gods for a particular task. With a special sword she has to fight a witch. Filmed in the Czech Republic for German TV (RTL).

DECEMBER 19

German release of Peter Jackson's *The Lord of the Rings: The Fellowship of the Ring*. The project was co-financed by German investor funds (also known as "stupid German money").

DECEMBER 31

Fünf Wochen im Ballon (Five Weeks in a Balloon) is the final entry in a series of Jules Verne puppet animated projects that Berlin-based Manfred Durniok produced in Shanghai.

In addition:

Ice Planet, pilot for an (unrealized) TV series, a mix of *Star Trek* and *Battlestar Galactica* produced by H5B5 Media AG. Dutch-born director Winrich Kolbe had indeed worked on American sci-fi series: besides *Galactica*, on *War of the Worlds*, *Star Trek*, *Space 2063*, *Soldier of Fortune, Inc.*, and *Threat Matrix*.

Swimming Pool—Der Tod feiert mit (Swimming Pool: Death Joins in the Celebration/The Pool): Teenager party in a swimming pool but there is a killer raining on their parade.

2002

Cinemas: 1844

FEBRUARY 21

666—Traue keinem, mit dem Du schläfst! (666: In Bed with the Devil): Goethe's *Faust* up to date in a comedy made by Rainer Matsutani with Jan Josef Liefers as Frank Faust and Armin Rhode as Mephisto II. Produced by Constantin Film.

MARCH 21

Resident Evil with Mila Jovovich was a German co-production (by Constantin Film) directed by Paul W. S. Anderson with interiors filmed at the former East German TV studios, now Studios Berlin Adlershof (and at various locations in Berlin and Potsdam): A virus has escaped in 'The Hive', a vast secret facility deep below the streets of "Raccoon City" turning the staff into flesh-eating zombies (thereby launching a series of sequels).

JULY 27

Mutation III (M III: Century of the Dead) was an amateur direct-to-video release written and directed by Timo Rose premiered at the Splatterday Night Festival in Saarbrücken.

SEPTEMBER 27

Bibi Blocksberg: A feature film version of Elfie Donnelly's series about a benevolent witch girl, this time fighting an evil witch named Rabia (portrayed by Corinna Harfouch). Hermine Huntgeburth directed.

OCTOBER 25

Jörg Buttgereit's TV documentary devoted to Godzilla and Toho: *Die Monsterinsel (Monster Island)*.

DECEMBER 5

Das Jesus Video (The Jesus Video/The Hunt for the Hidden Relic/Ancient Relic): TV movie based on a 1998 novel by Andreas Eschbach. During an archeological dig outside Jerusalem young Steffen Vogt finds a 2000-year-old skeleton and next to it a plastic bag with instructions for a video camera. There is some speculation about the skeleton as that of a time traveler who shot footage of Jesus Christ.

In addition:

Tattoo—Rette deine Haut (Tattoo: Save Your Skin) was clearly inspired by *The Silence of the Lambs.*

2003

JANUARY 16

Tag 26 (Day 26): Two survivors of a biological war. Andreas Samland made this movie as student of Deutsche Film- und Fernsehakademie Berlin.

JANUARY 30

The Antman (Antrage): Start of a Studio Babelsberg produced series of three B sci-fi flics titled *Planet B*. Starring Götz Otto, Lars Rudolph and DEFA's retired Indian chief Gojko Mitić.

Other Planet B entries were:

Mask Under Mask (Mortal Beauty—Fluch der Schönheit) by Markus Goller with Rita Lengyel as Alyssa de Espella, a sorceress who guards the secret of eternal youth.

Detective Lovelorn und die Rache des Pharao (Detective Lovelorn and the Revenge of the Pharaoh) directed by Thomas Frick starring a 3469 years-old mummy of a pharaoh (played by Reiner Schöne) ready to destroy the whole world. Turned out a commercial and critical failure (like the other films of the series), the last movie appearance of Horst Buchholz who was seen as Professor Svedenborg.

FEBRUARY 6

Anatomie 2 (Anatomy 2): According to director **Stefan Ruzowitzky**, "no film sequel of the American kind which sticks closely to the first part to guarantee, according to Hollywood calculations, 60 percent of the box-office gross of the predecessor. The project stimulated me only because I got the chance to do something different. This is no classic Gothic Horror Teenie subject like the first part but more of a psychological thriller filled with action. We choose a different approach but kept *Anatomy* as trademark for suspenseful entertainment."[77]

MARCH

Garden of Love (Born Undead) by Olaf Ittenbach: The ghosts of a brutally murdered family ask their grown-up daughter to find the killer.

MARCH 8

Nikos the Impaler, a Romanian barbarian who has risen from the dead, is the obverse of Vlad the Impaler. "Starring" (and directed by) Andreas Schnaas.

MARCH 29

Beyond the Limits by Olaf Ittenbach focuses on the tales of a gravedigger and a mysterious occult relic.

MAY 20

Premiere in Cannes: *Wolfzeit (Time of the Wolf)*. Austrian director Michael Haneke sets his post-apocalyptic drama in a time when all environment has been destroyed, water contaminated and animal life burned. French-Austrian-German co-production with Isabelle Huppert.

---

77   Jochen Müller, *Stefan Ruzowitzky zu "Anatomie 2": „Ein Abklatsch-Sequel reizt mich nicht."* In: Blickpunkt: Film, January 22, 2003.

JUNE 12

Geheimnisvolle Freundinnen (Mysterious Friends): ProSieben TV thriller about the weird experiences of four girlfriends after a séance.

JUNE 21

Hamlet_X: a labyrinth of experimental Shakespeare scenes with Meret Becker as Hamlet and Bela B. Felsenheimer as Maître des plaisirs. Made by Koppfilm at Berlin's Volksbühne am Rosa-Luxemburg-Platz.

JUNE 30

Arnold Schwarzenegger and *Terminator 3: Rise of the Machines* co-financed by IMF Internationale Medien und Film GmbH & Co. 3 Produktions KG.

SEPTEMBER 25

Animated feature film *Jester Till*: allegedly the story of one of Europe's best-loved folk tale characters, *Till Eulenspiegel*, doesn't resemble him at all and could be *Jester George* as well. The makeshift-Till of this movie is on his way to the bustling city of Boomstadt to visit his grandfather, the old wizard Marcus. Marcus and his faithful assistant, the owl Cornelius, are cooking up a magic potion of eternal life and happiness but their project is sabotaged by Dr. Death… This sure has nothing to do with the folk tales. Piet De Rycker, who had worked with the producer previously, told me that he once mentioned a *Till Eulenspiegel* project to him with animal characters, like Disney's *Robin Hood*.

OCTOBER 10

Apparatspott—Gerangel in Ruum un Tied (Apparatspott: Tussle in Space and Time): a new entry in Martin Hermann's ultra low-budget series of sci-fi parodies.

Bloodthirsty zombies rave in *House of the Dead* directed by Germany's self-stylized master of schlock, **Dr. Uwe Boll,** in an adaptation of the 1996 light gun arcade game of the same name produced by Sega. Short in Vancouver, Canada.

OCTOBER 16

Pumuckl und sein Zirkusabenteuer (Pumuckl's Circus Adventure): 2D animated hobgoblin Pumuckl is kidnapped by circus artists who want to exploit his invisibility in their show.

NOVEMBER 22

Küss' niemals einen Flaschengeist (Never Kiss a Genie) by Klaus Knoesel: Sat.1 produced fantasy comedy.

2004

JANUARY 1

Blueprint: Franka Potente as a composer who (due to an incurable illness) will be cloned to save her art for posterity. Based on a novel by Charlotte Kerner.

MARCH 18

Holger Tappe, who invested a heritage to found Ambient Entertainment in Hanover, and his friend Lenard Fritz Krawinkel joined forces to create the 3D-animated *Boo, Zino & the Snurks*, the goblin-like stars of a TV animation show, who strand in the reality of our world: *Back to Gaya*. Although it was the first feature-length 3D animated film produced in Germany and two American writers (Don McEnery and Bob Shaw who had some Disney and Pixar experience) were hired to polish Jan Berger's script, the result was only mildly successful.

APRIL 29

Der Teufel von Rudow (Nightmare in Suburbia): A series of murders in Rudow, a suburb of Berlin.

JUNE 12

Apokalypse Eis (Post Impact): TV movie with a comet causing a new ice age. Some survivors on the search for a device that promises hope for mankind.

JUNE 13

Los Angeles premiere of Anglo-American/Irish/German co-production of Jules Verne's *Around the World in 80 Days* produced at the Babelsberg Studios, this version starring Jackie Chan as Passepartout, Steve Coogan as Phileas Fogg and Arnold Schwarzenegger in a cameo as Prince Hapi.

JULY 22

(T)Raumschiff Surprise—Periode 1 (Dreamship Surprise: Period 1): Star Trek parody with director Michael "Bully" Herbig as Mr. Spuck, Christian Tramitz as Captain Jürgen T. Kork and Rick Kavanian as Schrotty (and the ship's physician, Pulle), three well-known German TV comedians:

The year is 2054. Mankind has settled on Mars. 250 years later, the descendants of the first settlers choose to return, striving to conquer the Earth and prepared to annihilate any life on the planet. All efforts seem futile: the invasion will take its course.

And still, Queen Metapha (Anja Kling) commands her people "not to bury the sand in their heads", as there seems to be one last flicker of hope: the crew of "Dreamship Surprise" (Michael Bully Herbig, Christian Tramitz, Rick Kavanian), who are to embark on a journey through time in order to undo the colonization of Mars. Yet the spaceship's crew members have a far more important mission on their minds: they are smack in the middle of their dance performance rehearsals for the "Miss Waikiki" competition and thus only reluctantly agree to take a taxi bound to the Earth. [78]

---

78 www.herbx.de

AUGUST 1

Casper Van Dien as Captain Abraham Van Helsing and **Udo Kier** as Captain Varna in *Dracula 3000*, premiered at the Estepona horror film festival. South African-German co-production.

AUGUST 12

Daniel der Zauberer (Daniel the Magician) with so-called German "superstar" Daniel Küblböck and director **Ulli Lommel** as late Grandpa Johnny Küblböck who waves the magic wand. Definitely: one of the worst movies ever.

AUGUST 23

World premiere in Tokyo: *Resident Evil: Apocalypse*.

SEPTEMBER 19

Lauras Stern (Laura's Star): Seven-year-old Laura is finding it difficult to make new friends after having moved to a new town. One evening, outside in a park, she finds a little star that has fallen from the nightly sky. She lovingly mends the little star's leg with a plaster, and thus begins a marvelous friendship. After a while, however, Laura realizes that the star is fading away on earth and that for its sake she has to let it go back up into the sky. 2D-animated feature Anime-style produced by Rothkirch Cartoon Film and Warner Bros. Germany. Based on the children's books by Klaus Baumgart and a TV series.

SEPTEMBER 30

Bibi Blocksberg und das Geheimnis der blauen Eulen (Bibi Blocksberg and the Secret of the Blue Owls): Bibi, the little witch, is going to help Elea, a girl wheelchair-bound since a tragic accident. Aunt Walpurgia mentions to her the legend of the "Solace Owls", magical owls with a healing power hidden in their blue coats.

OCTOBER 1

Tears of Kali, an ultra low budget entry written and directed by Andreas Marschall and compiled from a trio of independent short films: *Shakti*, *Devi* and *Kali*. The plot (early 1980s) deals with people interested in meditation and esoterism getting involved with the mysteries a fictitious cult based in India, the radical Taylor-Eriksson Group. Direct-to-DVD release distributed by Anolis Entertainment.

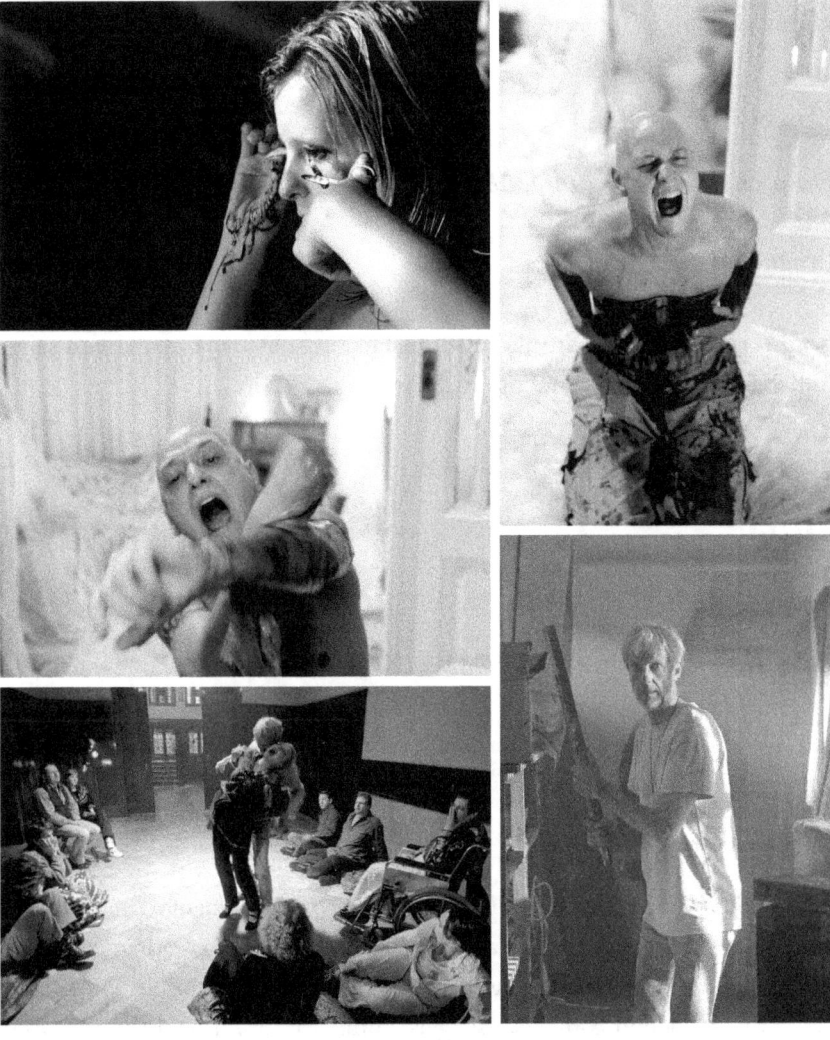

Tears of Kali | © 2004 Cut and Run Prod./Anolis Entertainment

OCTOBER 17

TV's *Hai-Alarm auf Mallorca (Shark Attack in the Mediterranean)* with strongman Ralf Moeller and a delayed *Jaws* substitute.

OCTOBER 28

7 Zwerge—Männer allein im Wald (7 Dwarves: Men Alone in the Wood) produced by and starring Otto Waalkes as one of the seven dwarves, Cosma Shiva Hagen as Snow White and her mother, Nina Hagen, as evil queen.

NOVEMBER 14

Der verzauberte Otter (The Enchanted Otter): TV fantasy filmed in Thuringia.

In addition:

Transport: Futuristic short film made at Hochschule für Film and Fernsehen in Babelsberg with outstanding model work.

2005

FEBRUARY 3

Alone in the Dark: **Uwe Boll's** film version of an Infogrames fantasy game of the same name. Boll shot in July 2003 in Vancouver starring Christian Slater as Edward Carnby, a private eye who specializes in supernatural phenomena.

FEBRUARY 5

Felix—Ein Hase auf Weltreise (Felix Around the World): Cinema compilation of an animated TV series starring a rabbit character known to German kids from merchandising products. Produced (and co-written) by Gabriele M. Walther, CEO of production company Caligari Film: "In 1997 I read the first *Felix* book to my nephew. He asked me if couldn't make *Felix* into a movie. Indeed,

I later purchased the media rights from the publisher and produced a TV series. [...] The publisher had initiated the property very cleverly. First there was the stuffed animal manufactured by Spiegelburg followed by the book. And then in the bookstores the books were offered with the stuffed animals. It is rather unusual to introduce a character like *Felix* without a media product. Usually, it is the other way round: first the movie, then the merchandising."[79]

MARCH 10

A woman pursued into the labyrinth of the London subway. The only reason German money was poured into this British *Creep* was the participation of Franka Potenta (*Run Lola Run*).

MARCH 25

Bibi Blocksberg—Eene Meene Eins, Zwei, Drei: Cinema compilation of animated TV episodes produced by Gerhard Hahn and Kiddinx Berlin.

APRIL 1

Oscar Wilde's immortal *Das Gespenst von Canterville (The Canterville Ghost)* as TV movie produced by Roxy Film with an animated ghost provided by Schesch Filmproduktion.

APRIL 21

Stürmisch verliebt (Perfect Weather for Love), TV sci-fi comedy.

APRIL 26

Mutter aus heiterem Himmel (Heaven & A Thing Called Love): Fantasy TV movie (Sat.1) by Nikolai Müllerschön.

---

79 Blickpunkt:Film. February 7, 2005.

JULY 28

Incredibly bad *Nibelungen* parody written by comedian Tom Gerhardt (who also starred as *Siegfried*) and Herman Weigel and directed by Sven Unterwaldt Jr. A reviewer on IMDb had the chutzpah to write: *Finally a funny German movie worth watching!*

JULY 31

Kampfansage—Der letzte Schüler (The Challenge): Post doomsday plot about a future world dominated by warlords. Jonas is the last surviving keeper of ancient martial arts dynasty.

AUGUST 18

Globi und der Schattenräuber (Globi and the Solen Shadows) by Robi Engler (director) and Tony Loeser (producer) is a strange mix of a Swiss cartoon logo, a parrot character created in the 1930s, and Japanese anime. None of both movies really works: Teenagers Lucinda and Benji are rock musicians. When the villain, Maestro, steals Benji's shadow, the boy can no longer play a note. Worse, he physically begins to fade away. Globi, the parrot character, tracks Maestro to a subterranean Gothic opera house where he discovers that the self-acclaimed "Phantom of the Opera" steals musicians' shadows in order to control all the world's music. Globi and his friends must reunite the shadows with their musicians to save the world's worth of music.

SEPTEMBER 2

U.S. release of *A Sound of Thunder* directed by Peter Hyams from a Time Travel short story by Ray Bradbury co-funded by Germans and starring some German actors (Armin Rohde and Heike Makatsch).

SEPTEMBER 4

Werner Herzog's *The Wild Blue Yonder* with Brad Dourif as alien who has escaped from his frozen world in the Andromeda Galaxy and now joins CIA in a period when mankind faces a climatic catastrophe and tries to find a home on another planet.

SEPTEMBER 9

Der kleine Eisbär 2—Die geheimnisvolle Insel (Little Polar Bear 2: The Mysterious Island): Little Polar Bear Lars and his friends travel from North to South Pole where they encounter a huge sea monster from antediluvian days and survive a volcanic eruption.

SEPTEMBER 15

Ein Luftikus zum Verlieben (Falling in Love with a Happy-Go-Lucky): TV movie written and directed by Helmut Metzger.

SEPTEMBER 18

Sheeba—Die dunkelste Seite der Macht (Sheeba: The Darkest Side of the Force): Video inspired by *Star Wars*.

OCTOBER 27

German release of *Doom* based on a video game series. Babelsberg Production Services as co-producer.

OCTOBER 23

Uwe Boll's *BloodRayne* features a female vampire who is going to kill the man who raped her mother. Kristanna Loken as Rayne with a supporting cast that consists of Geraldine Chaplin, Meat Loaf, **Udo Kier** and Ben Kingsley.

NOVEMBER 17

Moonlight Mountain: Around a desolate mountain the dead rise to frighten the living. Written and directed by Timo Rose.

DECEMBER 2

Zimmer 205—Traust du dich rein? (205: Room of Fear) by Rainer Matsutani at the Stockholm German Films Go North! Jennifer Ulrich as college student Katrin Nadolny thinks that something is wrong with her new dorm room.

DECEMBER 23

Uli Edel's pathetic mini-series TV version of *Die Nibelungen (Ring of the Nibelungs)*, only loosely based on mythology. Benno Fürmann as Siegfried. **Volker Engel** served as VFX director and co-producer.

DECEMBER 24

ZDF TV version of *Rotkäppchen (Little Red Riding Hood)*.

In addition:

A *Dungeon of Evil* is operated by a sadistic hermit.

2006

JANUARY 5

Herr der Diebe (The Thief Lord): A magical treasure with the power to spin time itself is the fantasy tool of a novel by Cornelia Funke who tells the story of a mysterious young "Thief Lord" and his gang of abandoned kids. Richard Claus directed.

FEBRUARY 14

Lapislazuli—Im Auge des Bären: A Neandertal boy named Bataa (Clarence Ryan) is revived by a meteorite crash in the Austrian Alps. Premiered at the Berlin International Film Festival.

FEBRUARY 16

Felix 2—Der Hase und die verflixte Zeitmaschine (Felix and the Time Machine): new cartoon adventures.

MARCH 16

Die Wolke (The Cloud) adapted by Marco Kreuzpaintner from Gudrun Pausewang's novel and directed by Gregor Schnitzler: An MCA occurs in a fictitious nuclear power plant near Schweinfurt.

MARCH 23

Gernot Roll's remake of *Der Räuber Hotzenplotz (The Robber Hotzenplotz)* with Armin Rohde as robber and Rufus Beck as Petrosilius Zwackelmann, the magician.

APRIL

Cannibal—Aus dem Tagebuch eines Kannibalen: A video devoted to cannibalistic obsession (*"from the diary of a cannibal"*) by a man featuring as "Marian Dora" who is said to have worked for **Ulli Lommel**.

Camp Corpses: This video promised *summer—sun—blood*.

APRIL 4

Chain Reaction, a video by Olaf Ittenbach: **Zombie Onslaught**.

APRIL 16

Das total verrückte Wunderauto (Charlie 2): TV movie about a boy and a car that is connected to the internet and develops a mind of its own.

MAY 18

Cannes screening of *Princess*, a Danish-German animation movie.

MAY 28

TV co-funded version of *Hansel and Gretel* shot in Thuringia and directed by Anne Wild.

Pro Sieben Märchenstunde (Pro Sieben Fairy-Tale Hour), a comedy TV series of fairy tales produced by Rat Pack for ProSieben Television. Visual Effects by Quadriga FX.

JUNE 11

A horror video titled *Zombie Commando* deals with the effects of a "Z virus".

JULY 20

Hui Buh—Das Schlossgespenst (Hui Buh: The Castle Ghost): Michael "Bully" Herbig acts it out in motion capture. His performance brings a castle ghost to life.

AUGUST 3

Urmel aus dem Eis (Impy's Island): Urmel (or Impy in the English-language version) is a baby dinosaur frozen since prehistoric times and revived in 3D animation by Ambient Entertainment. Based on a children's book by Max Kruse, son of puppet manufacturer Käthe Kruse.

AUGUST 26

Schule der kleinen Vampire (School for Vampires): 104-part TV series (ca. 12 minutes per episode) based on children's books by Jackie Niebisch and produced by Gerhard Hahn in cooperation with Cartoon One and Rai Fiction.

AUGUST 27

Thomas Kretschmann as cannibal in *Rohtenburg* by Martin Weisz, based on a true crime case, at the London FrightFest Film Festival. New U.S. title: *Grimm Love*.

SEPTEMBER

A satirical 3D-animated cartoon about Hitler, sitting on the toilet complaining about Churchill and singing in the bathtub, became an instant download hit in the internet: *Der Bonker* conceived by illustrator Walter Moers. Nevertheless, a planned animated feature film with Cartoon Adolf was shelved.

SEPTEMBER 14

Das Parfum—Die Geschichte eines Mörders (Perfume: The Story of a Murderer): Ben Whishaw as Jean-Baptiste Grenouille, a medieval perfumist searching for the ultimate scent. **Bernd Eichinger** produced and co-wrote, Tom Tykwer directed from a bestselling novel by Patrick Süskind. Dustin Hoffman had a supporting part.

SEPTEMBER 21

Oh, wie schön ist Panama (The Trip to Panama/Oh, How Beautiful Panama Is), animated children's movie based on a story by Janosch [Horst Eckert].

OCTOBER 5

Das kleine Arschloch und der alte Sack—Sterben ist Scheisse (The Little Bastard and the Old Fart: Death Sucks), feature-length animation comedy by Michael Schaack and Konrad Weise based on the comics by Walter Moers.

OCTOBER 26

7 Zwerge—Der Wald ist nicht genug (7 Dwarves: The Forest Is Not Enough) produced by and starring comedian Otto Waalkes as Bubi with his fellow dwarves played by Mirco Nontschew (Tschakko), Boris Aljinovic (Cloudy), Ralf Schmitz (Sunny), Gustav-Peter Wöhler (Cookie), Martin Schneider (Speedy) and Norbert Heisterkamp (Ralfie). Nina Hagen as witch and her daughter Cosma Shiva Hagen as Snow White.

NOVEMBER 16

Dead Eyes Open tells of six young people stranded in the midst of an unknown wilderness where they enter an odd fortress.

NOVEMBER 22

A man buried alive returns from the dead to take bloody revenge: **Uwe Boll's** *Seed*.

DECEMBER 14

Mondscheinkinder (Children of the Moon), a children's film by Manuela Stacke about a boy who wants to become an astronaut. Produced by Hochschule für Film und Fernsehen Munich.

DECEMBER 16

Westwood, California premiere of *Happily N'Ever After* (German release title: *Es war k'einmal im Märchenland*), a big-budget 3D-animated fairy-tale spoof produced by Berlin Animation Film, a company funded by investors won over by Dresdner Bank, and made especially for the American market where it was released by Lion's Gate. The movie failed totally when U.S. patrons discovered that it was no new *Shrek* but turned out a true *Schreck*.

DECEMBER 21

Das hässliche Entlein & ich (The Ugly Duckling and Me!): Hans Christian Andersen's tale animated with a new twist. Here it is a character named Ratso, a rat, who finds himself forced to take responsibility for the Ugly Duckling.

DECEMBER 26

Lauras Weihnachtsstern (Laura's Christmas Star): Direct-to-DVD release produced by Cartoon Film Berlin and Warner Bros. Germany with 3D animation outsourced to Beijing.

2007

JANUARY 16

2030—Aufstand der Alten (2030: Revolt of the Old): 3-episode ZDF miniseries: the collapse of the German and European social security system.

MARCH 19

Taiketsu (Babylon Z: The Last Apocalypse) set in the ruins of future Babylon. Written and directed by Sven Knüppel.

APRIL 27

Slasher (also known as *Chainsaw Slasher*): a savage lunatic in the German backwoods. Directed by Frank W. Montag.

Uwe Boll's *Seed* released in Canada: Max Seed is a mass murderer who survives his own execution to take revenge.

JUNE 18

Innere Werte (Sea Patrol), a ZDF TV movie.

JUNE 27

Unsuk Chin: Alice in Wonderland: Korean composer Unsuk Chin's opera of Lewis Carroll's tale at the Bavarian State Opera and on TV. Production design: Achim Freyer.

SEPTEMBER 20

Der kleine König Macius (Little King Macius): Preschool animation based on a character by Janusz Korczak who was killed by the Nazis 1942 in Treblinka.

Premiere in Las Vegas: *Resident Evil: Extinction*.

OCTOBER 18

Die drei Räuber (Three Robbers): Stephan Schesch's animated feature film production of a Tomi Ungerer book: Once upon a time there were three fierce robbers. In the dark of the night they walked the roads hidden under large black capes and tall black hats. The first had a blunderbuss. The second had a pepper blower. The third had a huge red axe. They terrified everyone and plundered everywhere they went. One bitter, particularly black night the three stopped a carriage that had but one passenger. Little orphan Tiffany was on her way to live with a wicked aunt. She was delighted to meet the robbers instead. Since there was no treasure to steal, the robbers bundled the girl in a warm cape and carried her away to their hideout… Stefan Arndt (X-Filme) and David Groenewold were co-producers.

OCTOBER 19

Everlasting Hate: More living dead stumbling through the forest.

OCTOBER 24

Hölle Hamburg (Hamburg Hell): The dead souls of the Comintern take possession of a filmmaker's consciousness.

OCTOBER 25

Michael "Bully" Herbig's parody of Sissi as 3D-animated feature film *Lissi und der wilde Kaiser (Lissi and the Wild Emperor)*, complete with a snowman.

Bukarest Fleisch (Bukarest Meat): Andy Fetscher's TV debut, co-funded by the Film Academy Baden-Württemberg in Ludwigsburg and Hessischer Rundfunk, leads to Romania where humans are literally turned through the meat grinder.

NOVEMBER 17

Road Rip: *One trip. One bad trip. One road trip.* Too tame for hardcore splatter fans.

NOVEMBER 29

Schwerter des Königs—Dungeon Siege (In the Name of the King: A Dungeon Siege Tale) by **Uwe Boll** with Jason Statham, John Rhys-Davis and Ron Perlman.

DECEMBER 11

Limited Games (Limited Games: The Curse of Störtebeker's Treasure): Six students and the bloodiest summer of their life.

In addition:

Dennis Jacobsen, Randa Chahoud and Oliver Jahn, three students of Deutsche Film- und Fernsehakademie in Berlin, based 14 short TV episodes of *Iljon Tichy: Raumpilot* on Stanisław Lem's *Star Diaries*.

A family of cannibals haunts the Black Forest in Timo Rose's video *Barricade*.

A group of young people on a "Scary Camping" tour: **Kadaver (Cadaver)**.

Tuberkulose (Tuberculosis) was meant as joke.

2008

JANUARY 1

Kleiner Dodo (Little Dodo): An orangutan boy fights climactic change that threatens the green rainforest. Dodo loves all the different sounds and noises and can imitate nearly every one of them: from splashing drops of water to chirping cicadas. One day he finds a violin, a "thingamabob", as Darwin, the wise old ape, calls it. When the river dries out and the animals start to suffer during a great drought, Dodo discovers the secret of the "thingamabob": music! 2D-animated fantasy adapted by Rolf Giesen from a book by Hans de Beer and Serena Romanelli. Produced by Cartoon Film and Warner Bros. Germany.

FEBRUARY 5

Das Wunder von Loch Ness (The Secret of Loch Ness): Boy searches for Loch Ness Monster. by Michael Rowitz. Rat Pack production for Sat.1 TV.

MARCH 28

Apparatspott—Dat mokt wie gistern (Apparatspott—we will do this yesterday), the third entry in the series.

Dard Divorce was made by slaughter assembly line filmmaker Olaf Ittenbach on weekends in his own house.

APRIL 24

Chasseurs de dragons (Die Drachenjäger): 3D-animated dragon hunters with animation handled by Trixter in Munich. Zoe is a little girl who believes in fairy tales. Not because she is naïve, but because she simply likes fairy tales. So in order to help her uncle get rid of a terrible dragon, Zoe decides she has to find some fairy-tale heroes. And when she meets Gwizdo and Lian Chu—a couple of two-bit, fly-by-night dragon hunters—well what the heck, she's going to believe in them anyway... Based on a French-Canadian animated TV series created by Arthur Qwak and produced by Futurikon and Tooncan.

MAY 1

3D-animated *Urmel voll in Fahrt (Impy's Wonderland)* by Ambient Entertainment (Holger Tappe) and Constantin Film (Reinhard Klooss).

MAY 2

Hamburg premiere of *Don't Wake the Dead* by Andreas Schnaas with Blind Dead Knights Templar and Nazi zombies rising from the graves.

MAY 14

Ari Folman's Flash animated *Waltz with Bashir* (co-financed by Razor Film Produktion Berlin and Medienboard Berlin-Brandenburg) in Cannes competition.

JUNE 19

Das Bonobo-Prinzip (The Bonobo Principle): sci-fi movie by Michael Sittner.

JULY 24

BloodRayne II: Deliverance, a video by **Uwe Boll**.

AUGUST 1

Virus Undead: Another zombie horror video written by Wolf Jahnke. It features an H5N1-like infection transmitted by diseased birds that causes corpses to reanimate in search of human prey. A medical student and his friends find themselves surrounded by them.

AUGUST 31

Die Jagd nach dem Schatz der Nibelungen (*The Search for the Treasure of the Nibelungen*, U.S. title: *The Charlemagne Code*): TV treasure hunt mystery directed by Ralf Huettner.

SEPTEMBER 22

Niko—Ein Rentier hebt ab (Niko & the Way to the Stars/The Flight Before Christmas): Niko, a young reindeer boy, knows that his Dad is a member of Santa's legendary Flying Forces, the coolest reindeer squad around. But he has never met his Father. Following an attack by the notorious Black Wolf's gang on his herd's peaceful home, Niko heads off on a desperate, dangerous mission through icy blizzards and across wild terrain to find his Dad and save Christmas. Scandinavian (Danish and Finnish) Xmas reindeer special, produced with German participation (Ulysses Filmproduktion Hamburg).

SEPTEMBER 25

Alone in the Dark II, a horror video produced by **Uwe Boll**.

OCTOBER 2

Hamburg premiere of *Jasper und das Limonadenkomplott (Jasper: Journey to the End of the World)*, an animated feature film about two penguin brothers, Jasper and Junior, who, with the help of 9-year-old Emma, retrieve the eggs of a threatened parrot species from the evil Dr. Block.

OCTOBER 9

Krabat: Remake directed by Marco Kreuzpaintner with David Kross as title character fighting evil master played by Christian Redl.

OCTOBER 16

Die Geschichte vom Brandner Kasper (The Story of Brandner Kasper): Remake with Franz Xaver Kroetz as 70-year-old Kasper Brandner who outwits Boanlkramer a.k.a. Death (played by Michael "Bully" Herbig). Directed by Joseph Vilsmaier.

Der Mondbär (The Moonbear): 3D-animated cinema version based on TV series from the previous year. The Moonbear looks like a cartoon and almost floats due to cheap China animation.

OCTOBER 24

Guitar Men: The Darkest Secret of Rock'n Roll, directed by Thomas Wind: When the Nazi regime finally collapsed in 1945, some of Hitler's top scientists decided to save the fruit of their labor, the plan for a lethal super weapon, and hide it inside as guitar.

Tortura: Survival in the darkness of the abandoned underground subways of Munich where, according to filmmaker Michael Effenberger, rogue cannibals and sadists have their residency.

NOVEMBER 15

Nerves by Ralf Möllenhoff: Xmas in a decaying suburb with a slaughterhouse still operating.

DECEMBER 11

Tintenherz (Inkheart): The father of a teenage girl has the dangerous ability to bring characters from books to life. Based on a novel by Cornelia Funke.

DECEMBER 20

Brüderchen und Schwesterchen (Brother and Sister), TV fairy tale with Odine John as little sister and Hans-Laurin Beyerling as little brother.

Tischlein deck dich (Table-Be-Set), TV fairy tale.

DECEMBER 25

Frau Holle (Mother Holly): TV movie by Bodo Fürneisen with Marianne Sägebrecht.

DECEMBER 26

TV version of *Das tapfere Schneiderlein (The Brave Little Tailor)* with Kostja Ullmann.

Arend Agthe's *Dornröschen (Sleeping Beauty)* on TV.

In addition:

Fluch des Vergessens (Curse of Forgetting): 47-minute horror film by Christoph Böll.

Infekt (Infection): Post doomsday horror video, fight for survival in a world populated by zombies. Written and directed by Michael Effenberger.

2009

Cinemas: 1744

JANUARY 5

Gonger—Das Böse vergisst nie: Evil Never Forgets. TV movie by Christian Theede.

JANUARY 28

Klischee—Mörderisches Halloween auf Malloraca (Cliché: Gory Halloween in Mallorca): *Hacked to Pieces… Butchered at Dawn!*

2012: 35-minute graduate film not to be confused with **Roland Emmerich's** American version of *2012*. Shown at the Max Ophüls Festival in Saarbrücken.

FEBRUARY 6

A remake of *Lippels Traum (Lippel's Dream)* screened at the Berlin International Film Festival (Generation Kplus): A shy 11-year-old boy seeks escape at night in his dreams, fleeing into an Oriental fairy-tale world.

FEBRUARY 9

Hexe Lilli: Der Drache und das magische Buch (Lilly the Witch: The Dragon and the Magic Book) with Trixter-animated dragon character. Adapted from Knister's [80] book and directed by **Stefan Ruzowitzky**.

MARCH

Beyond Remedy (working title simply: *Fear*) was first shown in Turkey and in other countries, including the United States, before DVD sales began in Germany on January 7, 2010: The story of six international medical students who went forth to learn what fear was.

MARCH 26

2D-animated *Prinzessin Lillifee (Princess Lillifee)* rules the enchanted kingdom of Pinkovia.

APRIL 7

Mörder kennen keine Grenzen (Time Warp): TV sci-fi.

---

80   Ludger Jochmann.

MAY 1

Melancholie der Engel (The Angels' Melancholia), an experimental horror film by "Marian Dora".

MAY 18

Antichrist by Lars von Trier shown at the Cannes Film Festival: As some locations in North Rhine-Westphalia (Germany) were used, Trier was co-funded by Filmstiftung Nordrhein-Westfalen in Düsseldorf (check **Robert Sigl's** Foreword to this book).

JUNE 11

Suffer and Die made by Philip Polcar for roughly € 2000.

JULY 23

Mullewapp—Das grosse Kinoabenteuer der Freunde (Mullewapp: The Big Cinema Adventure of the Friends): MotionWorks Halle-animated farmyard tale. The cinema version based on a TV series with characters created by Helme Heine.

SEPTEMBER 9

As a kid, German TV star comedian Michael "Bully" Herbig was thus fascinated with Japanese anime series *Wickie und die starken Männer (Vicky and the Strong Men/Chiisana Baikingu Bikke/Vicky the Viking)*, based on children's books by Runer Jonsson, that he decided to produce a live-action movie with Jonas Hämmerle as Viking boy going on adventure.

SEPTEMBER 24

Laura's Stern und der geheimnisvolle Drache Nian (Laura's Star and the Mysterious Dragon Nian): Set against the background of a rural Mongolian area and the Chinese capital offering awesome sights of past, present and future at the time of New Year's Spring Festival. Two girls, Laura born in the West (Germany) and Ling-Ling raised in the East (China), master their initial misunderstandings and with the help of a tiny, miracle-working Star become close friends.

Laura and family go to China. Laura's Mother, a cello player, is scheduled to appear in concert with a pipa player on stage at the New Year's Concert in the Opera. A faithful friend, a living tiny star that has befriended with Laura, is following the plane like a guardian angel. Hitting turbulences, however, the star gets lost somewhere over Inner Mongolia.

Laura feels totally alien in the big Chinese city Beijing after she has lost the Star while Ling-Ling misses her father, a renowned yak-researcher, who very often is out in the countryside and not at home. It is Ling-Ling on one of her rare trips to visit her father at a Field of Yaks located in a National Park who finds what she thinks is a sparkling glass object. Actually, it is Laura's Star that she brings to Beijing.

Meanwhile Laura and her family are shown around the huge concert hall Mom will appear. This also marks Laura's first encounter with Ling-Ling who has been pulled to the hall by the star's power. Ling-Ling's Aunt, by the way, is the pipa player who will be on stage with Laura's Mother. Fighting over the glowing gem, the Star, the girls realize that they have much in common and that they only have to share the sense of wonder that the Star opens up for them.

But before that is going to happen, there are trials and tribulations to test the seriousness of their friendship. In the Darkest Night of the Year a whole twilight world of imagination materializes. Although Laura is worried about her Star assuming that it might be blackened, the girls dare to face all dangers and, illuminated by the Star's magic and with the support of a makeshift Nian, overcome their fears to emerge as twin sisters.

Nian, a creature, half dog, half lion, has been awakened by the girls' initial dispute over the ownership of the miraculous Star although this Nian was only a costume to appear on stage with the musicians at New Year's Eve. Some stardust has fallen onto this Nian costume and made it alive. According to legend, Nian's mission is to scare people in the darkness of the last night of the old year. To their big surprise, Laura and Ling-Ling find out that the creature that once has been a costume is unaware of its menacing role and even is too scared himself to scare others.

Riding on the back of the Nian creature, tamed by cookies, the girls travel high above Beijing to defeat the Cloud of Darkness and save the Star from being blackened.

A giant firework celebrating New Year has the Black Cloud retread and brings the girls back to the reality of their families and to a springtime of star-blessed friendship.

On stage, Laura's Mother and Ling-Ling's Aunt have come to the finale. They end nicely keeping one last tone and look happily at each other and to their families sitting in the first row. The delighted audience applauds frenetically. Overjoyed, the two girls hug.

By their mutual care, the girls will grow to the understanding that a shared life is a prosperous life.

First Sino-German co-production in 3D (more than 50 % of the movie were produced in Beijing, a small percentage in India, the rest in Berlin, Germany). A sequel to *Laura's Star* (2004, that told how Laura and the Star became friends) that told how Laura and the star became friends. Famous Chinese pianist Lang Lang was delighted to take part in the production as he was started at an early age having seen a Tom & Jerry Cartoon, *Cat Concerto*.

In an earlier version the tiny Miracle Star didn't "crash" over Inner Mongolia but the Forbidden City in Beijing. On the roofs of the ancient buildings there are nine little stone dragons and one of them is brought to life by the power of stardust. This little creature befriends Ling-Ling, a little girl who attends a kung fu school. The climax was supposed to happen not in Beijing but on the Roof of the Earth, somewhere in Tibet, where a yak-cow gives birth to a calf.

However, as often happens in animation, there are many cooks involved and everybody seems to have ideas of his or her own.

Awards:

Gold Panda Award, Best domestic animated feature film, 2011

Gold Panda Award, Best Screenplay, 2011

OCTOBER 1

Studio Babelsberg-produced space opera *Pandorum* with Dennis Quaid and Ben Foster as astronauts.

OCTOBER 3

Break, a sadistic set slasher movie set in the Canadian woods, at the Sitges—Catalonian International Film Festival: *No Mercy, Just Pain!*

OCTOBER 10

La Petite Mort by Marcel Walz: Three friends on their way to Mallorca are mugged by an unknown and wind up at a restaurant called *Maison de la Petite Mort*.

OCTOBER 18 AND 19

Vulkan (Volcano): surprising volcanic activities in the Eiffel mountains in Germany. Two-part disaster movie produced by TeamWorx for RTL TV. VFX by Pixomondo.

Break | © Praetoria Productions/Anolis Entertainment

NOVEMBER 19

Tannöd, deep in the fir forest, is the proper location of a *Murder Farm* in Swiss-German co-production.

NOVEMBER 29

Mein Flaschengeist und ich (My Genie and Me) produced by Constantin Television for RTL.

DECEMBER 15

Erdora—Kapitel 1: Der Todeskreis (Erdora Chapter 1: The Circle of Death), a video by Philip Polcar.

DECEMBER 25

Suzanne von Borsody as evil witch who encaptures *Rapunzel* played by Luisa Wietzorek in a TV fairy tale directed by Bodo Fürneisen.

Roman Knižka as TV's *Puss in Boots: Der gestiefelte Kater*.

An Anglo-German animation short on BBC TV: *The Gruffalo* by Max Lang and Jakob Schuh based on the eponymous children's book.

DECEMBER 26

Lotte Flack as *Dornröschen (Sleeping Beauty)* and Hannelore Elsner as Maruna in a TV fairy tale directed by Oliver Dieckmann.

Gottfried John as King Gustav and Robert Stadlober as TV's *Rumpelstilzchen (Rumpelstiltskin)*.

The Grimm Brothers' *Gänsemagd (The Goose Girl)* on TV.

Deutschmond: Eerie creatures threaten Berlin in the 21st century. Directed by George Inci.

DECEMBER 28

Scientist discovers ancient *bible code*: *Der Bibelcode*. TV movie starred Cosma Shiva Hagen and Joachim Fuchsberger.

2010

Cinemas: 1714

JANUARY 2

Die Bremer Stadtmusikanten (The Bremen Town Musicians): TV version with the German voices of Peter Striebeck (donkey), Harald Schmidt (rooster), Hannelore Elsner (cat), and Bastian Pastewka (cat).

Die kluge Bauerntochter (The Smart Farmer's Daughter), TV fairy tale with Anna Maria Mühe.

JANUARY 28

A more or less (more: less) romantic date in the Brandenburg forests ends in a typical slasher orgy: *Bad End*.

FEBRUARY 1

Hepzibah—Sie holt dich im Schlaf (Hepzibah/The Village): TV thriller by **Robert Sigl**. An ordinary town in the east becomes the bizarre scene of a most terrifying trend. Seemingly happy girls are killing themselves on their 18th birthday. For Kirsten that fact does not deter her from traveling to the accursed Selmen trying to unearth the facts which had led to her adoption.

Her yearning for the truth buried in her past must be fulfilled quickly as the day of her 18th birthday is near...

MARCH 14

Dead Survivors, another zombie virus routine.

MARCH 15 AND 16

Two-part (180 minutes) TV movie *Die Grenze (The Frontier)* produced by teamWorx (Nico Hofmann) for Sat.1: What would happen if Germany would be divided again?

MARCH 20

No Reason by Olaf Ittenbach. Tagline: *Sometimes Death has no reason!*

APRIL

American, Swedish and German DVD premiere of **Uwe Boll's** *The Final Storm:* doomsday on a global scale, an almost Biblical deluge.

APRIL 29

Bloodthirsty murderer on the *Rampage* (directed by **Uwe Boll**).

APRIL 30

Kassel premiere of Ralf Kemper's *Toxic Lullaby*: After a bad drug trip Eloise wakes up amidst a nightmare of zombies.

MAY 1

Karl the Butcher vs. Axe (set in "post doomsday year" 2023 with a fight all against all) by Timo Rose and Andreas Schnaas announced as *Violent Shit*

4.0. Co-starring Moguewai Warriors, The Other, Gang Loco, Hirntot (Braindead), and Not Fragile.

MAY 4

Zurück zum Glück (Back to Luck): A second chance for Ines Wegner. Ines gets transported back in the past tries to re-direct her life. TV movie by Wolfgang Dinslage.

JULY

Attack of the Tromaggot: a common maggot transformed into a large flesh-eating worm. 81-minute amateur video.

JULY 15

Womb written and directed by Benedek Fliegauf at the German Film Week: a woman's consuming love forces her to bear the clone of her dead beloved.

AUGUST 16

Avantgarde by Marcel Walz: *Fashion Kills!* Special makeup effects by Marc Rohnstock.

SEPTEMBER 9

Rammbock: Berlin Undead. When Michael makes the trip from Vienna to Berlin to see his ex-girlfriend Gabi, he stumbles into a city that is in the grip of a terrible virus.

Black Death, an Anglo-German co-production. The 14th century: Only one single village populated of infidels is mysteriously spared by the plague.

SEPTEMBER 11

Leuenklinge: a sword & sorcerer fanfilm by Nicolas Mendrek based on RPG *The Dark Eye*. Shot at Lohra Castle in Thuringia.

SEPTEMBER 16

Resident Evil: Afterlife with Milla Jovovich.

SEPTEMBER 28

Das zweite Wunder von Loch Ness (The Secret of Loch Ness II), a Rat Pack production for Sat.1 TV. Apparently the first part (2008) was successful enough to come up with a sequel along the same lines. Lukas Schust repeats his part as a boy who is on the track of the Loch Ness Monster.

SEPTEMBER 30

Das Sandmännchen—Abenteuer im Traumland (The Sandman and the Lost Sand of Dreams): stop motion with Germany's TV Sandman set in a live-action frame (with a slight nod to **Michael Ende's** *NeverEnding Story*).

Miko dreams of being a captain. He is an imaginative little boy, but he is just as fearful. Miko is also the only hope the Sandman has to save the dreams of every child in the world. The Sandman's dream-making sand has been stolen by Habumar. Habumar is going to poison the sand and turn people's dreams into nightmares.

A mix-up sends Miko into the Sandman's world, where all dreams live on after we wake up.

Shot at a special (former exhibition) stage at Babelsberg Studios.

OCTOBER 7

Konferenz der Tiere (Animals United), officially based on Erich Kästner's book but in 3D animation more like *Madagascar*. Produced by Ambient Entertainment (Holger Tappe) and Constantin Film (Reinhard Klooss) and one of the worldwide most successful German animation films.

OCTOBER 15

La Isla by Michael Effenberger: Two sisters on a remote island (because it's a cheap movie). A voodoo priestess has dark visions—and the dead (and with them evil) return to earth. Some splatter effects created by Olaf Ittenbach.

OCTOBER 28

Wir sind die Nacht (The Dawn): female vampires in the night life of Berlin. Starring Karoline Herfurth, Nina Hoss and Jennifer Ulrich in a movie produced by Rat Pack and Constantin Film.

OCTOBER 30

The Color, a cinematic adaptation of H. P. Lovecraft's short novel *The Color Out of Space*: Jonathan Davis, an American, travels to Germany where his father was stationed after the war and finds the area poisoned by a meteorite.

SEPTEMBER 23

German sci-fi movie *Transfer—Der Traum vom ewigen Leben (Transfer: The Dream of Eternal Life)* entered Austin Fantastic Fest.

NOVEMBER 4

Die kommenden Tage (The Coming Days) written and directed by Lars Kraume with Bernadette Heerwagen and Daniel Brühl: doomsday panic over the few remaining oil fields in Asia.

NOVEMBER 7

Crash landing on the remote planet of *Nydenion*, German sci-fi mix.

DECEMBER 5

Necronos: Tower of Doom by Marc Rohnstock: Necronos is a mage who wants nothing else than to obliterate the whole mankind with the support of a blood demon, a witch and gruesome warrior demons. But first he needs a virgin witch…

DECEMBER 24

Aschenputtel (Cinderella), another TV version of the fairy tale made by Provobis for Zweites Deutsches Fernsehen.

DECEMBER 25

Das blaue Licht (The Blue Light), a Grimm fairy tale produced by German TV (Hessischer Rundfunk).

In addition:

This year splatter video producers Timo Rose and Andreas Schnaas joined forces and made a splatter comedy shocker *Unrated: The Movie*: Frank, an unsuccessful director, takes some amateur actresses to a forest hut to shoot a new movie. One of the props is the ancient *Book of Nightmares*…

Abnormis: "Stop screaming, I'm only slicing you."

Another video entry was titled *A Fucking Cruel Nightmare*.

2011

Cinemas: 1671

JANUARY 11

2030—Aufstand der Jungen (2030: Revolt of the Young): dystopian TV thriller by Jörg Lühdorff, a sequel to *2030—Aufstand der Alten (2030: Revolt of the Old*, 2007).

JANUARY 18

Restrisiko (Residual Risk): Sat.1 TV movie about an accident in a nuclear power plant.

JANUARY 20

Popular by Marcel Walz, a.k.a. *Maximum Violence*.

JANUARY 24

Unexpectedly, producer-distributor **Bernd Eichinger** suffered a heart attack. He died during a dinner with family and friends in Los Angeles. Since he attended film school in Munich, Bernd Eichinger's pet project was a 2nd remake of the *Nibelungs* and, becoming the head of the New Constantin Film that was established after the bankruptcy of the old company, followed that vain dream until his premature death in 2001: his first script titled *The Morning of Valhalla*, the final draft *Wrath*. Director Tom Tykwer who had read it, *"There he had picked a sandtrap as big as a swimming pool. If he would have made that movie, the critics would have crucified him."*[81]

FEBRUARY 3

Beijing premiere of ***Little Big Panda (Kleiner starker Panda)*** co-produced

---

81 Süddeutsche Zeitung, September 5, 2012.

by Benchmark Entertainment Picture Productions, Berlin/Angels Avenue/ Juventy Films/ORB Filmproduktion/Yi Sang Media in association with China Animation Comic Game Group Co. Ltd., Beijing and directed by Michael Schoemann and Greg Manwaring.

High in the majestic mountains the survival of the panda bears is under dire threat as humans (Chinese, not to be seen in the final movie) encroach on their environment. At the same time the supply of the pandas' cherished sole nutrient, bamboo shoots, is steadily dwindling away. Unfortunately, pandas become extremely apathetic when confronted with change and certainly need a hero to guide them out of misery.

The one they need is Manchu [Chinese version: Pandy], a little panda known as the "Chosen One", but stupidly he is rejected by his clan due to his hair-brained ideas but finally gains confidence and leads his community struggling for survival to a better environment, a New Promised Land of Bamboo.

Long and complicated production history. In China announced as the most expensive domestic animated feature film up to date (with a budget of more than US$50 million). Actually produced in Europe (Germany, Spain, Belgium) for less than US$10 million. Xiao Xiong Chen, a wealthy Chinese investor with no knowledge of animation but a network of good connections, bought into the project for a million and released the Chinese dubbing that included well-known voice talent via China Film Group with a big promotional campaign.

Picco is a raw drama set in a youth prison.

FEBRUARY 17

Hexe Lilli—Die Reise nach Mandolan (Lilly the Witch: The Journey to Mandolan). 3D-animated by Trixter Munich was Lilli's companion, Hector the little dragon.

FEBRUARY 25

Entropie (Entropy), low-budget direct-to-ivdeo release: *One man—four fates… and a whole world at the edge of chaos.*

FEBRUARY 26

Unrated 2: Scary as Hell by Andreas Schnaas and Timo Rose: The next object of a TV journalist named Abby Freitag who specializes in supernatural phenomena is a haunted house.

FEBRUARY

The Future, low-budget French-American-Anglo-German co-production written and directed by and starring Miranda July nominated for a Golden Bear, 61st Berlin International Film Festival: When Sophie and Jason decide to adopt a sick stray cat, their perspective of life changes radically, literally altering the course of space and time.

In the world of Miranda July, magic is possible. Did I mention that some of The Future *is narrated by the sick cat? In her films, the passage of time is not allowed to become routine.* […]

On the surface, this film is an enchanting meditation. At its core is the hard steel of individuality. [82]

MARCH 10

Iron Doors 3D: Man must escape from locked vault before he dies of dehydration. Filmed in Cologne.

Die Tigerentenbande—Der Film (The Gang of Tigers: The Movie), an animated feature film inspired by Janosch and produced by Papa Löwe Filmproduktion.

---

82 Roger Ebert, *Fluffy whimsy and a core of steel*. www.rogerebert.com.

MARCH 13

The Divide by Xavier Gens at the South by Southwest Film Festival. Lauren German and Michael Biehn as survivors of a nuclear attack locked in the basement of their apartment building. American-French-Canadian with German co-producers involved.

APRIL 4

Project Genesis: Crossclub 2, indie trash & splatter movie. Announced as being made by a bunch of people who most likely have watched Robert Rodriguez's *Planet Terror*.

MAY 1

Der Film deines Lebens (The Film of Your Life), a mystery drama by Sebastian Goder.

MAY 6

Uwe Boll's *BloodRayne: The Third Reich* at the Weekend of Fear Festival with a mix of vampires and Nazis. Shot in Zagreb, Croatia.

MAY 18

Melancholia by Lars von Trier was supported by Filmstiftung Nordrhein-Westfalen and premiered at the Cannes Film Festival.

JUNE 8

Nina sieht es…!!! (Nina Sees It…!!!): a fantasy comedy, TV movie by Rolf Silber.

JULY 28

Masks by Andreas Marschall at the Grossman Film and Wine Festival in Slovenia: In the 1970s Matteusz Gdula invented an acting method that was supposed to make every actor "shine". But lots of his students died. Gdula committed suicide. His method got banned. Decades later Stella, a struggling but rather untalented drama student, is accepted by the still working school. There she is eyewitness of some strange occurences and gets drawn into the bizarre and deadly web that surrounds the dark secret of the school.

The acting in this one is fantastic. Normally, it's hard to judge a foreign release but this film is well acted and it shows regardless of the language. […]

The story is a stylish murder mystery with a great ending and a lot of suspense throughout. I typically dislike giallos but this one knew exactly how to hold the viewer's attention. Finally, those of you looking for death will find it here. The film has several death scenes that take its time when it comes to the carnage. The kills are not rushed but stylishly drawn out to give the viewers their money's worth. No camera tricks and quick cuts where the viewer misses out here. Instead, the kills are done in front of us to enjoy.

The reviewer certainly is a splatter connoisseur. [83]

AUGUST 26

Uwe Boll presents *Schlaraffenhaus* by Marcel Walz, a *Sadistic Massacre*.

AUGUST 31

Sex, Dogz and Rock n Roll: action and animation by Braunschweig-based amateur and industrial film brothers Marc and Carsten Fehse.

SEPTEMBER 1

2D-animated *Prinzessin Lillifee und das kleine Einhorn (Princess Lillifee and the Little Unicorn)*.

---

83   Blacktooth, www.horrorsociety.com, October 30, 2016.

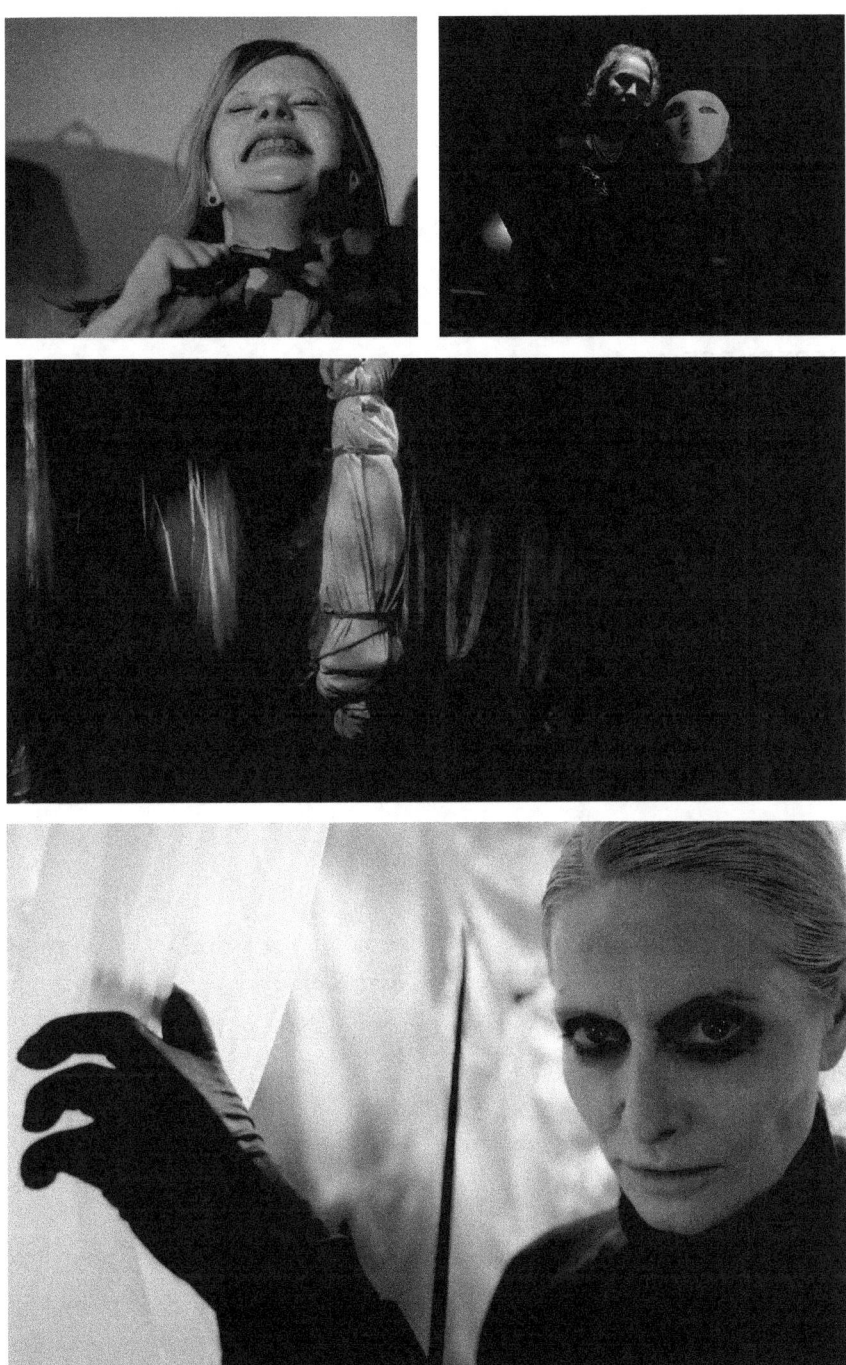

Masks | © Stormlight Films and Anolis Entertainment

SEPTEMBER 11

A German TV production made with domestic talent in China premiered in Toronto: *UFO in Her Eyes* directed by Xiaolu Guo from his own novel that deals with a supposed UFO sighting in a village in the South of China that (with the support of a millionaire) becomes a tourist spot. **Udo Kier** was cast as Steve Frost.

SEPTEMBER 15

Low-budget filmmaker Ulrike Ottinger entered a Japanese village *Unter Schnee (Under Snow)*.

SEPTEMBER 22

Tim Fehlbaum's *Hell*: People of the future (Hannah Herzsprung, Lars Eidinger) struggling to fight the devastasting effects of sun rays: *The Sun will burn you!* Production began at the Munich Film School in 2009 under the title *2016—Das Ende einer Nacht (2016: The End of a Night)*. The production was supported by **Roland Emmerich.**

SEPTEMBER 25

The dramatic world of Global Warming according to RTL TV: *Bermuda-Dreieck Nordsee (Bermuda-Triangle North Sea)*.

OCTOBER 13

Lauras Stern und die Traummonster (Laura's Star and the Dream Monsters), another entry in Klaus Baumgart's series of animated films (with a big chunk executed in China).

Der siebente Rabe (The Seventh Raven), a 72-minute silhouette film by Jörg Herrmann.

OCTOBER 20

Urban Explorer (The Depraved) by Andy Fetscher: *Discover the dark side of Berlin*. A venture into a subterranean world.

OCTOBER 27

Der letzte Angestellte (The Last Employee), low-budget ZDF TV film: A lawyer hired to liquidate a company is terrorized by a woman he had to fire. Special makeup effects by Olaf Ittenbach.

NOVEMBER 17

Extinction: The G.M.O. Chronicles: the survivors of a pandemic in the usual hurry to find a cure against turning into zombies.

NOVEMBER 24

Als der Weihnachtsmann vom Himmel fiel (When Santa Fell to Earth): Santa crashlands his sleigh having escaped the evil Gerold Goblynch who was named head of the Great Christmas Council. Based on a novel by Cornelia Funke and produced at MMC Studios in Cologne.

DECEMBER 24

Der Eisenhans (Iron John): TV fairy tale, produced by Provobis for Zweites Deutsches Fernsehen.

DECEMBER 25

Jorinde und Joringel, a TV fairy tale produced by Hessischer Rundfunk.

DECEMBER 26

Die zertanzten Schuhe (The Shoes that Were Danced to Pieces), a new TV version of the Grimm fairy tale.

DECEMBER 27

American-Canadian DVD premiere of **Uwe Boll's** fantasy *Schwerter des Königs —Zwei Welten (In the Name of the King: Two Worlds)* with Dolph Lundgren.

2012

Cinemas: 1652

JANUARY 12

Reality XL Realität ist ein Traum (Reality Is a Dream) with Heiner Lauterbach as Professor Konstantin Carus and the mystery of a particle accelerator that lets 23 of his colleagues disappear.

FEBRUARY 4

An archeologist discovers an ancient artifact and scroll that arte linked to a gateway of hell: *Legend of Hell* by Olaf Ittenbach.

FEBRUARY 11

Iron Sky premiered at Berlin International Film Festival, a Finnish-Australian-German co-production about Nazis on the Moon. Among the German actors are Götz Otto, **Udo Kier** and Tilo Prückner.

FEBRUARY 12

Martina Gedeck imprisoned somewhere in the countryside by an invisible *Wall*: Austrian-German co-production *Die Wand* was based on a 1963 novel by Marlen Haushofer.

MAY 18

Zombies from Outer Space with alien-zombies invading Bavaria. Location shooting in and around Landshut. Martin Faltermeier directed.

Savage Love by Olaf Ittenbach: Demons raid a brothel.

MAY 24

Janosch's *Komm, wir finden einen Schatz (Let's Find a Treasure)*, animated children's film made by Papa Löwe Filmproduktion.

JUNE 25

Cannibal Diner premiered in Essen: *Sie haben dich zum Fressen gern...*—*They love to eat you...*

OCTOBER 30

Mich gibt's nur zweimal (Mama ist ein Android/Robot Mom): TV comedy on testing high-tech household androids.

SEPTEMBER 6

Der kleine Rabe Socke (Raven the Little Rascal): Animated animal fable with a raven character from a book by Nele Moost.

SEPTEMBER 20

Resident Evil: Retribution co-funded by Constantin Film Munich.

OCTOBER 5

Radio Silence (On Air) at the Mile High Horror Film Festival: A serial killer called The Night Ripper plays cat and mouse with police and public.

NOVEMBER 1

Niko 2—Kleines Rentier, grosser Held (Niko 2: Little Brother, Big Trouble): Reindeer Niko has to save his little stepbrother Jonni who was kidnapped.

NOVEMBER 15

In 1849 a businessman on a Melville-esque sea voyage in the South Pacific battles a mysterious illness and shelters a runaway slave. In 1936 Robert Frobisher, a penniless young composer, flees Cambridge for Edinburgh to join the household of a vain and temperamental maestro. Four decades later an alternative-press journalist risks her life investigating safety problems at a nuclear power plant.

In our own day a feckless book publisher finds himself trapped in a nursing home. Sometime in the corporate, totalitarian future a member of the genetically engineered serving class, a fast-food worker named Sonmi-451, is drawn into rebellion, while in a still more distant, postapocalyptic, neo-tribal future (where Sonmi is worshipped as a deity), a Hawaiian goatherd. …

Cloud Atlas: Besides *Metropolis* the biggest financial flop in German fantasy film history. Distributors warned Berlin-based production company X-Filme to try and film David Mitchell's massively non-linear 2004 novel but Tom Tykwer and the Wachowskis (Lana and Andy) wouldn't listen, hired Tom Hanks and Halle Berry, spent an enormous money and produced one unintelligible movie that doesn't make sense if you don't know the book. Only in China a mild success.

Describing this movie, despite its lofty ambitions, can feel like an exercise in number crunching, and watching it is a bit like doing a series of math problems in your head. How do three directors parcel six plots into 172 minutes? [84]

And Roger Ebert wrote: *Even as I was watching* **Cloud Atlas** *the first time, I knew I would need to see it again. Now that I've seen it the second time, I know I'd like to see it a third time—but I no longer believe repeated viewings will solve anything. To borrow Churchill's description of Russia, "it is a riddle, wrapped in a mystery, inside an enigma."* [85]

---

84 A. O. Scott, Souls Tangled Up in Time. In: The New York Times, October 26, 2012.
85 Castles in the Sky. October 24, 2012. www.rogerebert.com/reviews/cloud-atlas-2012.

NOVEMBER 17

Plastic a.k.a. *Plastic Surgery Massacre* by Marcel Walz screened at the Austrian Fright Nights:

NOVEMBER

Grünes Gold (Green Gold): Claymation short about media manipulation concerning the Iraq war.

DECEMBER 25

Sibylle Tafel's TV version of *Rotkäppchen* with Edgar Selge as wolf and Amona Assmann as *Little Red Riding Hood*.

Sebastian Grobler followed with another Grimm tale: *Schneeweisschen und Rosenrot* with Sonja Gerhardt as Snow White and Liv Lisa Fries as Rose Red. Detlev Buck played the evil dwarf.

Jan Josef Liefers as *Baron Münchhausen* rides the cannonball in a 2-part TV movie (First-Channel TV).

DECEMBER 26

Hänsel und Gretel: TV version for First Channel TV. Anja Kling as the witch. Uwe Janson directed.

DECEMBER 27

Die Vampirschwestern: Two 12-year-old *Vampire Sisters*, Silvania Tepes (Marta Martin) and Dakaria Tepes (Laura Antonia Roge), have to adapt to the human world. Based on a book by Franziska Gehm. Produced by Claussen Wöbke Putz Filmproduktion and the German branch of Columbia Pictures.

2013

Cinemas: 1637

JANUARY 13

Ritter Rost—Eisenhart und voll verbeult: 3D-animated fantasy adventures of young *Knight Rusty* who resembles a walking cash register in a land made of scrap metal. Rusty must reclaim his honor after being accused of cheating in a jousting tournament. "Highlight" is the fight with a fire-breathing dragon. Based on an idea by Mark Slater.

A serial killer who murdered 23 young women at the beginning of WW1: *Bela Kiss: Prologue*.

JANUARY 22

Buenos Aires premiere of *Hansel & Gretel: Witch Hunters* with Jeremy Renner as Hansel and Gemma Arterton as Gretel killing witches all around. The American production was shot at Studio Babelsberg (participating as co-producers) and on location in Saxony and Braunschweig.

JANUARY 28

Blutsschwestern—Jung, magisch, tödlich (Blood Sisters: Young, Magical, Deadly): Supernatural TV horror movie produced by ProSieben. Working title: *Die Bibel des Blutes (The Bible of Blood)*.

FEBRUARY 7

The Forbidden Girl is a witch looking for the love of the young son of a fundamentalist pastor.

FEBRUARY

A young girl survives the end of the world, with most of mankind wiped out by a comet, rather economically for filmmaker Sebastian Fritzsch somewhere in the forest: *Endzeit (End of Time)*. Premiered at Berlin International Film Festival.

MARCH

The *Art Girls* of the title are three women from Berlin who, while preparing an exhibition sponsored by a biotech firm, experience symptoms of an evolutionary leap. Rather pretentious and dull.

MARCH 14

Der Mondmann: producer Stephan Schesch's underfinanced but sympathetic animation fantasy of a *Moon Man* visiting Earth. Based on a book by Tomi Ungerer.

Hai-Alarm am Müggelsee (Shark Alarm at Müggel Lake), a comedy written and directed by Leander Haussmann and Sven Regner. Certainly no competition for *Jaws*.

MARCH 21

Quiqueck & Hämat: Proll Out with two 3D-animated aliens orbiting earth to observe mankind.

MARCH

Der Schrottmann (The Scrapman): Three kids playing on the Scrapman's ground find movies where they can be part of. Short film by Fabian Driehorst made at Kunsthochschule für Medien in Cologne.

Die Frau in mir (*The Woman Inside*, working title: *Zur Sache, Macho!*), transsexual German TV fantasy commissioned by Sat.1.

APRIL 11

Thor—Ein hammermässiges Abenteuer (Legends of Valhalla: Thor), an animated feature film co-produced by Hamburg-based Ulysses Filmproduktion:

The young blacksmith Thor dreams of greatness, honor and respect but his mother has other plans for him. He is the son of Odin, the King of the Gods, and the villagers believe that they live under Odin's godly protection. In the meantime, Hel, the Queen of the Underworld, is brewing an evil plot that endangers both men and gods. The hammer Crusher ends up in Thor's hands and when giants swarm the land, capturing (among others) Thor's best friend Edda, Thor must step up in order to stand a chance against the evil forces.

APRIL 21

Raw—Der Fluch der Grete Müller (Raw: The Curse of Grete Müller) by Marcel Walz at the Vienna Fright Nights Film Festival. *Blair Witch Project* rip-off with teenagers who are going to shoot a documentary about the legend of Grete Müller in a haunted forest.

MAY 16

German co-funded *Der Kongress (The Congress)* is a very innovative idea by Ari Folman loosely based on a book by Stanisław Lem: An actress (played by an ageing Robin Wright) sells her likeness to Miramount Nagasaki (originally Paramount Nagasaki) to become an animated image within a polluted world. Screened at the Cannes Festival during Directors' Fortnight: *It says a lot about* **The Congress** *that it risks sowing such confusion, blurring the line between the actor and the character, inviting us to draw parallels between the confident, successful Wright and her gloomy, outmoded alter ego. Ostensibly, the film is science fiction—directed by the Israeli animator Ari Folman amnd spotlighting issues of intellectual property, internet avatars and the withering flesh. But, like the best SF,* **The Congress** *is actually about the here and now. We might not want to live in the world that is shows us. On some level, however, we already do.*[86]

---

86 The Guardian, August 7, 2014.

JULY 1

British DVD premiere of an **Uwe Boll** production: *Zombie Massacre* (in a Romanian town).

JULY

A film project was discussed by Thomas Eckelkamp, son of producer-distributor Hanns Eckelkamp, and writer Rolf Giesen: *Nosferatu vs. Dracula*.

A FIGHT FOR SUPREMACY BETWEEN IMMORTALS

KRONOS, *the all-devouring son of heaven and earth, the ancient leader of the titans who castrated his father Ouranus, was defeated by* **ZEUS**, *the lightning god, who condemned the "original" into Tartarus.*

In our story, **NOSFERATU**, *the ancient Lord of the Vampires, is like Kronos: a monstrous creature of destruction born from Hell, leading an army of death-bringing rats and a pandemonium of other creatures from the depths of the abyss to the surface of earth. His strongest weapon against mankind is the plague. His objective: Extinguish humans and their environment and make the surface of earth uninhabitable, make it like hell—no sun, no water, no hope, no life.*

DRACULA, *the skyborn vampire, represented by the wings of the bats, suave, seductive and erudite, uses modern tactics to defeat his gruesome ancestor and conceal his own identity, his equally gruesome origin and past.*

Unlike **NOSFERATU, DRACULA** *is a creature of light: a fallen angel condemned to live in darkness which he loathes and abhors. His main mistake: He wanted to become like God himself. His main goal is to overcome his shortfall and return into light—as new god and ruler of all heaven.*

DRACULA *wants to destroy in order to rebuild.* **NOSFERATU** *wants total destruction and chaos.*

The struggle for power and world domination is staged as final war between bats and rats.

AUGUST 12

Hollywood premiere of ***Chroniken der Unterwelt—City of Bones (The Mortal Instruments: City of Bones)*** directed by Harald Zwart from a screenplay by Jessica Postigo: A young woman joins a group of warriors in New York City who protect the world from demons. German-American-Canadian-British co-production based on a series by Cassandra Clare. German production partner was Constantin Film Munich.

AUGUST 18

Necrophile Passion (Necrophilic Passion) written and directed by Tom Heidenberg.

SEPTEMBER 19

Lost Place: An abandoned U.S. military radio tower station in the Palatinate forest (Pfälzerwald) with still horrible side effects.

SEPTEMBER 26

Keinohrhase und Zweiohrküken (Rabbit without Ears and Two-Eared Chick): preschool 3D animation based on a children's book by Klaus Baumgart and Til Schweiger.

OCTOBER 3

Helden—Wenn Dein Land Dich braucht (Heroes: The Fate of the World is in their Hands), TV movie that opens with a telecommunications satellite crashing into the Brandenburg Gate in Berlin.

NOVEMBER 7

Das kleine Gespenst: feature film with a 3D-animated version of Otfried Preussler's *Little Ghost* (and a nod to *Casper the Friendly Ghost*).

DECEMBER 19

TV fairy tale *Die goldene Gans (The Golden Goose)*.

DECEMBER 25

Grimm's *Vom Fischer und seiner Frau (The Fisherman and His Wife)* as TV movie directed by Christian Theede.

DECEMBER 26

Another TV version of Grimm Brothers' *Der Teufel mit den drei goldenen Haaren (The Devil with Three Golden Hair)* starring André M. Hennicke as the Devil.

TV-made *Die kleine Meerjungfrau (The Little Mermaid)* based on the fairy tale by Hans Christian Andersen with Zoe Moore as Undine, Ben Becker as her father, King of the Sea, and Ben's sister Meret Becker as Mydra the witch.

2014

Cinemas: 1630

Aloryon: fantasy film directed by Marcel Barion, sword & sorcery against the evil powers of darkness.

FEBRUARY 1

Seed 2 (produced by **Uwe Boll**): Serial killer Max Seed is back...

FEBRUARY 20

Technically well-made but story- and character-wise rather disappointing jungle adventures produced by Ambient Entertainment and Constantin Film: *Tarzan 3D*.

The animation is efficient but bland. The characters have all the expressiveness of plastic dolls.

The attempt at updating Edgar Rice Burroughs' much-filmed story and making it into a contemporary eco-fable is feeble in the extreme.

Even the chest-beating and vine-swinging are performed in half-hearted fashion. An absurdly portentous voice-over is used to plug the gaps in the story. […]

Johnny Weissmuller movies were much more fun than this. [87]

MARCH 13

Pettersson und Findus—Kleiner Quälgeist, grosse Freundschaft (Pettson and Findus: A Little Nuisance, a Great Friendship): Petersson is played by Ulrich Noethen while his cat friend Findus is 3D-animated.

APRIL 8

FPS: First Person Shooter at the Vienna Fright Nights Film Festival. The picture was filmed like an FPS game, fighting a scientist who has created a deadly virus and incidentally kidnapped your pregnant wife.

MAY 8

Raw 2—Das Tagebuch der Grete Müller (Raw 2: The Diary of Grete Müller) by Marcel Walz.

---

87 Geoffrey Macnab, *Tarzan 3D, film review: Big-budget German-made animation is utterly lacking in craft or wit*. In: Independent, May 1, 2014.

JULY 31

Die Fusion: A journey into an abstract *inner zone*. Low-budget movie with Nikolai (son of Klaus) Kinski as Dr. Antonius Cappa.

SEPTEMBER 11

Die Biene Maja—Der Kinofilm: Maya the Bee fighting the hornets—a revival of the Japanese anime series of the 1970s, 3D-animated.

SEPTEMBER 14

La Petite Mort II by Marcel Walz.

SEPTEMBER 16

The sword & sorcery world of *Omnia* explored in a hopeless plot.

SEPTEMBER 25

Der 7bte Zwerg (The 7th Dwarf), the 3D animated Story of the Seven Dwarves, mixing the fairy tales of *Snow White* and *Sleeping Beauty*: *The seven dwarves must wake Beauty from her slumber. And fast! Snow White's son has a mysterious illness that only Beauty can heal, if only the dwarves can make it to her birthday in time! The fight against the curse of evil Fairy Dellamorta is a race against time. Literally! Turning back the clock and travelling through time is easy. After all, this is supposed to be a fairy tale.*

Directed by Harald Siepermann (who died mid-production in 2013) and Boris Aljinovic, *The 7th Dwarf* is an animated extension of a franchise that includes two prior live-action features: *7 Dwarfs (2004)*, which was one of the most successful Teuton titles of that year, and its lower-grossing sequel, *7 Dwarfs: The Forest Is Not Enough (2006)*. Where those pictures freely sampled from the likes of "Snow White", "Little Red Riding Hood" and "Rumpelstiltskin", the new film largely riffs on "Sleeping Beauty" […] The dwarfs, by contrast, are a pretty inoffensive, forgettable bunch, whose names alone (i.e., Cloudy, Sunny, Cookie, Speedy) serve as a reminder of just how hard it has become to put an original spin on public-domain fairy tales outside the Disney studio auspices.[88]

Was the force mainly responsible for taking the project out of Siepermann's hand and spoiling it producer Douglas Welbat?

OCTOBER 16

Die Vampirschwestern 2—Fledermäuse im Bauch (Vampire Sisters 2: Bats in the Belly).

OCTOBER 30

Jakob, a young local police officer, encounters a sword-wielding *Samurai* in a movie written and directed by Till Kleinert.

Der kleine Medicus—Bodynauten auf geheimer Mission im Körper (The Litte Medic: Secret Mission of the Bodynauts/Rescue Rabbit): Fantastic Voyage styled educational fantasy (3D animation) based on a book by Dr. Dietrich Grönemeyer, the physician brother of German rock star Herbert Grönemeyer.

OCTOBER 31

Die Präsenz (The Presence) by Daniele Greco: A haunted castle becomes a deadly trap.

NOVEMBER 8

Spanish premiere of *Sueñan los androides (Androids Dream)* at the Seville European Film Festival. The movie was co-produced with German funding and released in Germany as *Androiden träumen*. Inspired by Philip K. Dick.

---

88 Justin Chang in: Variety July 30, 2015.

NOVEMBER 13

Damned on Earth: Belial, Prince of Hell, gets out of control. Amon, an ordinary Hell official, and sex-crazed Samsaveel are supposed to stop his riot. Written and directed by Ralf Kemper.

DECEMBER 18

Saphirblau (Blue Saphir): Time traveling mystery based on a book by Kerstin Gier. With Karl Walter Sprungala as William Shakespeare and Peter Simonischek as Count of St. Germain.

3D-animated *Coconut the Little Dragon: Der kleine Drache Kokosnuss.*

DECEMBER 25

Siebenschön: German TV movie produced in the Czech Republic based on a fairy tale by Ludwig Bechstein.

DECEMBER 26

Von einem, der auszog, das Fürchten zu lernen (The Story of the Youth Who Went Forth to Learn What Fear Was) by the Brothers Grimm made for TV.

2015

Cinemas: 1648

FEBRUARY 7

A student is chosen as teacher of a boy named Klaus who is kept by his parents in an isolated bunker mansion: *Der Bunker (The Bunker)* was presented at the Berlin International Film Festival (Perspektive Deutsches Kino).

FEBRUARY 28

Thanks to a potion Dr. Victor Wolffenstein, sort of a Frankenstein substitute, has become immortal but due to unwanted side effects (necrosis) is in constant need for new body parts: *The Curse of Doctor Wolffenstein* was written and directed by Marc Rohnstock.

APRIL 2

Erdora: Kapitel 2 Der Schattenkrieger (Erdora Chapter 2: The Shadow Warrior) by Philip Polcar and Michael Palm.

Gespensterjäger (Ghosthunters: On Icy Trails): Female comedian Anke Engelke as Hetty Cuminseed, a professional ghosthunter, and 11-year-old Tom Thompson are joined by a 3D-animated ghost. Animated by Michael Coldewey and his Munich Trixter gang.

Mara und der Feuerbringer (Mara and the Firebringer): a fifteen-year-old girl named Mara is going to stop the havoc Norse god Loki is about to spread all over the world. Produced by Rat Pack and Constantin Film.

APRIL 30

Raw 3—Die Offenbarung der Grete Müller (Raw 3: The Revelation of Grete Müller) by Marcel Walz.

MAY 2

5 Seasons, a horror video about child abuse by Olaf Ittenbach.

MAY 17

German Angst: Three horror episodes by Jörg Buttgereit (*Final Girl*), Michael Kosakowski (*Make a Wish*) and Andreas Marschall (*Alraune*).

MAY 19

Der kleine Rabe Socke 2—Das grosse Rennen (Raven the Little Rascal: The Big Race), 2D-animated sequel with the character created by Nele Moost, premiered at the Stuttgart Festival of Animation.

MAY 28

Disceptatio: Living in his imaginary world Connor fights for his love. Written and directed by Tim Gerrit Augurzke and Tobias Wolters.

JUNE 8

British release of *Zombie Massacre 2: Reich of the Dead* starring Nazi-created zombies versus American GIs. Produced by **Uwe Boll**.

JUNE 25

German release of the Danish-German co-production *Antboy 2: Die Rache der Red Fury*. Co-funded by Deutscher Filmförderfonds DFFF. (The 1st *Antboy* released in 2013 was completely Danish.)

JUNE 26

Boy 7, a sci-fi mystery thriller by Özgür Yildirim at the Munich International Film Festival: A teenager wakes up in a subway car suffering from complete memory loss.

JULY 16

Ooops! Die Arche ist weg… (Ooops! Noah Is Gone/All Creatures Big and Small): 3D-animated animal adventures on Noah's Ark with some ugly Nestrians as stowaways.

JULY 18

Der Himmel zwischen den Welten (The Sky Between the Worlds), TV movie by debutant Thomas André Szabó: Mia, a 17-year-old girl, realizes that she is going to play a key role at the Apocalypse.

AUGUST 10

Starting with the Locarno Film Festival, *Der Nachtmahr (The Nightmare)*, a Coming-of-age drama by AKIZ (i.e., Achim Bornhak), a graduate of Film Academy Baden-Württemberg, began to tour to the respective festivals: After a rave party another 17-year-old teenage girl has nightmares and is regularly visited by a horrible monster.

AUGUST 13

Hitman: Agent 47 (based on a computer game series) partly shot in Berlin and Brandenburg and therefore co-funded by Medienboard Berlin-Brandenburg.

SEPTEMBER 10

Therapie für einen Vampir/Der Vampir auf der Couch (Therapy for a Vampire): Tobias Moretti as vampire count Geza von Közsnöm enters psychotherapeutic sessions with Dr. Sigmund Freud (played by Karl Fischer).

OCTOBER 1

True Love Ways: Plagued by nightmares Séverine decides to separate from her boyfriend and enters a splatter romance in black and white.

OCTOBER 8

Er ist wieder da (Look Who's Back): *He* is no one else than Adolf Hitler who returns to nowadays Berlin and becomes a reality TV star. *He* is played by Oliver Masucci, who doesn't resemble Hitler that much but is a good actor.

Based on a bestselling book by Timur Vermes and directed by David Wnendt who studied at Film University Babelsberg:

"I think it's good and healthy to laugh about [Hitler]," says Wnendt. *"But there's a big difference whether you laugh about him as a person or whether you would belittle his crimes or if you laugh about the victims. That's a big difference."*

Wnendt believes it's better for Germans to laugh about Hitler than to demonize him.

"It was just normal people who elected [the Nazis], normal people who followed orders, and normal people who could've stopped him. And that didn't happen," Wnendt says. *"So the responsibility and also the historical fault is with the German people, with ordinary people."* [89]

OCTOBER 19

Creepy Campfire Stories on Halloweens Eve.

OCTOBER 23

8 Sekunden Ein Augenblick Unendlichkeit (8 Seconds: An Instant Infinity) at the Hof International Film Festival: Esra, a young Turkish woman living in Berlin, clashes with the rules imposed on her in real life and the world of her dreams.

NOVEMBER 5

Ritter Trenk (Trenk the Little Knight) is a ten-year-old boy who longs to become a medieval hero. Based on a children's book by Kirsten Boie and an equally 2D-animated series released to TV in 2011.

DECEMBER 3

Die Krone von Arkus (The Crown of Arkus), a German family fantasy film

---

[89] Carol Hills, *Yes, it's OK for Germans to laugh about Hitler.* In: The World, April 11, 2016.

released in the United States under the DVD title *The Malevolent Queen*. Filmed on location in Lower Saxony and Saxony-Anhalt. Written and directed by Franziska Pohlmann.

DECEMBER 17

Start of a series of films with young Felix Vorndran (played by Oskar Keymer) shrinking his school principal, then his parents and finally his friends: *Hilfe, ich hab meine Lehrerin geschrumpft (Help, I Shrunk My Teacher)*. Directed by Sven Unterwaldt Jr.

DECEMBER 25

Die Salzprinzessin (The Salt Princess), a Grimm fairy tale on TV.

DECEMBER 26

TV fairy tale *Hans im Glück (Hans in Luck)*.

2016

Cinemas: 1654

JANUARY 7

Unfriend by Simon Verhoeven: Cyberthriller about Laura, a psychology student, whose Facebook contacts turn into a nightmare. Directed by Simon Verhoeven, the son of actress Senta Berger and director Michael Verhoeven.

FEBRUARY 15

Molly Monster—Der Kinofilm (Molly Monster the Movie) premiered at the Generation section of Berlin International Film Festival. Molly Monster and her family are 2D-animated dinosaur caricatures created by Ted Sieger and originally launched at German preschool TV in 2009.

MARCH 18

Seekers: Found footage film about a group of geocachers who make a terrible discovery in a forest somewhere in Poland.

MAY 30

Das Spinnwebhaus (The Spiderwebhouse): Children abandoned by their mother left to their own imagination that transforms the house into a haunted castle.

JULY 14

Mullewapp—Eine schöne Schweinerei (Mullewapp: A Nice Mess): the sequel to the animated adventures of Johnny Mauser and his animal friends.

AUGUST 27

Ostzone: A haunted house in East Germany, a former clinic building, is bought by three young people, Linda, Marius and their friend Marie.

SEPTEMBER 1

König Laurin (King Laurin): Theo, the son of King Dietrich (played by Rufus Beck), befriends Dwarf King Laurin who enables him to win a tournament and save his father's kingdom.

SEPTEMBER 13

Premiere in Tokyo and Seoul: ***Resident Evil: The Final Chapter***.

SEPTEMBER 15

Rolf Losansky died in Potsdam.

OCTOBER 20

Remake of Wilhelm Hauff's *Das kalte Herz (The Cold Heart)* with Frederick Lau as Peter Munk, Milan Peschel as benevolent Glassman Spirit and Moritz Bleibtreu as evil Dutch Michael who is going to steal Peter's heart for a heart of stone. Directed by Johannes Naber. The screenplay was co-written by Andreas Marschall (*Tears of Kali*).

OCTOBER 28

Five film students watch an eerie UFO landing: *UFO—Es ist hier (UFO: It Is Here)* by Daniele Greco.

NOVEMBER 3

Pettersson und Findus 2—Das schönste Weihnachten überhaupt (Pettson and Findus: The Best Christmas Ever).

DECEMBER 10

A Cure for Wellness by Gore Verbinski was co-funded by Studio Babelsberg and thus received German subsidy money.

DECEMBER 18

Vampirschwestern 3—Reise nach Transsilvanien (Vampire Sisters 3: Journey to Transylvania).

DECEMBER 25

A TV fairty-tale remake of *Das singende, klingende Bäumchen (The Singing, Ringing Tree)*. The DEFA version of 1957 was far superior, by the way.

Primz Himmelblau und Fee Lupine (Prince Skyblue and Lupine the Fairy), another fairy-tale entry on TV.

In addition:

Hellstone: Welcome to Hell, a Creature Feature.

2017

Cinemas: 1672

JANUARY 19

Ritter Rost 2—Das Schrottkomplott (Knight Rusty 2: Full Metal Racket), a rather boring sequel to the original animated adventure released in 2013.

FEBRUARY 12

Überflieger—Kleine Vögel, grosses Geklapper (A Stork's Journey), an animated feature film at the Berlinale's Generation Section: Richard the Stork isn't a stork but a sparrow. Nevertheless, he is convinced that he is a stork, because he was raised by storks. When his foster family migrates to Africa, Richard is left behind. But the sparrow is determined to follow them to Africa.

Another entry at Berlinale (Generation): *Die Häschenschule—Jagd nach dem goldenen Ei (Rabbit School: Guardians of the Golden Egg)*: A modern version of an old German children's book favorite. Max Rabbit, a juvenile shoplifter from a big city, doesn't fit in the old-time school for Easter Rabbits in the middle of the woods. But with the help of rabbit girl Emmy he acquires the proper Easter Rabbits skill and challenges a sneaky family of foxes who are after a Golden Egg.

MARCH 18

Montrak: Vampire attack on Germany. Written and directed by Stefan Schwenk starring Dustin Semmelrogge.

JUNE 7

Antimarteria: sort of a fairy-tale drug movie directed by Spencer Berlin (i.e., Eric Remberg) in South Africa.

AUGUST 17

Bullyparade—Der Film: 5-part movie based on Michael "Bully" Herbig's TV popular sketch comedy show. One episode is based on characters from *(T) Raumschiff Surprise* and titled *Planet of Women*.

SEPTEMBER 2

Ulli Lommel died in Stuttgart.

NOVEMBER 2017

Special screening of a new series in Berlin: **Dark** developed by Wiedemann & Berg Television, the first original (science fiction thriller family drama) series for Netflix entirely authored, shot and produced in Germany, three seasons between 2017 and 2020.

The premise: When two children go missing in the small German town of Winden, its sinful past is exposed along with the double lives and fractured relationships that exist among the four families as they search for their kids. The plot is garnished with supernatural elements.

It's hardly a spoiler to say that **Dark** *concerns itself mostly with time travel. Characters travel between a few distinct eras of Winden's recent history, each 33 years apart.*

Their actions in each of these episodes, deliberate or otherwise, have knock-on effects that reverberate across the decades to cause some truly mind-boggling complications.
[…]

If the time travel elements can be confusing, then the motivations of the characters may not be. Everyone is acting out of love—romantic, paternal or otherwise. Unrequited, forbidden and first loves all feature throughout the three seasons, and the family relationships forged are utterly central to the show's narrative.[90]

OCTOBER 23

Der kleine Vampir (The Little Vampire 3D), a 3D-animated remake of Uli Edel's feature film from the year 2000: Two boys, American and vampire, unite against a notorious vampire hunter. Directed by Richard Claus and Karsten Kiilerich.

2018

Cinemas: 1672

JANUARY 18

Hilfe, ich habe meine Eltern geschrumpft (Help, I Shrunk [sic!] *My Parents)*: Felix and his schoolmates try to undo the shrinking of their parents. VFX by Pixomondo.

FEBRUARY 15

Wes Anderson's puppet stop motion feature *Isle of Dogs*, co-funded by Studio Babelsberg, opened the Berlin International Film Festival. For festival director Dieter Kosslick this hadn't to do with a passion for animation but more with friendship with director Wes Anderson. After all, Anderson came from the world of "real", of "legitimate" movies (*Grand Budapest Hotel*). And there was the chance of getting some big-name voice actors like Jeff Goldblum, Tilda Swinton, Scarlett Johansson and Bill Murray to walk on Kosslick's sponsored red carpet. But it was understood as a signal too. Many guests were surprised

---

90 Michael Stuichbery, *Dark: Why it's time to binge Netflix's successful original German series*. July 1, 2020. www.thelocal.de

that a so-called "A" Festival would open with a film like that. Why, of all people, an acknowledged live-action director would descend (!) to the world of stop motion?

It's well known that for Wes Anderson, the world is one big toy box. His new picture is set in a near-future Japan, where Kobayashi (voiced by Kunichi Nomura, one of the film's co-writers), the corrupt mayor of fictional city Megasaki, has taken draconian measures to curb the spread of various canine diseases, including the dreaded "snout fever". He orders all Megasaki's dogs to be exiled to a bleak island, essentially a huge offshore trashpile.

Dogs are treated like garbage. But then Atari comes, the 12-year old son of the dog-hating, cat-loving mayor, to save his beloved dog.

The puppet dogs' expressive eyes may occasionally well up with tars, but if there's one thing that **Isle of Dogs** *isn't, it's twee; Anderson and his story collaborators, who also include Roman Coppola and Jason Schwartzman, firmly eschew the Japanese cult of kawaii, or cuteness.*[91]

If you watch the stop-motion films produced by institutions like the Laika *studio (*Coraline *and* The Corpse Bride*) or Aardman Animations (*Wallace and Gromit*), you'll see their work is all about the minutiae and manipulating even the smallest design elements.*

And Anderson, no matter if he's working in stop-motion or live-action, is positively obsessed with minutiae. He loves all the tiny components of mise en scène that seem trifling in a vacuum. He's in utmost control of every bit of visual information that appears in each frame. And like an animator, he'll often use his total mastery over the frame to exaggerate affects, lending even his live-action films a cartoonish quality.[92]

---

91   *Isle of Dogs review—Wes Anderson's scintillating stop-motion has bite.* The Guardian, February 15, 2018.
92   Andy Crump, *How Wes Anderson sneaks stop-motion animation into every film he makes.* March 28, 2018. www.theweek.com

The reviewer goes so far as to call the fable about dogs, pro-cat bureaucracy, and trash-strewn wastelands an *abundant homage to the great Japanese filmmaker Akira Kurosawa.*

This praise seems really outrageous for animation, but it's also a much-needed plea for the possibilities of dimensional animation. Indeed, the film is a mix of two Japanese filmmakers: Kurosawa and Hayao Miyazaki.

Isle of Dogs was two years in the making. A crew of 670 handled 1,000 puppets: 500 dogs and 500 humans.

We tried to do everything we can in the camera, Anderson explained, and I don't think there is anything in the whole movie that you would call CG.[93]

And Anderson explained that it's definitely not a children's movie. For some children it could be even disturbing. And he points out the acceptance of animation in Japan within the adult community: *Miyazaki is Spielberg-level in popularity.*

FEBRUARY 20

Luz, a young female cabdriver, is pursued by a demonic entity. The graduate work of Cologne media student Tilman Singer was shown at the 68th Berlin International Film Festival.

FEBRUARY 22

Heilstätten (U.S. DVD release: *Haunted Hospital*) leads a group of YouTube influencers into the eerie sanatorium of Beelitz (actually filmed at Heilstätte Grabowsee in Oranienburg).

---

93 *Wes Anderson on the Politics 'Isle of Dogs' and a Return to Stop-Motion.* In: Variety, February 15, 2018.

FEBRUARY 23

Mute, an Anglo-German internet release co-produced by Studio Babelsberg. Future Berlin as science-fiction Casablanca.

MARCH 1

Die Biene Maja—Die Honigspiele (Maya the Bee: The Honey Games): a disappointment concerning content and box office.

MARCH 29

Michael Ende's popular book *Jim Knopf und Lukas der Lokomotivführer (Jim Button and Luke the Engine Driver)* as live-action film made at Babelsberg studios with lots of CGI and effects animation, maybe a little too much for Ende's original.

APRIL 13

Village People—Tod aus dem All (Village People: Death from Outer Space) by Armin Schnürle. Special Effects: Olaf Ittenbach.

MAY 24

Luis & die Aliens (Luis and the Aliens), an animated feature developed by Christoph and Wolfgang Lauenstein and produced by Ulysses Filmproduktion: a rather Americanized little boy's encounter of the third kind. Luis is eleven years old and a lonely kid. But then he finds real friends in an awesome trio of crazy aliens that has crash-landed on earth. The aliens fix the boy's life in a most unusual way.

JUNE

Hamburg-based company Brave New Work GmbH announced an ambitious animation project to be directed by Ali Soozandeh tentatively titled *Angst, a cinematic graphic novel set against the backdrop of the Great Depression Berlin*

1931–32 is a city of contrasts, where war cripples end up in the gutter and pimps look like Adolf Hitler—or Hitler looks like a pimp.

Elli, a 16-year-old girl, who lives in a traditional working-class residential area, dreams of a career on stage, in the movies, in the spotlight. She can sing, she can dance. One day she makes the acquaintance of a painter and adventurer who might be the right one to give her career a boost. What she doesn't know is that he is also a notorious Black Magician. Edward Alexander seems fascinated enough by the young girl that he asks her to visit him and become part of his circle of Black Magic. Edward Alexander was to be modeled after Aleister Crowley. The story was conceived by Rolf Giesen.

JUNE 13

Die sagenhaften Vier/Marnies Welt (Marnie's World), a modern-day retelling of the Bremen Town Musicians by Christoph and Wolfgang Lauenstein, shown at the Annecy International Animation Film Festival.

JUNE 16

Unterwerfung (Submission): TV movie based on a novel by Michel Houellebecq set in Paris 2022.

SEPTEMBER 9

High Life at the Toronto International Film Festival: Survival in deep space. French-American-Polish-Anglo-German co-production with Juliette Binoche and Robert Pattinson. Interiors filmed in Cologne.

OCTOBER 11

Abgeschnitten (Cut Off) based on a novel by Sebastian Fitzek, a thriller set in the vicinity of Forensic Pathology. Moritz Bleibtreu and Lars Eidinger were cast in the leads. Co-produced by Bela B. (Dirk) Felsenheimer.

OCTOBER 18

Skin Creepers: The Jensen Brothers, two unsuccessful filmmakers, are going to make a pornographic movie—when they realize that something is wrong with their actress: *They wanted to get inside her—but something else was already there...* The girl is possessed by a demon: *The Exorcist Meets Evil Dead!!*

DECEMBER 6

Tabaluga: 3D animation featuring a little green dragon created by pop singer Peter Maffay and ice princess Lilli who have to fight an evil wizard and save the world from a terrible snowman named Arktos.

DECEMBER 8

Rootwood at the Chicago International Genre Film Festival: Jessica and William, two students who host a podcast *Spooky Hour*, are hired by a Hollywood producer to shoot a documentary about the Curse of the Wooden Devil.

DECEMBER 24

Der süsse Brei (The Sweet Porridge), TV version of Grimm's fairy tale.

2019

Cinemas: 1734

FEBRUARY 9

Der goldene Handschuh (The Golden Glove) based on a novel by Heinz Strunk and directed by Fatih Akan, born in Hamburg to Turkish parents, in his own words a horror afficionado since his teenage years, is a fictitious biography of Hamburg's serial killer Fritz Honka (1935-1998). The film was screened, without any chance, in competition at the Berlin International Film Festival.

MARCH 3

First Berlin screening of *Iron Sky 2: The Coming Race,* a Finnish-Belgian-German co-production. With Earth devastated by a nuclear war, the former Nazi Moonbase has become the last refuge. To save mankind the heroes have to enter Hollow Earth and fight the vril, an ancient reptilian race. The trailer had Hitler riding on a T-Rex.

AUGUST 22

A zombie virus infects all German cities—except Weimar and Jena: *Endzeit (Ever After)*.

OCTOBER 24

Bayala—Das magische Elfenabenteuer (Bayala: A Magical Adventure): Since the day the dragons disappeared, the magic of Bayala has been vanishing. Hope is reborn when a dragon egg is found with the young dragon ready to hatch. But his parents must be the first the newly born is supposed to see, otherwise the magic line will be broken. Young sun-elf Surah sets out on a dangerous mission with her twin sister and some friends to reunite the baby dragon with his parents. Co-produced by Ulysses, Telepool and Universum Film.

DECEMBER 12

Der kleine Rabe Socke 3—Suche nach dem verlorenen Schatz (Raven the Little Rascal: Hunt for the Lost Treasure).

DECEMBER 24

Schneewittchen und der Zauber der Zwerge (Snow White and the Magic of the Dwarfs), TV movie by The Chau Ngo with Tijan Marei as Snow White.

In addition:

Love & 50 Megatons by Cornelius Schick. Not only technically (a firework of different techniques: models, matte paintings, green screen, on-set live tracking, real-time game engines) but plot-wise too a challenging, superior 43-minute graduate film made this year at Film Academy Baden-Württemberg that seems to be inspired by story elements of Orwell's *1984* as well as Kubrick's *Dr. Strangelove*: A love story between a man and a bomb.

In a fictitious world a wall goes through a country and its capital. Both sides face each other irreconcilably. In this environment Paul, a 40-year-old rocket scientist, falls in love with Mary. Like him, she is not absorbed with the political differences of both sides. But Mary is not an ordinary woman. Actually, Mary is an intercontinental rocket, 30 meters high and weighing 110 tons with a 50-megaton-nuclear warhead at its tip.

2020

The Year of the Corona Pandemic:

Many release dates had to be delayed due to lockdown which included cinemas.

JANUARY 11

Deathcember: an anthology of 24 short films with macabre content.

FEBRUARY 23

Undine premiered at Berlin International Film Festival: Christian Petzold's modern-day version of the ancient myth: Undine (played by Paula Beer) has to kill the man who left her and then return to the water from whence she came.

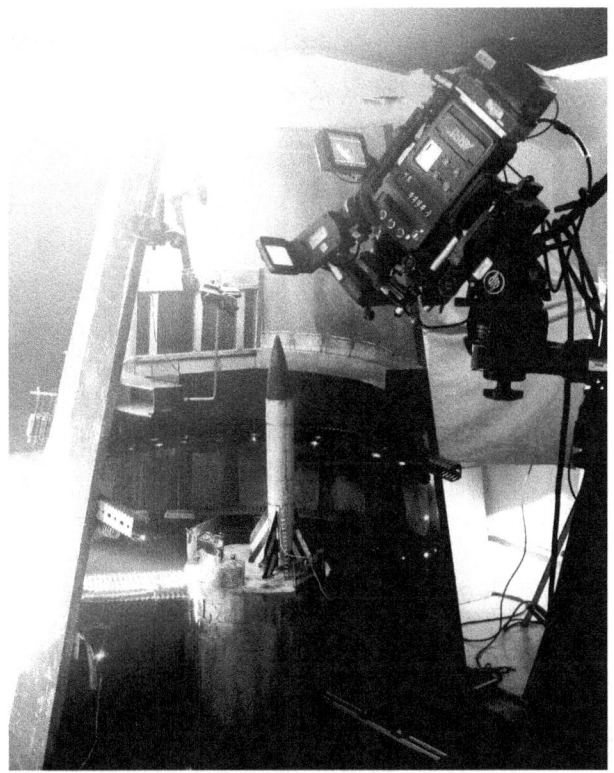

Making of *Love & 50 Megatons* | Courtesy of Cornelius Schick

MARCH 5

Die Känguru-Chroniken (The Kangaroo Chronicles) based on a radio comedy series and books by Marc-Uwe Kling. In the feature film version director Dani Levy mixed live action with a 3D animated kangaroo. Produced by X-Filme Creative Pool in association with ZDF and Trixter (computer animated elements).

JUNE

Matrix 4 co-written and directed by Lana Wachowski, the latest in the sci-fi mega-franchise jointly produced by Warner Bros. and Village Roadshow Pictures, started production on the Babelsberg lot.

AUGUST

Constantin Film announced a Netflix series based on their *Resident Evil* franchise: Two youths living in New Racoon City are infected by the T-virus. 8 episodes running 60 minutes each.

AUGUST 27

After many years in production, a poor man's *Sharknado* titled *Sky Sharks* by Marc Fehse and his brother Carsten finally screened at the Fright Fest in London:

A team of Arctic geologists stumbles across an abandoned laboratory in which the Nazis developed an incredible and brutal secret weapon during the final months of WW2.

Deep in the ice, the team accidentally awakes a deadly army of flying zombie sharks ridden by genetically mutated, undead super-humans, who are unleashed into the skies, wreaking their bloodthirsty revenge on any aircraft that takes to the air.

An elite task force is assembled to take on this deadly threat and stop the Sky Sharks from conquering the air, but as time runs out, the task force realises they will have to fight fire with fire, and the stage is set for the greatest flying super-mutant zombie shark air battle the world has ever seen... [94]

According to its production history, *Sky Sharks* is definitely patchwork filmed whenever some funding or actors were available:

While it's true not every film needs to have a wealth of substance—some of my favorite films are loved for their visual fidelity alone—what most do need, regardless of genre, is consistency, flow, and, if we're lucky, interesting characters. **Sky Sharks** *struggles with these elements in a big way. The favoring of visual spectacle over substance isn't necessarily what bothers me here, though. Rather, it's the lack of actual scenes that move the story forward or introduce who these characters are. […]*

Sky Sharks *might be a disastrous mess of a film in terms of structure and consistency, but it's a drop-dead gorgeous mess.* [95]

SEPTEMBER 24

Ooops! 2—Land in Sicht (Ooops: The Adventure Continues): 3D-animated sequel taking place among the animals on Noah's Ark. The uneasy peace between carnivores and herbivores could break down at any second. After a series of unfortunate events, Finny and Leah, the Nestrian and the Grymp, are washed overboard, along with the last food supplies. On board of a makeshift raft, they are joined by Jelly, a chatty young jellyfish. Buffeted by a violent storm, the three are plunged into the depths of the ocean. Leah and Jelly find themselves on a remote island while Finny wakes up under the shadow of a belching volcano. Directed by Toby Genkel and Sean McCormack.

---

94   https://moviesandmania.com > 2015/01/23 > sky-sharks-2016-german-comedy-action-horror-movie-by-marc-fehse-cast-plot-trailer/.
95   Jeffrey W. Hollingsworth, *'Sky Sharks' is a Visual Fest of Complete and Utter Absurdity*. August 28, 2020. www.killerhorrorcritic.com/reviewsnews/frightfest-2020-review-sky-sharks-is-a-visual-feast-of-complete-and-utter-absurdity.

OCTOBER 1

The live-action sequel of **Michael Ende's** adventures of Jim Knopf: *Jim Knopf und die Wilde 13 (Jim Button and the Wild 13)* again directed by Dennis Gansel. In "The Land That Mustn't Be" Jim Button discovers that, as a matter of fact, he is Prince Myrrh of Jamballa who had been kidnapped by a gang of pirates calling themselves the Wild 13 (who are actually only 12). Eventually Jamballa re-emerges out of the waves when the former Wild 13 sink "The Land That Mustn't Be".

OCTOBER 11

The third season of German TV series *Babylon Berlin* (created by by Tom Tykwer, Achim von Borries and Hendrik Handloegten from Volker Kutscher's detective novels) dealt partly with occultism in the Weimar Republic (Fraternitas Saturni), presented a murdering caped "Phantom" in a movie studio (Babelsberg) and had a strange *Caligari*-like scientist who dreams of creating the new man, a "Man Machine".

OCTOBER 15

Drachenreiter (Dragon Rider) on a 3D-animated journey through the Himalayas in search for the Rim of Heaven. Based on a book by Cornelia Funke.

OCTOBER 28

The first entry in a German sci-fi TV series that is supposed to explore the future: *Exit*, based on a short story by Simon Urban, has a challenging topic: digital copies of humans that survive the death of the originals—but Sebastian Marka's direction is rather tedious. As second entry a love story between a human and a hubot is announced: *Ich bin dein Mensch (I Am Your Human)*.

DECEMBER 3
(RELEASE DATE FINALLY DELAYED DUE TO CORONA)

Monster Hunter: Fantasy action thriller by Paul W. S. Anderson with Milla

Jovovich based on a video game series, co-produced by Constantin Film Munich.

DECEMBER 10
(RELEASE DATE FINALLY DELAYED DUE TO CORONA)

Warner Bros. Germany followed Disney's example with a live-action version of the 2004 animated feature *Lauras Stern (Laura's Star)*.

Die Hexenprinzessin (The Witch Princess) on TV.

In preproduction:

A ZDF TV series (8 episodes) based on Frank Schätzing's ecological thriller *Der Schwarm (The Swarm)*.

2021

JANUARY 6
(RELEASE DATE FINALLY DELAYED DUE TO CORONA)

Hilfe, ich hab meine Freunde geschrumpft (Help! I Shrunk My Friends): The ghost of his school introduces Felix to the secret of shrinking. The boy has nothin' better to do than to shrink his friends who have screwed up a recent date. Third part of the *I Have Shrunk* series, this entry directed by Granz Henman.

APRIL

Die Häschenschule 2—Der grosse Eierklau (Rabbit School 2: The Big Egg Stealing).

JUNE

Tides (also known as *Haven: Above Sky*) by Tim Fehlbaum: When Earth became uninhabitable for humans, the ruling elite settled the planet Kepler

209. But its atmosphere makes the new inhabitants sterile. Two generations later, a program is to determine whether life on Earth is possible again: Mission Ulysses II is supposed to bring certainty. The space capsule gets out of control when it enters Earth's atmosphere. Female astronaut Blake (played by Nora Arnezeder) is the only one who survives the landing—but she realizes that she is not alone on Earth. A struggle for survival begins, and Blake must make choices that will determine the fate of all humanity.

In addition:

One of the most ambitious 3D animation projects in production during Corona pandemic in Germany was *Peterchens Mondfahrt (Little Peter's Journey to the Moon),* based on the classic children's story by Gerdt von Bassewitz, first performed in 1912 as a play, as a book published in 1915: the tale of two children, Peter and his sister Anneli, who help a May beetle named Mr. Zoomzeman to retrieve his missing sixth leg from the cruel Man in the Moon.

Other 3D animation projects to be released:

The Amazing Maurice based on a book by Terry Pratchett.

Memory Hotel, an adult stop-motion puppet film by Heinrich Sabl, in production for almost 20 years and constantly in danger of not getting finished: 1945. On the last night of the Great War, little Sophie loses her parents in an unholy battle over a small hotel somewhere on the outskirts of town. The victorious Red Army takes up quarters in the hotel. Soviet soldier Vasili, who has lost an arm in the assault, becomes the proprietor, Sophie the kitchen help. Sabl's film project tells the story of Sophie and her stubborn yet courageous fight for the happiness she was denied as a child.

Mia und ich—Der Film (Mia and Me: The Movie): A girl is transformed into an elf in the magic land of Centopia. Based on Gerhard Hahn's TV series and produced by Studio 100 Munich, with some of the 3D animation outsourced to India.

INSTEAD OF AN AFTERWORD

please allow me to comment on a new epoch: a virtual age that is accelerated by the Corona Crisis while I type these words:

THE ORWELLIAN AGE OF PHANTOMOLOGY

THE INFINITE *BLOB* OF THE MYSTERIOUS *AVENGERS*

The first science fiction movie I ever saw in my life (in 1959) was either *The Blob* produced by Jack H. Harris: Indescribable! Indestructible! Nothing Can Stop It! or *The Mysterians*, the King Bros. release of the revanchist Japanese Earth Defense Forces made by Ishiro Honda and Eiji Tsuburaya. And I know how shocked I was when I saw a few years later (and older) the radioactively distorted shadows on the walls of an outer space laboratory: all that remained of the unlucky Venusian aggressors in the East-German Stanisław Lem pic *First Spaceship on Venus* that sure had influenced Gene Roddenberry in creating *Star Trek*.

In China the movies are being called *electric shadowplays (dianguang yingxi)*:

From the early days of mankind shadows seemed to men to be something magic. The spirits of the dead were called shadows, and the underworld was named the Kingdom of Shadows and was looked upon with awe and horror. [96]

Peter Schlemihl comes to mind, who sold his shadow to the Devil for a bottomless wallet. (Loosely based on Stanisław Lem, Ari Folman made a modern-day

---

96 Lotte Reiniger, *Shadow Theatres and Shadow Films*. London and New York: B.T. Batsford Ltd. and Watson-Guptill, 1970, p. 11.

film of that story: His *Congress* shows Robin Wright selling her image and identity to Miramount Studios.)

Today the "Devil" has various names. He turns up as *Google, YouTube, Facebook, Netflix*. All of them are not German, not even European or American. They are global! At least in the media there are no borders to nations anymore. The shadows sold to this "Devil" are our digitized *Avatars*. Instead of a bottomless wallet we get, as reward, "disneyfied" entertainment "at its finest".

Like a gigantic vacuum cleaner (at least before COVID-19), the *Walt Disney Empire* is absorbing all franchises that one could wish for: besides their own Mouse-eared brands and theme parks in the United States, France, Japan, and China there are the *Star Wars* series, 21st Century Fox and, of course, the *Marvel Cinematic Universe*.

Almost sixty years after my early childhood *Blob* experience, in early 2018, I watched *The Avengers: Infinity War*, which saw me dumbfounded. The picture is about a Titan named Thanos who looks like a muscle-bound trucker. This digitized guy is going to challenge the universe and needs the complete army of Marvel superheroes to stop him: Thor, Captain America, Young Spider-Man, Iron Man, Black Panther, Vision, Groot, The Incredible Hulk, Falcon, the Scarlet Witch, Star-Lord, Doc Strange, Stan Lee (right before his demise) in his obligatory 15-second cameo, you name them, too many to count them. One of them is named War Machine! All the shadows from the age of virtual comics are together for people who cannot get enough.

One of my favorite writers, the late Urs Widmer, titled one of his stories: *Shit im Kopf—A Brain Full of Shit*. Nuff said!

I felt like H. G. Wells when he saw and reviewed Fritz Lang's *Metropolis*. He said that recently he had seen the silliest film and couldn't believe that it would be possible to make one sillier. It gave, Wells assured, in one eddying concentration almost every possible foolishness, cliché, platitude, and muddlement about mechanical progress and progress in general served up with a sauce of sentimentality that is all its own. Never for a moment did one believe any of this foolish story. In no moment was there anything amusing or convincing in its dreary series of strained events. To the Godfather of Science Fiction, the costly project was immensely and strangely dull. [97]

After I had seen that giant pile of shit called *Infinity War*, I said to myself that I had seen enough blockbuster "science fiction" for the rest of my life—and with Corona I got sick even of my first love, the cinema. I remember those prophetic words by French noir filmmaker Jean-Pierre Melville (who passed away in 1973): *Cinema will end in 2020!*

THE POD PEOPLE OF FUTUREWORLD

With blockbuster CGI = *Computer Generated Imagery*, it's not so much the content, not the substance, it's the form, or to quote Marshall McLuhan: the medium itself that is the message. The minimalist substance is less important than the fascination with the technological aspects of the medium that sometimes absorbs and "devours" the viewer. The form is the mass of digital platforms that are currently performing and globalizing American Nightmare.

The digital media transform the simulation of non-existing realistic worlds to a daily affair. What digital simulation has achieved is not so much realism, it is *photo*-realism. It's an incredible world of make-believe. The objective is not to copy our sensuous and physical experience but the image of it. Eventually, as Pandora's Box is opened already, out of it will emerge the world dominion of image worship. There is no distance anymore to fantasy content. Fantasy isn't any more special. It's down-to-earth and plain, like a daydream. We get the shit into our brain.

Everything has to become "lifelike". That was the main goal right from the beginning. It was not about good acting. It was about capturing the image of man as naturalistic as possible. Everything was meant to be absolutely lifelike and "authentic" (the non-word not only of the year but of the decade).

---

97 H. G. Wells in: The New York Times. April 17, 1927.

Biomechanics organizations monitored and registered the human body's motions for medical research. Multiple cameras were synced to a computer, reflective or bright markers placed on the body's main points of motion (elbows, wrists, knees) in order to track movements.

The video game industry was among the first to introduce this system to the entertainment industry, and John Dykstra used it for creating a digital double of Val Kilmer in *Batman Forever* (1995), produced by Tim Burton and directed by Joel Schumacher.

The process reminds of a story written by Jack Finney in 1954: *The Body Snatchers*. It was four times filmed, the first version *Invasion of the Body Snatchers* directed by Don Siegel, and also inspired a bunch of dopier imitations like *Invasion of the Pod People*. Back then, in Cold War McCarthyism, the Pod People were meant to represent the "Communist Menace". But there is a deeper meaning.

Finney's "pod people" you will find everywhere in society: unspeakable "demons" who are going to take possession of friends, parents, relatives, spouses, neighbors. According to Finney, even lovers turn inexplicably cold, succumb to depression or become victims of dementia—and we fear that we are next in line to lose our mind and soul!

Synthetic actors, the *Synthespians* of digital imagery, might not only absorb our physical identity and movements but even will command artificial intelligence someday which would make their appearance in an interactive scenario much more interesting and unpredictable. In interactive environments that are by now more successful than the story-wise analogue, still linear product of the movie industry one better works with digital actors, as they most easily transfer from one medium to another. More than 1,000 actresses and actors so far have been scanned already and digitized by a Los Angeles-based company. These Avatars will populate a virtual playground of games while we, the "originals", will be transformed into donkeys.

THE DECOMPOSITION OF IMAGES

The technology of the Age of Virtualization mediates a little of that feeling of omnipotence that Stanley Kubrick described when he glorified a Christ-like Star Child at the end of *2001: A Space Odyssey*. In new media we are no more viewers and consumers but participate *actively*. Or so we think.

In Cyber Age the magic word to open Sesame is no more analogue, no more Cinema or TV but Cross Media, IPTV, Mobile Phone, iPad, ADSL. TV etc. Everything and everybody are subject to a global matrix. In the beginning it was just a typewriter in front of a TV set. Today it is a life design which fulfills the visions of religion. Anything can be copied: digitally—be it reasonable or tasteless. Like an ancient God you can cross life forms, animals and humans and create your own *Chronicles of Narnia*: talking lions, centaurs with ponytail, winged unicorns and more exotic chimera. According to the viral marketing of a Swiss chocolate manufacturer the future of cows is purple.

The mediator between the products of the human brain and global reality is the internet. This digital network is so to speak a by-product of the 1969 ARPANET, a project of the *Advanced Research Projekt Agency (ARPA)* installed by the United States Ministry of Defense.

Helmut Herbst, professor and filmmaker, developed a theory about what he called the decomposition of images that began with Robertson's *Phantasmagoriae*, ghostly Magic lantern projections in the 19th century, and reached its final stage with the internet. To put such images into a general store with drawers or transform it into a box office at the entrance of a cinema is like nailing a pudding to the wall.

George Lucas once postulated to "democratize" the means of producing semi-professional images. The result is to be seen on YouTube, a rather young medium that already contains billions of moving images in its brief history. The population boom led to an explosion of (mostly amateurish) images. Everybody seems to feel a vocation to participate in that cult. Mediocrity has become the main competition of the professionals.

CYBERPUNK

In William Gibson's *Neuromancer* vision of Cyberpunk Virtual Reality humans virtually become part of the computer world:

…a "consensual hallucination" created by millions of connected computers. This network can be "jacked" into, while in the real world characters flit from Tokyo to the Sprawl, an urban agglomeration running down the east coast of the US. Gritty urban clinics carry out horrendous sounding plastic surgery. A junkie-hacker, Case, is coaxed into hacking the system of a major corporation. What once seemed impossibly futuristic is now eerily familiar.

"Neuromancer," says novelist and blogger Cory Doctorow, "remains a vividly imagined allegory for the world of the 1980s, when the first seeds of massive, globalised wealth-disparity were planted, and when the inchoate rumblings of technological rebellion were first felt. A generation later, we're living in a future that is both nothing like the Gibson future and instantly recognizable as its less stylish, less romantic cousin. Instead of zaibatsus [large conglomerates] run by faceless salarymen, we have doctrinaire thrusting young neocons and neoliberals who want to treat everything from schools to hospitals as businesses.[98]

Raymond Kurzweil, Google's chief futurist and Director of Engineering, claims that we are close to linking our brains with AI. This wouldn't make our brain obsolete, though: *By linking our brains to cloud computers, humans could expand the limits of our own computing ability—and eventually, upload our own brains to the cloud.*[99] Kurzweil hopes that in the 2030s or 2040s our thinking will be predominately non-biological and that we will be able to fully back up our brains. (*Back up with shit?* we might ask provocatively.)

Larry Page, Google's co-founder, hopes that the functions of the search engine will become someday part of the human brain. Google, of course, will be the supranational institution to select these implants.

---

98   Ed Cumming, *William Gibson: the man who saw tomorrow*. In: The Guardian, 28 July 2014.
99   CBC—June 9, 2015. Cit. From Kurzweil Accelerating Intelligence. Kurzweil in the Press

Raúl Rojas, Professor of Artificial Intelligence, Free University Berlin, however considers the Silicon Valley visions of coming singularity illusory and phantasmal. *"We are far apart from understanding the brain left alone surpass it."* [100] But this is not the question. These ideas are being thought and merely this makes them real. *Artificial Vision, Brain-computer interfaces (BCI)* and *Mind-machine interfaces (MMI)* are science fact. The attack on the human brain is well underway. *The Amazing Transparent Man* is not only a film title by Edgar G. Ulmer but, beginning with Facebook, Naked Scanner, Surveillance Cameras and Flying Eyes Drones, a desirable concept for global totalitarianism. Destination: open the human subconscious mind. And—hard to believe—people are asking for mind control: to fight worldwide terrorism and gain more security within a seemingly golden, virtual cage. I once heard a YouTube executive speak about the assets they had: *living people!* These platforms and "cultural industries" are truly collecting scalps or brains to make money. Will we belong to YouTube or Google?

PHANTOMOLOGY: A LIFE PLAN FOR THE DIGITAL AGE

Half a century ago, Stanisław Lem, who wrote *The Astronauts*, the 1951 novel the DEFA film *First Spaceship on Venus* was based on that had shocked me as an innocent child, had a vision about the consequences of what we call today thoughtlessly *Virtual Reality*. He termed this vision *Phantomology* which describes a (waking) state in which fiction and reality become indistinguishable.

What can a person, connected to a phantomatic generator, experience? Everything. He can scale mountain cliffs, walk without a space suit or oxygen mask on the surface of the Moon, in a clanking armor he can lead a faithful posse to conquer medieval forts or the North Pole. He can be adulated by crowds as a marathon winner or as the greatest poet of all time and accept the Nobel Prize from the hands of a Swedish King, indulge in the requited love of Mme. Pompadour, duel with Iago to avenge Othello, or get stabbed himself by Mafia hitmen. He can also grow enormous eagle wings and fly; or else become a fish and live his life on the coral reef; as an immense shark he can pursue schools of prey with jaws wide open, more! he can

---

100 Spiegel Online, June 23, 2015.

snatch swimming people, chew them up with a gusto and then digest in a tranquil nook of his underwater cavern. [101]

Lem was not that much worried about the technology itself but about the consequences of deception, the mix of reality and fiction. Where does the vision begin, where does it end? How high is the level of immersion? We should be concerned about the social consequences of the global standardization of such a mind control. Not the user will have the power but whoever will control him or her.

3D animation and digital games are only a piece of jigsaw in a global concept. Europe for instance stands for variety but not for interactive randomness. We cannot suspend or delay a process, but we want to save our poetry, our music, our culture. Meanwhile, however, we are volunteering as human guinea pigs in the new age of Orwellian monitoring. For digital entertainment, social media like Twitter and Facebook, onlinebanking and eBay and a mountain of trash and advertisements we offer our brains and access to our subconscious mind. We are praying to one day become "immortal" virtual people with fully developed virtual nervous systems, run by an artificial intelligence that sure will not be liberal but "reasonably" autocratic. Daniel Francis Galouye's *Simulacron 3* was published in 1964. It's a prophetic work. Dr. Nick Bostrom, philosopher and director of the Future of Humanity Institute, Faculty of Philosophy, Oxford University, takes some inspiration from Galouye's vision:

Many works of science fiction as well as some forecasts by serious technologists and futurologists predict that enormous amounts of computing power will be available in the future. Let us suppose for a moment that these predictions are correct. One thing that later generations might do with their super-powerful computers is run detailed simulations of their forebears or of people like their forebears. Because their computers would be so powerful, they could run a great many such simulations. Suppose that these simulated people are conscious (as they would be if the simulations would be sufficiently fine-grained and if a certain quite widely accepted position in the philosophy of mind is correct). Then it could be the case that the vast majority of

---

101   Stanisław Lem, *Summa Technologiae [Sum of Technology]*. Wydawnictwo Literackie, 1964.

minds like ours do not belong to the original race but rather to people simulated by the advanced descendants of an original race. It is then possible to argue that, if this were the case, we would be rational to think that we are likely among the simulated minds rather than among the original biological ones. Therefore, if we don't think that we are currently living in a computer simulation, we are not entitled to believe that we will have descendants who will run lots of such simulations of their forebears. That is the basic idea.[102]

The future determines inevitably our present age.

Germany has lost the race for the future. The digitization of the country went too slow. Technological necessities were neglected and left for Asia or America. In this regard even Finland is better off than Germany. The moving images of the future will be different—different from the content of this book...

POSTSCRIPT

To avoid misunderstandings concerning the respectability of this book, we have omitted two documentary films based on works by Erich von Däniken: **Erinnerungen an die Zukunft** (**Chariots of the Gods**, 1970) and **Botschaft der Götter** (**Mysteries of the Gods**, 1976).

---

102   Nick Bostrom, *Are You Living in a Computer Simulation?* Abstract. Published in Philosophical Quarterly (2003), Vol. 53, No. 211, p. 243.

BIBLIOGRAPHY

Agde, Günter, *Flimmernde Versprechen. Geschichte des deutschen Werbefilms im Kino seit 1897*. Berlin: Verlag Neues Berlin, 1998.

Alpers, Hans Joachim/Fuchs, Werner/Hahn, Ronald M./Jeschke, Wolfgang, *Lexikon der Science Fiction Literatur*. 2 volumes. Munich: Heyne, 1991.

Alt, Dirk, *»Der Farbfilm marschiert!«: Frühe Farbfilmverfahren und ihr Einsatz durch die NS-Propaganda 1933-1940*. Book edition of a master thesis, 2007. Munich: belleville, 2013.

Andriopoulos, Stefan, *Ghostly Apparitions: German Idealism, the Gothic Novel, and Optical Media*. New York: Zone Books, 2013.

Aster, Christian von, *Horror-Lexikon. Von Addams Family bis Zombieworld. Die Motive des Schreckens in Film, Literatur und Wirklichkeit*. Berlin: Lexikon Imprint Verlag, 2002.

Aurich, Rolf/Jacobsen, Wolfgang/Schnauber, Cornelius, *Fritz Lang*. Berlin: Jovis, 2001.

Baumann, Hans D., *Horror. Die Lust am Grauen*. Weinheim: Beltz, 1989.

Bayer, Udo, *Carl Laemmle und die Universal: Eine transatlantische Biografie*. Würzburg: Königshausen u. Neumann, 2013.

Belach, Helga/Bock, Hans-Michael [eds.], *Das Wachsfigurenkabinett. Drehbuch von Henrik Galeen zu Paul Lenis Film von 1923*. Munich: edition text + kritik, 1994.

Belach, Helga/Bock, Hans-Michael [eds.], *Das Cabinet des Dr. Caligari. Das Drehbuch von Carl Mayer und Hans Janowitz zu Robert Wienes Film von 1919/20*. Munich: edition text + kritik, 1996.

Belach, Helga/Jacobsen, Wolfgang, *Richard Oswald*. Munich: edition text + kritik, 1992.

Berger, Eberhard/Giera, Joachim [eds.], *77 Märchenfilme. Ein Filmführer für jung und alt*. Berlin: Henschelverlag, 1990.

Berriatúa, Luciano, *Los proverbios chinos de F. W. Murnau*. Madrid: Filmoteca Espanola, Instituto de las Artes, 1990-92.

Blettenberg, Detlef, *Murnaus Vermächtnis*. Cologne: DuMont Buchverlag, 2010.

Bock, Hans-Michael [ed.], *CineGraph: Lexikon zum deutschsprachigen Film*. Munich: edition text + kritik, 1984-

Bock, Hans-Michael/Jacobsen, Wolfgang [eds.], *Henrik Galeen*. Film-Materialien 2. Eine Publikation mit Unterstützung der Initiative KOMMUNALES KINO Hamburg e.V. (METROPOLIS). Hamburg-Berlin, May 1992.

Bock, Hans-Michael [compilation], *Paul Leni. Grafik Theater Film*. Catalogue for an exhibition. Frankfurt am Main: Deutsches Filmmuseum, 1986.

Bogdanovich, Peter: *Fritz Lang in America*. London: Studio Vista, 1967.

Bozza, Mike/Herrmann, Michael [eds.], *Schattenbilder—Lichtgestalten: Das Kino von Fritz Lang und F. W. Murnau*. Filmstudien. Bielefeld: transcript Verlag, 2009.

Brennicke, Ilona/Hembus, Joe: *Klassiker des deutschen Stummfilms. 1910-1930*. Munich: Goldmann, 1983.

Brill, Olaf, *Der CALIGARI-Komplex*. Munich: belleville, 2012.

Brockmann, Stephen, *A Critical History of German Film*. Rochester, NY: Camden House, 2010.

Coates, Paul, *The Gorgon's Gaze: German Cinema, Expressionism, and the Image of Horror*. Cambridge: Cambridge University Press, 1994.

Copper, Basil, *The Vampire in Legend, Fact and Art*. London: Corgi Books, 1975.

Courtade, Pierre, *Cinéma Expressioniste*. Paris: Henri Veyrier, 1984.

Craig, Rob, *It Came from 1957: A Critical Guide to the Year's Science Fiction, Fantasy and Horror Films*. Jefferson, North Carolina, and London 2013: McFarland & Company, Inc., Publishers.

Dahlke, Günther/Karl, Günter [eds.], *Deutsche Spielfilme von den Anfängen bis 1933. Ein Filmführer*. Berlin/GDR: Henschelverlag, 1988.

David, Christian, *Kinski. Die Biographie*. Berlin: Aufbau-Verlag, 2008.

Davidowic, Klaus S., *Film als Midrasch: der Golem, Dybbuks und andere kabbalistische Elemente im populären Kino*. Göttingen: V&R unipress, 2017.

Dettmar, Ute/Pecher, Claudia Maria/Schlesinger, Ron [eds.], *Märchen im Medienwechsel. Zur Geschichte und Gegenwart des Märchenfilms*. Stuttgart: Metzler, 2018.

Eickhoff, Stefan, *Max Schreck. Gespenstertheater*. Munich: belleville, 2009.

Eisner, Lotte H., *The Haunted Screen. Expressionism in the German Cinema and the Influence of Max Reinhardt*. Berkeley: University of California Press, 1969.

Eisner, Lotte H., *Murnau*. London: Secker & Warburg, 1973. Frankfurt am Main: Kommunales Kino, 1979.

Eisner, Lotte H., *Ich hatte einst ein schönes Vaterland. Memoiren*. Foreword by Werner Herzog. Heidelberg: Das Wunderhorn, 1984.

Eisner, Lotte H., *Fritz Lang*. London: Secker & Warburg, 1976. Cambridge, Massachusetts: Da Capo Press, 1986.

Elsaesser, Thomas, *Metropolis—Der Filmklassiker von Fritz Lang*. Hamburg: Europa Verlag, 2000.

Elsaesser, Thomas, *Weimar Cinema and After: Germany's Historical Imaginary*. New York: Routledge, 2000.

Endler, Cornelia Anett, *Es war einmal… im Dritten Reich. Die Märchenfilmproduktion für den nationalsozialistischen Unterricht*. Frankfurt am Main: Peter Lang GmbH, Internationaler Verlag der Wissenschaften, 2006.

Erich Kettelhut. Der Schatten des Architekten. Deutsche Kinemathek Museum für Film und Fernsehen. Munich: belleville, 2009.

Everson, William K., *Classics of the Horror Film: From the Days of the Silent Film to The Exorcist*. Secaucus, NJ: Citadel Press, 1974.

Ewers, Hanns Heinz, *Der Student von Prag*. Berlin: Dom, 1930.

Farin, Michael/Schmid, Hans [eds.], *NOSFERATU: Eine Symphonie des Grauens*. Munich: belleville, 2018.

Fleischer, Uwe/Trimpert, Helge [eds.], *Wie haben Sie's gemacht?—Babelsberger Kameramänner öffnen ihre Trickkiste*. Marburg: Schüren, 2004.

Flückiger, Barbara, *Visual Effects. Filmbilder aus dem Computer*. Marburg: Schüren, 2008.

Fraenkel, Heinrich, *Unsterblicher Film*. 2 volumes. Munich: Kindler Verlag, Volume 1: 1956, Volume 2: 1957.

Friedrich, Andreas [ed.], *Filmgenres. Fantasy- und Märchenfilm*. Stuttgart: Reclam, 2003.

Friedrich Wilhelm Murnau. Die privaten Fotografien 1926-1931. Berlin, Amerika, Südsee. Catalogue. Berlin: Schwulenmuseum, 2013.

Fritz Langs Metropolis. Deutsche Kinemathek Museum für Film und Fernsehen. Munich: belleville, 2010.

Fröhlich, Gustav, *Waren das Zeiten. Mein Film-Heldenleben*. Munich/Berlin: Herbig, 1983.

Gehler, Fred/Kasten, Ullrich, *Friedrich Wilhelm Murnau*. Berlin: Henschel-Verlag, 1990.

Gehler, Fred/Kasten, Ullrich, *Fritz Lang: Die Stimme von Metropolis*. Berlin: Henschel-Verlag, 1990.

Gehr, Herbert/Ott, Stephan, *Film-Design. Visual Effects für Kino und Fernsehen*. Bergisch Gladbach: Lübbe, 2001.

Geser, Guntram, *Fritz Lang, Metropolis und Die Frau im Mond. Zukunftsfilm und Zukunftstechnik in der Stabilisierungszeit der Weimarer Republik*. Meitingen. Corian, 1999.

Giesen, Rolf, *Der phantastische Film*. 2 volumes. Schondorf am Ammersee: Roloff und Seesslen, 1980.

Giesen, Rolf, *Science-fiction. 50 Klassiker des SF-Films*. Schondorf am Ammersee: Roloff und Seesslen, 1980.

Giesen, Rolf, *Lexikon des phantastischen Films*. 2 volumes. Berlin; Frankfurt/M; Vienna: Ullstein, 1984. [New edition: Munich: Apex Verlag, 2018].

Giesen, Rolf, *Special Effects. King Kong, Orphée und die Reise zum Mond.* Deutsche Kinemathek and Internationale Filmfestspiele Berlin. Ebersberg: Edition 8 ½, 1985.

Giesen, Rolf, *Sagenhafte Welten. Der phantastische Film*. Munich: Heyne, 1990.

Giesen, Rolf/Meglin, Claudia, *Künstliche Welten*. Hamburg: Europa Verlag, 2000.

Giesen, Rolf, *Lexikon der Special Effects*. Berlin: Lexikon Imprint, 2001.

Giesen, Rolf, *Lexikon des Trick- und Animationsfilms*. Berlin: Lexikon Imprint, 2003.

Giesen, Rolf, *Special Effects Artists: A Worldwide Biographical Dictionary of the Pre-Digital Era with a Filmography*. Jefferson, North Carolina, and London: McFarland & Company, Publishers, Inc., 2008.

Giesen, Rolf/Storm, J.P., *Animation Under the Swastika: Trickfilm in Nazi Germany, 1933-1945*. Jefferson, North Carolina, and London: McFarland & Company, Publishers, Inc., 2012.

Giesen, Rolf, *The Nosferatu Story: The Seminal Horror Film, Its Predecessors and Its Enduring Legacy*. Jefferson, North Carolina: McFarland & Company, Publishers, Inc., 2019.

Giesen, Rolf, *Bienenstich und Hakenkreuz. Zeichentrick aus Dachau—die Deutsche Zeichenfilm GmbH*. Frankenthal: Mühlbeyer Filmbuchverlag, 2020.

Giesen, Rolf, *Hitler's Third Reich of the Movies*. Orlando, FL: BearManor Media, 2020.

Gilloch, Graeme, *Siegfried Kracauer: Our Companion in Misfortune*. Cambridge, UK/Malden, MA: Polity Press, 2015.

Grafe, Frieda/Patalas, Enno [eds.], *Licht aus Berlin. Lang Lubitsch Murnau*. Berlin: Brinkmann u. Bose, 2003.

Grafe, Frieda/Patalas, Enno/Prinzler, Hans Helmut, *Fritz Lang*. Edited by Wolfram Schütte. Munich: Hanser, 1976.

Grant, Barry Keith [ed.], *Fritz Lang Interviews. Conversations with Filmmakers*. Jackson: University Press of Mississippi, 2003.

Grob, Norbert, *Fritz Lang: "Ich bin ein Augenmensch"*. Berlin: Propyläen Verlag, 2014.

Habel, F.-B., *Das grosse Lexikon der DEFA-Spielfilme. Die vollständige Dokumentation aller DEFA-Spielfilme von 1964 bis 1993*. Berlin: Schwarzkopf & Schwarzkopf, 2000.

Hahn, Ronald M./Giesen, Rolf, *Das neue Lexikon des Fantasy-Films*. Berlin: Lexikon Imprint 2001.

Hahn, Ronald M./Giesen, Rolf, *Das neue Lexikon des Horrorfilms*. Berlin: Lexikon Imprint,

Hahn, Ronald M./Jansen Volker, *Lexikon des Science Fiction Films*. Foreword by Rolf Giesen. Munich: Heyne, 1997.

Halle, Randall, Pittsburgh, *Chainsaws and Neo-Nazis: Contemporary German Horror Film Production*. GFL: German as a foreign language.

Hanisch, Michael, *Auf den Spuren der Filmgeschichte. Berliner Schauplätze*. Berlin: Henschel Verlag, 1991.

Happ, Alfred, *Lotte Reiniger. 1899-1981; Schöpferin einer neuen Silhouettenkunst*. Tübingen: Universitätsstadt Tübingen—Fachbereich Kunst und Kultur, 2004.

Hardt, Ursula, *From Caligari to California: Eric Pommer's Life in the International Film Wars*. Providence/Oxford: Berghahn Books, 1996.

Hartwig, Helmut, *Die Grausamkeit der Bilder. Horror und Faszination in alten und neuen Medien*. Weinheim: Quadriga, 1986.

Herzog, Werner, *Vom Gehen im Eis: München-Paris 23.11. bis 14. 12. 1974*. Frankfurt/Main: Fischer, 2009.

Hilger, Josef, *Raumpatrouille. Die phantastischen Abenteuer des Raumschiffes ORION. Berlin: Schwarzkopf & Schwarzkopf*.

Jackson, Kevin, *Nosferatu—Eine Symphonie des Grauens*. A BFI book. London: British Film Institute, 2013.

Jacobsen, Wolfgang, *Erich Pommer. Ein Produzent macht Filmgeschichte*. Berlin: Argon, 1999.

Jacobsen, Wolfgang [ed.], *Babelsberg. Ein Filmstudio 1912-1992*. Berlin: Argon, 1992.

Jacobsen, Wolfgang, *Siodmak Bros. Berlin—Paris—London—Hollywood*. Berlin: Argon, 1998.

Jacobsen, Wolfgang, *Erich Pommer: Filmproduzent zwischen Kunst, Industrie und Unterhaltung*. Jüdische Miniaturen. Berlin: Hentrich und Hentrich Verlag, 2017.

Jacobsen, Wolfgang/Prümm, Karl/Wenz, Benno [eds.], *Willy Haas. Der Kritiker als Mitproduzent. Texte zum Film 1920-1933*. Berlin: Edition Hentrich, 1991.

Jacobsen, Wolfgang/Sudendorf, Werner [eds.], *Metropolis—Ein filmisches Laboratorium der modernen Architektur/A Cinematic Laboratory for Modern Architecture*. Stuttgart and London: Edition Axel Menges, 2000.

Jensen, Paul, *The Cinema of Fritz Lang*. New York: Barnes, 1969.

Jung, Fernand/Weil, Claudius/Seesslen, Georg, *Der Horrorfilm*. Munich: Roloff und Seesslen, 1977.

Kaes, Anton, *Shell Shock Cinema: Weimar Culture and the Wounds of War*. Princeton and Oxford: Princeton University Press, 2009.

Kagelmann, André, *Der Krieg und die Frau. Thea von Harbous Erzählwerk zum Ersten Weltkrieg*. Kassel: MEDIA-Net, 2009.

Kalbus, Oskar, *Vom Werden deutscher Filmkunst*. 2 volumes: *Der Stummfilm*; *Der Tonfilm*. Altona-Bahrenfeld: Cigaretten-Bilderdienst, 1935.

Kasten, Jürgen/Loacker, Armin [eds.], *Richard Oswald. Kino zwischen Spektakel, Aufklärung und Unterhaltung*. Vienna: verlag filmarchiv austria, 2005.

Kasten, Jürgen/Keitz, Ursula von/Lang, Frederik/Stiasny Philipp [eds.], *Ufa international. Ein deutscher Filmkonzern mit globalen Ambitionen*. Munich: edition text + kritik, 2020.

Keiner, Reinhold, *Hanns Heinz Ewers und der Phantastische Film*. Studien zur Filmgeschichte 4. Hildesheim: Georg Olms Verlag, 1988. E-Book: Kassel 2012.

Keiner, Reinhold, *Thea von Harbou und der deutsche Film bis 1933*. Hildesheim/Zurich/New York: Georg Olms Verlag, 1984.

Kennel, Herma, *Als die Comics laufen lernten. Der Trickfilmer Wolfgang Kaskeline zwischen Werbekunst und Propaganda*. Berlin: be-bra Verlag, 2020.

Knigge, Andreas C., *Fortsetzung folgt. Comic-Kultur in Deutschland*. Frankfurt am Main/Berlin/Vienna: Ullstein, 1986.

Koop, Volker, *Warum Hitler King Kong liebte, aber den Deutschen Micky Maus verbot. Hitlers geheime Filmleidenschaft*. Berlin: be-bra, 2015.

Kracauer, Siegfried, *From Caligari to Hitler: A Psychological History of the German Film*. Princeton, NJ: Princeton University Press, 1974.

Kreimeier, Klaus, *The Ufa Story: A History of Germany's Greatest Film Company*. Translated by Robert and Rita Kimber. Berkeley/Los Angeles/London: University of California Press, 1999.

Kugel, Wilfried, *Der Unverantwortliche. Das Leben des Hanns Heinz Ewers*. Dusseldorf: Grupello-Verlag, 1992.

Eric Kurlander, *Hitler's Monsters: A Supernatural History of the Third Reich*. New Haven, Connecticut: Yale University Press, 2017.

Kurtz, Rudolf, *Expressionismus und Film*. Berlin: Verlag der Lichtbild-Bühne, 1926. Reprint: Zurich 2007.

Kurtz, Rudolf, *Expressionism and Film*. New Barnet, Herts: John Libbey Publishing Ltd., 2016. English translation of German original *Expressionismus und Film*.

Kyrou, Ado, *Le Surréalisme au cinema*. Paris: Le Terrain Vague, 1963.

Lamprecht, Gerhard, *Deutsche Stummfilme*. 9 Bände: 1903-1912; 1913-1914; 1915-1916; 1917-1918; 1919; 1920; 1921-1922; 1923-1926; 1927-1931. Deutsche Kinemathek e.V. Berlin 1967-69.

Lange, Britta, *Die Entdeckung Deutschlands. Science-Fiction als Propaganda*. Berlin: Verbrecherverlag, 2014.

Leiser, Erwin, *"Deutschland erwache!" Propaganda im Film des Dritten Reiches*. Reinbek/Hamburg: Rowohlt, 1968.

Lorenz, Christoph F., *Lexikon der Science-Fiction-Literatur seit 1900. Mit einem Blick auf Osteuropa*. Frankfurt/Main: Peter Lang, 2016.

Lotte Reiniger: Silhouettenfilm und Schattentheater. Exhibition June 2-August 17, 1979. Catalogue: Margit Downar. Munich: Puppentheatermuseum im Münchner Stadtmuseum, 1979.

Lotte Reiniger: Schattentheater—Schattenpuppen—Schattenfilm. Eine Anleitung. Tübingen: texte verlag, 1981.

Mack, Max, *Die zappelnde Leinwand. Ein Filmbuch*. Berlin: Dr. Ensler & Co., 1916.

Manvell, Roger, *Masterworks of the German Cinema*. London: Lorrimer, 1973.

Martini, Wolfgang, *Das Filmgesicht: Paul Wegener*. Munich: Curt J.C. Andersen, 1928.

McGilligan, Patrick, *Fritz Lang: The Nature of the Beast*. New York: St Martin's Press, 1997.

McNally, Raymond T./Florescu, Radu, *In Search of Dracula: The History of Dracula and Vampires*. Boston: Mariner Books, 1994.

Mecki, Märchen & Schnurren. Die Puppenfilme der Gebrüder Diehl. Frankfurt am Main: Deutsches Filmmuseum, 1994.

Möller, Kai, *Paul Wegener. Sein Leben und seine Rollen. Ein Buch von ihm und über ihn*. Hamburg: Rowohlt Verlag, 1954.

Nagl, Tobias, *Die unheimliche Maschine. Rasse und Repräsentation im Weimarer Kino*. Munich: edition text + kritik, 2009.

Nicolella, Henry/Soister, John T., *The Horror and Fantasy Films of Paul Wegener*. Duncan, Oklahoma: BearManor Media, 2012.

Noa, Wolfgang, *Paul Wegener*. Berlin/GDR: Henschelverlag, 1964.

Nosferatu: A Symphony of Horror—A Film by F. W. Murnau: A Shot-by-Shot Presentation by Roy A. Sites M.L.A. CreateSpace Independent Publishing Platform 2014.

Opfermann, H[ans] C[arl]/Kramer, Georg, *Die neue Trickfilm-Schule: Ein Lehr- und Nachschlagebuch für Filmamateure, Film- und Fernsehfachleute und den filmtechnischen Nachwuchs*. Seebruck/Chiemsee: Heering, 1963.

Parrill, William B., *European Silent Film on Video: A Critical Guide*. Jefferson, North Carolina, and London: McFarland & Company, Publishers, Inc., 2006.

Patalas, Enno, *Metropolis in/aus Trümmern—Eine Filmgeschichte*. Berlin: Bertz und Fischer Verlag, 2001.

Petzold, Volker, *Das große Ost-West-Sandmännchenlexikon*. Berlin: Verlag für Berlin-Brandenburg, 2009.

Petzold, Volker, *Das Sandmännchen: Alles über unseren Fernsehstar*. Hamburg: edel Edition, 2009.

Pfeiffer, Herbert, *Paul Wegener*. Berlin: Rembrandt-Verlag, 1957.

Pirie, David, *Vampir-Filmkult*. Gütersloh: Prisma, 1977.

Prinzler, Hans Helmut [ed.], *Friedrich Wilhelm Murnau—Ein Melancholiker des Films*. Berlin: Bertz und Fischer Verlag, 2003.

Prinzler, Hans Helmut, *Chronik des deutschen Films 1895-1994*. Stuttgart and Weimar: Verlag J. B. Metzler, 1995.

Rathmann, Claudia, *Was gibt's denn da zu lachen? Lustige Zeichentrickserien und ihre Rezeption durch Kinder unter besonderer Berücksichtigung der präsentierten Gewalt*. Munich: Nomos, 2009.

Reff, Werner/Varsarhelyi, Istvan, *Filmtrick, Trickfilm*. Leipzig: Fotokinoverlag, 1980.

Reichow, Joachim, *Plaudereien über den Zeichen-Puppentrickfilm*. Berlin/GDR: Henschelverlag, 1966.

Reiniger, Lotte, *Shadow Theatres and Shadow Films*. London and New York: B. T. Batsford Ltd. and Watson-Guptill, 1970.

Richard Oswald. Produzent und Regisseur. A CineGraph Book. Compiled by Hans-Michael Bock, Wolfgang Jacobsen and Jörg Schöning. Editors: Helga Belach and Wolfgang Jacobsen. Munich: edition text + kritik, 1990.

Riess, Curt, *Das gab's nur einmal. Das Buch der schönsten Filme unseres Lebens*. Hamburg: Verlag der Sternbücher, 1956.

Roffat, Sébastien, *Propagandes animées: le dessin animé politique entre 1933 et 1945*. Paris: Bazaar & Co, 2010.

Saunders, Thomas J., *Hollywood in Berlin: American Cinema and Weimar Germany*. Berkeley: University of California Press, 1994.

Schäfer, Horst [ed.], *Lexikon des Kinder- und Jugendfilms im Kino, im Fernsehen und auf Video*. Meitingen: Corian, 1998-

Schenk, Ralf/Scholz, Sabine [eds.], *Die Trick-Fabrik. DEFA-Animationsfilme 1955-1990*. Deutsches Institut für Animationsfilm (DIAF). Berlin: Bertz und Fischer Verlag, 2003.

Schlesinger, Ron, *Rotkäppchen im Dritten Reich. Die deutsche Märchenfilmproduktion zwischen 1933 und 1945. Ein Überblick*. 3rd revised edition. DEFA-Stiftung. Berlin 2013.

Schoemann, Annika, *Animation in Deutschland. Von den Anfängen bis zur Gegenwart 1909-2001*. Sankt Augustin: Gardez, 2003.

Schönemann, Heide, *Fritz Lang: Filmbilder Vorbilder*. Berlin: Edition Hentrich, 1992.

Schönemann, Heide, *Paul Wegener. Frühe Moderne im Film*. Stuttgart/London: Edition Axel Menges, 2003.

Schonger, Hubert [ed.], *Kamera läuft... 25 Jahre Schongerfilm. Ein Almanach zum 25-jährigen Bestehen der Schongerfilm*. Inning am Ammersee 1950.

Seeber, Guido, *Der Trickfilm in seinen grundsätzlichen Möglichkeiten. Eine praktische und theoretische Darstellung der photographischen Filmtricks*. Berlin: Verlag der »Lichtbildbühne«, 1927. Reprint: Frankfurt am Main: Kommunales Kino, 1979.

Seesslen, Georg/Weil, Claudius, *Kino des Phantastischen*. Reinbek/Hamburg: Rowohlt, 1980.

Seesslen, Georg, *Kino des Utopischen*. Reinbek/Hamburg: Rowohlt, 1980.

Shephard, Jim, *Nosferatu in Love*. London: Faber & Faber, 1998.

Siodmak, Curt, *Unter Wolfsmenschen. Vol. 1, Europa*. Editorial consultant: Rolf Giesen. Bonn: Weidle, 1995.

Skal, David J., *Hollywood Gothic: The Tangled Web of Dracula From Novel To Stage To Screen*. New York: Farrar, Straus and Giroux, 2004.

Skal, David J., *Something in the Blood: The Untold Story of Bram Stoker, the Man Who Wrote Dracula*. New York/London: Liveright Publishing Corporation, 2016.

Soister, John T./Nicolella, Henry/Battle, Patrick Wilks, *Conrad Veidt on Screen. A Comprehensive Illustrated Filmography*. Jefferson, North Carolina, and London: McFarland & Company, Publishers, Inc., 2002.

Stiasny, Philipp, *Spannung, Tiefsinn, Sensationen. Das populäre Kino in Deutschland und der Krieg, 1914-1929*. Dissertation zur Erlangung des akademischen Grades Doctor philosophiae. Humboldt-Universität zu Berlin Philosophische Fakultät II Institut für deutsche Literatur. Berlin, September 7, 2006. First Referee: Prof. Dr. Erhard Schütz. Second Referee: Prof. Dr. Bernd Sösemann.

Stiglegger, Marcus, *Grenzüberschreitungen. Exkursionen in den Abgrund der Filmgeschichte. Der Horrorfilm*. Berlin: Martin Schmitz Verlag, 2018.

Storm, J.P./Dressler, Michael, *Im Reiche der Micky Maus. Walt Disney in Deutschland 1927-1945*. Catalogue for an exhibition of Filmmuseum Potsdam. Berlin: Henschel-Verlag, 1991.

Straschek, Günter Peter, *Handbuch wider das Kino*. Frankfurt am Main: Suhrkamp, 1975.

Strauss, Stefan, *Albin Grau: Biografie und Œuvre*. December 22, 2010. Inaugural Dissertation. Ruhr Universität Bochum, Fakultät füt Philologie. First Referee: Prof. Dr. Wolfgang Beidenhoff. Second Referee: Prof. Dr. Peter M. Spangenberg.

Struck, Wolfgang, *Die Eroberung der Phantasie. Kolonialismus, Literatur und Film zwischen deutschem Kaiserreich und Weimarer Republik*. Göttingen: V & R Unipress, 2010.

Stüler, Alexander/Hotschewar, Marijan V., *Filmtricks und Trickfilme*. Halle: Knapp, 1937.

Strzelczyk, Florentine, *Motors and Machines, Robots and Rockets: Harry Piel and Sci-Fi Film in the Third Reich*. In: German Studies Review Vol. 27, No. 3. The John Hopkins University Press, October 2004.

Taschenbuch des Kameramannes für Lehr- und Nachschlagezwecke. Berlin 1928.

Töteberg, Michael, *Fritz Lang*. Reinbek/Hamburg: Rowohlt, 1985.

Trebbin, Frank, *Die Angst sitzt neben dir*. Berlin: self-published, 1990.

Urwand, Ben, *The Collaboration: Hollywood's Pact with Hitler.* Harvard University Press 2013.

Vana, Gerhard, *Metropolis. Modell und Mimesis.* Berlin: Gebr. Mann Verlag, 2001.

Verband der Deutschen Filmclubs e. V. [ed.], *Retrospektive Fritz Lang. Dokumentation.* Compiled by Dr. Gerd Albrecht. 1964.

Völker, Klaus [ed.], *Künstliche Menschen. Dichtungen und Dokumente über Golems, Homunculi, Androiden und liebende Statuen.* Munich: Hanser, 1971.

Youngkin, Stephen D./Bigwood, Jones/Cabana Jr., Raymond, *The Films of Peter Lorre.* Secaucus, New Jersey: Citadel, 1982.

Wegener, Paul, *Der Golem, wie er in die Welt kam.* Berlin: Scherl, 1921.

Weimarer Kino—neu gesehen. Deutsche Kinemathek—Museum für Film und Fernsehen. Berlin: Bertz und Fischer Verlag, 2018.

Weiss, Harald, *Der Flug der Biene Maja durch die Welt der Medien. Buch, Film, Hörspiel und Zeichentrickserie.* Wiesbaden: Harrassowitz Verlag, 2012.

Wetzel, Kraft/Hagemann, Peter A., *Liebe, Tod und Technik. Kino des Phantastischen 1933-1945.* Berlin: Verlag Volker Spiess, 1977.

Wohlrabe, Jürgen [ed.], *60 Jahre Jugendfilm, 1934-1994.* Leitword by Dr. Helmut Kohl. Berlin: Nicolai, 1994.

Zglinicki, Friedrich von, *Der Weg des Films.* Hildesheim/New York: Olms Presse, 1956.

INDEX

Names

Abel, Alfred 6, 49, 84, 86, 111, 147

Achmann, Werner 248

Achternbusch, Herbert 299, 325

Ackerman, Forrest J[ames] 207, 305, 323

Ackermann, Curt 226

Adametz, Addi [Adele] 209

Adjani, Isabelle 288, 295

Adlon., Percy 330

Adorf, Mario 323

Agthe, Arend 384

Akin, Fatih 355, 434

AKIZ *see* Bornhak, Achim

Albers, Hans VI, 86, 98, 133, 138, 168, 169

Alberty, Karl-Otto 267

Albes, Emil 31

Albin, Hans 237

Aldor, Bernd 46, 48

Aldrich, Robert 281

Alékan, Henri 312

Alexander, Kurt 79

Alexandrow, Eugen 343

Aljinovic, Boris 376, 417

Alonso, Chelo 248

Alpers, Hans Joachim 257

Altmann, Max 22, 26

Altorjay, Gábor 302

Ander, Charlotte 98

Anders, Christian 295

Andersen, Hans Christian 72, 103, 201, 217, 278, 376, 415

Anderson, Daniel 348

Anderson, Poul 331

Anderson, Paul W. S. 360, 440

Anderson, Wes 429-431

Andonov, Ivan 267

Andra, Fern 63

Angst, Richard 222

Antel, Franz 210

Arendt, Elke 209, 213

Arent, Eddie 218, 234, 286

Armendariz, Pedro 233

Armstrong, Michael 259

Arndt, Stefan 378

Arnezeder, Nora 442

Arnheim, Valy 96

Arnim, Achim von 54

Arnold, August 70

Arrabal, Fernando 292

Arterton, Gemma 410

Askin, Leon 275

Askonas, Paul 68

Assmann, Amona

Assmann, Arno 191

Atwood, Margaret 319

Augurzke, Tim Gerrit 421

August, Amadeus 301

Augustinski, Peer 307

Aulinger, Elise 186

Aust, Peter 273

Bach, Vivi 252

Bacher, Hans 310

Bär, Rainer 300

Baky, Josef von 193

Balázs, Béla 129, 189

Balsamo, Joseph 68

Balser, Ewald 218

Balzac, Honoré de 153

Bamberger, Franz 14

Baran, Paul Alexander 264

Bardot, Brigitte 211

Barion, Marcel 415

Barke, Lothar 264

Barker, Lex 226, 230, 249, 252

Barkowsky, Helmut 264

Barrie, Nigel 97

Barry, Iris 103

Barrymore, John 63

Barthel, Waldfried 195

Barthel, Kurt Walter 204

Bartholomae, Hubert 307

Bartholomä, Luise 120

Bartok, Eva 248

Bartosch, Berthold 124
Bartsch, J. Joachim
Barylli, Gabriel 307
Basinger, Kim 351
Bassermann, Albert 26, 125
Bassewitz, Gerdt von 220, 322, 442
Bates, Alan 320
Báthory, Erzsébet 263
Bauer, Alfred 197
Baumgart, Klaus 365, 404, 414
Baur, Sebastian 282
Bava, Mario 267, 269
Baxter, John 323
Bayrhanmer, Gustl 297
Beauvais, Peter 265
Bechstein, Ludwig 419
Beck, Rufus 354, 373, 425
Beck, Walter 262, 299, 308, 314
Becker, Ben 415
Becker, Meret 363, 415
Becker, Theodor 40
Bedřich, Václav 311
Beer, Paula 436
Beethoven, Ludwig van 168
Behn-Grund, Friedl 198
Behrendt, Gerhard 216, 219
Belling, Rudolf 34
Bendow, Wilhelm 98, 168
Benn, Gottfried 139
Bennent, Heinz 295
Benoit, Pierre 132
Benson, E. F. 307
Berben, Iris 262
Berber, Ady (Adolf) 225
Berber, Anita 18, 50, 53, 54, 68, 84, 117
Beregi, Sr., Oscar 134
Berg, Alex *see* Reinecker, Herbert

Bergen, Arthur 37
Berger, Grete 27
Berger, Jan 364
Berger, Ludwig 14, 89, 158, 258
Berger, Senta 255, 424
Berger, William 275
Bergman, Ingmar 282–283
Bergman, Michel 323
Berkévicz, Ulla 293
Berlin, Spencer *see* Remberg, Eric
Berndl, Christa 186
Berneis, Peter 237
Bernhardt, Kurt (Curtis) 137
Berry, Halle 408
Beyer, Erich 249
Beyer, Uwe 249
Beyerling, Hans-Laurin 383
Biberti, Ilse 307
Biehn, Michael 401
Biensfeldt, Paul
Bildt, Paul 76, 196
Biltz, Karl Peter 258
Bing, Adolf 69
Bing, Ignatz 69
Binoche, Juliette 433
Birgel, Willy 156
Blackwell, Sr., Carlyle 119
Black, Jack 333
Bläck Fööss 310
Bláha, Zdenek 258
Blanchar, Pierre 138
Blanco, Roberto 286
Blase, Wilhelm 149
Blasko, Béla Ferenc Dezső *see* Lugosi, Béla
Blech, Hans-Christian 258
Bleibtreu, Moritz 426, 433
Bleiweiss, Celino 277

Blümel, Peter 216
Bluhm, Walter 207
Blumenberg, Hans-Christoph 308, 358
Blumenschein, Tabea 286
Blythe, Betty 98
Bocanová, Mahulena 337
Bodenstein, Christel 214
Böcklin, Arnold 38
Böhm, Karlheinz 227
Böhm, Suse 209
Boehner, Fritz 138
Böll, Christoph 384
Bös, Paul 213
Böttge, Bruno J. 201
Böttger, Fritz 222
Bogart, Humphrey 137
Bogdanovich, Peter 223
Bohnen, Michael 138, 168
Boie, Kirsten 423
Bois, Curt 224
Bokel, Radost 309
Boll, Uwe 245, 330, 364, 368, 371, 377, 379, 381, 382, 393, 401, 402, 406, 413, 415, 421
Bollmann, Horst 225
Bolváry, Géza von 119
Bonne, André 199
Bonsels, Waldemar 108, 171
Boorman, John 358
Boos, Walter 273
Bornhak, Achim 422
Borresholm, Boris von 229, 244
Borries, Achim von 440
Borsche, Dieter 225, 234, 235, 236, 248
Borsody, Eduard von 156
Borsody, Suzanne von 391
Bostrom, Nick 450

Bowen, Elizabeth 307

Boyd, Stephen 286

Boyer, Charles 133

Brace, Bill 227

Bradbury, Ray 370

Brahm, John [Hans] V

Brandis, Jonathan 321

Brandner, Uwe 260, 264

Brandon, Henry 26, 234, 319

Brandt, Heinrich 88

Brauer, Jürgen 305, 339

Braun, Magnus von 25

Braun, Michael 247

Braun, Wernher von 25, 120, 205, 222, 247, 282

Brauner, Artur 48, 222, 223, 226, 230, 231, 232, 235, 236, 238, 248-249, 250, 255, 265, 293, 356

Brausewetter, Hans 168

Brav, Ludwig

Brdečka, Jiři 181

Brecht, Bert 88, 202, 277

Breiner, Holger 342

Bresee, Bobbie 323

Bresee, Frank 323

Brice, Pierre 249

Bringmann, Peter F. 336

Brockmann, Jochen 218

Brösel *see* Feldmann, Rötger

Browne, Roscoe Lee 281

Brückner, Thomas 354

Brühl, Daniel 396

Brühl, Heidi 234

Brühne, Lothar 184

Brunckhorst, Natja 327

Brunel, Adrian 103

Buchholz, Horst 329, 361

Buck, Detlev 409

Bürstein, Rudolf *see* Meinert, Rudolf

Büttner, Wolfgang 258, 306

Bulwer-Lytton, Edward V, 68, 78-79

Burggraf, Waldfried *see* Forster, Friedrich

Burke, Sam 250

Burton, Richard 267

Burton, Tim 446

Busch, Wilhelm 197, 210

Bussmann, Gisela 157

Buttgereit, Jörg 304, 313, 319, 323, 329, 337, 360, 420

Cadenbach, Joachim 256

Camerini, Mario 195

Čapek, Karel 111

Caro, Marc 334

Carow, Heiner 239

Carradine, David 283

Carradine, John 276

Carreras, Michael 278

Carrière, Matthieu 275

Carroll, Lewis 377

Carstensen, Margit 271, 295, 327

Caven, Ingrid 271

Cervi, Gino 221

Cézanne, Paul 162

Chabrol, Claude 320

Chahoud, Randa 379

Chamisso, Adelbert von 1, 27, 69, 253

Chan, Jackie 365

Chaney, Lon 130, 280

Chaney, Jr., Lon [Creighton Chaney] 171

Chaplin, Geraldine 371

Charell, Erik 54

Chen Xiao Xiong 399

Chin, Un-suk 377

Chmara, Grigori 90

Chrisander, Nils Olaf 37

Christian, Paul *see* Hubschmid, Paul

Christmann, Karl-Heinz 331

Churchill, Winston 408

Clair, René 189

Clare, Cassandra 414

Clarin, Hans 201, 297

Claus, Richard 372, 429

Clausen, Jürgen 161

Clausnitzer, Niels 209, 213

Cleef, Karla von 187

Clifford, Frank 189

Coldewey, Michael 340, 420

Columbus, Christopher 326

Compton, David G. 293

Constantine, Eddie 262, 265

Coogan, Steve 365

Coppola, Roman 430

Corman, Roger 226, 229, 235, 252, 255

Cotten, Joseph 267, 281

Courtland, Jerome 248

Craven, Wes 348

Crawford, Joan 137

Cristiani, Quirino

Cronenberg, David IX, X

Crowley, Aleister 43, 96, 101, 110, 433

Cürlis, Hans 53

Curtiz, Michael *see* Kertész, Mihály

Czibulka, Alfons von 54

Däniken, Erich von 451

Dafoe, Willem 329, 349, 350

Dagover, Lil 11, 74, 293

Dall, Karl 259

D'Amato, Joe 318

Dammbeck, Lutz 329

Damon, Mark 303

Danforth, Jim 227

Danning, Sybil [Sybille Danninger] 263

D'Arcy, Alexander 222

Dark, Jason *see* Rellergerd, Helmut

Darlton, Clark *see* Ernsting, Walter

Daub, Ewald 137

Daudert, Erich 157

Dautert, F. F. E. 192

Davidson, Paul 4, 28, 35, 42, 47, 114

Davis, Bette 137

Deane, Hamilton 216

De Balzac, Honoré 153

De Beer, Hans 357, 380

Decarli, Bruno 40, 46

De Casseres, Benjamin 121

DeCordova, Leander 98

De la Motte Fouqué, Friedrich 273

De Laurentiis, Dino 282-283

DeLuise, Dom 326

De Mol, John 339

De Rycker, Piet 345, 363

De Saint-Exupéry, Antoine 322

de Vogt, Carl 51

Defoe, Daniel 307

Degener, Friedrich 71

Degermark, Pia 263

Deitch, Gene 311

Delis, Daniela Maria 309

Delmare, Fred 278

Delon, Nathalie 267

Deltgen, René 156

Delvaux, Paul 332

Demme, Jonathan 348

Demongeot, Mylène 212

Desmond, Olga

Desni, Xenia 97

Deutsch, Ernst 72

Deyle, Matthias 311

Dick, Philip K[indred] 418

Dickens, Charles 301

Dieckmann, Heinrich ("Enrico") 17, 67, 71, 74, 77, 87, 215

Dieckmann, Karl Leopold Ferdinand 17

Dieckmann, Martha Elise Agnes 17

Dieckmann, Oliver 391

Diehl, Ferdinand 19, 126, 129, 131, 141, 147, 148, 156, 195, 197, 199, 260, 305, 327

Diehl, Hermann 131, 147, 148, 195, 197, 199, 260

Diehl, Paul 147

Dieterle, William (Wilhelm) 115, 142, 221

Dietrich, Erwin C. 125, 279-280, 337

Dietrich, Marlene 351

Diffring, Anton 275

Dillenz, Richard 175

Dinslage, Wolfgang 394

Disney, Walt 122, 140, 148, 149, 154, 164, 166, 175, 181, 197, 205, 233, 258, 317

Ditzen, Rudolf Wilhelm Friedrich *see* Fallada, Hans

Dmytryk, Edward 267

Dnjeprow, Anatolij 276

Dobson, Frank 103

Doctorow, Cory 448

Dominik, Hans 5, 155, 187, 251

Dommartin, Solveig 324

Donnelly, Elfie 340, 360

Donovan, Paul 340-341

Dor, Karin 249, 252

"Dora, Marian" 373, 386

Dorn, Dieter 314

Dorris, Anita 114

Douglas, Kirk 195, 248

Douglas, Melvyn 281

Dourif, Brad 370

Doyle, Arthur Conan 36, 232

Drache, Heinz 247

Dressler, Holm 314

Dreyer, Carl Theodor 130, 131, 268

Driehorst, Fabian 411

Dullea, Keir 255

Dumas, Alexandre

Du Maurier, George 114

Dupont, Ewald André 53, 106

Durning, Charles 281

Durniok, Manfred 307, 317, 338, 340, 343, 359

Dux, Eckart 214

Dykstra, John 446

Ebert, Heiko 282, 312

Ebert, Roger 408

Eckelkamp, Hanns 234, 343, 356, 413

Eckelkamp, Thomas 413

Eckert, Horst *see* Janosch [Horst Eckert]

Edel, Alfred 266

Edel, Uli 353, 372, 429

Eden, Barbara 325

Edwards, Amelia 307

Effenberger, Michael 383, 384, 396

Egede-Nissen, Aud 84

Eggeling, Viking 96, 98, 101

Eggers, Robert

Ehmck, Gustav 272, 286

Eibenschütz, Lia 89

Eichinger, Bernd 192, 252, 301, 303, 306, 375, 398

Eidinger, Lars 404, 433

Einstein, Albert 113

Eis, Egon 218

Eisenstein, Sergej M. 98

Eisler, Hanns 212

Eisner, Lotte H[enriette] 16, 199, 200, 263, 288, 301

Ekman, Gösta 109

Elsner, Hannelore 252, 258, 391, 392

Elster, Else 133

Emilfork, Daniel 334

Emmerich, Roland V, 207, 302, 304, 307, 320, 331, 337, 346, 357, 385, 404, 432

Ende, Edgar 120

Ende, Michael 120, 227, 231, 303, 309, 321, 332, 334, 395, 440

Endfield, Cyril (Cy) 255

Engel, Curt A. 192, 195

Engel, Erich 88, 196

Engel, Volker 244, 337, 372

Engelke, Anke 420

Engelmann, Andrews 168

Engels, Erich 132

Engler, Robi 370

Englisch, Lucie

Ensor, James 332

Erdmann, Hans 9, 74, 79, 167

Erler, Rainer 135, 224, 231, 234, 260, 274, 276, 283, 287, 291, 294, 301, 307, 309, 316, 323

Ernemann, Heinrich

Ernsting, Walter 207, 226

Eschbach, Andreas 360

Essel, Franz 213

Esser, Paul 224, 252, 263

Ewald, Hans 126

Ewers, Hanns Heinz 5, 24, 25, 27, 28, 29, 30, 43, 54, 62, 80, 88, 116, 131, 143, 167, 198, 199

Ewert, Heidi 203

Falk, Peter 329

Falkenberg, Paul 176

Fallada, Hans 305

Faltermeier, Martin 406

Fassbinder, Rainer Werner VI, 187, 262, 265, 266, 269-270, 271, 298

Fehlbaum, Tim 404, 441

Fehling, Jürgen 152

Fehse, Carsten 402, 438

Fehse, Marc 402, 438

Feld, Hans 60

Feld, Rudi 97

Feldmann, Rötger 322

Felmy, Hansjörg 236

Felsenheimer, Bela B. (Dirk Albert) 355, 363, 433

Felsenstein, Walter 230, 261

Fendel, Rosemarie 274

Fethke, Jan 22

Fetscher, Andy 379, 405

Feuchtwanger, Lion

Feuillade, Louis 308

Feyder, Jacques 132

Fieber, Gerhard 206

Fiedler, Bea 292

Fiedler, Bernd 348

Fiedler, Erich 143

Figdor, Karl 221

Finch, John

Fink, Hugo 31

Finney, Jack 446

Fipper, Heiko 343

Firmans, Josef

Fischer, Gisela 274

Fischer, Hans see Fischerkoesen, Hans

Fischer, Kai 252

Fischer, Karl 422

Fischer, Samuel 27

Fischerkoesen, Hans 171, 173, 174, 183, 184, 185

Fischinger, Hans 151

Fischinger, Oskar 18, 120, 141, 151, 172, 250

Fisher, David Lee

Fisher, Terence 231

Fitz, Florian 339

Fitzek, Sebastian 433

Flack, Lotte 391

Flaherty, Robert 127

Fleischer, Max 164, 183

Fleischmann, Peter 292, 319

Flick, Horst 270

Flickenschildt, Elisabeth 273

Fliegauf, Benedikt 394

Flimm, Jürgen 298, 315

Florey, Robert V

Fodor, Ladislas 236

Fønss, Olaf 39, 75

Förnbacher, Helmut 275

Förster, Alfred 207, 213

Förster, Anna 338

Folman, Ari 381, 412, 443

Forster, Friedrich 186

Forster, Rudolf 236

Foster, Ben 389

Foster, Hal 340

Fouqué, Friedrich de la Motte

Fox, Edward 340

Fox, William 108

Francesco, Silvio 323

Francis, Freddie 231, 263

Franck, Walter 139

Franco, Jess 254, 265, 279, 294, 297

Frank, Horst 217, 283, 284

Franke, Dieter 294

Fratzscher, Peter 341

Frei, Gerhard 210

Freud, Sigmund 23-24

Freund, Karl 12, 31, 40, 111, 257, 358

Freund, Peter 358

Frey, A. M. 89

Freyer, Achim 237, 377

Fric, Martin 181

Frick, Thomas 361

Fricke, Peter 263

Friedrich, Götz 230

Friedrichsen, Uwe 284

Fries, Liv Lisa 409

Fritsch, Willy 142

Fritzsch, Sebastian 411

Fritzsche, Sonja

Froboess, Cornelia 314

Fröbe, Gert 226, 230, 248, 251, 272, 286

Froelich, Carl 26

Fuchs, Gaby 258

Fuchsberger, Joachim 218, 225, 234, 245, 254, 257, 392

Fühmann, Franz 237, 239

Fürmann, Benno 349, 372

Fürneisen, Bodo 305, 384, 391

Fulci, Lucio 318, 344

Funk, Walter 168

Funke, Cornelia 372, 383, 405, 440

Furneaux, Yvonne 238

Fux, Herbert 259, 286

Gable, Clark 255

Gad, Urban 25, 76, 82

Gärtner, Claus-Theo 284

Gagarin, Yuri Alekseyevich 225

Galeen, Henrik 6, 21, 24, 48, 96, 110, 116, 133, 157, 176, 192

Gallun, Raymond Z. 207

Galouye, Daniel Francis 271, 346, 450

Gansel, Dennis 440

Ganz, Bruno 288, 312, 329

Garko, Gianni 292

Gaus, Bodo 229

Gavioli, Gino 272

Gavioli, Roberto 272

Gedeck, Martina 406

Gehm, Franziska 409

Gehring, Viktor 186

Geike, Willi 345, 357

Geissendörfer, Hans W[ilhelm] 260

Geissler, Dieter 267, 303, 332, 333, 339, 343

Gemser, Laura 296

Genkel, Toby 439

Gens, Xavier 401

Genschow, Fritz 20, 21, 147, 201, 203, 205, 207, 210, 214, 219, 220, 235, 282, 302

Genschow, Gabriel 302, 344

Genschow, Marina 302

George, Götz 253, 254, 335, 336

George, Heinrich 98

Gérard, Henriette 130

Gerhardt, Sonja 409

Gerhardt, Tom 370

Gerlach, Wolf 233

German, Lauren 401

Germer, Karl 101

Gernsback, Hugo

Gerron, Kurt 148

Gerson, Dora 148

Gert, Valeska 98

Gesang, Isidor *see* Gottowt, John

Geschonneck, Erwin 196, 215, 291

Gesek, Ludwig

Geyer, Karl August 24

Gibson, William 448

Giehse, Therese 196, 277

Gier, Kerstin 419

Giesen, Rolf 291, 300, 301, 305, 306, 310, 327, 330, 343, 344, 352, 380, 413, 433

Gilksyon, Terry 256

Giller, Walter 286

Gilliam, Terry 315

Girotti, Mario 249

Gliese, Rochus 13, 42, 69, 124, 287

Glowna, Vadim 282

Godard, Jean-Luc 345

Godden, Rudi 151

Goder, Sebastian 401

Goebbels, Joseph 127, 134, 144, 146, 164, 166, 168, 170, 171, 182-183, 186, 199

Göring, Hermann 183

Goethe, Johann Wolfgang von 1, 2, 79, 175, 223, 317

Goetzke, Bernhard 10, 74, 75, 84, 90, 168, 196, 238

Golan, Menahem 293

Goldblum, Jeff 429

Goldammer, Gerhard 226

Goldmann, Rachel Lea Rosi 5

Goldmann, Wilhelm 5

Goller, Markus 361

Golling, Alexander 209

Gonska, Mascha 275

Gorbachev, Mikhail 329

Gordon, Richard 215, 217

Gorges, Ingolf 280

Gotthelf, Jeremias 72

Gottlieb, Franz Josef 237, 259

Gottowt, John 8, 27, 62, 64, 132, 167

Gottschalk, Thomas 314

Gould, Symon 118, 124, 125

Graatkjær, Axel

Granach, Alexander 12, 13, 27, 80, 81, 89, 90, 98, 114,

Grassmann, Werner 306

Grau, Albin 10, 19, 43, 64, 67, 71, 72, 74, 87, 88, 89, 97, 102, 108, 116, 264

Graunke, Kurt 216

Greco, Daniel 418, 426

Greenbaum, Jules 26, 36

Greene, Graham 206

Gregor, Freddy see Wendlandt, Horst

Gremm, Wolf 298

Griem, Helmut 292, 314

Grimm, Jakob 1, 3, 49, 121, 123, 147, 157, 166, 202, 209, 227, 259, 264, 267, 278, 283, 284, 285, 291, 292, 294, 319, 338, 391, 397, 405, 409, 415, 419, 424, 434

Grimm, Wilhelm 1, 3, 49, 121, 123, 147, 157, 166, 202, 209, 227, 259, 264, 267, 278, 283, 284, 285, 291, 292, 294, 319, 338, 391, 397, 405, 409, 415, 419, 424, 434

Grimmelshausen, Hans Jakob Christoffel von 239

Grobler, Sebastian 409

Grönemeyer, Dietrich 418

Grönemeyer, Herbert 418

Groenewold, David 378

Gronach, Jessaja see Granach, Alexander

Gronau, Ernst 64

Groschopp, Richard 138

Grosskurth, Kurt 267

Grothe, Sven 274

Grube, Elisabeth 79

Gründgens, Gustaf 136-137, 223

Grüninger, Joachim 357

Grune, Karl 115

Guckel, Hans Erdmann Timotheos see Erdmann, Hans

Gülergün, Mehmet 236

Gülstorff, Max 44, 50

Günther, Egon 320

Günther, Erich 210, 237, 282, 305, 312, 337, 344

Guo Xiaolu 404

Gusner, Iris 277

Guter, Johannes 97

Guthke, Frank 265, 274

Gutmann, Nathaniel 344

Gutterer, Leopold 168

Haack, Käthe 168

Haarmann, Fritz 269, 335

Haas, Waltraud 199

Haas, Willly 133

Habbema, Cox 267, 280

Hächler, Horst 273

Hämmerle, Jonas 386

Hagen, Antje 274

Hagen, Cosma Shiva 368, 376, 392

Hagen, Louis 106

Hagen, Nina 368, 376

Hagens, Gunther von 349

Haggard, H[enry] Rider 98

Hahn, Gerhard 322, 340, 358, 369, 374, 442

Halbe, Max 139

Haller, Richard 247

Hallervorden, Dieter 261

Hallwachs, Hans Peter 308

Haltaufderheide, Elke 268

Hameister, Willy 58

Handke, Peter 312

Handloegten, Hendrik 440

Haneke, Michael 326, 362

Hanfstaengl, Ernst "Putzi" 43

Hanisch, Otto 261

Hanks, Tom 408

Hanoszek, Karl 222

Hansen, Joachim 271

Harbou, Thea von 11, 65, 74, 83, 86, 87, 90, 101, 134, 138, 203

Hardwicke, Cedric 156

Harfouch, Corinna 360

Harisch, Klaus 357

Harlan, Veit 148, 196, 197, 211, 217

Harmstorf, Raimund 263

Harnack, Falk 218

Harris, Jack H. 443

Harryhausen, Diana 327

Harryhausen, Ray 216, 230, 233, 236, 238, 300, 305, 327, 329, 330, 337, 347, 351-353

Hartl, Karl 138

Hartmann, Paul 136

Hartwig, Wolf C. 217, 222

Harvey, Laurence 227

Haskin, Byron 211, 233

Hasse, O[tto] E[duard] 238

Hasselhoff, David 314

Hauff, Wilhelm 69, 87-88, 89, 126, 196, 201, 202, 216, 287, 426

Hauptmann, Gerhart 138

Haushofer, Marlen 406

Haussmann, Leander 411

Havenstein, Klaus 255, 256

He Yumen 317

Hebbel, Friedrich 154

Heck, Dieter Thomas 261, 302

Heckroth, Hein 220, 224

Hedrich, Dagmar 273

Heering, Lutz 300

Heerwagen, Bernadette 396

Hegen [Hegenbarth], Hannes 344

Hegesa, Grit

Heidenberg, Tom 414

Heine, Anselma 53

Heine, Helme 386

Heinrich, Brigitte 280

Heinz, Wolfgang 75

Heisterkamp, Norbert

Held, Hans 158, 159, 175, 191

Heller, André 299

Heller, Dagmar 274

Helm, Brigitte 22, 111, 115, 116, 125, 132, 138, 207, 337

Hempel, Johannes (Jan) 201, 228

Henckels, Paul 148

Hendriks, Paul 257

Henman, Granz 441

Hennicke, André M. 415

Henniger, Rolf 249

Hentsch, Jürgen 335

Herbig, Michael "Bully" 365, 374, 378, 383, 386, 428

Herbst, Helmut 140, 273, 276, 447

Herfurth, Karoline 396

Hermann, Martin 347, 363

Herrmann, Bernard 216

Herrmann, Jörg 404

Herwig, Ursula 235

Herzog (Stipetić), Werner VI, 167, 263, 288, 370

Herzsprung, Hannah 404

Hessling, Hans 166

Heydrich, Reinhard 177

Hierl, Werner 248

Hill, Terence *see* Girotti, Mario

Hilpert, Heinz 141, 153, 190

Himmler, Heinrich 183

Hindenburg, Paul von 133

Hippler, Fritz 159, 168

Hirschfield, Jeffrey 340

Hirschmeier, Alfred 221. 240

Hirtz, Dagmar 354

Hitchcock, Alfred 89, 224

Hitler, Adolf 43, 54, 85, 133, 137, 139, 141, 143, 146, 152, 165, 167, 176, 183, 248, 249, 301, 383, 422-423, 433, 435

Ho Chi Minh 202

Hölscher, Heinz 213

Hörbiger, Hanns 193

Hörbiger, Paul 193, 199

Hoffman, Dustin 375

Hoffmann, Carl 224

Hoffmann, E. T. A. 2, 35, 37, 67, 80, 111, 206, 258, 280, 329

Hoffmann, Frank 304

Hoffmann, Kurt 224

Hofkirchner, Wilhelm Arpad Peter *see* Hoven, Adrian

Hofmann, Eduard 181

Hofmann, Ernst 27

Hofmann, Nico 335, 393

Hohensee, Bettina 312

Holk, Heinrich *see* Dieckmann, Heinrich ("Enrico")

Holl, Gussy 51

Hollmann, Patrick 328

Holm, Claus 248

Holt, Hans 199

Holt, Renate von 251

Holtz, Reinhold Johann 154

Holz, Fritz 34

Holzmeister, Judith 199

Homer 195

Honda, Ishiro 443

Hong Hu Zhao 340

Honka, Fritz 434

Honold, Rolf 247

Hoppe, Rolf 273

Horn, Willi 147

Horney, Brigitte 156, 168

Hoss, Nina 396

Houellebecq, Michel 433

Houwer, Rob 259

Hoven, Adrian 85, 237, 254, 259, 263, 268, 295

Howard, Karin 321, 344

Howard, Tom 234

Huber, Grischa 265

Hubschmid, Paul 352

Huettner, Ralf 312, 314, 327, 382

Hugenberg, Alfred 168

Hugo, Victor 117

Hummell, Oliver 351

Humpe, Inga 303

Humperdinck, Engelbert 21

Hunte, Otto 91

Huntgeburth, Hermine 360

Huppert, Isabelle 362

Huppertz, Gottfried 11, 146

Hurt, William 324

Huston, John 255, 309

Huttula, Gerhard 21, 169, 201, 206, 213

Huxley, Aldous 297

Huyck, Willard 285

Hyams, Peter 370

Hyer, Martha 221

Illés, Eugen 50

Ilna, Elisabeth 203

Inci, Georg 392

Ingram, Rex 110

Ionesco, Eugène 232

Ittenbach, Olaf 318, 328, 341, 356, 358, 362, 373, 380, 393, 396, 405, 406, 407, 420, 432

Itzenplitz, Eberhard 273

Iwerks, Ub 122

Jackson, Peter 359

Jacobs, W. W. 307

Jacobsen, Dennis 379

Jacques, Norbert 83

Jahn, Oliver 379

Jahnen, Margaret 234

Jahnke, Stephan

Jahnke, Wolf 321, 381

Jannings, Emil 10, 34, 44, 48, 64, 96, 108-109, 127, 194

Janosch [Horst Eckert] 375, 407

Janowitz, Hans 13, 29, 49, 55, 63, 203

Janson, Uwe 409

Janson, Victor 36, 39, 168

Janssen, Walter 139

Jasný, Voytech 297

Jazay, Daniel 342

Jedele, Helmut 218

Jeunet, Jean-Pierre 334

Jeffries, Lang 252

Jittlov, Mike 323

Jochmann, Ludger see Knister

Johansson, Scarlett 429

John, Georg 46

John, Gottfried 271, 391

John, Odine 383

Johnson, Brian 303

Johst, Hanns 139

Jonsson, Rune 386

Jovovich, Mila 360, 395, 440-441

Jürgens, Curd 199, 222, 293

Jugo, Jenny 191-192

Juhnke, Harald 230

Julino, Florian 230

July, Miranda 400

Jung, Jürgen 260

Junghans, Wolfram 108

Jungk, Robert 132

Junkersdorf, Eberhard 340

Kästner, Erich 168, 258, 396

Käutner, Helmut 188, 191, 238

Kafka, Franz 72. 276

Kaiser, Wolf 210

Kaiser-Titz, Erich 39

Kalanag see Schreiber, Helmut

Kalaš, Jilis 181

Kalinke, Ernst Wilhelm 249

Kandel, Josef 181

Kant, Uwe 281

Karbe, Margrith Helena 179

Kardan, Alexander 87

Karloff, Boris 66

Karloff, Sara 323

Karlowa, Elma 271

Karlstadt, Liesl 88

Karmakar, Romuald 335

Karp, Willy 201

Kaschnitz, Marie Luise 307

Katz, Steven 350

Kaufmann, Christine 271, 302

Kauka, Rolf 230, 236, 272

Kavanian, Rick (Richard Horatio) 365

Kayssler, Friedrich 35, 138

Keglevic, Peter 311

Kehlmann, Michael 273

Keienburg, Ernst 140

Keitel, Harvey 293

Keller, Inge 251

Keller, Marion 189

Kellermann, Bernhard 6, 27, 35, 136, 197

Kemp, Paul 142

Kemper, Ralf 393, 419

Kermbach, Otto 79

Kern, Peter 271, 286, 327

Kerner, Charlotte 364

Kerp, Theo 322

Kerr, Charlotte 274

Kertész, Mihály 68

Kestin, Erich 256

Kettelhut, Erich 14, 91-92, 112, 223, 291

Keyhoe, Donald E. 260

Keymer, Oskar 424

Kiebach, Hans Jürgen 294

Kier, Udo 181, 259, 271, 272, 302, 307, 327, 334, 336, 340, 366, 371, 404, 406

Kierska, Marga 51

Kierspe, Udo see Kier, Udo

Kiilerich, Karsten 429

Kilmer, Val 446

Kindermann, Helmo 213

Kindler, Klaus 235

King, Frank 233. 443

King, Herman 233

King, Maurice 233, 443

King, Stephen 47

Kingsley, Ben 371

Kinski, Klaus VI, 110, 225, 234, 235, 237, 251, 270, 280, 288-290, 325

Kinski, Nastassja 224, 278, 329

Kinski, Nikolai 290, 417

Kipling, Rudyard 116

Kirch, Leo 309, 322

Kirsten, Brigitte 251

Kirsten, Ralf 251

Klante, Diethard 291

Klauss, Jürgen (Karl) 304

Klein, Bernhard 64

Klein, César 64

Klein, Gerhard 215

Klein-Rogge, Rudolf 11, 83, 87, 93, 95, 111, 134, 135, 137, 138, 206

Kleinau, Willy A. 205, 206

Kleinbach, Heinrich von *see* Brandon, Henry

Kleinert, Till 418

Kleist, Heinrich von 142, 152

Klemke, Werner 329

Klemm, Rudi 118

Kling, Anja 365, 409

Kling, Marc-Uwe 438

Klinkhammer, Carl 249

Klitzsch, Ludwig 168

Klooss, Reinhard 381, 396

Klopfenstein, Clemens 306, 316

Kluge, Alexander VI, 230, 264, 266

Knapp, Max 212

Knef, Hildegard 198, 293

Knister [Ludger Jochmann] 385

Knižka, Roman 391

Knoesel, Klaus 331, 339, 364

Knötzsch, Hans 231

Knorr, Manfred 268

Knüppel, Sven 377

Kobler, Erich 209

Koch, Marianne 248

Köhler, Manfred R. 251, 263

König, Ralf 337

Körber, Maria 197

Körner, Lothar 29

Koerner von Gustorf, Florian 329

Kohlhaase, Wolfgang 221

Kohner, Paul 19, 134, 313

Kohut, Walter 260, 274

Kolbe, Winrich 359

Kolditz, Gottfried 86, 216, 225, 228, 235, 261, 279, 291, 298

Kolin, Nikolaij 119

Kopp, Martin 71

Kopsch, Julius 146

Korczak, Janusz 378

Korda, Alexander 158, 168

Korén, Juliane 262

Korittke, Oliver 355

Kornblum, Hans Walter 88, 102, 117

Kortner, Fritz 67, 89, 124

Korytowski, Manfred 299

Kosakowski, Michael 420

Koschella, Josef 296

Kosslick, Dieter 429

Kothenschulte, Daniel 256

Kracauer, Siegfried 12, 189, 248

Kraft, Evelyne 286

Kraft, Robert 4, 38

Kräly, Hans 48

Krahl, Hilde 199

Kranz, George 311

Kratzert, Hans 273, 320

Kraume, Lars 396

Krause, Georg 222

Krauss, Werner 10, 28, 41, 44, 55, 61, 89, 90, 96, 98, 104, 110, 219

Krawinkel, Lenard Fritz 364

Kreidolf, Ernst 160

Kretschmann, Thomas 340, 375

Kreuzpaintner, Marco 373, 382

Kristl, Vlado 230, 251

Kroetz, Franz Xaver 383

Kross, David 382

Krüger, Christiane 274

Krüger, Gerhard 149, 160

Krüger, Hardy 211

Krüger Jr., Hardy 356

Krüger, Richard 201, 214

Krüger, Werner 207

Krumm, Paul Albert 260

Krug, Manfred 251

Krug, Wilhelm 146

Kruse, Käthe 374

Kruse, Max 374

Kubaschewski, Ilse 192, 286

Kubin, Alfred 55, 271

Kubitschek, Ruth-Maria 307

Kubrick, Stanley 102, 255, 261, 262, 281, 436, 447

Küblböck, Daniel 366

Kühnberg, Leontine 39, 67

Kümel, Harry 263

Küntzel, Martha 101

Kunert, Günther 304

Kunstmann, Doris 354

Kunstmann, Ernst 192, 196, 206, 217, 219

Kuntze, Reimar 98

Kurosawa, Akira 303, 431

Kurzweil, Raymond 448

Kutscher, Volker 440

Kutter, Anton 147, 159

Kyser, Hans 90

Ladengast, Walter 274, 288

Laemmle, Carl, Sr. 4, 114, 153

Lakomy, Torsten 342

Lamprecht, Gerhard

Lamprecht, Günter 271

Lancaster, Burt 281, 322

Landgrebe, Gudrun 323, 328

Landgut, Inge 138

Landshoff, Ruth 79

Lang, Anton 13

Lang, Fritz 13, 46, 51, 74, 83, 84, 85, 90-93, 96, 96, 101, 110, 120, 127, 134, 176, 179, 203, 211, 223, 225, 226, 248, 279, 444

Lang, Max 391

Lang, Pauline 13

Lang Lang 388

Lange, Hellmuth 258

Lange, Karl (Carl) 218, 251

Langhans, Rainer 265, 292

Larsen, Trygve *see* Eis, Egon

Larsen, Viggo 31

Laser, Dieter 280, 284

Lasswitz, Kurd 3, 25, 23

Latal, Stanislav 181

Lau, Frederick 426

Laube, Birger 349

Lauenstein, Christoph 320, 432, 433

Lauenstein, Wolfgang 320, 432, 433

Laughton, Charles 137

Laurel, Stan 207

Lauterbach, Heiner 406

Lavi, Daliah 226

Lee, Christopher 231, 246, 247, 252, 254, 278

Lee, Stan 444

Le Fanu, Joseph Sheridan V, 130

Léger, Fernand 98

Lehn, Georg 213

Lehndorff, Veruschka von 303

Leipnitz, Harald 247, 251, 252

Leitner, Angela von 207

Lem, Stanisław VI, 219, 220, 284, 379, 412, 443, 449-450

Lemmel, Dieter 245

Lengyel, Rita 361

Leni, Paul V, 10, 47, 96, 114, 117, 120

Lenica, Jan 232, 244, 255

Levi, Paul Josef *see* Leni, Paul

Levka, Uta 255

Levy, Dani 438

Levy, Gabriel 138

Lewis, Matthew Gregory 280

Ley, Robert 168, 183

Lichtenheldt, Nicole 311

Liebeneiner, Wolfgang 199, 263

Liebknecht, Karl 84

Liebmann, Robert 53

Liefers, Jan Josef 359, 409

Lieven, Albert 253

Liljedahl, Marie 258

Linda, Curt 258-259, 327, 333, 341

Lincke, Paul 239

Lindau, Paul 26

Lindenberg, Udo 303

Lingen, Theo 286

Lipnicki, Jonathan 353

Lippschitz, Arnold 132

Lisewski, Stefan 288

Lisi, Virna 267

List, Niki 322

Loanic, Minhoï Geneviève 290

Lobel, Bruni 274

Loeser, Tony 282, 312, 343, 370

Loevy, Pauline 5

Loewenstein, László *see* Lorre, Peter

Löwenthal, Peggy *see* Longard, Peggy

Löwitsch, Klaus 271

Lohman, Augie (August J.) 234

Loken, Kristanna 371

Lom, Herbert 249, 250, 259

Lommel, Ludwig Manfred 186-187

Lommel, Ulli (Ulrich Manfred) 186-187, 265, 269-270, 271, 366, 373, 428

Loncraine, Richard 307

Longard, Peggy 76

Loos, Anna 355

Loos, Theodor 90, 103, 133

Lopez, Jennifer 351

Lorey, Guillarmo 87

Lorre, Peter 20, 127, 133, 138, 237, 269

Losansky, Rolf 126, 237, 274, 282, 298, 301, 311, 329, 344, 425

Lothar, Hans 231

Lovecraft, H[oward] P[hillips] 396

Lowitz, Siegfried 218

Lubitsch, Ernst 14, 27, 35, 39, 46, 48, 79, 188

Lucas, George 285, 447

Ludendorff, Erich 170

Ludwig, Ernst 39

Ludwig, Rolf 217, 226

Lüders, Günther 210

Lühdorff, Jörg 398

Lühr, Peter 281

Lütge, Karl 62

Lugosi, Béla 8, 63, 81, 132, 171, 210, 225, 355

Lukschy, Wolfgang 225

Lundgren, Dolph 406

Lustig, Konrad 209

Lutz, Joseph Maria 193

Luxemburg, Rosa 84

Lygum, Per 339, 343

Maar, Paul 323

MacDonald, Peter 332

Mack, Max 10, 26, 32, 269

MacLaughlin, John 307

MacPhail, Angus 119

Maertens, Kai 348

Märthesheimer, Peter 260, 271, 356

Maetzig, Kurt 220, 221

Maffay, Peter 434

Magritte, René 332

Mahler, Miriam 282

Mainz, Friedrich A[ugust] 222

Maire, Fred 274

Makatsch, Heike 355, 370

Malkovich, John 350

Malle, Louis 277

Mandel, Rena 130

Mandl, Julius Otto *see* May, Joe

Manera, Jesús Franco *see* Franco, Jess

Mangano, Silvana 195

Mann, Thomas 299

Manwaring, Greg 399

Marei, Tijan 435

Margheriti, Antonio 253

Marian, Ferdinand 168

Marka, Sebastian 440

Marks, Kurt 262, 305

Marlow, Maria 249, 250

Marschall, Andreas 367, 401, 420, 426

Marshall, Bruce 225

Martin, Karlheinz 67, 72

Martin, Marta 409

Marx, Karl 323

Masina, Giuelietta 306

Massary, Fritzi 35

Massey, Anna 255

Masucci, Oliver 422

Maté, Rudolph 130

Matheson, Richard 255

Mátray, Ernst 28

Matsutani, Rainer 334, 341, 359, 372

Maugham, W. Somerset 110

Maurischat, Fritz

Maurus, Gerda 120

May, Joe 6, 30, 46, 56, 65, 75, 156, 203, 221

May, Eva 65

May, Karl 249

May, Mia 9, 46, 56, 65, 294

Mayer, Carl 16, 49, 55, 62, 89, 171

Mayer-Horckel, Ferdinand Philip *see* Mayne, Ferdy

Mayne, Ferdy [Ferdinand] 37, 263, 323, 341

McCormack, Sean 439

McEnery, Don 364

McLuhan, Marshall 445

Meat Loaf 371

Mechau, Emil 137

Meddings, Derek 321

Meinert, Rudolf 8, 31, 37, 57, 58, 61, 63

Meinrad, Josef 199, 272

Melchior, Ib J[ørgen] 250

Méliès, Georges 22, 305

Mell, Marisa 275

Melville, Jean-Pierre 445

Mendrek, Nicolas 395

Menge, Wolfgang 261, 269

Menotti, Gian Carlo 257

Menz, Dieter 255

Menzel, Gerhard 249

Merhige, E[dmund] Elias 349, 350

Mesina, Ines 79

Messter, Oskar 3, 17, 18, 26, 40, 47, 65, 179

Metzger, Helmut 371

Metzner, Ernö 90, 98

Meyer, Anja 357

Meyer, Günter 288, 299, 312, 323, 326, 342, 345-346, 349

Meyer, Gustav *see* Meyrink, Gustav

Meyer, Jan-Hendrik 343

Meyer, Kai 345-346

Meyer, Maria 4

Meyer, Otto 205

Meyer, Russ 336

Meyerinck, Hubert von 137, 252

Meyrink, Gustav 4, 34, 54, 132

Mezger, Theo 247

Michael, Marion 211, 214

Micheluzzi, Victor 68

Mierendorff, Hans 62, 71

Miller, Arthur 212

Miller, Dick 229

Miller, George [Scottish director] 321

Miller, George [Australian director] 321

Miller, Hugh 103

Millowitsch, Mariele 354

Millowitsch, Willy 252

Minetti, Hans-Peter 291

Minko, Natalie 328

Minks, Wilfried 293

Mitchell, David 408

Mitchell, Cameron 252

Mitić, Gojko 261, 361

Miyazaki, Hayao 431

Mocky, Jean-Pierre 300

Möhl, Friedrich Karl 101

Möhring, Wotan Wilke 354, 355

Möllendorff, Horst von 171, 173, 174, 179, 181, 182, 183, 184-185, 186

Möllenhoff, Ralf, 383

Möller, Gunnar 157, 193

Möller, Ralf 368

Moers, Walter 347, 375

Moik, Lutz 196

Moissi, Alexander 29-30

Moissi, Bettina 191

Molo, Walter von 139

Mondi, Bruno 196

Mondry, Eberhard 235

Montag, Frank W. 377

Montagu, Ivor 89, 103, 118

Montand, Yves 212

Montgomery, Tyron 339

Moore, Zoe 415

Moorse, George 144, 265, 271, 275, 281, 306, 344

Moost, Nele 407, 421

Mora, Hella 204

Morena, Erna 62

Moretti, Tobias 422

Moritz, William 172, 173

Morrissey, Paul 271, 272

Mosbacher, Peter 245

Moser, Hans 199

Moszkowicz, Martin 311

Moyer, Stephen 340

Mozart, Wolfgang Amadeus 341

Mühe, Anna Maria 392

Mühe, Ulrich 326

Mühlen-Schulte, Georg 139

Müller, Georg 25

Müller, Hans 326

Müller, Paul Alfred 134

Müller, Pauline see Synd, Lu

Müller, Robby 324

Müller, Stefan

Müller-Stahl, Armin 309, 331

Müller-Westernhagen, Marius 336

Müllerschön, Nikolai 309, 369

Müntefering, Gert K. 296, 310

Münzenberg, Willi 98

Müthel, Lothar 27

Muren, Dennis 305

Murnau, Friedrich Wilhelm V, VI, 12, 24, 26, 27, 32, 47, 62, 64, 72, 75, 77, 79, 86, 108, 109, 118, 126, 127, 171, 263, 301, 349, 350

Murray, Bill 429

Muschalek, Jürgen 302

Mycroft, Walter C. 103

Myler, Lok see Müller, Paul Afred

Myrthenhzweig, Moritz see Mack, Max

Naber, Johannes 426

Nabokov, Vladimir 270

Nakaszynski, Klaus Günter Karl see Kinski, Klaus

Nalder, Reggie 211, 259

Natividad, Kitten 336

Nauckhoff, Rolf von 213, 252

Naujoks, Ingo 336

Naumann, Horst 235

Neff, Hildegarde see Knef, Hildegard

Negri, Pola 48

Neill, Sam 295

Nemec, Jan 276

Nemetz, Max 73

Nestroy, Johann 27, 86, 210

Nesvadba, Josef 246

Neuberger, Hans 145

Neuhäuser, Holger 331

Neumann, Hans 48, 90, 98

Neumann, Karl 166, 174

Neuss, Alwin 31, 32

Neusser, Erich 146

Ngo, The Chau 435

Niebisch, Jackie 374

Nielsen, Asta 25, 44, 62, 90, 99

Nielsen, Hans 189

Nischwitz, Theo 224, 248

Noa, Manfred 90

Noethen, Ulrich 416

Noever, Hans 260

Nolan, Jaime see Böttger, Fritz

Nomura, Kunichi 430

Nontschew, Mirco 376

Nordhoff, Flo [Baron Florenz von Fuchs-Nordhoff] 215, 217

Nosbusch, Désirée 298

Nowottnick-Genschow, Rita-Maria 207, 302

Nowotny[-Genschow], Rita-Maria see Nowottnick-Genschow, Rita-Maria

Nussbaum, Raphael 234

Oberländer, Hans 36

Obermaier, Uschi 265

Oberth, Hermann 120, 260

O'Brien, Willis 126

Ode [Odemar], Erik 90

Odemar, Fritz 136

Oehmichen, Walter 189, 202, 209

Offenbach, Jacques 37

Ohrt, Christoph M. 334

Olsen, Rolf 276

Ornstein, Richard W. see Oswald, Richard

Orwell, George VI, 297, 300, 436

Ostermayr, Peter 50

Oswald, Richard 6, 15, 31, 32, 35, 37, 41, 42, 44, 46, 50, 53, 54, 62, 67, 76, 79, 119, 125, 132, 235

Ott, Edgar 255, 256

Ottinger, Ulrike 286, 296, 303, 404

Otto, Götz 361, 406

Pabst, Erich 67

Pabst, Georg Wilhelm 104, 127, 132, 195

Padrón, Juan 307

Page, Larry 448

Pal, George 126, 127, 161, 162, 163, 164, 211, 227, 305

Palm, Michael 420

Palmer, Lilli 255

Pankejeff, Sergei 23-24

Panneck, Sebastian 328

Panzer, Wolfgang 306

Parker, Eleanor 211
Parker, Percy G. *see* Hoven, Adrian
Parr, Julian 207
Paryla, Katja 288
Pasetti, Peter 304
Pastewka, Bastian 392
Pattinson, Robert 433
Patzak, Peter 275
Paul, Albert 39
Pavanelli, Livio C. 119
Pavlidis, Carlos 309
Pekny, Romuald 314
Pempeit, Lilo 271
Perak, Rudolf 183
Perlinger, Sissi 334
Perlman, Ron 334, 379
Peroff, Paul Nikolaus 121
Perrault, Charles 319
Perschy, Maria 236
Peschel, Milan 426
Peters, Werner 234
Petersen, Jürgen 184-185
Petersen, Wolfgang VI, 152, 161, 269, 280, 307
Peterson, Lorne 305
Petersson, Harald G. 247, 249
Petri, Ilse 145
Petzold, Christian 436
Pfenninger, Rudolf 101, 136
Pfister, Josef 175
Pfleger, Hermine *see* May, Mia
Philipsen, Constantin Preben 195, 218, 226, 253
Pick, Lupu 48
Piel, Harry (Heinrich) 14, 15, 34, 36, 39, 62, 64, 66, 129, 136, 137, 139, 155, 232
Pils, Heide 301
Pinschewer, Julius 118

Pinter, Harold 319
Piontek, Klaus 285
Piper, Tommy 293
Pirinçci, Akif 333
Platte, Rudolf 253
Plautus, Maccius 142
Pleva, Jörg 274
Plumpe, Friedrich Wilhelm *see* Murnau, Friedrich Wilhelm
Pocci, Franz von 195
Poe, Edgar Allan 27, 35, 51, 53, 80, 132, 252
Poelzig, Hans 4, 66, 99, 145
Pohl, Michael 356
Pohland, Hans Jürgen 259, 293
Pohlmann, Franziska 424
Pohris, Herbert 161
Polanski, Roman 263, 345
Polcar, Philip 386, 391, 420
Polidori, John V
Pollock, Channing 114
Pommer, Anna 12
Pommer, Erich 12, 34, 59, 60, 61, 63, 96, 97, 104, 121, 127, 188, 247
Pommer, Gustav 12
Ponto, Erich 193
Porten, Henny 206
Possardt, Werner 309
Potente, Franka 349, 364, 369
Praetorius, Johannes
Prager, Wilhelm 69, 86
Pratchett, Terry 442
Preiss, Wolfgang 221. 223, 226, 230, 237
Presle, Micheline 221
Preussler, Otfried 272, 327, 415
Price, Vincent 156, 226, 229
Prochnow, Jürgen 280, 284
Prostigo, Jessica 414

Prückner, Tilo 292, 406
Puhlmann, Willi 186
Pulver, Liselotte 224, 252
Pulwer, Leon 311
Purzer, Manfred 257
Quadflieg, Will 223, 248
Quaid, Dennis 389
Qualtinger, Helmut 246
Quian Yunda 338
Quinn, Anthony 195
Raab, Kurt 269, 270, 271
Rabben, Mascha 271, 272
Rabenalt, Arthur Maria 189, 198
Raboldt, Toni 87
Radloff, Angela von 273
Raeder, Gustav 151
Rätz, Günter 295
Raimund, Ferdinand 315
Rains, Claude 136
Rameau, Emil 48
Rameau, Hans 136
Rasch, Carlos 261
Rasp, Fritz 13, 46, 98, 116, 120, 131, 280
Rau, Andrea 263
Reagan, Ronald 137
Redl, Christian 382
Reeves, Michael 259
Regner, Sven 411
Regnier, Charles 234
Rehkopf, Paul 71
Reicher, Ernst 30, 31, 35
Reicher, Frank 30
Reichmann, Wolfgang 231, 294
Reimann, Walter 57, 58, 59
Reincke, Heinz 286
Reinecker, Herbert 247, 251, 252
Reinert, Robert

Reinhardt, Max 5, 21, 24, 26, 27, 28, 44, 99, 109, 142

Reiniger, Lotte (Charlotte) 17, 18, 49, 53, 69, 72, 77, 87, 106-107, 117, 124, 126, 140, 142, 296, 305

Reinl, Harald 22, 218, 226, 230, 246, 249, 252, 309

Reisch, Günter 221

Reitz, Edgar 258, 266

Rellergerd, Helmut 270, 339

Remberg, Eric 428

Renard, Maurice 98

Renner, Jeremy 410

Resch, Ingrid 274, 275

Reschke, Ernst 79

Resemann, Léon 26

Reuber-Staier, Eva 258

Reyer, Walter 248

Rhode, Armin 359, 370, 373

Rhomberg, Rudolf 252

Rhys-Davies, John 331, 379

Rice Burroughs, Edgar 416

Richardson, Natasha 319

Richter, Hans [actor] 224, 252

Richter, Hans [artist] 99, 117

Richter, Jason James 332

Richter, Jochen 286

Richter, Paul 84, 90, 92, 93, 131

Richtsfeld, Richard 294

Riefenstahl, Leni 129, 152-153, 226

Riethmüller, Heinrich 255-256

Rikli, Martin 145, 148

Rilla, Walter 82, 238, 245

Rimbaud, Arthur 260

Rippert, Otto 4, 39, 51, 156

Rittau, Günther 111, 112

Ritter, Karl 122

Robertson [Étienne-Gaspard Robert] 447

Robison, Artur (Arthur) 11, 44, 142, 143

Robinson, Ann 323

Roddenberry, Gene 221, 443

Rodrian, Fred 329

Rodriguez, Robert 401

Roehler, Oskar 327

Röhrig, Walter 57, 59

Roellenbleg, Heinrich 171

Roellinghoff, Charlie (Karl Gottlieb Josef) 126

Roge, Laura Antonia 409

Roger, Friedrich Waldemar 116, 123, 125, 216

Rohm, Maria 254

Rohmer, Sax 246, 247

Rohnstock, Marc 394, 397, 420

Rojas, Raúl 449

Roll, Gernot 373

Romanelli, Serena 380

Rooney, Mickey 326

Rose, Timo 360, 371, 379, 393, 397, 400

Rosegger, Peter 90

Rosner, Erwin 62

Roth, Rose Renée 274

Rothkirch, Thilo Graf 345, 357

Rowitz, Michael 380

Rudolph, Lars 361

Rücker, Günter 221

Rückert, Friedrich 160

Rühmann, Heinz 181, 190, 219, 329

Rütting, Barbara 248

Ruland, Tina 337

Ruppel, Karl-Ludwig 215, 217, 219, 224, 230

Russek, Rita 354

Rutkowski, Heidelore 158

Ruttmann, Walter 11, 70, 98, 165

Ruzowitzky, Stefan 228, 348, 356, 362, 385

Ryan, Clarence 372

Rye, Stellan 6, 28, 29, 32

Sabl, Heinrich 442

Sabu 221

Sadoul, Georges

Sägebrecht, Marianne 384

Sais, Tatjana 252

Šajtinac, Boris 259

Salmonova, Lyda 42, 45, 69

Samel, Udo 337

Samland, Andreas 361

Samuelson, G. B. 98

Sander, Otto 312, 329

Sanders Brahms, Helma 272

Sandrock, Adele 142

Sartre, Jean-Paul 212

Savalas, Telly 269

Schaack, Michael 333, 375

Schaaf, Johannes 271, 309

Schacht, Hjalmar 109

Schäffer, Georg Sylvester 85

Schätzing, Frank 441

Schafmeister, Heinrich 338

Schall, Ekkehard 215, 279

Schamoni, Peter 229, 230

Schamoni, Thomas 260

Schatz, Friedhelm 330, 340

Schau, Jürgen 348

Scheer, Karl Herbert 226, 253

Scheerbart, Paul 3, 35, 64

Scheff, Werner 50

Schenkel, Carl 292

Schesch, Stephan 378, 411

Schick, Cornelius 436

Schikaneder, Emanuel 341

Schiller, Friedrich von 88

Schilling, Niklaus 268, 299

Schillings, Max von 82

Schirk, Heinz 283

Schittenhelm, Brigitte *see* Helm, Brigitte

Schlegel, Margarete 82

Schleicher, Kurt 183

Schlettow, Hans Adalbert 50, 84, 90, 132

Schley, Karl Maria 274

Schlingensief, Christof 321, 327, 336

Schlöndorff, Volker 319

Schmenger, Ursula 315

Schmidt, Gerhard 276

Schmidt, Harald 392

Schmidt, Wolf 211

Schmidt-Reichwein, Jörg

Schmidtchen, Kurt 210

Schmitz, Ralf 376

Schmitz, Sybille 130, 144

Schnaas, Andreas 318, 325, 328, 338, 343, 344, 356, 362, 381, 393, 397, 400

Schneer, Charles H[irsch] 222, 337

Schneider, Dr. 83

Schneider, Helmuth 234

Schneider, Martin 376

Schneider, Romy 248, 293

Schnell, Georg Heinrich 50, 65, 85, 88

Schnell, Reinald 321

Schnitzler, Gregor 373

Schnürle, Armin 432

Schoemann, Michael 313, 326, 344, 399

Schön, Margarete 90, 103

Schöne, Reiner 361

Schönherr, Dietmar 247, 328

Schonger, Hubert 16, 17, 148, 154, 155, 157, 158, 160, 166, 187, 190, 191, 193, 195, 201, 202, 203, 204, 209, 212, 213, 218, 226, 228, 229

Schongerfilm *see* Schonger, Hubert

Schramm, Erica 267

Schreck, Max 6, 70, 73, 75, 79, 81, 88, 115, 130, 137, 144, 145, 349, 350

Schreiber, Helmut 116, 151

Schröder, Greta (Margarete) 14, 28, 37, 81, 82, 95

Schroeter, Werner 271

Schüfftan, Eugen 14, 103, 104, 106, 147, 206, 234

Schühly, Thomas 335

Schündler, Rudolf 273

Schünzel, Reinhold 11, 44, 50, 51, 53, 54, 68, 142, 204

Schürenberg, Siegfried 255

Schützendorf, Guido 48

Schuh, Jakob 391

Schultze, Kristian 210

Schultze, Norbert 154, 210

Schultze, Jr., Norbert 210

Schulz, Herbert K. 210, 231

Schulze, H[ugo] O[tto] 112, 127

Schulze-Mittendorf, Walter 111

Schumacher, Ernst Mathias 88, 104

Schumacher, Joel 446

Schumann, Curt 145

Schust, Lukas 395

Schwartzman, Jason 430

Schwarzenegger, Arnold 363, 365

Schwarzkopf, Klaus 304

Schweiger, Til 414

Schweighöfer, Matthias 354

Schwenk, Stefan 327

Schwind, Wolfgang Ritter von 166

Seeber, Clemens 6

Seeber, Guido 6, 22, 23, 25, 27, 48, 98, 99, 104, 157

Seelig, Matthias 335, 336

Seibold, Willy 87, 88

Seibt, Siegfried 222, 288

Seifert., Kurt 151

Seitz, Sr., Franz 70

Seitz, Jr., Franz 299

Selge, Edgar 409

Semmelrogge, Dustin 427

Semmelrogge, Martin 355

Semyonov, Viktor 278

Senftleben, Günter 234

Servais, Raoul 332

Seubert, Martha *see* Dagover, Lil

Seybold, Katrin 306

Seyrig, Delphine 263, 303

Shakespeare, William 28, 97, 98, 281, 419

Shaw, Bob 364

Sheckley, Robert 260

Shelley, Mary W. V, 39

Sieber, Wolfgang 345

Siefert, Gertrud 29

Siegel, Don 446

Sieger, Ted 424

Siepermann, Harald 310, 417, 418

Sigl, Robert IX, 230, 318, 334, 341, 345-346, 348, 354, 386, 392

Signoret, Simone 212

Silber, Rolf 401

Silvestri, Umberto 195

Simmons, Dan XI

Simon, Michel 217

Simon, Rainer 267

Simonischek, Peter 419

Simson, Marianne 154, 168

Singer, Tilman 431

Siodmak, Curt (Kurt) V, 20, 59, 133, 138, 156, 166, 171, 231, 232, 283, 305, 337,

Siodmak, Robert 20

Sittner, Michael 381

Skladanowsky, Max 16, 156

Slater, Christian 368

Slater, Mark 410

Slezak, Leo 168

Smolowa, Sibyl 50

Sommer, Elke 267, 269, 349

Sommer-Bodenburg, Angela 353

Soozandeh, Ali 432

Speelmans, Hermann 168

Spiegl, Walter 207

Spiehs, Karl 292, 314

Spielberg, Steven 339, 431

Spiess, Helmut 204, 210

Sprungala, Karl Walter 419

Stacke, Manuela 376

Stadler, Heiner 306

Stadlober, Robert 391

Statham, Jason 379

Stanton, Harry Dean 293

Stapenhorst, Günther 198

Starewicz, Władysław 143, 146

Stark, Curt A. 26

Staudte, Wolfgang 132, 202

Stauss, Emil Georg von 47, 170

Steckel, Leonard 129

Stefani, Francesco 87, 201, 210-211, 214, 318

Steinbicker, Reinhart 141

Steiner-Prag, Hugo 34

Steinrück, Albert 53, 65, 115

Stellmach, Thomas 339

Stemmle, Robert Adolf 155, 235

Stenbock-Fermor, Alexander 221

Steppat, Ilse 251

Stern, Ernst

Steuben, Joe 344

Stevens, Brinke 323

Stevenson, Robert Louis V, 26, 53, 63, 132, 141, 199, 265, 338

Stockmann, Franz J. 333

Stoker, Bram [Abraham] V, 22, 41, 68, 81, 83, 95, 260, 288

Stoker, Florence 83, 85, 86, 95, 101, 103, 117, 118, 146

Storch, Wenzel 328

Stordel, Kurt 144, 145, 149-150, 153, 191

Storm, J. P. 173

Storm, Theodor 158, 280

Storz, Oliver 307

Strack, Günter 274

Stranka, Erwin 270, 281

Stranz, Fred 70

Strauss, Johann 199

Stravinsky, Igor 234

Stresemann, Gustav 109

Striebeck, Peter 392

Strigel, Claus 355

Strobl, Karl Hans 54

Stroheim, Erich von 198

Stoss, Raymond 231

Strugatsky, Arkady 319

Strugatsky, Boris 319

Strunk, Heinz 434

Sturm, Hans 69, 99

Süskind, Patrick 375

Summers, Walter 98

Sutherland, Donald 330

Swift, Jonathan 103

Swinton, Tilda 429

Syberberg, Hans Jürgen 283

Sydow, Max von 293

Sydow, Rolf von 204

Synd, Lu 44, 45

Szabó, István 317

Szabó, Thomas André 422

Tafel, Sibylle 409

Talamonti, Rinaldo 286

Tani, Yoko 221

Tappe, Holger 364, 381, 396

Tappert, Horst 295

Tavernier, Bertrand 293

Teege, Joachim 251, 252

Teigler, Rolf 347

Theede, Christian 384, 415

Theumer, Ernst Ritter von 252

Thiele, Hertha 135

Thiele, Rolf 258, 273

Thimig, Hermann 74

Thomalla, Georg 224

Thomalla, Kurt 123

Thome, Rudolf 260, 262

Thompson, Carlos 221

Thompson, Tom 420

Thoms, Dietrich 213

Tichy, Wolfram 341

Tiller, Nadja 308

Tillgner, Hans Heinrich *see* Clifford, Frank

Timme, Philipp 338

Tischmeyer, Heinz 160, 190

Todd, Bobby 191, 213

Toelle, Tom 260

Tors, Ivan 138

Tost, Hans 156

Towers, Harry Alan 245, 247, 251

Tränker, Heinrich 96, 97, 101

Tramitz, Christian 365

Trautmann, Ludwig 36, 39

Treumann, Karl 31

Treumann, Wanda 31

Trier, Lars von XI, 386, 401

Trivas, Victor 217

Tsuburaya, Eiji 443

Twardowski, Hans Heinrich von 64

Tykwer, Tom 245, 342, 375, 398, 408, 440

Uhlen, Susanne 325

Ullman, Liv 283

Ullmann, Kostja 384

Ulmer, Edgar G[eorg] 66, 449

Ulrich, Jennifer 372, 396

Ungerer, Tomi 378, 411

Unterwaldt Jr., Sven 370, 424

Urban, Simon 440

Urchs, Wolfgang 229, 233, 313, 322, 339

Uschkurat, Werner 235

Ustinov, Peter 137

Vagenshtain, Angel 267

Vajda, Ladislao 219

Valente, Caterina 323

Valentin, Barbara 271

Valentin, Karl 88

Vallentin, Hermann 35, 39, 82

Vallis, Lo 43

Van Dien, Casper 366

Van Dreelen, John 268

Van Eyck, Peter 223, 235, 238

Van Gogh, Vincent 306

Varnbüler, Karl von 4

Veidt, Conrad 14, 15, 27, 32, 44, 46, 50, 51, 53, 54, 55, 61, 62, 63, 68, 75, 96, 98, 109, 110, 117, 133, 158, 171

Veit, Karl L. 260

Ventura, Lino 220

Verbinski, Gore XI, 426

Verdi, Giuseppe 227

Verhoeven, Michael 286, 424

Verhoeven, Paul 196

Verhoeven, Simon 424

Vermes, Timur 423

Verne, Jules 4, 36, 50, 62, 110, 340, 343

Vernon, Howard 254

Vesper, Will 139

Vespermann, Kurt 137

Vidal, Gore 237

Vilsmaier, Joseph 383

Vogel, Frank 226

Vohrer, Alfred 254, 257

Voigt, Jürgen 273

Vollbrecht, Karl 91-92, 211

Vorlicek, Vaclav 337, 347

Vuillermoz, Emile 93

Waalkes, Otto 301, 357, 368, 375

Wachowski, Andy 408

Wachowski, Lana 408, 438

Wackernagel, Katharina 354

Waffenschmied, Otto 139

Wagenstein, Angel see Vagenshtain, Angel

Waggner, George 166

Wagner, Elsa 157

Wagner, Fritz Arno 10, 82, 142, 215

Wagner, Richard 238

Wahlöö, Peer 298

Wajda, Andrzej 303

Walbrook, Anton see Wohlbrück, Adolf

Waldau, Gustav 168

Waldleitner, Luggi [Ludwig] 263, 280, 314

Waldon, Louis 265, 271

Walker, Paul 142, 158

Wallace, Bryan Edgar 235, 236, 238

Wallace, Edgar VI, 119, 131, 195, 210, 218, 225, 226, 231, 234, 237, 238, 246, 247, 251, 252, 253, 254, 257

Wallburg, Otto 148

Walters, Thorley 231

Walther, Gabriele M. 368

Waltz, Christoph 341

Walz, Marcel 389, 398, 402, 409, 412, 416, 417, 420

Wangenheim, Gustav von 67, 82

Wanka, Rolf 234

Warm, Hermann 12, 35, 55, 56, 59, 130, 218, 278

Warren, Bill 323

Warsitz, Lothar 138

Wauer, Wilhelm 35

Wawrzycke, Otto see Waffenschmied, Otto

Wecker, Gero 214

Weeks, Rollo 353

Wegener, Paul 5, 21, 27, 28, 32, 33, 38, 42, 45, 46, 49, 53, 54, 65, 66, 69, 95, 99-100, 110, 114, 115, 116, 125, 132, 145, 190, 287

Weidemann, Heinrich 192

Weigel, Hans 301

Weigel, Herman 152, 301, 370

Weiler, Kurt 237, 282

Weise, Konrad 375

Weiss, Gustav 101

Weissmuller, Johnny 249, 416

Weisz, Martin 375

Welbat, Douglas 418

Welch, Raquel 267

Welles, Mel 252

Welles, Orson 217

Wells, H[erbert] G[eorge] V, 39, 76, 111, 113, 136, 258, 304, 444

Wenders, Wim 187, 306, 324, 329

Wendlandt, Horst 82, 237, 238, 245, 251, 254, 283, 301, 309, 334

Wendlandt, Matthias 334

Wendt, Elisabeth 154

Wepper, Fritz 213

Werckmeister, Hans 64

Werner, Ilse 168

Werner, Karl 29

Wernicke, Otto 139

Wery, Carl 147, 193

Wessel, Horst 110, 131

Wettcke, Thorsten 355

Weyher, Ruth 89

Whale, James 136

Wheatley, Dennis 278

Whishaw, Ben 375

Whitlock, Albert 305, 321

Wicki, Bernhard 225, 293

Widmark, Richard 278, 281

Widmer, Urs 444

Widtmann, Heinz 22, 26

Wieck, Dorothea 135, 143

Wieder, Hanne 224

Wieman, Mathias 129, 135

Wiene, Karl 5

Wiene, Robert 5, 40, 49, 55, 57, 58, 60, 63, 89, 90, 98, 124, 148

Wiens, Paul 226

Wiesenberg, Heinrich *see* Galeen, Henrik

Wiesner, C. U. 288

Wietzorek, Luisa 391

Wild, Anne 374

Wilde, Oscar 46, 238, 369

Wildenbruch, Ernst von 40

Wildgruber, Ulrich 292

Wilhelm, Hans F. 209

Wilhelm, Rolf 250, 274

Williams, Guy 233

Williams, John 307

Willis, Bert 306

Wind, Thomas 336, 383

Winkelmann, Adolf 303

Winkler, Angela 326

Winkler, Max 185

Winterstein, Eduard von 50, 129, 168, 221

Wirth, Franz Peter 210

Wirth, Mizzi 36

Wischnewski, Siegfried 249

Witt, Uwe 203

Wittke, Jr., Paul 127

Wittlinger, Karl 273

Wnendt, David 423

Wöhler, Gustav-Peter 376

Woelz, Georg 149

Wörner, Nathalia 344

Wohl, Ludwig von 75

Wohlbrück, Adolf 143

Wohlrabe, Jürgen

Wohlrabe, Willy 154

Wolff, Gerry 321

Wolff, Peter 132

Wolff, Sylvia 315

Wolkoff, Alexander 119

Wolter, Ralf 292

Wolters, Tobias 421

Wray, Fay 197

Wright, Robin 412, 444

Wronker-Flatow, Manfred 83

Wünsch, Peter 357

Wyborny, Klaus 273

Wysbar, Eva 144

Wysbar, Frank 135, 144

Yildirim, Özgür 421

York, Eugen 207

Zavitz, Lee 234

Zamyatin, Yevgeny 297

Zbonek, Edwin 236

Zech, Rosel 292

Zeglio, Primo 252

Zehe, Kurt 166

Zehetbauer, Rolf 248, 327

Zeman, Karel 315

Zengerling, Alf (Alfons) 9, 117, 120, 121, 123, 128, 142, 145, 154, 158, 201, 225

Zharikov, Yevgeni 261

Zhuang Minjin 317

Ziehfuss, Edmund 112

Ziemann, Sonja 255

Ziesemer, Edgar S[rigio] 48

Zihlmann, Max 260

Zoré, Ingrid 294

Zschoche, Herrmann 267

Zulawski, Andrzej 295

Zwart, Harald 414

Titles

A [cutout animation] 244-245

À Nous la Liberté 189

Abenteuer des Dr. Kircheisen, Die [The Adventures of Dr. Kircheisen] 74

Abenteuer des Freiherrn von Münchhausen—Eine Winterreise, Die [The Adventures of Baron Münchhausen: A Winter Journey] 175, 176

Abenteuer des Prinzen Achmed, Die [The Adventures of Prince Achmed] 106-107, 108

Abenteuer mit Blasius [Adventure with Blasius] 276

Abenteuer von Pico und Columbus, Die [The Adventures of Pico and Columbus] 326

Abgeschnitten [Cut Off] 433

Abnormis 397

Abrafaxe Unter Schwarzer Flagge, Die [The Abrafaxe: Under the Black Flag] 358

Absolute Film, Der [Absolute Film] 98, 99

8 Sekunden Ein Augenblick Unendlichkeit [8 Seconds: An Instant Infinity] 423

Adam II 255

Adventures of Baron Munchausen, The 315

Ahasver 46

Aktion Abendsonne [Campaign Evening Sun, 1979] 291

Alfred J. Kwak [TV series] 320

Algol eine Tragödie der Macht [Algol: Tragedy of Power] 64

All Creatures Big and Small see *Ooops! Die Arche ist weg… [Ooops! Noah Is Gone]*

Alone in the Dark 368

Alone in the Dark II 382

Aloryon 415

Alpha und Asphalt [Alpha and Asphalt] 274

Alraune (1928) 116

Alraune (1930) 125-126

Alraune (1952) 198-199

Alraune. Die Geschichte eines lebenden Wesens [novel] 25

Alraune, die Henkerstochter, genannt die rote Henne 50

Alraune und der Golem [Alraune and the Golem] 54

Als der Weihnachtsmann vom Himmel fiel [When Santa Fell to Earth] 405

Am Rande der Welt [At the Edge of the World] 115

Amazing Maurice, The 442

Amazing Transparent Man, The 449

Amerika—Europa im Luftschiff. Ein Zukunftsbild aus dem Jahre 2000 [America—Europe in an Airship: A Vision of the Future in Year 2000] 29

Amoklauf [Rampage] 330

Amphitryon 142

Amphitryon [TV] 298

Anatomie [Anatomy] 348-349

Anatomie 2 [Anatomy 2] 362

Ancient Relic see *Jesus Video, Das [The Jesus Video, TV]*

Andere, Der (1913) [The Other] 26, 269

Andere, Der (1930) [The Other] 124

Andere Student von Prag, Der [The Other Student of Prague] 31

Andy Warhol's Dracula 272

Andy Warhol's Frankenstein 271

Angst [project] 432-433

Angst essen Seele auf [Fear Eats the Soul] 270

Animals United see *Konferenz der Tiere (2010)*

Anna und Elisabeth 135

Antboy 2 421

Anthropophagous 2000 344

Antichrist XI, 386

Antimarteria 428

Antman, The [Antrage] 361

Apfel ist ab, Der [The Apple Fell] 191

Apokalypse Eis [Post Impact, TV] 365

Apparatspott, De [The Apparatspott] 347

Apparatspott—Gerangel in Ruum un Tied [Apparatspott: Tussle in Space and Time] 363

Apparatspott—Dat mokt wie gistern [Apparatspott: we will do this yesterday] 380

Apple, The 293-294

Arche, Die [The Ark] 50

Arche Noah Prinzip, Das [The Noah's Ark Principle] 302-303

Arme Müllersbursch und das Kätzchen, Der [The Poor Miller's Boy and the Kitten] 264

Armer Hansi [Poor Hansi] 174-175

Around the World in 80 Days (2004) 365

Artificial Worlds [exhibition] see Künstliche Welten

Art Girls 411

Arzt ohne Gewissen [Doctor without Scruples] 218

Aschenbrödel (1915) [Cinderella] 36

Aschenbrödel (1916) [Cinderella] 44

Aschenbrödel (1931) [Cinderella] 128

Aschenputtel (1923) [Cinderella] 87

Aschenputtel (1955) [Cinderella] 207

Aschenputtel (2010) [Cinderella, TV] 397

Asterix and the Big Fight see Asterix Operation Hinkelstein

Asterix, Mickey Mouse & Co. [exhibition] 308

Asterix Operation Hinkelstein (Le Coup de Menhir/Asterix and the Big Fight) 317

Asteroidenjäger [Asteroid Hunters, novel] 261

Astronauci [The Astronauts, novel] 449

Astronauts, The see Astronauci

L'Atlantide see Herrin von Atlantis, Die

Attack of the Killer Tomatoes 301

Attack of the Tromaggot 394

Aufruhr im Schlaraffenland [Trouble in the Land of Milk and Honey] 213

Augen der Mumie Ma, Die [The Eyes of the Mummy] 48

Augen des Ole Brandis, Die [The Eyes of Ole Brandis] 29-30

Aus der Urzeit der Erde [From Primordial Times] 126

Automärchen [Motoring Tales] 300

Avantgarde 394

Avengers: Infinity Wars, The 444, 445

Aufruhr im Schlaraffenland [Trouble in the Land of Milk and Honey]

Babylon—Im Bett mit dem Teufel [Babylon: In Bed with the Devil] 327

Babylon Berlin [TV series] 440

Back to Gaya 364

Bad End 392

Bär von Baskerville, Der [The Bear of the Baskervilles] 36

Bärenhäuter, Der [The Bear-Skinned Man] 308

Balance 320

Barn Dance, The 121

Baron Münchhausen 409

Baron Prášil [Baron Münchhausen] 315

Barricade 379

Batman Forever 446

Battleship Potemkin 98

Battlestar Galactia [TV] 359

Bayala—Das magische Elfenabenteuer [Bayala: A Magical Adventure] 435

Befehl aus dem Dunkel see Kaiju Daisenso

Begotten 350

Bela Kiss: Prologue 410

Ben-Hur 225

Benjamin Blümchen [Benjamin the Elephant] 340

Bennys Video 326

Berlin Snuff 336

Bermuda-Dreieck Nordsee [Bermuda-Triangle North Sea, TV] 404

Besuch auf einem kleinen Planeten [Visit to a Small Planet, TV] 263

Besuch bei Van Gogh [Visit with Van Gogh] 306

Beyond Remedy 385

Beyond the Limits 362

Bibelcode, Der [The Bible Code] 392

Bibi Blocksberg 360

Bibi Blocksberg—Eene Meene Eins, Zwei, Drei 369

Bibi Blocksberg und das Geheimnis der blauen Eulen [*Bibi Blocksberg and the Secret of the Blue Owls*] 366

Biene Maja—Der Kinofilm, Die [*Maya the Bee: The Movie*] 417

Biene Maja—Die Honigspiele, Die [*Maya the Bee: The Honey Games*] 432

Biene Maja und ihre Abenteuer, Die [*The Adventures of Maya the Bee, book*] 108, 171

Biene Maja und ihre Abenteuer, Die [*The Adventures of Maya the Bee, movie*] 108

Biest im Bodensee, Das [*The Beast in the Lake*] 343

Big Mess, The see *Grosse Verhau, Der*

Bildnis des Dorian Gray, Das (1917) [*The Picture of Dorian Gray*] 46

Bis ans Ende der Welt [*Until the End of the World*] 323-324

Bitteren Tränen der Petra von Kant, Die [*The Bitter Tears of Petra von Kant*] 270

Black Cat, The [story] 53, 132

Black Cat, The (1934) 66

Black Death 394

Black Emanuelle 296

Black Indies, The [novel] 110

Black Moon 277

Black Past 318

Blackest Heart see *Deutsche Kettensägen-Massaker, Das* [*The German Chainsaw Massacre*]

Blade af Satans bog 55

Blair Witch Project, The 351

Blaubart [*Bluebeard*, project] 88

Blaue Licht, Das (1932) [*The Blue Light*] 129

Blaue Licht, Das (1976) [*The Blue Light*] 277-278

Blaue Licht, Das (2010) [*The Blue Light*] 397

Blaue Hand, Die [*Creature with the Blue Hand*] 251

Blaue Palais, Das [*The Blue Palace*, TV series] 274

Bless the Child 351

Blob, The 443, 444

Blood Demon, The see *Schlangengrube und das Pendel, Die*

Blood of Fu Manchu, The [*Der Todeskuss des Dr. Fu Man Chu*] 254

BloodRayne 371

BloodRayne: The Third Reich 401

BloodRayne II: Deliverance 381

Bloody Dead, The see *Blaue Hand, Die*

Bloody Moon see *Säge des Todes, Die* [*The Saw of Death*]

Bluebeard [*Blaubart*] 267

Blueprint 364

Blümlein Wunderhold, Das [*Little Flower Wunderhold*] 195

Blumen für den Mann im Mond [*Flowers for the Man in the Moon*] 274

Blutendes Deutschland [*Bleeding Germany*] 134

Blutsschwestern—Jung, magisch, tödlich [*Blood Sisters: Young, Magical, Deadly*] 410

Body Snatchers, The [short story] 446

Böse Geist Lumpaci Vagabundus, Der [*The Evil Ghost Lumpaci Vagabundus/Lumpaci the Vagabond*] 86

Bonker, Der 375

Bonobo-Prinzip, Das [*The Bonobo Principle*] 381

Boo 132

Boo, Zino & the Snurks see *Back to Gaya*

Boogeyman, The 265

Boot, Das [*The Boat*] 303

Botschaft der Götter [*Mysteries of the Gods*] 451

Bottle Imp, The [story] 141, 199, 338

Boy 7 421

Brain, The see *Toter sucht seinen Mörder, Ein*

Break 389, 390

Bremer Stadtmusikanten, Die (1944) [*The Bremen Town Musicians*, project] 179-180

Bremer Stadtmusikanten, Die (1959) [*The Bremen Town Musicians*] 218-219

Bremer Stadtmusikanten, Die (1970) [*The Bremen Town Musicians*] 260

Bremer Stadtmusikanten, Die (2010) [*The Bremen Town Musicians*] 392

Brides of Fu Manchu, The [*Die dreizehn Sklavinnen des Dr. Fu Man Chu*] 247

Brüderchen und Schwesterchen (1929) [Brother and Sister] 121

Brüderchen und Schwesterchen (2008) [Brother and Sister, TV] 382

Bucket of Blood, A see *Vermächtnis des Professor Bondi, Das*

Bucklige und die Tänzerin, Der [The Hunchback and the Dancer] 62

Bucklige von Soho, Der [The Hunchback of Soho] 247

Bukarest Fleisch [Bukarest Meat, TV] 379

Bullyparade—Der Film 428

Bunker, Der [The Bunker] 419

Burning Moon, The 328

Butcher, The 325

By Rocket to the Moon see *Frau im Mond [Woman or Girl in the Moon]*

Cabinet des Dr. Caligari, Das [The Cabinet of Dr. Caligari] V, 10, 16, 29, 55-61, 62, 130, 171, 218, 278, 327

Camp Corpses 373

Cannibal - Aus dem Tagebuch eines Kannibalen 373

Cannibal Diner 407

Captain Cosmotic 343

Captain Sindbad 233-234

Cardillac 258

Carmilla [novel] 130

Carnival Story 233

Casa dell'esorcismo, La [The House of Exorcism/Der Teuflische] 275

Casper the Friendly Ghost 415

Castle, The [novel, fragment]

Cat and the Canary, The 114

Cat Creeps, The 132

Cell, The 351

Chain Reaction 373

Chainsaw Slasher see *Slasher*

Charlemagne Code, The see *Jagd nach dem Schatz der Nibelungen, Die [The Search for the Treasure of the Nibelungen]*

Chasseurs de dragons [Dragon Hunters, TV series] 380-381

Chasseurs de dragons [Dragon Hunters, movie] 380-381

Checkpoint Charly see *Warum die Ufos unseren Salat klauen [Why the UFOs Steal Our Lettuce]*

Chef wünscht keine Zeugen, Der [The Chief Wants No Survivors/No Survivors, Please] 237

Chemie und Liebe [Chemistry and Love] 189

Chiisana Baikingu Bikke see *Wickie und die starken Männer [Vicky and the Strong Men]*

Children of the Night [novel] XI

Chinesische Nachtigall, Die [The Chinese Nightingale] 118

Christiane F. - Wir Kinder vom Bahnhof Zoo 152

Chronicles of Narnia, The 447

Chroniken der Unterwelt—City of Bones [The Mortal Instruments: City of Bones] 414

Cinderella 197

Cité de Enfants Perdus, La [Die Stadt der verlorenen Kinder/The City of Lost Children] 334

Close Encounters of the Third Kind 352

Cloud Atlas VI, 60, 408

Color, The 396

Color out of Space, The [short novel] 396

Coraline 430

Corpse Bride, The 430

Coup de Menhir, Le see *Asterix Operation Hinkelstein*

Creep 369

Creepy Campfire Stories 423

Crucible, The [drama] 212

Cure for Wellness, A XI, 426

Curse of Doctor Wolffenstein, The 420

Dämonenhochzeit, Die [The Demon's Wedding] 339

Dam Busters, The 285

Dame, der Teufel und die Probiermamsell, Die [The Lady, the Waitress and the Devil] 49

Damned on Earth 419

Dampfross steigt, Das 123

Dance of the Vampires 37

Daniel der Zauberer [Daniel the Magician] 366

Dard Divorce 380

Dark [TV series] 428-429

Dark Area, The 351

Dawn, The see Wir sind die Nacht

De Sade 255

Dead Eyes Open 376

Dead Survivors 393

Death Watch see Gekaufte Tod, Der

Deathcember 436

Decoder 302

Delegation, Die [The Delegation] 260

Demonium 356

Depraved, The see Urban Explorer

Des Satans nackte Sklavin see Nackte und der Satan, Die

Destiny see Müde Tod, Der [The Weary Death/Behind the Wall]

Detective Lovelorn und die Rache des Pharao [Detective Lovelorn and the Revenge of the Pharao] 361

Deutsche Kettensägen-Massaker, Das [The German Chainsaw Massacre] 321-322

Deutschmond 392

Diable en bouteille, Le see Liebe, Tod und Teufel

Diagonal-Symphonie [Symphonie Diagonale] 96

Dich schickt der Himmel [You Are Heaven Sent, TV] 355

Digedags in grauer Vorzeit, Die [Prehistoric Digedags/ The Digedags in the Dim and Distant Past] 344

Ding im Schloss, Das [The Thing in the Castle] 291

Dir zuliebe 181

Disceptatio 421

Divide, The 401

Doktor Dolittle und seine Tiere [Dr. Dolittle and his Animals] 117

Doktor Faustus 299

Don Kihot 230

Donovan's Brain [novel] 231

Don't Wake the Dead 381

Doom 371

Dorian Gray im Spiegel der Boulevardpresse [Dorian Gray in the Mirror of the Yellow Press] 303

Dornröschen (1910) [Sleeping Beauty] 24

Dornröschen (1917) [Sleeping Beauty] 47

Dornröschen (1922) [Sleeping Beauty] 87

Dornröschen (1936) [Sleeping Beauty] 145

Dornröschen (1936) [Sleeping Beauty, animation] 145

Dornröschen (1955) [Sleeping Beauty] 207

Dornröschen (1971) [Sleeping Beauty] 262

Dornröschen (2008) [Sleeping Beauty, TV] 384

Dornröschen (2009) [Sleeping Beauty, TV] 391

Dr. Jekyll and Mr. Hyde [novel] V

Dr. Jekyll and Mr. Hyde [movie, 1920] V, 63

Dr. M 320

Dr. Mabuse, der Spieler [Dr. Mabuse, the Gambler] VI, 83-84, 85, 223, 291

Dr. Mabuse competition [project] 356

Dr. Satansohn 39

Dr. Strangelove 436

Drache Daniel, Der [Daniel the Dragon] 320

Drachenjäger, Die see Chasseurs de dragons [Dragon Hunters]

Drachenreiter [Dragon Rider] 440

Dracula [novel] V, 22, 41, 68, 81, 260

Dracula [stage play] 216

Dracula [movie, 1931] 132

Dracula [movie, 1958] 216

Dracula 3000 366

Drakula halála 68

Dreht euch nicht um, der Golem geht rum oder Das Zeitalter der Musse [Don't Turn Around, the Golem Walks or: The Era of Vacancy, TV, 2 parts] 265

Drei Haselnüsse für Aschenputtel [Three Wishes for Cinderella] 337

Drei Räuber, Die [Three Robbers] 378

Dungeon of Evil 372

Earth vs. the Flying Saucers 260, 337

Einladung zur Enthauptung [Invitation to a Beheading, TV] 270

Eisbraut, Die 29

Eisenhans, Der (1988) [Iron John] 314

Eisenhans, Der (2011) [Iron John] 405

Eleagabal Kuperus [novel] 54

Elektromensch, Der [The Electro-Man] see Grosse Wette, Die [The Big Bet]

Elixiere des Teufels, Die [The Devil's Elixirs, novel] 2, 280

Elixiere des Teufels, Die [The Devil's Elixirs, movie] 280

Emil and the Detectives 258

Endzeit (2013) [End of Time] 410-411

Endzeit (2019) [Ever After] 435

Enemy Mine 307

Engel mit dem Saitenspiel, Der [The Angel with the String Play] 181

Entdeckung Deutschlands, Die [The Discovoery of Germany] 45

Entropie [Entropy] 400

Eolomea 267-268

Er ist wieder da [Look Who's Back] 422-423

Erdora—Kapitel 1: Der Todeskreis [Erdora Chapter 1: The Circle of Death] 391

Erdora—Kapitel 2: Der Schattenkrieger [Erdora Chapter 2: The Shadow Warrior] 420

Erinnerungen an die Zukunft [Chariots of the Gods] 451

Erotic Adventures of Hansel and Gretel, The see *Hänsel und Gretel verliefen sich im Wald [Lass uns knuspern, Mäuschen]*

Erster April 2000 [April 1, 2000] 199

Es ist nicht leicht, ein Gott zu sein [Hard to Be a God] 319

E.T. the Extra-Terrestrial 307, 309

Eurydike—Die Braut aus dem Jenseits [Eurydice, the Bride from the Netherworld, TV] 286

Everlasting Hate 378

Ewige Jude, Der [The Eternal Jew] 159-160

Exit [TV] 440

Extinction: The G.M.O. Chronicles 405

Fabel von King Kong—Ein amerikanischer Trick- und Sensationsfilm, Die see *King Kong*

Face of Fu Manchu, The [Ich, Dr. Fu Man Chu] 245-246

Fährmann Maria [Ferryman Maria] 144

Falsche Prinz, Der [The False Prince] 86

Falscher Verdacht Haytabo 265-266

Fan, Der [The Fan] 298

Fantastival [film festival] 300

Fantomas 83

Fata Morgana 263

Father Noah's Ark [Die Arche Noah] 140

Faust [play] 1, 2, 27, 79

Faust (1926) VI, 108-109, 327

Faust (1960) 223

Faust—Vom Himmel durch die Welt zur Hölle [Faust: The Movie] 314

Felidae 333

Felix—Ein Hase auf Weltreise [Felix Around the World] 368-369

Felix 2—Der Hase und die verflixte Zeitmaschine [Fekix and the Time Machine] 373

Felix und der Wolf [Felix and the Wolf] 314

Feuerzeug, Das [Tinder—The Box] 217

Fiend without a Face [Ungeheuer ohne Gesicht] 214-215, 217

Film deines Lebens, Der [The Film of Your Life] 401

Final Storm., The 393

Firebird [ballet] 234

First Man into Space 217

First Men in the Moon 238

First Spaceship on Venus see *Schweigende Stern, Der [The Silent Star/Planet of the Dead]*

5 Seasons 420

Flaschenteufel, Der (1952) [The Bottle Imp] 199

Flaschenteufel. Der (1971) [The Bottle Imp, TV] 265

Flashback—Mörderische Ferien [Flashback] 349

Fledermaus, Die [operetta] 199

Fleisch [Spare Parts, TV] 291

Fliegende Auto, Das [The Flying Car] 64

Fliegende Holländer, Der [The Flying Dutchman] 48

Fliegende Holländer, Der [The Flying Dutchman, opera film] 238

Fliegende Koffer, Der [The Flying Trunk] 72

Fliegende Windmühle, Die [The Flying Windmill] 295

Flight Before Christmas, The see *Niko—Ein Rentier hebt ab [Niko & the Way to the Stars]*

Fluch, Der [The Curse] 314

Fluch der grünen Augen, Der [The Curse of the Green Eyes] 237

Fluch des Vergessens [Curse of Forgetting] 384

Forbidden Girl, The 410

F.P. 1 antwortet nicht [F.P. 1 Doesn't Answer] 133, 155

FPS: First Person Shooter 416

Frankenstein [novel] 26, 39

Frankenstein [movie, 1931] V, 66, 131, 132

Frankenstein Meets the Wolf Man 171

Frau Holle (1906) [Mother Holly] 21

Frau Holle (1907) [Mother Holly] 22

Frau Holle (1928) [Mother Holly] 117

Frau Holle (1948) [Mother Holly] 190

Frau Holle (1953) [Mother Holly] 201

Frau Holle (1961) [Mother Holly] 228

Frau Holle (1963) [Mother Holly] 235

Frau Holle (2008) [Mother Holly, TV] 384

Frau im Mond [Woman or *Girl in the Moon]* 120

Frau in mir, Die [The Woman Inside, TV] 411

Frau Luna [TV] 239

Frau Venus und ihr Teufel [Lady Venus and her Devil] 251

Fräulein von Scuderi, Das [novel] 206, 258

Fräulein von Scuderi, Das [movie] 206-207

Freak Orlando 296

Freitag, der 13: Das unheimliche Haus, 2. Teil [Friday the 13th/Black Friday: The Scary House, 2nd Part] 44

From Caligari to Hitler [book] 189

Frosch mit der Maske, Der [Face of the Frog] 218

Froschkönig, Der (1940) [The Frog Prince] 158

Froschkönig, Der (1954) [The Frog Prince] 205

Froschkönig, Der (1988) [The Frog Prince] 314

Fucking Cruel Nightmare, A 397

Fünf Wochen im Ballon [Five Weeks in a Balloon] 359

Furcht [Fear] 46

Furchtlosen Vier, Die [The Fearless Four] 340

Fusion, Die [Inner Zone] 417

Future, The 400

Gänsehirtin am Brunnen, Die [The Goose-Girl at the Well, TV] 292

Gänsemagd, Die (1957) [The Goose Girl] 214

Gänsemagd, Die (2009) [The Goose Girl, TV] 391

Galathea 142

Galoschen des Glücks, Die [The Magic Shoes] 308

Game of Thrones 90

Garden of Love [Born Undead] 362

Gartenzwerge, Die [The Garden Dwarves] 229

Gebissen wird nur nachts—das Happening der Vampire [The Vampire Happening] 263

Geburt der Hexe [Birth of the Witch, TV] 293

Gefängnis auf dem Meeresgrunde, Das [The Prison on the Ocean Floor] 66

Geheimagent, Der [The Secret Agent] 129

Geheimnis der M-Strahlen, Das [The Mystery of the M Rays] 31

Geheimnios von D.14, Das [The Mystery of D.14] 34

Geheimnis des blauen Zimmers, Das [The Secret of the Blue Room] 132-133

Geheimnisse des Orients [Secrets of the Orient] 119

Geheimnisse einer Seele [Secrets of a Soul] 104

Geheimnisvolle Freundinnen [Mysterious Friends, TV] 363

Geheimnisvolle Spiegel, Der [The Mysterious Mirror] 116

Geheimnisvolle Streichholzdose, Die [A Match Box Mystery] 22

Geheimnisvolle Villa, Die [The Mysterious Villa]

Geisterjäger John Sinclair [Ghosthunter John Sinclair, pulp series] 270

Geisterjäger John Sinclair [Ghosthunter John Sinclair, TV feature] 339

Geisterjäger John Sinclair [Ghosthunter John Sinclair, TV series] 348

Geisterseher, Der [The Ghost Seer] 88

Geisterstunde, Die see *Skeleton Dance*

Gekaufte Tod, Der [Death Watch] 293

Genuine 63-64

German Angst 420

Geschichte der Dienerin, Die [The Handmaid's Tale] 319

Geschichte vom armen Hassan, Die [The Story of Poor Hassan] 215

Geschichte vom Brandner Kasper, Die [The Story of Brandner Kasper] 382-383

Geschichte vom goldenen Taler, Die [The Fairy Tale of the Golden Thaler, TV] 305

Geschichte vom kleinen Muck, Die [The Story of Little Muck] 202

Gespenst, Das [The Ghost] 299

Gespenst von Canterville, Das (1964) [The Canterville Ghost, TV] 238

Gespenst von Canterville, Das (1965) [The Canterville Ghost, TV] 245

Gespenst von Canterville, Das (2005) [The Canterville Ghost, TV] 369

Gespenstergeschichten [Ghost Stories, TV series] 306-307

Gespensterjäger [Ghosthunters: On Icy Trails] 420

Gestiefelte Kater, Der (1935) [Puss in Boots] 142, 150

Gestiefelte Kater, Der (1948) [Puss in Boots, marionette play] 189

Gestiefelte Kater, Der (2009) [Puss in Boots, TV] 391

Gestohlene Herz, Das [The Stolen Heart] 140

Getreue Roboter, Der [The Faithful Robot, TV] 284

Gevatter Tod [Godfather Death, TV] 294

Giantland [Micky im Lande der Riesen] 140

Gli orrori del castello di Norimberga [Baron Blood] 267

Globi und der Schattenräuber [Globi and the Stolen Shadows] 370

Goblet of Gore 338

Göttlicher Job, Ein [A Goddamn Job] 355

Gold (1921-22) [project] 74

Gold (1934) 138, 155

Goldene Ding, Das [The Golden Thing] 266

Goldene Gans, Die (1953) [The Golden Goose] 202

Goldene Gans, Die (2013) [The Golden Goose, TV] 415

Goldene Handschuh, Der [The Golden Glove] 434

Goldene Jurte, Die [The Golden Yurt] 225

Goldene Pest, Die [The Golden Plague] 76

Golem, Der [The Golem, novel] 34

Golem, Der (1915) [The Golem, movie] 32-34

Golem film project (1943) 176-179

Golem und die Tänzerin, Der [Golem and the Dancer/The Golem and the Dancing Girl] 45

Golem, wie er in die Welt kam, Der [The Golem: How He Came into the World] V, 65-66

Gonger, Der [ballad] 26

Gonger—Das Böse vergisst nie [Gonger: Evil Never Forgets] 384

Goonies, The 307

Gorilla von Soho, Der [The Gorilla Gang] 254

Graf Dracula (beisst jetzt) in Oberbayern [Dracula Blows his Cool] 292

Graf Habenichts [Puss in Boots] 144

Graf von Cagliostro, Der [The Count of Cagliostro] 68

Grand Budapest Hotel 429

Grenze, Die [The Frontier, TV, 2 parts] 393

Grimm Love see Rohtenburg

Grimms Märchen von lüsternen Pärchen [Grimm's Fairy Tales for Adults] 258

Gritta von Rattenzuhausbeiuns [Gritta of the Rat's Castle] 305

Grosse Käseverschwörung, Die [The Great Cheese Conspiracy, TV] 310

Grosse König, Der [The Great King] 196

Grosse Verhau, Der [The Big Mess] VI, 264

Grosse Wette, Die [The Big Bet] 35-36

Grosser graublauer Vogel, Ein [A Big Grey-Blue Bird] 260

Grüne Stern, Der [The Green Star] 301

Grüne Wolke, Die [The Green Cloud/The Last Man Alive] 355

Grünes Gold [Green Gold] 409

Gruffalo, The 391

Gruft mit dem Rätselschloss, Die [The Curse of the Hidden Vault] 237

Guitar Men: The Darkest Secret of Rock'n Roll 383

Gulliver's Travels [project] 104-106

Gulliver's Travels (1939) 164

Guru kommt, Ein [Here Comes the Guru, TV] 294

H. P. Lovecraft: Schatten aus der Zeit [The Shadow Out of Time, TV] 275

Habakuk [comic strip] 127

Hänsel und Gretel (1897) [Hansel and Gretel] 17

Hänsel und Gretel (1907) [Hansel and Gretel] 21, 22

Hänsel und Gretel (1921) [Hansel and Gretel] 69

Hänsel und Gretel (1940) [Hansel and Gretel] 157

Hänsel und Gretel (1954) [Hansel and Gretel, Genschow version] 203

Hänsel und Gretel (1954) [Hansel and Gretel, Schonger version] 204

Hänsel und Gretel (2006) [Hansel and Gretel, TV] 374

Hänsel und Gretel (2012) [Hansel and Gretel, TV] 409

Hänsel und Gretel im Zauberwald [The Magic Forest] 343

Hänsel und Gretel verliefen sich im Wald [Lass uns knuspern, Mäuschen] 259

Häschenschule—Jagd nach dem goldenen Ei, Die [Rabbit School: Guardians of the Golden Egg] 427

Häschenschule 2—Der grosse Eierklau, Die [Rabbit School 2: The Big Egg Stealing] 441

Hässliche Entlein und ich, Das [The Ugly Duckling & Me] 376

Hai-Alarm am Müggelsee [Shark Alarm at Müggel Lake] 411

Hai-Alarm auf Mallorca [Shark Attack in the Mediterranean, TV] 368

Halde, Die [The Rubbish Tip] 27

Hamburger Krankheit, Die [The Hamburg Plague/The Hamburg Syndrome] 292

Hamlet [play] 152

Hamlet_X 363

Hand, Die [story] 53

Hanneles Himmelfahrt (1922) [The Assumption of Hannele] 82

Hanneles Himmelfahrt (1934) [The Assumption of Hannele] 138

Hans im Glück (1949) [Hans in Luc,k] 193, 194

Hans im Glück (1976) [Hans in Luck] 280

Hans im Glück (1999) [Hans in Luck] 344

Hans im Glück (2015) [Hans in Luck] 424

Hans Röckle und der Teufel [Hans Röckle and the Devil] 273

Hans Trutz im Schlaraffenland [Hans Trutz in the Land of Milk and Honey] 46

Hansel & Gretel: Witch Hunters 410

Hansemanns Traumfahrt [Hansemann's Dream Journey] 149

Happily N'Ever After [Es war k'einmal im Märchenland] 376

Harald 338

Harold und die Geister [Harold and the Ghosts] 333

Harry Hill im Banne der Todesstrahlen [Harry Hill Under the Spell of Death Rays] 96

Hase und der Igel, Der [The Hare and the Hedgehog, TV] 299

Hasenherz [The Coward] 312

Hatschipuh 311

Haus zum Mond, Das [The House to the Moon] 67

Hausgeist, Der [The Household Ghost, TV series] 325

Haven: Above Sky see Tides

Haytabo see Falscher Verdacht Haytabo

Head, The see Nackte und der Satan, Die

Head of Janus, The see Der Januskopf

Heart of Stone see Kalte Herz, Das (1950)

Heiligenschein, Der [The Halo] 283

Heilstätten [Haunted Hospital] 431

Heinzelmännchen, Die (1939) [The Brownies] 155

Helden—Wenn Dein Land Dich braucht [Heroes: The Fate of the World is in their Hands, TV] 414

Helena [Helen of Troy] 90

HeliCops [TV series] 342

Hell 404

Hellstone: Welcome to Hell 427

Henker von London, Der [The Mad Executioner] 235-236

Hepzibah 392-393

Herr der Diebe [The Thief Lord] 372

Herr der Welt (1913) [Master of the World] 29

Herr der Welt, Der (1934) [The Master of the World] 138-139

Herr vom anderen Stern, Der [The Man from Another Star] 190

Herrin der Welt [Mistress of the World, 2 parts] 221-222

Herrin von Atlantis, Die [L'Atlantide] 132

Herrliche Zeiten im Spessart [Glorious Times in the Spessart] 252

Herzog Ernst [Duke Ernest] 329

Hex [novel] 346

Hexe Lilli: Der Drache und das magische Buch [Lilly the Witch: The Dragon and the Magic Book] 385

Hexe Lilli: Die Reise nach Mandolan [Lilly the Witch: The Journey to Mandolan] 399

Hexen [Witches] 204

Hexen bis aufs Blut gequält [Mark of the Devil] 259

Hexen geschändet und zu Tode gequält [Mark of the Devil II] 2, 268

Hexen von Salem, Die/Les sorcières de Salem [The Witches of Salem] 212

Hexenprinzessin, Die [The Witch Princess, TV] 441

Hexer, Der (1932) [The Witcher/The Ringer] 131

Hexer, Der (1956) [The Witcher/The Ringer, TV] 210

Hexer, Der (1962) [The Witcher/The Ringer, TV] 231

Hexer, Der (1963) [The Witcher/The Ringer, TV] 234

Hexer, Der (1964) [The Mysterious Magician] 238

High Crusade, The 331

High Life 433

Hilde Warren und der Tod [Hilde Warren and Death] 46

Hilfe! Ich bin ein Fisch [Hjælp! Jeg er en fisk/Help! I'm a Fish] 355

Hilfe, ich habe meine Eltern geschrumpft [Help, I Shrunk My Parents] 429

Hilfe! Ich hab meine Freunde geschrumpft [Help, I Shrunk My Friends] 441

Hilfe! Ich hab meine Lehrerin geschrumpft [Help, I Shrunk My Teacher] 424

Hilfe, Hilfe, die Globolinks 257

Himmel über Berlin, Der [The Sky Over Berlin/Wings of Desire] 312, 329

Himmel zwischen den Welten, Der [The Sky Between the Worlds] 422

Hiob 50

Hitler, ein Film aus Deutschland [Hitler: A Film from Germany] 283

Hitman: Agent 47 422

Hochzeit im Korallenmeer [Wedding in the Coral Sea] 181

Hölle Hamburg [Hamburg Hell] 378

Höllenträume [Dreams of Hell, project] 74

Hoffmanns Erzählungen (1916) [The Tales of Hoffmann] 37

Hoffmanns Erzählungen (1970) [The Tales of Hoffmann] 261

Holgi—Der böseste Junge der Welt [Holgi, the Most Meanest Boy in the World] 349

Hollow Man 351

Hollywood Monster [Ghost Chase] 311

Homunculus 39-40, 156

Homunkulieschen 43

Homunkulieschen wird Filmdiva [Homunkulieschen Becomes a Screen Goddess] 43

Horror Heaven 304

Horst Wessel [novel] 131

Hot Dogs: Wau—wir sind reich [Millionaire Dogs] 344

Hound of the Baskervilles, The see Hund von Baskerville, Der

House of the Dead 364

House of Usher 226

House of Wax 229

Hui Buh—Das Schlossgespenst [Hui Buh: The Castle Ghost] 374

Hund von der Baskerville, Der (1914) [The Hound of the Baskervilles] V, 31

Hund von Baskerville, Der (1929) [The Hound of the Baskervilles] 119

Hund von Blackwood Castle, Der [The Monster of Blackwood Castle] 253-254

Hunt for the Hidden Relic, The see Jesus Video, Das [The Jesus Video, TV]

I Aim at the Stars [Ich greife nach den Sternen] 222

I Know the Way to the Hofbräuhaus 325

Ice Planet [TV] 359

Ich bin dein Mensch [I Am Your Human, TV] 440

Ich liebe dich, ich töte dich [I Love You, I Kill You] 264

Ideale Untermieter, Der [The Ideal Lodger] 211

Iljon Tichy—Raumpilot [Ilyon Tichy, Space Pilot, TV series] 379

Im Banne des Unheimlichen [The Zombie Walks] 254

Im Express-Zuge zum Mars [Express Train to Mars] 86

Im Schloss der blutigen Begierde [Castle of Bloody Lust/Castle of the Creeping Flesh] 254

Im Stahlnetz des Dr. Mabuse [The Return of Dr. Mabuse] 226

Im Staub der Sterne [In the Dust of the Stars] 279

Immer wieder Glück [Always Lucky] 195

Immortuus see *Non Mortuus*

In der Arche ist der Wurm drin [Stowaways on the Ark] 313

In der Welt des Unsichtbaren 41

In jenen Tagen [In Those Days] 188

In Schneekönigs Reich [In the Kingdom of the Snow King] 104

In weiter Ferne, so nah! [Faraway, So Close] 329

Independence Day VI, 337-338, 352, 357

Indische Grabmal, Das (1921) [The Indian Tomb] 75

Infekt [Infection] 384

Innere Werte [Sea Patrol, TV] 377

I.N.R.I. 90

Insel der Angst, Die [The Island of Fear, TV] 354

Insel der Krebse, Die [Crabs on the Island, TV] 276

Insel der Seligen, Die [Island of Bliss, The] 28

Insel der Verschollenen, Die [The Island of the Lost] V, 76

Invasion der Spaghetti-Monster, Die [Invasion of the Spaghetti Monsters, project] 301

Invasion of the Body Snatchers 446

Invisible Man, The [1933] 136

Invisible Man, The [project, 1939] 155

Invisible Man Returns, The 156

Iron Doors 3D 400

Iron Sky 406

Iron Sky 2: The Coming Race 435

Isabella von Ägypten, Kaiser Karl des Fünften erste Jugendliebe [novel] 54

Isla, La 396

Isla de la Muerte, La [Das Geheimnis der Todesinsel/ Island of the Doomed] 252

Island of Dr. Moreau, The [novel] V, 76

Island of Lost Souls V

Isle of Dogs 429-431

Jack the Ripper 279-280

Jagd nach dem Glück, Die [The Pursuit of Happiness] 124

Jagd nach dem Schatz der Nibelungen, Die [The Search for the Treasure of the Nibelungen] 382

Januskopf, Der [The Head of Janus] 63

Jason and the Argonauts 236

Jasper und das Limonadenkomplott [Jasper: Journey to the End of the World] 382

Jedermann seine eigene Jazzband 123

Jeepers Creepers 356

Jester Till 363

Jesus Video, Das [The Jesus Video, TV] 360

Jim Knopf und die Wilde 13 (1962) [Jim Button and the Wild 13, TV series] 231

Jim Knopf und die Wilde 13 (2020) [Jim Button and the Wild 13] 440

Jim Knopf und Lukas der Lokomotivführer (1961) [Jim Button and Luke the Engine Driver, TV series] 227

Jim Knopf und Lukas der Lokomotivführer (2018) [Jim Button and Luke the Engine Driver] 432

Joey 304, 307

John Llewellyn Hamiltons Ende [novel] 29

John Sinclair see *Geisterjäger John Sinclair*

Jonathan 260

Jorinde und Joringel 405

Jud Süss [Jew Suss] 168, 196, 211, 217

Jules Verne's Rocket to the Moon 251

Jungle Book, The [collection of stories] 116

Jungle Book, The [Das Dschungelbuch, movie] 255-256, 258

Jurassic Park 352

Kadaver [Cadaver] 379

Känguru-Chroniken, Die 438

Käpt'n Blaubär—Der Film [Captain Bluebear: The Movie] 347

Kaiju Daisenso [Invasion of the Astro-Monster/Befehl aus dem Dunkel] 251

Kalif Storch (1923) [Caliph Stork] 87-88

Kalif Storch (1931) [Caliph Stork] 126

Kalif Storch (1949) [Caliph Stork, animation, project] 191

Kalte Herz, Das (1924) [The Cold Heart] 89

Kalte Herz, Das (1950) [The Cold Heart] 196

Kalte Herz, Das (2016) [The Cold Heart] 426

Kaltenbach Papiere, Die [The Kaltenbach Papers] 323

Kamikaze 1989 298

Kampfansage—Der letzte Schüler [The Challenge] 370

Karl the Butcher vs. Axe [Violent Shit 4.0] 393-394

Kasper reist ins Märchenland/Kaspers Reise ins Märchenland [Kasper's Trip to Fairy Tale Land] 192, 193

Kaspers Reise um die Welt [Kasper's Trip Round the World] 195

Kasper's Reise zu den Zwergen [Kasper's Journey to the Dwarfs] 204

Katzenjammer Kids [comic strip] 197

Kein Blut für Erich [No Blood for Erich, project] 334

Keinohrhase und Zweiohrküken [Rabbit without Ears and Two-Eared Chick] 414

Kerabans phantastische Reise [Jue jiang de Kailaban/ Keraban's Fantastic Voyage] 339-340

King Kong 30, 137, 197-198, 306, 329

King Kong und die weisse Frau see *King Kong*

King Kongs Faust [King Kong's Fist] 306

Kiss My Blood 342

Kleine Arschloch und der alte Sack,—Sterben ist Scheisse, Das [The Little Bastard and the Old Fart: Death Sucks] 375

Kleine Däumling, Der [Tom Thumb] 187

Kleine Drache Kokosnuss, Der [Coconut the Little Dragon] 419

Kleine Eisbär—Der Kinofilm, Der [Little Polar Bear] 357

Kleine Eisbär 2—Die geheimnisvolle Insel, Der [Little Polar Bear 2: The Mysterious Island] 371

Kleine Gespenst, Das (1992) [The Little Ghost] 327

Kleine Gespenst, Das (2013) [The Little Ghost] 415

Kleine Häwelmann, Der (1940) [The Little Haverman] 158

Kleine Häwelmann, Der (1956) [The Little Haverman] 210

Kleine Lok, Die [The Little Fire Engine] 206

Kleine König Macius, Der [Little King Macius] 378

Kleine Königstragödie, Eine [A Little King's Tragedy] 138

Kleine Medicus—Bodynauten auf geheimer Mission im Körper, Der [The Little Medic: Secret Mission of the Bodynauts/Rescue Rabbit] 418

Kleine Meerjungfrau, Die [The Little Mermaid] 415

Kleine Muck, Der (1921) [Little Muck] 69

Kleine Muck, Der (1944) [Little Muck] 186

Kleine Prinz, Der [The Little Prince, TV] 322

Kleine Rabe Socke, Der [Raven the Little Rascal] 407

Kleine Rabe Socke 2—Das grosse Rennen, Der [Raven the Little Rascal: The Big Race] 421

Kleine Rabe Socke 3—Suche nach dem verlorenen Schatz, Der Der [Raven the Little Rascal: Hunt for the Lost Treasure] 435

Kleine Rebellion 136

Kleine Vampir, Der (2000) [The Little Vampire] 353

Kleine Vampir, Der (2017) [The Little Vampire 3D] 429

Kleine Zauberer und die grosse 5, Der [The Little Magician and the Big Bad Mark] 281

Kleine Zauberflöte, Die [The Little Magic Flute] 341

Kleiner Dodo [Little Dodo] 380

Kleiner starker Panda [Little Big Panda] 398-399

Klischee—Mörderisches Halloween auf Mallorca [Cliché: Gory Halloween in Mallorca] 384

Kluge Bauerntochter, Die [The Smart Farmer's Daughter] 392

König Laurin [King Laurin] 425

König Phantasielos [King Uninspired, TV] 322

Kolberg 196, 210, 217

Komabrutale Duell, Das [The Comabrutal Duel] 343

Komm, wir finden einen Schatz [Let's Find a Treasure] 407

Kommando Störtebeker [Störtebeker the Command] 357

Kommenden Tage, Die [The Coming Days] 396

Komposition in Blau [Composition in Blue] 141

Kondom des Grauens [Killer Condom] 337

Konferenz der Tiere [book] 258-259

Konferenz der Tiere (1969) [Conference of Animals] 258-259

Konferenz der Tiere (2010) [Animals United] 396

Kongress, Der [The Congress] 412, 444

Konzert für Bratpfanne und Orchester [Concerto for Frying-Pan and Orchestra] 275

Krabat (2008) 382

Kraftmeyer, Der [The Bruiser] 35

Krone von Arkus, Die [The Crown of Arkus] 423-424

Künstliche Welten [exhibition] 351-353

Küss mich, Frosch [Kiss Me, Frog, TV] 354

Küss' niemals einen Flaschengeist [Never Kiss a Genie] 364

Kurfürstendamm 15, 62

Kvitebjørn Kong Valemon [Der Eisbärkönig] 325

Lady Dracula 286

Lange Ritt zur Schule, Der [The Long Ride to School] 298

Lapislazuli—Im Auge des Bären 372

Lauras Stern (2004) [Laura's Star] 366

Lauras Stern (2020) [Laura's Star] 441

Lauras Stern und der geheimnisvolle Drache Nian [Laura's Star and the Mysterious Dragon Nian] 386-389

Lauras Stern und die Traummonster [Laura's Star and the Dream Monsters] 404

Lauras Weihnachtsstern [Laura's Christmas Star] 377

Laurin X, 318-319

Lebende Buddhas [Living Buddhas] 99-100, 110

Lebende Rätsel, Das [The Living Enigma] 39

L'Ecran Démoniaque [Die dämonische Leinwand/The Haunted Screen, book] 199-200

Legend of Hell 406

Legende von der heiligen Simplicia, Die [The Legend of Saint Simplicia] 65

Legion of the Dead 356

Lenya—Die grösste Kriegerin aller Zeiten [Lenya, the Greatest Warrior of All Time, TV] 358

Letzte Angestellte, Der [The Last Employee, TV] 405

Letzten Menschen, Die [The Last Men] 50

Letzten Tage von Gomorrha, Die [The Last Days of Gomorrha] 272

Leuenklinge 395

Lèvres rouges, Les/Blut an den Lippen [Daughters of Darkness] 263

Lexx: The Dark Zone 340-341

Liane, das Mädchen aus dem Urwald [Liane, Jungle Goddess] 211

Liane—die weisse Sklavin [Liane, the White Slave] 214

Lichtspiel Opus 1 70

Liebe, Tod und Teufel [Love, Death, and Devil] 141

Lili Marleen [song] 210

Limited Games [Limited Games: The Curse of Störtebeker's Treasure] 379

Lindenstrasse [TV series] 344

Lippels Traum (1991) [Lippel's Dream] 323

Lippels Traum (2009) [Lippel's Dream] 385

Lisa e il diavolo [Lisa and the Devil/Lisa und der Teufel] 269

Lissi und der wilde Kaiser [Lissi and the Wild Emperor] 378

Loft 306

Lola rennt [Run Lola Run] 342, 369

Lord of the Rings: The Fellowship of the Ring, The 359

Lorenz im Land der Lügner [Lorenz in the Land of Liars] 339

Lost in Space [TV series] 268

Lost Place 414

Lost World, The 96, 126

Love and 50 Megatons 436, 437

Love Me and the World Is Mine 106

Lucifer 85

Luftikus zum Verlieben, Ein [Falling in Love with a Happy-Go-Lucky, TV] 371

Luftpirat und sein lenkbares Luftschiff, Der [Captain Mors the Air Pirate, pulp series] 62

Luftpiraten, Die [The Air Pirates] 62

Luis & die Aliens [Luis and the Aliens] 432

Lumpaci Vagabundus (1913) 27

Lumpazivagabundus (1956) 210

Lumpazivagabundus (1965) 246

Lustige Palette—Im Reiche der Micky Maus, Die [The Funny Palette: In the Reich of Mickey Mouse] 140

Luz 431

M 127

Macao oder die Rückseite des Meeres 316

Mad Max 321

Madagascar 396

Madame X 286

Mädchen aus der Feenwelt oder Der Bauer als Millionär, Das [The Peasant as Millionaire, TV] 315

Mädchen mit den Feuerzeugen, Das [Cripples Go Christmas] 312

Mädchen mit den Schwefelhölzern, Das (1925) [The Girl with the Matchsticks/The Little Match Girl] 103-104

Mädchen mit den Schwefelhölzern, Das (1953) [The Girl with the Matchsticks/The Little Match Girl] 201

Märchen: Purzel, Brumm und Quack, Ein [A Fairy Tale: Purzel, Brumm and Quack] 149-151

Märchenbraut, Die [Arabela, TV series] 296

Magdalena, vom Teufel besessen [Magdalena, Possessed by the Devil] 273

Magic Fishbone, The [children's story] 301

Magic Sticks 311

Magic Voyage, The see *Abenteuer von Pico und Columbus, Die [The Adventures of Pico and Columbus]*

Magician, The 110

Magnetic Monster, The 138

Mains d'Orlac, Les [novel] 98

Mainzelmännchen, Die [Little Mainz Men, TV characters] 233

Making Contact see *Joey*

Malevolent Queen, The see *Krone von Arkus, Die [The Crown of Arkus]*

Man Eater 344

Man in Space [TV] 205

Man Who Laughs, The 117

Mann geht durch die Wand, Ein [The Man Who Walked Through the Wall] 219

Mann mit dem Objektiv, Der [Man with the Objective] 226

Mara und der Feuerbringer [Mara and the Firebringer] 420

Maria d'Oro und Bello Blue [Once Upon a Time] 271-272

Mark of the Devil see *Hexen bis aufs Blut gequält*

Mask Under Mask [Mortal Beauty—Fluch der Schönheit] 361

Maske des Todes, Die [The Mask of Death] 62

Masks 401-402, 403

Masque of the Red Death, The [story] 51

Master of the World 352

Matrix 4 438

Max und Moritz 210-211

Maximum see *Popular*

Medusa [project] XI

Mein Flaschengeist und ich [My Genie and Me, TV] 391

Meister Eder und sein Pumuckl 297

Meisterdieb, Der [The Master Thief] 285

Melancholia 401

Melancholie der Engel [The Angels' Melancholia] 386

Memory Hotel 442

Mephisto 317

Merkwürdige Geschichten [TV series] 262

Metropolis VI, 60, 101, 102, 104, 110-114, 116, 127, 133, 134, 146, 147, 291, 408, 444

Mia und ich—Der Film [Mia and Me: The Movie] 442

Mich gibt's nur zweimal [Mama ist ein Android/Robot Mom, TV] 407

Mickey's Mechanical Man [Die mechanische Micky Maus] 140

Midsummer Night's Dream, A (1935) 142

Million, Le 189

Millionenspiel, Das [The Game of Millions] 260-261

Mirakel der Liebe [She] 98

Mission Stardust see *Perry Rhodan: SOS aus dem Weltall*

Mönch mit der Peitsche, Der [The Monk with a Whip] 252

Mörder kennen keine Grenzen [Time Warp, TV] 385

Molly Monster—Der Kinofilm [Molly Monster the Movie] 424

Momo 309

Mondbär, Der [The Moonbear] 383

Mondmann, Der [Moon Man] 411

Mondscheinkinder [Children of the Moon] 376

Monk, The [novel] 280

Monster Hunter 440-441

Monsterinsel, Die [Monster Island] 360

Montrak 427

Moon 44 320

Moonlight Mountain 371

Moritz in der Litfasssäule [Moritz in the Advertising Pillar] 301

Morning of Valhalla, The see *Wrath*

Mother Courage [Mutter Courage, play] 202

Müde Tod, Der [The Weary Death/Behind the Wall] 74, 203

Münchhausen VI, 168-170, 175, 193

Mullewapp—Das grosse Kinoabenteuer der Freunde [Mullewapp: The Big Cinema Adventure of the Friends] 386

Mullewapp—Eine schöne Schweinerei [Mullewapp: A Nice Mess] 425

Mumie, Die [The Mummy] 30

Murder Farm, The see *Tannöd*

Murderous Vacation see *Flashback—Mörderische Ferien*

Murders in the Rue Morgue [movie] V

Murks, Die [The Goofs, project] 310-311

Mutation III [M III: Century of the Dead] 360

Mute 432

Mutter aus heiterem Himmel [Heaven & A Thing Called Love, TV] 369

Mutter Courage [Mother Courage]

My Lovely Monster 323

Mysterians, The [Chikyu Boeigun] 443

Mysterien eines Frisiersalons, Die [Mysteries of a Barbershop] 88

Mysterious Island 230

Nachlass, Der [The Legacy, TV] 287

Nacht der Erkenntnis see *Schatten*

Nächte des Entsetzens [Nights of Terror] 44

Nachtgestalten [Night Creatures] 54

Nachtmahr, Der [The Nightmare] 422

Nachtschatten [Nightshade] 268

Nackte und der Satan, Die [The Naked and the Satan] 217-218, 222

Naked Jungle, The 211

Naked Wytche, The see *Hänsel und Gretel verliefen sich im Wald [Lass uns knuspern, Mäuschen]*

Nashörner, Die [Rhinoceros] 232

Nature Girl and the Slaver see *Liane—die weisse Sklavin [Liane, the White Slave]*

Necronomicon - Geträumte Sünden 254

Necronos: Tower of Doom 397

Necrophile Passion [Necrophilic Passion] 414

Necropolis see *Stargate*

NEKRomantik 313

NEKRomantik 2: Die Rückkehr der lebenden Toten [The Return of the Living Dead] 323-324

Nerves 383

Neues vom Hexer [Again the Ringer] 245

Neues vom Räuber Hotzenplotz [The Latest on Robber Hotzenplotz] 286

Neuromancer [novel] 448

NeverEnding Story, The see *Unendliche Geschichte, Die*

NEWS—Bericht über eine Reise in eine strahlende Zukunft [Journey to a Glowing Future] 309-310

Nibelungen, Die (1924) 90-95, 103, 134, 146, 223, 291

Nibelungen, Die [remake suggested by Hitler] 146

Nibelungen, Die (1966, 2 parts) 248-250

Nibelungen - Der Fluch des Drachen, Die (2005) [Ring of the Nibelungs, TV] 372

Niccolò Paganini [project]

Night Before Christmas, The [Die Nacht vor dem Weihnachtsabend] 140

Night of the Vampires see *Fluch der grünen Augen, Der [The Curse of the Green Eyes]*

Niko—Ein Rentier hebt ab [Niko & the Way to the Stars] 382

Niko 2—Kleines Rentier, grosser Held [Niko 2: Little Brother, Big Trouble] 407

Nikos the Impaler 362

Nina sieht es…!!! [Nina Sees It….!!!] 401

1982: Gutenbach [TV] 286

1984 [novel] 436

No Reason 393

Nobody [film series] 85

Non Mortuus [project] 68, 74, 78-79

Nosferatu—eine Symphonie des Grauens [Nosferatu: A Symphony of Horror] V, 6, 8, 9, 13, 14, 17, 41, 47, 67, 71, 72, 73, 74-75, 76, 77, 78, 79-82, 83, 85, 86, 88, 95, 101, 103, 116, 117, 118, 119, 121, 123, 124, 125, 130, 132, 136, 167, 215, 216, 237, 288, 349

Nosferatu—Phantom der Nacht VI, 288-290

Nosferatu the Vampire see *Nosferatu - eine Symphonie des Grauens*

Nosferatu, the Vampyre see *Nosferatu—Phantom der Nacht*

Nosferatu vs. Dracula [project idea] 413-414

Nuclear Conspiracy, The see *NEWS—Bericht über eine Reise in eine strahlende Zukunft* [*Journey to a Glowing Future*]

Nur über meine Leiche [*Over My Dead Body*] 335

Nydenion 397

Oberst cigarette advertising film 127-128

Oberst Redl 317

Oh, wie schön ist Panama [*The Trip to Panama/Oh, How Beautiful Panama Is*] 375

Olle Hexe [*Ole Witch*] 323

Olympia 152

Omnia 417

Ooops! Die Arche ist weg… [*Ooops! Noah Is Gone*] 421

Ooops! 2—Land in Sicht [*Ooops: The Adventure Continues*] 439

Operation Ganymed [*TV*] 283-284

Opry House, The [*Im Tiervarieté*] 123

Opus 3 98

Opus 4 98

Orchideen des Wahnsinns [*Orchids of Madness*] 309

Orchideengarten, Der [magazine] 54

Original Sin, The see *Apfel ist ab, Der* [*The Apple Fell*]

Orlacs Hände [*The Hands of Orlac*] 98

Ornament des verliebten Herzens, Das [*The Ornament of the Lovestruck Heart*] 53

Ostzone 425

Our Heavenly Bodies see *Wunder der Schöpfung*

Pan 271

Pandorum 389

Pankow '95 [*TV*] 302

Papageno 142

Parapsycho—Spektrum der Angst [*Parapsycho: Spectrum of Fear*] 275

Parent Trap, The 258

Parfum—Die Geschichte eines Mörders, Das [*Perfume: The Story of a Murderer*] 375

Passionsspiele [*Passion Plays*] 21

Peau de chagrin, La [novel] 153

Penthesilea [project] 152-153

Perinbaba [*Frau Holle/Mother Holly*] 306

Perry Rhodan [pulp series] 226, 247

Perry Rhodan: SOS aus dem Weltall [*Mission Stardust*] 252-253

Pest in Florenz, Die [*The Plague of Florence*] 51-52

Peter Schlemihls wundersame Geschichte [*Peter Schlemihl's Strange and Wonderful History*, art fairy tale] 1, 27, 69

Peter Schlemihls wundersame Geschichte [*Peter Schlemihl's Strange and Wonderful History*, TV] 253, 443

Peterchens Mondfahrt (1959) [*Little Peter's Journey to the Moon*, TV] 220

Peterchens Mondfahrt (1990) [*Peter in Magicland*] 322

Peterchens Mondfahrt (1992) [TV mini-series] 328

Peterchens Mondfahrt (2021) [*Little Peter's Journey to the Moon*] 442

Petite Mort, La 389

Petite Mort II, La 417

Pettersson und Findus—Das schönste Weihnachten überhaupt [*Pettson and Findus: The Best Christmas Ever*] 426

Pettersson und Findus—Kleiner Quälgeist, grosse Freundschaft [*Pettson and Findus: A Little Nuisance, a Great Friendship*] 416

Phantastische Film, Der [thesis] 291

Phantastische Welt des Matthew Madson, Die [*The Fantastic World of Matthew Madson*] 273

Phantom 86

Phantom der Oper, Das (1916) [*The Phantom of the Opera*] 37

Phantom of the Opera, The (1991) [TV] 322

Phantom von Soho, Das [*The Phantom of Soho*] 236

Phenomenology and Psychology of Cartoon Films, The [thesis] 154

Picco 399

Pied Piper, The [*Der Rattenfänger von Hameln*] 140

Pinocchio (1940) 164

Pit and the Pendulum, The [story] 252

Pitsch und Patsch 136

Planet der Kannibalen [*Planet of the Cannibals*] 358

Planet der toten Seelen [War of the Satellites] 235

Planet Terror 401

Plastic a.k.a. Plastic Surgery Massacre 409

Plutonium 287

Poltergeist 307

Popular 398

Possession 295

Präsenz, Die [The Presence] 418

Preis, Der [The Prize/Soft Error, TV] 300

Premutos: Der gefallene Engel [The Fallen Angel] 341

Prince Valiant [Prinz Eisenherz] 340

Princess 374

Prinz Himmelblau und Fee Lupine [Prince Skyblue and Lupine the Fairy, TV] 426

Prinz hinter den sieben Meeren, Der [The Prince Beyond the Seven Seas] 299

Prinz Keo. Der Raub der Mumie [Prince Keo: The Rape of the Mummy] 53

Prinzessin auf der Erbse, Die [The Princess and the Pea] 201

Prinzessin Lillifee [Princess Lillifee] 385

Prinzessin Lillifee und das kleine Einhorn [Princess Lillifee and the Little Unicorn] 402

Pro Sieben Märchenstunde [Pro Sieben Fairy-Tale Hour, TV series] 374

Project Genesis: Crossclub 2 401

Prophezeiung, Die see Bless the Child

Prosit Neujahr! [Happy New Year] 22

Prosperos Traum [Prospero's Dream] 281-282

Pumuckl und der blaue Klabauter [Pumuckl and the Blue Ship's Kobold] 330

Pumuckl und sein Zirkusabenteuer [Pumuckl's Circus Adventure] 364

Puppenmacher von Kiang-Ning, Der [The Puppet Maker of Kiang Ning] 89

Puppetoons 127

Purpurlinie, Die [The Purple Line] 217

Purzel, der Zwerg und der Riese vom Berg [Purzel the Dwarf and the Giant from the Mountains] 153

Quelle, Die [The Source] 287

Quest 339

Quick macht Hochzeit [Quick Marries, unfinished project] 165

Quiqueck & Hämat: Proll Out 411

Radio Silence—Der Tod hört mit 407

Rätsel von Piskov, Das [The Piskov Mystery, TV] 258

Räuber Hotzenplotz, Der (1974) [The Robber Hotzenplotz] 272

Räuber Hotzenplotz, Der (2006) [The Robber Hotzenplotz] 373

Rammbock: Berlin Undead 394

Rampage 393

Ramper der Tiermensch [The Strange Case of Captain Ramper] 115

Rapunzel (1897) 17

Rapunzel (1907) 22

Rapunzel (2009, TV) 391

Rapunzel oder Der Zauber der Tränen [Rapunzel or: The Magic of Tears, TV] 315

Rattenfänger, Der [The Pied Piper] 49

Rattenfänger von Hameln, Der (1910) [The Pied Piper of Hamelin] 24

Raumpatrouille (TV) [Space Patrol] VI, 247-248

Raw—Der Fluch der Grete Müller [Raw: The Curse of Grete Müller] 412

Raw 2—Das Tagebuch der Grete Müller [Raw 2: The Diary of Grete Müller] 416

Raw 3—Die Offenbarung der Grete Müller [Raw 3: The Revelation of Grete Müller] 420

Ray Harryhausen's World of Myth and Legend [project] 347

Reality XL Realität ist ein Traum [Reality Is a Dream] 406

Red Shoes, The 224

Regentrude, Die [The Rainmaiden] 280

Reineke Fuchs (1937) [Le Roman de Renard] 146-147

Reineke Fuchs (1989) [Reynard the Fox] 317

Reise ins Jenseits—Die Welt des Übernatürlichen [Journey Into the Beyond] 276-277

Reise nach dem Mond, Die [The Journey to the Moon, project] 143

Reise um die Erde in 80 Tagen, Die (1919) [Around the World in 80 Days] 50

Reise um die Erde in 80 Tagen, Die (1998) [Around the World in 80 Days] 343

Repulsion 345

Resident Evil 360

Resident Evil [TV series] 438

Resident Evil: Afterlife 395

Resident Evil: Apocalypse 366

Resident Evil: Extinction 378

Resident Evil: Retribution 407

Resident Evil: The Final Chapter 425

Restrisiko [Residual Risk, TV] 398

Rhythmus 21 99

Rigoletto [opera] 227

Ring of the Nibelungs see *Nibelungen – Der Fluch des Drachen, Die*

Ritter Rost—Eisenhart und voll verbeult [Knight Rusty] 410

Ritter Rost 2—Das Schrottkomplott [Knight Rusty 2: Full Metal Racket] 427

Ritter Trenk [Trenk the Knight] 423

Riverplay 358

Road Rip 379

Robert und Bertram [Robert and Bertram] 151

Robin Hood 363

Robinson Crusoe on Mars 307

Rohtenburg 375

Rootwood 434

Rote Sonne [Red Sun] 260

Rotkäppchen (1928) [Little Red Riding Hood] 116

Rotkäppchen (1948) [Little Red Riding Hood] 191

Rotkäppchen (1953) [Little Red Riding Hood] 201

Rotkäppchen (1954) [Little Red Riding Hood] 204

Rotkäppchen (1962) [Little Red Riding Hood] 230

Rotkäppchen (2005) [Little Red Riding Hood, TV] 372

Rotkäppchen (2012) [Little Red Riding Hood, TV] 409

Rotkäppchen und der Wolf [Little Red Riding Hood and the Wolf] 147

Rübezahl [unfinished animation project] 165

Rübezahl—Herr der Berge [Rübezahl: Ruler of the Mountains] 213

Rübezahls Hochzeit [Rübezahl's Wedding] 42

Rückkehr der Zeitmaschine, Die [The Return of the Time Machine, TV] 304

Ruf der Sibylla, Der [The Call of Sibylla] 306

Rumpelstilzchen (1940) [Rumpelstiltskin] 158

Rumpelstilzchen (1955) [Rumpelstiltskin] 207

Rumpelstilzchen (2009) [Rumpelstiltskin] 391

R.U.R. [play] 111

Sadistic Massacre see *Schlaraffenhaus*

Säge des Todes, Die [The Saw of Death] 294

Sag' endlich ja! see *Träum' nicht, Annette! [Don't Dream, Annette!]*

Sagenhaften Vier, Die/Marnies Welt [Marnie's World] 433

Salzprinzessin, Die [The Salt Princess, TV] 424

Samurai, Der [The Samurai] 418

Sandmännchen, Das (1955) [The Sandman] 207

Sandmännchen—Abenteuer im Traumland, Das [The Sandman and the Lost Sand of Dreams] 395

Sandmann/Sandmännchen (1959) [Sandman, East German TV character]

Sandmann/Sandmännchen (1962) [Sandman, West German TV character] 231

Sandmann, Der (1993) [The Sandman] 329

Sandmann, Der (1995) [The Sandman, TV] 335

Saphirblau [Blue Saphir] 419

Saptaparna [project] 74

Satanas 55

Satans sorger [The Sorrows of Satan, novel] 55

Savage Love 407

Schatten [Shadows] 88, 89, 123

Schatten des Meeres, Der [Specter of the Sea] 26

Schlangenei, Das [The Serpent's Egg] 282-283

Schlangengrube und das Pendel, Die [The Snake Pit and the Pendulum] 252

Schlaraffenhaus 402

Schneemann, Der [The Snowman] VI, 181-185

Schneemann für Afrika, Ein [A Snowman for Africa] 282

Schneeweisschen und Rosenrot (1938) [Snow White and Rose Red] 148-149

Schneeweisschen und Rosenrot (1979) [Snow White and Rose Red] 291

Schneeweisschen und Rosenrot (1984) [Snow White and Rose Red] 302

Schneeweisschen und Rosenrot (2012) [Snow White and Rose Red] 409

Schneewittchen (1907) [Snow White] 22

Schneewittchen (1928) [Snow White] 117

Schneewittchen (1959) [Snow White, TV, 2 parts] 219-220

Schneewittchen (1961) [Snow White] 228

Schneewittchen und das Geheimnis der Zwerge [Snow White and the Secret of the Dwarfs] 328

Schneewittchen und der Zauber der Zwerge [Snow White and the Magic of the Dwarfs, TV] 435

Schneewittchen und die sieben Zwerge (1939) [Snow White and the Seven Dwarfs] 154

Schneewittchen und die sieben Zwerge (1955) [Snow White and the Seven Dwarfs] 208-209

Schneewittchen und die sieben Zwerge (1996) [Snow White and the Seven Dwarfs] 338

Schöne Ende dieser Welt, Das [The Beautiful End of this World] 301

Schöne und das Tier, Die [Beauty and the Beast, TV] 300

School of Fear see *Sieben Tage Frist [Seven Days Grace]*

School's Out see *Schrei—denn ich werde dich töten [Scream—For I Will Kill You, TV]*

School's Out 2 see *Insel der Angst, Die [The Island of Fear, TV]*

Schramm

Schrei—denn ich werde dich töten [Scream—For I Will Kill You, TV] 345-346

Schrottmann, Der [The Scrapman] 411

Schule der kleinen Vampire [School for Vampires, TV series] 374

Schulgespenst, Das [The School Ghost] 311-312

Schwarm, Der [The Swarm, TV series in preproduction] 441

Schwarze Abt, Der [The Black Abbott] 234

Schwarze Mühle, Die [The Black Mill] 277

Schwarze Spinne, Die [The Black Spider] 72

Schweigende Stern, Der [The Silent Star/Planet of the Dead] 220-221, 443, 449

Schweinchen Dick [Porky Pig] 269

Schwerter des Königs—Dungeon Siege [In the Name of the King: A Dungeon Siege Tale] 379

Schwerter des Königs - Zwei Welten [In the Name of the King: Two Worlds] 406

Scotland Yard jagt Dr. Mabuse [Dr. Mabuse vs. Scotland Yard] 235

Sherlock Holmes und die sieben Zwerge [Sherlock Holmes and the Seven Dwarfs, TV]

Scream 346

666 - Traue keinem, mit dem Du schläfst! 359

Sechse kommen durch die ganze Welt [How Six Men Got on in the World] 267

Seed 376, 377

Seed 2: The New Breed 415

Seekers 425

Seekönigin, Die [Queen of the Lake] 347

Seelenwanderung [Transmigration of Souls] 231

Seltsame Geschichte des Brandner Kaspar, Die [The Strange Story of Brandner Kaspar] 193

Seltsame Historia von den Schiltbürgern, Die [The Strange Story of the Inhabitants of Schiltsburg] 228

Seltsamer Fall, Ein [A Strange Case] 32

Serenade, The [ballet pantomime] 79

Serpent's Egg, The see *Schlangenei, Das*

Seven Journeys see *In jenen Tagen [In Those Days]*

Seventh Victim, The [novel] 260

7th Voyage of Sinbad, The [Sindbads siebente Reise] 216, 233

Sex, Dogz and Rock n Roll 402

Shadow of the Vampire 349-351

Shalom Pharaoh 298

Sharknado 438

She [novel] 98

She [movie] see *Mirakel der Liebe [She]*

Sheeba—Die dunkelste Seite der Macht [Sheeba: The Darkest Side of the Force] 371

Sherlock Holmes und das Halsband des Todes [Sherlock Holmes and the Deadly Necklace] 231-232

Sherlock Holmes und die sieben Zwerge [Sherlock Homes and the Seven Dwarfs, TV series] 326, 334

Shit im Kopf [story] 444

Sie tötete in Ekstase [She Killed in Ecstasy] 265

Sieben Monde [Seven Moons] 341

Sieben Raben, Die [The Seven Ravens] 147

Sieben Tage Frist [Seven Days Grace] 257

7 Zwerge—Männer allein im Wald [7 Dwarves: Men Alone in the Wood] 368

7 Zwerge—Der Wald ist nicht genug [7 Dwarves: The Forest Is Not Enough] 375-376, 417

Siebente Rabe, Der [The Seventh Raven] 404

7bte Zwerg, Der [The 7th Dwarf] 417-418

Siebenschön 419

Siebtelbauern, Die 348

Siegfried 370

Siegfried und das sagenhafte Liebesleben der Nibelungen [The Long Swift Sword of Siegfried/The Lustful Barbarian] 263

Signale—Ein Weltraumabenteuer [Signals: An Adventure in Space] 261-262, 267

Silence of the Lambs, The 348

Simplicius Simplicissimus [project] 239-244

Simulacron 3 [novel] 271, 450

Singende, klingende Bäumchen, Das (1957) [The Singing, Ringing Tree] 214

Singende, klingende Bäumchen, Das (2016) [The Singing, Ringing Tree, TV] 426

666—Traue keinem, mit dem Du schläfst! [666: In Bed with the Devil]

Skeleton Dance [Die Geisterstunde] 122, 123

Skin Creepers 434

Sky Sharks 438-439

Slasher 377

Smog [TV] 269

Snow White and the Seven Dwarfs (1937) 148, 151, 154, 164

Soldier of Fortune, Inc. [TV series] 359

Sommer der Liebe [Summer of Love] 328

Sommer des Samurai, Der [The Summer of the Samurai] 308

Sommernachtstraum, Ein [A Midsummer Night's Dream/Wood Love] 98

Sommernachtstraum in unserer Zeit, Ein [A Midsummer Night's Dream in Our Time] 28

Sonne, Erde und Mond [Sun, Earth and Moon] 148

Sound of Thunder, A 370

Space Patrol see *Raumpatrouille*

Space 2063 [TV series] 359

Special Effects [retrospective and exhibition] 305

Spider-Man 352

Spinnen, Die [The Spiders] 51, 55

Spinnwebhaus, Das [The Spiderwebhouse] 425

Springtime [Im wunderschönen Monat Mai] 123

Spuk [story] 53

Spuk aus der Gruft [Spooky Crypt] 342

Spuk im Hause des Professors, Der [Spook in the House of the Professor/Trapped by the Camera] 31

Spuk im Hochhaus [Spooky in a Skyscraper] 299

Spuk im Schloss see *Cat and the Canary, The*

Spuk im Schloss (1947) [Ghost in the Castle] 188

Spuk im Reich der Schatten 349

Spuk mit Max und Moritz [Spook with Max and Moritz] 197

Spuk unterm Riesenrad [Spooky under the Ferris Wheel] 288

Spuk von draussen [Spook from Outside, TV] 312

Spukschloss im Spessart, Das [The Haunted Castle] 224

Stachelier: Der junge Engländer, Das 216

Staplerfahrer Klaus—Der erste Arbeitstag [Forklift Driver Klaus: The First Day on the Job] 355

Star Diaries, The [novel] 379

Star Trek [TV series] 221, 247, 347, 359, 443

Star Trek IV: The Voyage Home 352

Star Tresh—The De-Generation 345

Star Wars [Krieg der Sterne] 268, 285, 307, 444

Stargate 304

Steamboat Willie [Ein Schiff streicht durch die Wellen] 123

Steinerne Phantom, Das [The Phantom of Stone, project] 133

Steinerne Reiter, Der [The Stone Rider] 87

Stella Stellaris [TV miniseries] 334

Stern fällt vom Himmel, Ein [A Star Falls from the Sky, novel] 155

Stern von Bethlehem, Der [The Star of Bethlehem Störtebekers Geheimnis see Limited Games] 77

Sterntaler (1929) [Star Money] 120

Sterntaler (1940) [Star Money] 158

Störenfried, Der [The Intruder] 158-159

Story von Monty Spinnerratz, Die [A Rat's Tale] 339

Strange Case of Captain Ramper, The see *Ramper, der Tiermensch*

Strange Case of Dr. Jekyll and Mr. Hyde, The [novel] see *Dr. Jekyll and Mr. Hyde [novel]*

Stranger, The 217

Struwwelpeter 205

Student von Prag, Der (1913) [The Student of Prague] 27-28, 29, 110, 167

Student von Prag, Der (1926) [The Student of Prague] 110

Student von Prag, Der (1935) [The Student of Prague] 143

Stürmisch verliebt [Perfect Weather for Love, TV] 369

Stunde des Skorpions [Hour of the Scorpion, TV miniseries] 256

Sturzflieger, Die [The Crush Pilots] 336

Succubus see *Necronomicon*

Suche nach dem wunderbaren Vögelchen, Die [Quest for the Bird of Many Colors] 237

Sueñan los androides [Androids Dream/Androiden träumen] 418

Sünderin, Die [The Sinner] 249

Süsse Brei, Der (1940) [Sweet Porridge] 157

Süsse Brei, Der (2018) [Sweet Porridge, TV] 434

Suffer and Die 386

Suicide Club, The [story] 53, 132

Sun Koh—Der Erbe von Atlantis [Sun Koh: The Heir of Atlantis, pulp series] 134

Super 303

Supergirl. Das Mädchen von den Sternen [Supergirl: The Girl from the Stars] 262

Susanne und der Zauberring [Susanne and the Magic Ring] 270

Svengali 114

Swimming Pool—Der Tod feiert mit [Swimming Pool: Death Joins in the Celebration/The Pool] 359

Synthetischer Film oder Wie das Monster KING KONG von Fantasie und Präzision gezeugt wurde [Synthetic Film or: How the Monster KING KONG was created by imagination and precision] 276

System of Dr. Tarr and Professor Fether, The [story] 132

Tabaluga 434

Tag 26 [Day 26] 361

Taiketsu [Babylon Z: The Last Apocalypse] 377

Tal der Schatten, Das [The Valley of Shadows] 344

Tales of the Vikings [TV series] 249

Tannöd 391

Tanz der Farben [Dance of the Colors] 151

Tapfere Schneiderlein, Das (1941) [The Brave Little Tailor] 166

Tapfere Schneiderlein, Das (1956) [The Brave Little Tailor] 210

Tapfere Schneiderlein, Das (1960) [The Brave Little Tailor, TV] 224

Tapfere Schneiderlein, Das (1964) [The Brave Little Tailor] 237

Tapfere Schneiderlein, Das (1981) [The Brave Little Tailor, TV] 296

Tapfere Schneiderlein, Das (2008) [The Brave Little Tailor, TV] 384

Tarantel, Die [The Tarantula] 65

Tattoo—Rette deine Haut [Tattoo: Save Your Skin] 361

Tarzan 3D 416

Tausend Augen des Dr. Mabuse, Die [The 1,000 Eyes of Dr. Mabuse] 223

Taxandria 332

Tears of Kali 367

Telegate spot (2001) 356-357

Telerop 2009—Es ist noch was zu retten [TV series] 273-274

Tempest, The [play] 97, 281

Tenant, The 345

Terminator 3: Rise of the Machines 363

Terror 2000—Intensivstation Deutschland [Terror 2000: Intensive Care Unit Germany] 327

Testament des Dr. Mabuse, Das (1932) [The Testament of Dr. Mabuse/The Last Will of Dr. Mabuse] 134-135, 223, 225, 230

Testament des Dr. Mabuse, Das (1962) [The Terror of Dr. Mabuse/The Testament of Dr. Mabuse] 230

Teufel mit den drei goldenen Haaren, Der (1955) [The Devil with Three Golden Hair] 209

Teufel mit den drei goldenen Haaren, Der (2013) [The Devil with Three Golden Hair, TV] 415

Teufel muss weg, Der [The Devil Must Go, TV] 216

Teufel vom Mühlenberg, Der [The Devil from Mill Mountain] 205-206

Teufel von Rudow, Der [Nightmare in Suburbia] 365

Teufelskirche, Die [The Devil's Church] 71

Therapie für einen Vampir [Therapy for a Vampire] 422

Thief of Bagdad, The 158, 168

Thirteenth Floor, The 346

Thor—Ein hammermässiges Abenteuer [Legends of Valhalla: Thor] 412

Those Fantastic Flying Fools see *Jules Verne's Rocket to the Moon*

Those Magnificent Men in Their Flying Machines 251

Threat Matrix [TV series] 359

Three Little Pigs [Die drei kleinen Schweinchen] 140

Tides 441-442

Tigerentenbande—Der Film, Die [The Gang of Tigers: The Movie] 400

Till Eulenspiegel see *Jester Till*

Tilo Voss [project] 139-140

Time Machine, The [novel] 111, 258

Time Travelers, The 250

Tintenherz [Inkheart] 383

Tischlein deck dich (1956) [The Wishing-Table] 210

Tischlein deck dich (2008) [Table-Be-Set, TV] 383

Tischlein deck dich, Esel streck dich, Knüppel aus dem Sack! (1921) [The Wishing-Table, the Gold-Ass, & the Cudgel in the Sack] 76

Tischlein deck dich, Eselein streck dich, Knüppel aus dem Sack (1938) [The Wishing-Table, the Gold-Ass, & the Cudgel in the Sack] 148

Titanenkampf [Titan Struggle] 39

To the Devil… a Daughter [Die Braut des Satans] 278

Tobias Totz und sein Löwe [Tobias Totz and his Lion] 345

Tochter Ahasvers, Die [Ahasver's Daughter] 76

Tochter Ahasvers: Höllenreigen, Die [Ahasver's Daughter, 2nd part] 76

Todesgöttin des Liebescamps, Die [Love Camp] 295-296

Todesking, Der 319

Todesstrahlen des Dr. Mabuse, Die [The Death Ray Mirror of Dr. Mabuse] 238

Todesvisionen—Geisterstunde [Deadly Visions—Witching Hour] 316

Tolldreiste Kerle in rasselnden Raketen see *Jules Verne's Rocket to the Moon*

Too Young for Men see *Ideale Untermieter, Der [The Ideal Lodger]*

Torn Curtain 224

Tortura 383

Torture Chamber of Dr. Sadism, The see *Schlangengrube und das Pendel, Die [The Snake Pit and the Pendulum]*

Total verrückte Wunderauto, Das [Charlie 2, TV] 373

Toten Augen von London, Die [The Dead Eyes of London] 225

Toten erwachen, Die [The Dead Awake] 35

Totentanz [Dance of Death] 25

Toter hing im Netz, Ein [Horrors of Spider Island] 222

Toter sucht seinen Mörder, Ein [The Brain] 231

Totmacher, Der [The Deathmaker] 335

Toxic Lullaby 393

Träum' nicht, Annette! [Don't Dream, Annette!] 191-192

Transfer—Der Traum vom ewigen Leben [Transfer: The Dream of Eternal Life] 396

Transport 368

Trapped by the Camera see *Spuk im Hause des Professors, Der*

Traumstadt [Dream City] 271

(T)Raumschiff Surprise—Periode 1 [Dreamship Surprise: Period 1] 365, 428

Trickfilm in seinen grundsätzlichen Möglichkeiten, Der [book] 99

True Love Ways 422

Tuberkulose [Tuberculosis] 379

Tumba de los Muertos vivientes, La [Der Abgrund der lebenden Toten/The Treasure of the Living Dead] 297

Tunnel, Der [The Tunnel, novel] 35

Tunnel, Der (1915) [The Tunnel] 35

Tunnel, Der (1933) [The Tunnel] 136-137

Turm des Schweigens, Der [The Tower of Silence] 97

Twilight's Last Gleaming [Das Ultimatum] 281

2001: A Space Odyssey 102, 255, 261, 447

Überflieger—Kleine Vögel, grosses Geklapper [A Stork's Journey] 427

UFO—Es ist hier [UFO: It Is Here] 426

UFO in Her Eyes 404

Ulysses [project] 195

Ulysses (1954) 195

Un certain Monsieur Jo 217

Unbesiegbaren, Die [The Unconquered] 354

Unbewohnte Haus, Das [The Uninhabited House, novel] 89

Und das Wissen ist der Tod [The Knowledge of Death] 37

Und wandern sollst du ruhelos… [You will Be a Restless Wanderer…] 35

Undine 436

Undine 74 273

Unendliche Geschichte, Die [The NeverEnding Story] VI, 152, 303, 321, 327

Unendliche Geschichte 2: Auf der Suche nach Phantásien, Die [The NeverEnding Story II: The Next Chapter] 321

Unendliche Geschichte 3: Rettung aus Phantásien, Die [The NeverEnding Story III: Return to Fantasia] 332-333

Unendliche Geschichte, Die [The NeverEnding Story, animation series] 333

Unendlicher Weltenraum [Infinite Outer Space] 145

Unfriend 424

Ungeheuer von Kamimura, Das [The Monster of Kamimura] 121

Ungeheuer von London City, Das [The Monster of London City] 238

Unheimliche Chinese, Der [The Uncanny Chinese] 70

Unheimliche Geschichten (1919) [Eerie Tales/Tales of Terror] 53

Unheimliche Geschichten (1932) [Tales of Horror] 132

Unheimliche Geschichten [TV series] 297

Unheimliche Haus, Das [The Scary House] 41-42

Unheimliche Mönch, Der [The Sinister Monk] 246

Unheimlichen Hände des Dr. Orlac, Die see *Orlacs Hände*

Unheimlichen Wünsche, Die [The Sinister Wish] 153

United Trash [The Slit] 336

Unnatural… The Fruit of Evil see *Alraune (1952)*

Unrated: The Movie 397

Unrated 2: Scary as Hell 400

Unser Sandmännchen [Our Sandman, TV] 219

Unsichtbare, Der (1921) 71

Unsichtbare, Der (1939) [The Invisible Man, project]

Unsichtbare, Der (1963) [The Invisible Terror] 234

Unsichtbare Mensch, Der [The Invisible Man] 86

Unsichtbaren Krallen des Dr. Mabuse, Die [The Invisible Dr. Mabuse] 230

Unsichtbarer geht durch die Stadt, Ein [An Invisible Man Walks the City] 136

Unsuk Chin: Alice in Wonderland [opera, TV] 377

Unter Schnee [Under Snow] 404

Unternehmen Proxima Centauri [Operation Proxima Centauri] 232

Unterwerfung [Submission, TV] 433

Urban Explorer 405

Urban Scumbags vs. Countryside Zombies 328

Urmel aus dem Eis [Impy's Island] 374

Urmel voll in Fahrt [Impy's Wonderland] 381

Utopen, Die [The Utopes] 251

Vampir [novel] 63

Vampir [magazine] 268

Vampir auf der Couch see *Therapie für einen Vampir [Therapy for a Vampire]*

Vampira [TV] 265

¡Vampiros En La Habana! [Krieg der Vampire] 307

Vampirschwestern, Die [The Vampire Sisters] 409

Vampirschwestern 2—Fledermäuse im Bauch, Die [Vampire Sisters 2: Bats in the Belly] 418

Vampirschwestern 3—Reise nach Transsilvanien [Vampire Sisters 3: Journey to Transylvania] 426

Vampyr, Der [The Vampyre] 70

Vampyr - Der Traum des Allan Gray 130-131, 237, 278

Vampyr des Schlosses, Der [The Vampire of the Castle] 35

Vampyros Lesbos 265

Verfluchten, Die see *House of Usher*

Verlorene Schatten, Der [The Lost Shadow] 69

Verlorene Schuh, Der [The Lost Shoe] 89

Vermächtnis des Professor Bondi, Das 229

Vertauschte Königin, Die [The Reversed Queen] 304

Vertauschte Prinz, Der [The Reversed Prince, TV. 2 parts] 235

Verwandlung, Die [The Transformation, TV] 276

Verwitterte Melodie, Die [Weather-Beaten Melody] 171-174, 182, 183, 184, 186

Verzauberte Otter, Der [The Enchanted Otter] 368

Verzauberte Prinzessin, Die [The Enchanted Princess] 154-155

Vicky the Viking see *Wickie und die starken Männer [Vicky and the Strong Men]*

Village, The see *Hepzibah*

Village People—Tod aus dem All [Village People: Death from Outer Space] 432

Violent Shit 318

Violent Shit II: Mother Hold My Hand 328

Violent Shit III: Infantry of Doom 343

Violent Shit 4.0 see *Karl the Butcher vs. Axe* 318

Virus Undead 381

Vision of a United Totalitarian State, A [novel] 297

Vom Bäumlein, das andere Blätter hat gewollt [The Little Tree That Longed for Other Leaves] 160

Vom Fischer und seiner Frau [The Fisherman and His Wife, TV] 415

Von einem, der auszog, das Fürchten zu lernen [The Story of the Youth Who Went Forth to Learn What Fear Was, TV] 419

Von einem, der auszog, das Gruseln zu lernen (1935) [The Story of the Youth Who Went Forth to Learn What Fear Was] 141

Von einem, der auszog, das Gruseln zu lernen (1963) [The Story of the Youth Who Went Forth to Learn What Fear Was, TV] 234

Von morgens bis mitternachts [From Morn to Midnight] 72

Vormittags-Spuk [Ghosts Before Breakfast] 117

Vortex 356

Vulkan [Volcano, TV] 389

Wachsfigurenkabinett, Das [Waxworks] 96

Wahnsinn [Madness] 51

Waldhaus, Das [The Hut in the Forest] 123

Wallace and Gromit 430

Waltz with Bashir 381

Wand, Die [The Wall] 406

Wandernde Licht, Das [The Wandering Light] 40

Wann ist der Mond eigentlich rund? 347

War of the Satellites see *Planet der toten Seelen*

War of the Worlds [TV series] 359

Warning Shadows see *Schatten [Shadows]*

Warum die Ufos unseren Salat klauen [Why the UFOs Steal Our Lettuce] 293

Weihnachten mit Willy Wuff [Christmas with Willy Wuff, TV] 333

Weihnachten mit Willy Wuff 2—Eine Mama für Lieschen [Christmas with Willy Wuff: A Mom for Lieschen, TV] 336

Weihnachten mit Willy Wuff 3 [Christmas with Willy Wuff 3] 340

Welt am Draht [World on a Wire] VI, 271

Welt ohne Maske, Die [World Without a Mask] 137

Weltraumschiff I startet [Space Ship I Starts] 147, 155, 159

Weltraumschiff 18 [Space Ship 18] 155-156

Weltspiegel, Der [The World Mirror] 48

Wenn Du einmal Dein Herz verschenkst 121

Wenn du gross bist, lieber Adam [When You Grow Up, Dear Adam] 320–321

Wer reisst denn gleich vor'm Teufel aus? [Who's Afraid of the Devil?] 283

Werner—Beinhart! 322

Wettlauf zwischen dem Hasen und dem Igel, Der [The Race between the Hare and the Hedgehog] 148

When the Sleeper Wakes [novel] 39

Whom the Gods Wish to Destroy see *Nibelungen, Die (1966)*

Wichtelmänner, Die [Heinzelmännchen/Brownies] 123

Wickie und die starken Männer [Vicky and the Strong Men, TV series and movie] 386

Wiesenzwerge, Die [The Meadow Dwarves] 160-161

Wild Blue Yonder, The 370-371

Willi Tobler und der Untergang der 6. Flotte [Willi Tobler and the Decline of the 6th Fleet] 266

William Voss. Der Millionendieb [William Voss, the Million Thief] 37

William Wilson [novel] 27

Wings of Desire see *Himmel über Berlin, Der [The Sky Over Berlin]*

Wir [We, TV] 297

Wir sind die Nacht [The Dawn] 396

Witchfinder General 259-260

Wolf Man, The 59, 166

Wolf und die 7 Geisslein, Der (1939) [The Wolf and the Seven Little Goats] 156

Wolf und die sieben Geisslein, Der (1953) [The Wolf and the Seven Little Goats] 201

Wolf und die sieben jungen Geisslein, Der (1956) [The Wolf and the Seven Little Goats] 212

Wolfzeit [TIme of the Wolf] 362

Wolke, Die [The Cloud] 373

Womb 394

Wonderful World of the Brothers Grimm, The 227-228

Wrath [project] 398

Würger, Der [The Wrecker] 119

Würger der Welt, Der [The Strangler of the World] 53

Wuk der Fuchs [Vuk] 299

Wunder der Schöpfung [Miracle of Creation/In the World of the Stars] 102-103

Wunder des gezeichneten Tones, Das 136

Wunder des Malachias, Das [The Miracle of Father Malachia] 225

Wunder von Loch Ness, Das [The Secret of Loch Ness] 380

Wunderlampe des Hradschin, Die [The Magic Lamp of the Prague Castle] 38

Wundersamen Abenteuer des kleinen Mutz, Die [The Miraculous Adventures of Little Mutz] 138

Wupp lernt Gruseln [Wupp Learns What Fear Is] 131

Xaver und sein ausserirdischer Freund [Xaver and his Extra-Terrestrial Friend] 309

Yoghi, Der [The Yoghi] 42

Younger and Younger 330

Zärtliche Chaoten II [Lovable Zanies II] 313-314

Zärtlichkeit der Wölfe, Die [Tenderness of the Wolves] 269-270

Zanoni [novel] V, 68, 79

Zauberbuch, Das [The Magic Book] 337

Zaubergräte, Die [The Magic Fishbone, TV] 301

Zauberlehrling, Der [The Sorcerer's Apprentice] 175

Zaubermännchen, Das [The Dwarf Magician] 222

Zehn kleine Negerlein 204

Zeichen und Wunder [Signs and Miracles] 299

Zertanzten Schuhe, Die (1977) [The Shoes that Were Danced to Pieces, TV] 284

Zertanzten Schuhe, Die (2011) [The Shoes that Were Danced to Pieces, TV] 405

Zimmer 205—Traust du dich rein? [205: Room of Fear] 372

Zirri—Das Wolkenschaf [Cirri, the Cloud Lamb] 329

Zombie Commando 374

Zombie Massacre 413

Zombie Massacre 2: Reich of the Dead 421

Zombie '90: Extreme Pestilence 325

Zombie Onslaught see *Chain Reaction*

Zombie: The Resurrection 342

Zombies from Outer Space 406

Zorro [TV series] 233

Ztracená tvář [The Lost Face] 246

Zucker—Eine wirklich süsse Katastrophe [Sugar] 316

Zurück zum Glück [Back to Luck, TV] 394

Zwei vom Blitz getroffen [Two Striked by Thunderbolt, TV] 354

2012 385

2030—Aufstand der Alten [2030: Revolt of the Old, TV] 377

2030—Aufstand der Jungen [2030: Revolt of the Young, TV] 398

Zweite Wunder von Loch Ness, Das [The Secret of Loch Ness II] 395

Zwerg Nase (1953) [Nose, the Dwarf/Dwarf Nose] 201

Zwerg Nase (1978) [Nose the Dwarf, TV] 287

Zwischen Mars und Erde [Between Mars and Earth] 101

Zwischenfall im Weltall [Incident in Outer Space, project] 155

Zwischpaduri, der Strolch [Zwischpaduri the Rascal] 129

Zwölfte Stunde, Die [The Twelfth Hour] 123-124, 125, 126, 216